Instructor's Edition

BRIDGES
A READER FOR WRITERS

Instructor's Edition

BRIDGES
A READER FOR WRITERS

Sylvia A. Holladay
Hillsborough Community College

PEARSON
Prentice
Hall

Upper Saddle River, NJ 07458

Editorial Director: Leah Jewell
Executive Editor:
  Craig Campanella
Editorial Assistant: Joan Polk
Marketing Manager: Kate Stewart
Marketing Assistant: Kara Pottle
Production Liaison:
  Marianne Peters-Riordan
Permissions Supervisor: Ronald Fox
Permissions Researcher: Annette Coolidge

Manufacturing Buyer: Benjamin Smith
Cover Art Director: Jayne Conte
Cover Design: Bruce Kenselaar
Cover Photo: Ian Adams
  Photography
Composition/Full-Service Project
Management: GGS Book Services,
  Atlantic Highlands
Printer/Binder: R.R. Donnelley
  and Sons

Credits and acknowledgments borrowed from other sources and reproduced, with permission, in this textbook are listed starting on page 347.

10 9 8 7 6 5 4 3 2 1

BRIEF CONTENTS

CONTENTS

PART 2   READINGS FOR WRITERS   51

CHAPTER 4 Home and Family   52

One can never leave home. One carries the hopes and dreams of home eternally just under the skin.

—MAYA ANGELOU

CHAPTER 6 Education   126

> *If a nation expects to be ignorant and free, in a state of civilization, it expects what never was and never will be.*
>
> —THOMAS JEFFERSON

CHAPTER 9 Popular Culture   234

It has become appallingly obvious that our technology has exceeded our
humanity.

—ALBERT EINSTEIN

Alternate Table of Contents for Part II: Rhetorical Patterns

Following is an Alternate Table of Contents According to Rhetorical Pattern. Listed here are selections in which this pattern is emphasized. There are other selections in the Reader that may exhibit the pattern in combination with others or use it to develop another pattern.

Narration and Description

Example and Enumeration

Cause and Effect

Comparison and Contrast

Argument

Lyric Poetry

Alternate Table of Contents for Part II: Sources of Ideas for Writing

Reading and Research

Conversation and Interview

Preface

In Bertice Berry's autobiography *Bertice: The World According to Me,* she writes that "By changing the emotions that are evoked, [she] tries to interrupt the tapes in people's heads" and adds "Herein lies the possibility to create change." When I first conceived the idea for this textbook, I had not read Berry's book, but I had a similar idea: I wanted to prepare a textbook that would change the emotions and attitudes as well as increase the knowledge and improve the competencies of students entering college writing courses. When I did read her book, I realized that what I hope to do is "change the tapes" in students' heads. I want students to hear positive, not negative, voices in their heads, voices that encourage, not discourage, them in their attempts to improve their writing abilities.

Bridges: A Reader for Writers is a reader intended to provide positive activities and thoughts for students in beginning composition courses in college. Throughout the textbook, the cognitive is integrated with the affective to help students develop writing skills, build confidence, and cope with writing apprehension. The selections provide varied opportunities for students to read, discuss, and practice the processes and patterns of writing. The book encourages feedback from classmates as well as the instructor at all stages of the writing process. The study aids help students understand the bridges and interconnections among the four aspects of the communications process—speaking, listening, reading, and writing.

It may be used with a handbook or rhetoric.

The emphasis is on writing from experience and helping students to realize that they have a broad range of experience from which to find topics, to discover evidence for writing, to write for a variety of audiences, and to construct both expository and argumentative essays for adult readers. The selections in this anthology—essays (both professional and student), poems, short stories—are brief and on topics of easy access and high interest to entering students in order to stimulate their thought and discussion. Drawn from a variety of authors and sources, the selections are appropriate for students of diverse backgrounds, abilities, interests, and goals. They are arranged topically, but two alternate tables of contents—rhetorical patterns and sources of ideas for writers—are also included. The study aids at the end of each selection include not only questions for vocabulary study, comprehension, and discussion, but also suggestions for practice in effective word choice, grammatical patterns, sentence patterns, paragraphing, and essay construction to help students improve their writing.

At the end of the course, I hope that the tapes in students' heads will be changed—that they will say, "I now understand better what I have to do to write more effectively," "I have improved my writing ability and want to continue to improve," and "I realize that although most writing is hard work, it can be fun and rewarding."

Many people contribute to a project such as this one, and I would like to thank all of them. First, I want to thank my students and colleagues—past and present; much that I have learned from them is reflected in this book. A special thanks goes to Craig Campanella, Senior Editor for English at Prentice-Hall/Pearson Education, for his confidence in me and guidance in this project. Gail Linton, Prentice Hall Sales Representative in Florida, provided encouragement and liaison. Other important members of the Prentice-Hall staff include Joan Polk, Editorial Assistant; Kate Stewart, Marketing Manager; and Marianne Peters-Riordan, Production Liaison. In addition, I want to thank Kelly Keeler, Production Editor at GGS Production Services, who worked closely and patiently with me on the copyediting and production of the final manuscript. Thanks also to others who worked on the preparation of the final manuscript: Sharon O'Donnell, copy editor; Lynn von Hassel, proofreader; and Annette Coolidge, permissions editor.

The busy, concerned instructors who took time to review the early manuscript and make helpful comments have made a valuable contribution to this textbook. Thanks to Dorothy Bonser, Owens Community College; Derek Bowe, Oakwood College; Danielle Marie Carney, Cerritos College; Eric Cash, Abraham Baldwin College; Heidi Goen-Salter, Diablo Valley College; Karen Hackley, Houston Community College; Deonne Kunkel, Diablo Valley College; Deborah Morrott, Utah Valley State College; Jo Ann Pavlevitch, University of Houston; Iris Rozencwajg, Houston Community College; Julie Segedy, Chabot College; Carla Witt, California Polytechnic; William Allen, UMass—Lowell; Danielle Carney, Cerritos College; Cindy Casper, Norwalk Community College; and Rosie Branciforte, International Academy of Design.

Finally, I thank King Edward the Pom, Miss Mindy the Poodle, Sugar Bear the Pom, and the newest member of our household Sargeant Pugsli the Pug for loving companionship during my long hours at the desk and computer and for enjoyable diversions when I needed them. Most of all, I thank my husband Thomas E. Hicks, Sr., for his love and patience throughout this project and all my other academic endeavors.

SYLVIA A. HOLLADAY

Instructor's Edition

BRIDGES

A READER FOR WRITERS

PART 1

Communicating and Writing in College

Your opinion is the best and most personal thing you can offer, so why pretend that it doesn't consist of confusion and panic as well as whatever intelligence and solid instincts you might have.

—BARRY FARRELL

Suggestions for Journal Entries

1. Where do you prefer to write?
2. When—what time of day—is best for you to write?
3. What type of writing do you enjoy most?
4. What problems do you have in writing?
5. What is your history in writing? For instance, what courses and practice have you had in writing?
6. Tell about an English teacher you liked.
7. Tell about an English teacher you did not like.
8. What are your goals for this course? What do you hope to learn?
9. Do you have writing anxiety, math anxiety, or test anxiety? If so, how does it affect you?
10. Do you like to keep a diary? Why or why not?

CHAPTER ONE

Introduction to Students

You Are a Writer

You are a writer. You have been writing all your life. In the past you have written lists of things to do or remember; notes and diaries for yourself; letters, e-mails, and instant messages (IMs) to friends and relatives, reports and papers for classes in school. You have filled out application forms, and perhaps written resumes and letters of application to get a job. On the job, you may have written notes, lists, orders, summaries, inventories, and reports for your boss. You probably have written an autobiographical blurb for the yearbook or a letter of complaint to a business. Yes, *you are a writer.*

In the future you will write more, much more. In college classes you will take notes on class lectures and visiting speakers, write summaries of books and articles that you read, and write outlines for papers and speeches of your own. You will write essays, essay exams, lab reports, and research papers. On your job you will write more notes, letters, summaries, and reports. In this age of electronic technology, you will write e-mail messages on your computer and order products online. You may write computer programs. Peter Drucker, an expert in business management, states that the higher up in a company or a career field you go, the more writing you will be required to do. By entering college, you have indicated that you want to move up in your work, and writing well can help you achieve your goal. Yes, *you have been a writer, you are a writer now, and you will be a writer in the future.*

You Can Improve Your Writing

Although you may not write as well as you want to write or as well as some others may expect you to write, you are a writer, and you should think of yourself as a writer. Keep a positive attitude. The better writer you become, the more successful you will be in college and on the job. With the desire to improve, the willingness to practice, and the advice of an experienced writer—your instructor—you can improve your writing. Here are a few tips to help you.

1. Think of writing as a *process of composing*, a series of related steps that often overlap to put your ideas together so that you can communicate effectively with readers.
2. Be aware of your audience, the readers that you intend to read what you write.
3. Write about what you know, something you have experienced, or something you have thought about and have discussed with others, or something on which you can find information.
4. Make your writing easy for your readers to follow and understand by putting your ideas in order; by connecting your ideas with signposts and other transitional devices; and by developing your ideas with plenty of evidence, explanations, and examples.
5. Take time to rethink and revise as well as to proofread and edit what you write.

LESSENING WRITING ANXIETY

Some people have *writing anxiety*, similar to test anxiety or math anxiety or computer anxiety, especially if the writing task is an assignment on which they will be evaluated. If you are one of these people, your hands get clammy when you start to write, your mind goes blank or you become confused, and you think you just can't complete a writing task or at least can't do it satisfactorily. You may not be able to get rid of your writing anxiety, but you can learn to cope with it and prevent it from interfering with your improving your writing. Here are a few tips to help you cope with writing anxiety.

- Don't try to be perfect. Realize that writing is messy, that it takes time, and that even experienced writers must proofread, revise, and edit.
- Break a large assignment into small steps.
- Get your ideas down on paper before you start changing and correcting.
- Budget your time wisely, and give yourself plenty of time to complete the writing satisfactorily.
- Study, review, and practice language skills (spelling, grammar, sentence structure, word choice, punctuation, capitalization) as needed to make the correct forms habitual.

Remember: *Think of yourself as a writer*. Have confidence that with effort and time you can improve your writing ability.

Why Reading is Important for Writers

You have probably already discovered that in school and on the job, writing and reading go together. Often what you write is based on what you have read—perhaps a college textbook, a job manual, or research in a library or on the Internet. Therefore, your ability to comprehend what you read is crucial to success in college and on the job.

First, reading stimulates you to think and talk and remember. It encourages you to probe your memory and to make connections between what you read and what you have experienced and already know. It increases your knowledge.

Second, reading helps you find something of importance *to you* to write about. If you are having trouble finding something to write about, you can read essays on topics of interest to you, such as horror movies or ice skating or being shy, or essays on subjects about contemporary life and society, such as American family life or divorce or leisure activities. Reading helps you recall memorable events that have happened to you and can help you solve some of your personal problems. Discussing what you read with other people—friends, family members, classmates—will help you remember forgotten details.

Third, reading provides examples and models of writing strategies and patterns. Therefore, you should read for technique (the way a passage is written) as well as content (what the passage is about). If you want to write about an experience from your childhood, you can study narrative essays by other writers to see how they have written about their experiences—how they have organized and developed their writings. If you want to convince your boss to give you a raise, you can read to see what persuasive techniques other writers have used to convince their readers and try similar techniques on your boss. Reading also provides examples of effective sentence patterns, grammatical patterns, word usage, and even punctuation. You can try some of these language techniques to enhance your own writing.

You Can Be Successful in This Class

One of the first steps in improving your writing and reading is taking this course and doing your best in it. Good study habits will help you in this class and throughout college. They include:

1. Recognize the importance of reading and writing for you *personally*.
2. Complete all the reading and writing assignments for the class.

3. Budget your time carefully. Begin each reading or writing task in plenty of time so that you can complete it without hurrying. Rushing through an assignment causes you to be careless and lessens your comprehension and recall.
4. Attend class regularly. Don't be absent unless absolutely necessary.
5. Be punctual in class attendance. Usually important information is covered at the beginning of the class period.
6. Keep up with the assignments, and don't get behind. Write down all assignments carefully and accurately. Always come to class prepared (with textbook, notebook, notebook paper, two pens, a paperback dictionary, and your completed assignment).
7. Take good notes in class—clear, complete, legible. Include in your notes everything that the instructor puts on the board, record the main ideas of lectures and discussions, and either mark in your textbook or take notes on what you read in your textbooks.
8. Participate in class discussions, and ask questions when you don't understand something. Get yourself involved in what is going on.
9. Be patient with yourself. Realize that reading and writing well take time, and be willing to devote the necessary time to doing the job well.
10. Above all, think of yourself as a *reader* and as a *writer* who can improve.

How to Use This Textbook

This textbook is for you to use in a beginning college writing course. It is primarily a reader to supplement your textbooks and study materials on composing skills and language skills.

Part I "Communicating and Writing in College" provides information on communicating in college courses, with an emphasis on writing. Part I contains three chapters. Chapter 1 introduces you to the textbook and gives tips on how to succeed in this class. Chapter 2 discusses briefly the communication process and then walks you through the important tasks of taking notes, annotating, outlining, and summarizing what you read. Chapter 3 focuses on special types of writing for college.

Part II "Readings for Writers" is a collection of readings to help you with your writing. It contains selections on eight topics that are familiar and interesting to you—home and family; youth and age; education; gender roles and relationships; dreams, goals, decisions; popular culture, the world of work, and science and technology. Each chapter contains poems, essays, and a short story on the subject. The selections are brief, and they provide a diversity of opinions and approaches to the general topic. These selections will stimulate you to think and talk and remember, thus helping you discover ideas for your own writings, and also will provide models and examples of strategies for writing and techniques for language use.

Each selection is accompanied by specific study aids that will help you understand and respond to what you read, discover something to write about, and comprehend and practice strategies for writing and techniques for language use that will help you improve your writing. Each begins with a brief **headnote** about the author and the specific subject of the selection so that you will know where she is coming from. A **Vocabulary Study** may precede the selection and list words that you need to know in order to comprehend the reading selection. Following the selection are questions for **Comprehension and Discussion**, questions on **Language and Technique**, and **Suggestions for Writing**. These suggestions include practice in construction of sentences, paragraphs, and essays. Even if your instructor does not assign all the study aids, you will benefit from doing them and keeping them in a journal of your ideas and writings. The entries in your journal will not only give you practice in writing but will also give you a start on later class assignments.

Other aids make the textbook easy for you to use. The lines in the poems and the paragraphs in the essays and short stories are numbered so that you can find words and sentences quickly when you are studying or discussing a selection or writing about it.

In addition to the main "Contents" found at the front of the textbook, two alternative tables of contents are also included: (1) the "Alternate Table of Contents for Part II: Rhetorical Patterns," which categorizes the selections by narration and description, example and enumeration, cause and effect, comparison and contrast, analysis and classification, process, definition, problem to solution, and argument; and (2) the "Alternate Table of Contents for Part II: Sources of Ideas for Writing," which categorizes the selections according to the author's sources of information: experience and memory, observation, reading and research, and conversation and interview.

TIPS FOR USING THIS TEXTBOOK

Following are a few tips to help you get the most out of this textbook.

Studying Vocabulary

You can't understand what you read unless you know the literal meanings of the words in the passage. Therefore, be sure to look up the meanings of any vocabulary words listed at the beginning of the selection as well as any words that you come across during the reading that you do not know. Because many words in the English language can have more than one meaning, be sure to consider the context in which the word is used and be aware of both the word's denotation (dictionary definition) and connotation (all the associations the word carries in addition to its literal meaning).

Reading for Comprehension

When you study each selection, you should comprehend and analyze it *before* you evaluate or judge it. Sometimes a reader makes the mistake of jumping to a hasty conclusion about something she or he has read: "I don't agree with it, so it is not a good piece." The study aids at the end of each selection will lead you to understand and analyze what you read.

As you read a selection, you should first scan it. Note the title, and try to figure out what it means and how it may be related to the reading passage. Then read the introductory paragraph or section, glance through the first sentence of each paragraph and the subheadings if any, and read the last paragraph. Next go back and read the selection carefully. Note important transitional markers (such as "my point is," "to sum up," "first," "second," "last," "therefore," "consequently," "however," etc.), and distinguish between general statements and examples. As you read, underline or highlight important points or jot down your thoughts in the margins. Writing journal entries of your reading responses is also a good idea. Answer each study question following the selection and be prepared to discuss these questions in class with your classmates. Then complete the Suggestions for Writing as assigned by your instructor.

Discussing What You Read

Talking about what you read with your classmates and friends can help you write well. First, talking about reading will stimulate you to think about a topic, think about it more deeply, and perhaps consider it from an angle that you have not considered before. Second, it will help you discover that you *do* know something about a subject; in fact, often you will discover that you know more than you think you do. Third, it will help you remember events, ideas, and details that you may have forgotten. It will help you pull them from the depths of your memory and your subconscious. When you do remember forgotten points, jot them in your journal or your class notebook so that you will not forget them again. Fourth, talking about reading will encourage you to articulate your opinions and positions, and to find specific evidence to explain your beliefs to people who agree with you and to defend them to those who do not agree with you. Thus, talking with others is excellent preparation for writing.

Writing About What You Read

Much of what you write for this class will be based on what you read. There are several ways you can use reading to help you write better. First, reading will stimulate you to think and will help you remember. As you read, you will find that you often identify with something the author says. You may say to yourself, "That reminds me of when. . . ," or "I remember once when something similar happened to me," or "I know somebody like that," or "I agree with this statement," or "But that comment is absolutely wrong." In fact, carrying on a silent conversation with the author not only helps you to comprehend the selection but also helps you discover something to write about. Make notations of your responses either in the textbook or in your journal. In addition, the reading selections demonstrate for you various writing strategies and language techniques that other writers use effectively to present their ideas. Then you can imitate and adapt the techniques for your own use. Finally, you can use information that you find in your readings to support your ideas in your writings. In fact, most argumentative writing and research reports are based on reading.

Throughout the textbook you will find suggestions for journal entries. A *journal* is a record of notes and ideas for later writings that are longer and more polished. It is similar to a diary in that it is written primarily for yourself, but it goes further than a diary: it not only indicates what happens but also includes your reactions to and thoughts about what happens. Journal entries are *freewriting*—that is, you record events and thoughts as they come to you without worrying about organization or order of the items, and without proofreading and editing or correcting language skills (such as capitalization, spelling, punctuation, grammar, sentence structure, word choice), and without revising for rhetorical skills (such as clarity, unity, organization, transitions). However, if you plan to share your journal entries with your classmates or if your instructor asks you to turn in some of the entries, you should proofread, edit, and revise those entries to share with others. In addition, your instructor may ask you to focus your freewritings from time to time; that is, focus on one subject instead of freewriting on whatever comes to mind. A journal can be a valuable resource of ideas for writings, so keep your journal up-to-date and complete. Bring it with you to every class because you will be using it for various class activities.

Remember, *you are a writer*, and with focused effort *you can become a better writer*. Be confident in yourself so that you can learn a lot in this course and improve your writing ability.

CHAPTER TWO

Responding to What You Read and Hear

Communicating: Sending and Receiving

Although communicating is a complex process, it is a familiar process—like writing—that you perform regularly. So just as you are a writer, you are also a communicator. Just as you are trying to improve your ability to write in this course, you are also in the process of improving your ability to communicate. In fact, writing is an aspect of the communications process.

THE PROCESS OF COMMUNICATING

Communications is the process through which one person (the sender) attempts to transfer his or her thoughts and feelings to another person (the receiver) and through which one person attempts to understand what is going on in another person's head. The sender may use speaking or writing to send a message to another person, and the receiver tries to understand the message through listening or reading.

COMPLEXITY OF THE PROCESS OF COMMUNICATIONS

Several factors contribute to the complexity of communicating, but three are particularly important to you as a college student in a composition course.

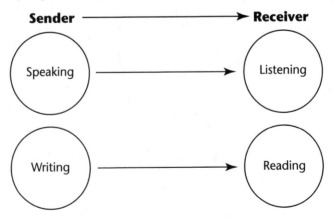

Process of Communications

First, the meanings of some words that the sender uses may be unfamiliar or unknown to the receiver. This situation often occurs when two people from different backgrounds and different educations attempt to communicate. Think of how frequently you do not understand what your doctor or lawyer or accountant tells you, or how confused you are when you try to communicate to someone of another generation or cultural group.

Second, the process of communications may be confusing because words do not always mean the same thing to the sender (the speaker or writer) as to the receiver (the listener or reader). Confusion or even blocked communication occurs especially when the sender and the receiver have different connotations (suggestions or emotions attached to the word) because of differences in experience. For example, if a child has a puppy who becomes his constant companion, he will have pleasant connotations of the word *dog*. However, if the child is bitten by the dog, he may become afraid of dogs and develop unpleasant connotations of the word *dog*.

Three, writing is further complicated by the fact that the receiver (the reader) is not in the presence of the sender (the writer). Therefore, the writer cannot see how the reader is responding: the writer cannot see the eyes, facial expressions, and body language, all of which provide clues to the speaker as to whether the listener understands the message.

As a result of these three factors, the writer must anticipate areas of confusion or difficulty for readers and use various techniques to compensate for these problems. For example, a good writer uses specific, precise diction or words; defines unfamiliar terms in context; and provides examples to clarify assertions. As a composition student, you will learn to anticipate possible problems that can impede communication and to avoid the bad habits that cause these problems. You should not ignore your audience and write primarily for yourself, but you should be familiar with and aware of your intended readers. You should not use vague words, but use precise, specific, concise language. You should not write generalization after generalization, but provide evidence and examples to support and clarify each generalization. Finally, you will use Standard English for spelling and grammar.

Taking Notes

One of the most important types of writing you will do in college is note-taking. Effective note-taking is one of the most important study habits for a college student to learn. You will take notes on what you hear and on what you read.

TAKING NOTES AS A LISTENER IN CLASS

As a college student, you will receive much important information through listening, so you need to take notes to help you remember what you hear in class. Because so much information comes into your brain through your senses—sight, smell, taste, hearing, and touch—and because of the way your memory works, you cannot expect to retain or remember everything, so you are selective. You usually remember the things that are interesting and important *to you*. Sometimes those ideas and instructions are not the same as those of your instructors. Therefore, if you have not already done so, you need to learn to take usable notes on what you hear. Here are a few tips to get you started.

1. Be prepared. Study the assignment to be familiar with the ideas discussed, follow the lecture, and ask questions on anything you do not understand.

2. Listen actively, not passively. Concentrate on what is going on; don't daydream or start thinking about your worries. Block those thoughts, and become involved in what your instructor or your classmates are talking about, take part in the discussion, and ask questions. If the subject does not seem interesting to you, remember that you have to develop interest in the ideas and processes of any course you are taking in order to pass the course. In addition, participate for your own learning, not to impress your instructor and your classmates.

3. Take notes on what you hear. Writing down what you hear reinforces what you hear and helps you to remember.

4. Take notes only on the important points. Do not attempt to record everything you hear in class—that's impossible. So what is important? First, write down everything that your instructor writes on the board. If she thinks something is important enough to write on the board, it is important enough to keep in your notes. Also, record everything that your instructor repeats or emphasizes. In addition, record only the main ideas and only enough examples to help you remember the discussion or refer to your textbook.

5. Be complete enough to be clear. Make your notes complete enough to be clear when you review them a week later to complete an assignment or three weeks later when you review for a test.

6. Be flexible. Don't allow the form of the notes to become more important than the content. The notes are for you, no one else, so messiness

and incorrect outline form—even misspelled words or grammatical errors—are okay.

TAKING NOTES AS A READER IN COLLEGE

Besides taking notes on what you hear and becoming a better listener in college classes, you will also take notes on what you read and try to become a better reader. The tips for receiving through listening also apply to receiving effectively through reading.

1. Be prepared. Scan the complete section—chapter, section, essay, poem, short story—before you start to read so that you can anticipate the important information.
2. Read actively, not passively. Become involved in what you read. Carry on a conversation with the author—ask questions, agree, argue. Make notes in the margins if you have your own copy.
3. Take notes to help you comprehend and remember what you read. Jot down the important points. Outline, paraphrase, or summarize the passage. Distinguish between the general statements, the explanations, and the illustrations. Another way to take notes on what you read is to annotate it: that is, highlight and make marginal notes to yourself if you have your own copy. In professional publications, headings and subheadings help you follow the ideas and keep them straight in your mind.
   Note: When you read to research a topic, use a special form for your notes and the citations for your sources. If your instructor does not tell you what form to use, use the Modern Language Association (MLA) style, a style generally accepted among scholars, teachers, and editors. You will find explanation and examples of MLA style in almost any English handbook or online.
4. Be clear. Remember that you will need to be able to understand your notes days or even weeks after your reading.
5. Be flexible. Do not allow the form of your notes to become more important than the ideas.

Many of the activities in this course will help you become a better note-taker on what you hear as well as what you read.

Annotating What You Read

Annotating what you read is a helpful technique for comprehension and study. To *annotate* means to mark a selection and make notes to yourself. Below is a sample annotated passage from *The Big Change* by Frederick Lewis Allen, a historical book similar to the history textbooks for your college courses. Allen traces the causes and effects of the Great Depression of the 1920s and 1930s, one of the greatest economic crises to face the United States. In this excerpt the author explains how the Depression affected people, but he writes without expressing his opinions or emotions.

The Great Depression

Frederick Lewis Allen

Intro:
Historical
anecdote
traces be-
ginning of
Depression

1   On the morning of October, 24, 1929, the towering structure of American prosperity cracked wide open. For many days the prices of stocks on the New York Stock Exchange had been sliding faster and faster downhill; that morning they broke in a wild panic. The leading bankers of New York met at the House of Morgan to form a buying pool to support the market; Richard Whitney, brother of a leading Morgan partner, thereupon crossed the street to the great hall of the Stock Exchange and put in orders to buy United States Steel at 205; and for a time prices rallied. Pierpont Morgan had halted the Panic of 1907. Surely this panic, too, would yield to the organized confidence of the great men of the world of finance.

What?
Check

C & C
to past

2   But within a few days it was clear that they could no more stop the flood of selling than Dame Partington could sweep back the Atlantic Ocean. On it went, session after session. On the worst day, October 29, over sixteen million shares of stock were thrown on the market by frantic sellers. And it was not until November 13 that order was restored.

?

Under-
standable!

3   In the course of a few brief weeks, thirty billion dollars in paper values had vanished into thin air—an amount of money larger than the national debt at that time. The whole credit structure of the American economy had been shaken more severely than anybody then dared guess. The legend of Wall Street leadership had been punctured. And the Great Depression was on its way.

Wow!

Good image

4   At first business and industry in general did not seem to have been gravely affected. Everybody assured everybody else that nothing really important had happened, and during the spring of 1930 there was actually a Little Bull Market of considerable proportions. But in May this spurt was at an end. And then there began an almost uninterrupted two-year decline, not only in security prices, but also—an infinitely more serious matter—in the volume of American business: a vicious circle of ebbing sales, followed by declining² corporate income, followed by attempts to restore that income by cutting³ salaries and wages and laying⁴ off men, which caused increased⁵ unemployment and further⁶ reduced sales, which led to increased ⁷business losses, which led to further ⁸wage cutting and further firing⁹ of men, and so on toward disaster.

EFFECTS
Causal chain of events

?

Bad Effect on security prices

Effects on biz

1-Lower sales

2-Less corporate income

3-Cutting salaries

4-Laying off workers

Yes! Must have been

5-Increased unemployment

6-More reduction in sales

7-More biz losses

8-More wage cuts

9-More firing

↓

DISASTER

5   During these bewildering years President Hoover at first tried to organize national optimism by summoning business executives to Washington to declare that conditions were fundamentally sound and that there would be no wage cutting. This didn't work. Then for a time he was inactive, trusting to the supposedly self-correcting processes of the market. These didn't work. Then, convinced that the financial panic which was simultaneously raging in Europe was the worst source of trouble,

Attempts to solve problems by Pres. Hoover

1

2

3

Another causal chain of events

he organized an international moratorium in war debts and reparations—a fine stroke of diplomacy which alleviated matters only briefly. Then he set up the Reconstruction Finance Corporation to bring federal aid to hard-pressed banks and businesses—while steadfastly refusing, as a matter of principle, to put federal funds at the disposal of individual persons who were in trouble. Just when it seemed as if recovery were at hand, in the winter of 1932–1933, the American banking system went into a tailspin; even the RFC solution hadn't worked. The result was one of the most remarkable coincidences of American history. It was on March 4, 1933—the very day that Hoover left the White House and Franklin D. Roosevelt entered it—that the banking system of the United States ground to a complete halt. An able and highly intelligent President, committed to orthodox economic theories which were generally considered enlightened, had become one of the tragic victims of the collapse of the going system.

4

5

BAM!

Imagine!

Summary—
Result

Actions
by Pres.
Roosevelt
to start
recovery

6   Whereupon Roosevelt, declaring in his cheerfully resolute Inaugural Address that "the only thing we have to fear is fear itself," swept into a tornado of action—successfully reopening the banks and initiating that lively, helter-skelter, and often self-contradictory program of reform, relief, and stimulation which was to keep the country in a dither during the middle nineteen-thirties and bring at least a measure of recovery.

Practice. Annotate one of the following essays from this textbook: "Teenagers Are Not Becoming More Violent" by Mike Males (p. 109), or "It's Not Just a Phase" by Katherine E. Zondlo (p. 120).

Outlining What You Read

Outlining is another technique that can help you comprehend and remember what you read. It can also help you plan an essay before you write it. Following is an outline of the excerpt from Frederick Lewis Allen.

The Great Depression

Thesis: The Great Depression which started in 1929 kept the United States in a dither through the middle nineteen-thirties.

Introduction: The events that led up to the Great Depression (1–3)
I. The effects of the Stock Market Crash on October 29, 1929 (4)
   A. Positive effects
      1. Assurances that nothing really important had happened
      2. Rally in Bull Market
   B. Negative effects
      1. Decline in security prices
      2. A downward spiral of effects on American business
         a. Fewer sales
         b. Less corporate income
         c. Lower salaries and wages
         d. Laying off workers
         e. Increased unemployment
         f. More reduction in sales
         g. More business losses
         h. More wage cuts
         i. More firings
         j. Disaster
II. Attempts to remedy the situation (4–5)
   A. Unsuccessful attempts by President Hoover
      1. Organizing national optimism
      2. Leaving the solution to the self-correcting process of the market
      3. Organizing an international moratorium in war debts and reparations
      4. Setting up the Reconstruction Finance Corporation
      5. Refusing to allow individuals to use federal funds

  B. Actions by President Roosevelt
   1. Reopening banks
   2. Initiating program of reform, relief, and stimulation

Practice. Outline one of the following essays in this textbook: "From Forced Technology to High Tech/High Touch" by John Naisbitt (p. 320), or "Friends, Good Friends—And Such Good Friends" by Judith Viorst (p. 162).

Summarizing What You Read

Writing a summary of a passage is another effective way to check your comprehension of what you read and to have a brief version for review. A *summary* is a condensation of the original, expressing the meaning in your own words. You summarize what the author says, but do not include all the explanations and examples that are in the original. Neither should you include any of your own interpretations or comments; just stick to what the author says. A summary is brief, usually 10 to 20 percent the length of the original. Here are a few tips to help you write a summary:

1. Read the entire passage first without marking or taking notes or beginning to summarize.
2. Identify the author's main point. It may be stated as a thesis sentence or it may be implied.
3. Identify and mark the major divisions of the passage.
4. Summarize section by section, not line by line or sentence by sentence.
5. When you complete the summary, compare it with the original to make sure you have not misinterpreted the author.

Following is a summary of the passage by Frederick Lewis Allen.

The Great Depression began on October 29, 1929, with the collapse of the New York Stock Exchange. Leading bankers tried to stop the collapse but could not. For a short time it seemed that there had been no negative effects, but soon it was evident that the American economy had been badly shaken. The negative effects on security prices and on business continued to increase. Although President Hoover tried to correct the downward spiral of the economy, his efforts were unsuccessful, and he became a victim of the collapse. When Roosevelt became president, he instituted a cycle of reform, relief, and stimulation, but recovery was very slow. [107 words]

Practice. Write a summary of one of the following essays from this textbook: "Relationships 101" from *Time Magazine* (p. 137), or "No Shame in My Game" by Katherine S. Newman (p. 281).

CHAPTER THREE

Writing in College

In addition to writing in response to what you hear and read in college, you will do a lot of writing of other types—journals, paragraphs, essays, essay tests, summaries, lab reports, research papers, perhaps poems and short stories. Chapter 2 provided brief explanations and examples of notes, annotations, outlines, and summaries. In this chapter are a few guidelines for other types of writing that you will do in this class: (1) the journal, (2) the paraphrase, (3) the synopsis, (4) the academic paragraph, and (5) the academic essay.

The Journal

As described earlier (p. 8), a *journal* is your personal record of responses to and notes and ideas about what happens in your life. It includes your reactions to and thoughts about what happens, your interpretation of events. Journal entries are freewriting in which you record events and thoughts as they come to you without worrying about form and style. However, if your instructor asks you to turn in selected journal entries, you should clean them up a bit. A journal can be a valuable resource of ideas for writing, so date each entry, and keep your journal up-to-date and complete. Bring it with you to every class meeting because you will be using it for class activities.

There are two basic types of journal entries. One is a *reflective record* of your thoughts and responses to what is going on in the world or what is happening in your life. An entry may be drawn from your memory or it may be your response to a current event.

Reflective Journal Entry by a Professional Writer

Henry David Thoreau

The other day I rowed in my boat a free, even lovely young lady, and, as I plied the oars, she sat in the stern, and there was nothing but she between me and the sky. So might all our lives be picturesque if they were free enough, but mean relations and prejudices intervene to shut out the sky, and we never see a man as simple and distinct as the man-weathercock on a steeple. [1840]

Nothing was ever so unfamiliar and startling to me as my own thoughts. [1840]

A man's life should be a stately march to a sweet but unheard music, and when to his fellows it seem irregular and inharmonious, he will only be stepping to a livelier measure, or his nicer ear hurry him into a thousand symphonies and concordant variations. There will be no halt ever, but at most a marching on his post, or such a pause as is richer than any sound, when the melody runs into such depth and wildness as to be no longer heard, but implicitly consented to with the arduous times, for then the music will not fail to swell into greater sweetness and volume, and itself rule the movement it inspired. [1840]

Reflective Journal Entry

Student Writer

There is a big commotion going on about whether colleges should have a playoff game or not. Why not? What are the objections. I don't know. Can't even imagine. Colleges are different from the pros sure, but how can a champion team be declared by votes of biased sportswriters. That's not logical. High schools, football & basketball & I think baseball teams play a state championship game. Even little league baseball. And there's the big 4 in college basketball. That was held in my city a few years ago, but I was too busy with other things to go. Guess I wasn't that interested. I'd be interested in a college football championship game though. If I couldn't afford to go as would be probable I'd watch on TV.

Practice. Write a personal journal entry on one of the topics below.

- A beautiful or picturesque scene that you have seen recently (see Thoreau).
- Your thoughts about what life is (see Thoreau).
- Your thoughts about what life should be (see Thoreau).
- A current problem or controversy in your college or in one of the local secondary or elementary schools. (see Student Writer above.)

The second type of journal entry is *reader response*. In this type of entry, you record your personal responses to something you have read—what you think of as you read the selection. For example, the setting may remind you of somewhere you have been, one of the characters may remind you of someone you know, or you may get upset by what happens. It is best to write this type of journal entry immediately after your first reading, while the events and ideas are fresh in your mind. When you write either type of entry—reflective or reader response—write down whatever comes to your mind. Do not try to be analytical or critical at this point, and do not worry about unity or grammar.

Reader Response Journal Entry Based on a Nonfiction Prose Selection

When I read the piece by Allen on the Depression (pp. 14–16), I thought about all the tales my great-grandparents used to tell me. Grandpa was in college but had to drop out. Grandma was in business school and didn't get to study as much as she wanted to. They got married in the early 30s and their first years were very hard. They had jobs in the factory but still had trouble making ends meet. It didn't even end until the war started. I remember that Grandpa had steak every Saturday night after that because he didn't have enough money during the Depression to buy meat.

Reader Response Journal Entry Based on a Literary Selection

The poem "Neutral Tones" by Thomas Hardy (p. 161) makes me sad. It's so cold and bleak and the characters are so unhappy. It reminded me of the last time I saw Jim. We didn't break up that night, but we broke up several months after he left the next morning. That night it was cold and rainy. I was tired and hungry. We argued a lot and I had a déjà vu. Wierd feeling. Maybe a warning of what was gonna happen. But déjà vu is about the past, not future. I just feel for the sad lovers in this poem and the memories they have of the winter cold and the cold in their hearts. And their eyes. Like Jim.

The purpose of a journal is to keep a record of your ideas and reactions for later reference and use in writing structured, edited compositions for other people to read.

Practice. Write a reader response journal entry on one of the following poems.

- "The Fury of Overshoes" by Anne Sexton (p. 90)
- "On Aging" by Maya Angelou (p.93)
- "Theme for English B" by Langston Hughes (p. 127)
- "Indian Movie, New Jersey" by Chitra Banerjee Divarkaruni (p. 235)

The Paraphrase

A *paraphrase* is a restatement of the original, line by line or sentence by sentence, in your own words. You may use a paraphrase of nonfiction—exposition or argument—in study or research notes, or a paraphrase of a poem in the explication (explanation) of the meaning. Following are a few tips for writing a paraphrase:

1. In preparation for writing a paraphrase, read the passage several times to comprehend the passage thoroughly.
2. Look up the meanings of any unfamiliar words or words that seem to be used in an unusual sense, and write them down so that you will not forget them.
3. Identify the main idea (topic sentence in a paragraph or thesis sentence in an essay or chapter or theme of a poem), and write it down.
4. Identify the structure of the passage (main points, subpoints, examples).
5. Referring to the passage, write the paraphrase, using your own words but not adding any of your own ideas, responses, or interpretations. You may have difficulty keeping your opinions out of the paraphrase, but you should save them for an essay of response or interpretation.
6. When you have completed the paraphrase, check it against the original to ensure that you have conveyed the author's meaning accurately and that you have not paraphrased too close to the source.

PARAPHRASING AN EXPOSITORY SELECTION

Following is a paragraph taken from Eric Berne's *The Structure and Dynamics of Organizations and Groups:*

> There are three types of leadership, corresponding to the three aspects of the group structure. The responsible leader is the front

man, the man who fills the role of leader in the organizational structure. The effective leader, who makes the actual decisions, may or may not have a role in the organizational structure. He may be the man in the back room, but he is the most important person in the individual structure. The psychological leader is the one who is most powerful in the private structures of the members and occupies the leadership slot in their group imagoes. All three types of leadership may be invested in the same individual, but there are all sorts of combinations. Thus, in the British Government, the Prime Minister is the responsible and effective leader, and the monarch is the psychological leader, and the ward boss is the effective leader. In certain criminal groups the front men are the responsible leaders, while another man who has no fixed role in the organizational structure is the effective and psychological leader.

Sample Paraphrase of the Berne Paragraph

Group or organizational structure can be divided into three types of leadership. One is the responsible leader who is visible to members or employees and to the public. The second type is the effective leader who actually makes the important decisions for the group. The psychological leader is one to whom the group looks for leadership and guidance. These three aspects of leadership may exist in one person or in several people in various combinations. For example, the British Prime Minister is the responsible and effective leader, but the king or queen is the psychological leader. Another example is criminal groups in which the front men are visible and responsible, but the psychological leader is someone else who may not even have a position in the group structure.

Practice. Write a paraphrase of one of the following paragraphs from this textbook: paragraph 10 from "The Anxiety Button" by Kitty Oliver (p. 102), paragraph 6 from "Media Literacy Education" by Elizabeth Thoman (p. 255), or paragraph 2 from "Mind-Expanding Machines" by Bruce Bower (p. 326).

PARAPHRASING A POEM

Following is a poem "Oh, My Love Is Like a Red, Red Rose," written by Robert Burns, an eighteenth century Scottish poet:

Oh, My Love Is Like A Red, Red Rose

Robert Burns

Oh, my love is like a red, red rose
    That's newly sprung in June;
My love is like the melody
    That's sweetly played in tune.

So fair art thou, my bonny lass,
    So deep in love am I;
And I will love thee still, my dear,
    Till a' the seas gang* dry.   *go

Till a' the seas gang dry, my dear,
    And the rocks melt wi' the sun;
And I will love thee still, my dear,
    While the sands o' life shall run.

And fare thee weel, my only love!
    And fare thee weel awhile!
And I will come again, my love
    Though it were ten thousand mile

Paraphrase of the Burns Poem

The woman I love is like a beautiful flower that has just bloomed. She is like beautiful, sweet music. My pretty girl, you are so lovely, and I am so much in love with you. I will love you until the seas have no water in them and until the rocks dissolve and turn to liquid from the heat. And I will still love you, my darling, when my life is over. So, for now, goodbye to you, the only one I love. I will be gone a while, but I promise you I will come to see you again even if I have to travel a long, long distance.

Practice. Write a paraphrase of one of the following poems from this textbook: "The Gift" by Li-Young Lee (p. 53), "The Fury of Overshoes" by Anne Sexton (p. 90), or "Theme for English B" by Langston Hughes (p. 127).

The Synopsis

A *synopsis* is a special type of summary; it is the summary of the plot of a story—a short story, a novel, a drama, a narrative poem, or a narrative essay. In a synopsis you tell what happens to whom where and when. Similar to writing a summary or a paraphrase, you include only the main points, use your own words, do not include any of your ideas or interpretations, and condense the story to a fraction of the original. Following is an example of a synopsis.

Synopsis of the Short Story "The Chaser" by John Collier (pp. 186–189)

Alan Austen nervously walked up the noisy stairs and finally found the name he was searching for in the dim light. He went into a small, sparsely furnished room where an old man was reading a newspaper. After the man greeted Alan by name, Alan asked him if he had a special mixture. The man replied he had lots of mixtures and one very special expensive one that he called a life cleaner. Alan wanted a less expensive love potion, and the old man sold him a strong, permanent one that would make his girlfriend extremely attentive and jealous of him. Alan was very pleased with the results that the old man described, so he bought it. Alan said goodbye, but the old man replied so long, expecting to see Alan again. [132 words]

Practice. Write a synopsis of one of the following short stories from this textbook: "A Clean, Well-Lighted Place" by Ernest Hemingway (p. 114), or "Charles" by Shirley Jackson (p. 146), or "A&P" by John Updike (p. 297).

The Academic Paragraph

A body paragraph in academic writing is an essay in miniature. It is part of a whole, part of a larger composition. An *academic paragraph* is defined as a unit or division of an essay, composition, or report; it expresses a thought or point relevant to a whole but is complete in itself. It is 100 or more words if developed adequately. The academic paragraph has the same characteristics as an essay but on a smaller scope.

Just as an essay has an introduction, body, and conclusion, a paragraph has a beginning, a middle, and an end. First, the academic paragraph begins with a *topic sentence*, a statement of the subject and slant of the paragraph unit. The topic sentence is to the paragraph as the *thesis sentence* is to the essay. It is the introduction to the paragraph. The topic sentence has the same characteristics as a thesis sentence:

- one sentence (not a fragment and not two sentences)
- unified (one idea expressed in one independent clause)
- restricted (limited to one idea that can be adequately developed in a paragraph)
- precise and clear (states the meaning with no ambiguity and no confusion)
- concise (not wordy)

The topic sentence differs from the thesis sentence in that it is smaller in scope and purpose: it does not attempt to cover as much as a thesis does. Second, just as an essay has a body, a paragraph also has a body. The paragraph breaks the topic idea into parts and develops each part with specific details and examples. Third, a paragraph ends with a clincher sentence that reaffirms the topic sentence. Sometimes the clincher is omitted if there is a sense of finality to the paragraph without it, but when you are writing for composition classes in college, you should use a clincher sentence. The same rhetorical modes and methods of development are used in both a paragraph and an essay. Just as transitional words and phrases are used to connect paragraphs in an essay, transitions are used to connect the sentences in a paragraph.

Following are a few examples of academically structured paragraphs written by professional writers. Following is an example by N. Scott Momaday from his essay "To the Singing, To the Drums."

Narrative-Descriptive Paragraph

Topic sentence

Details arranged spatially and chronologically

The celebration is on the north side. We turn down into a dark depression, a large hollow among trees. It is full of camps and cars and people. At first there are children. According to some centrifugal social force, children function on the periphery. They run about, making festival noises. Firecrackers are snapping all around. We park and I make ready; the girls help me with my regalia. I am already wearing white trousers and moccasins. Now I tie the black velvet sash around my waist, placing the beaded tassels at my right leg. The bandoleer of red beans, which was my grandfather's, goes over my left shoulder, the V at my right hip. I decide to carry the blanket over my arm until I join the dancers; no sense in wrapping up in this heat. There is deep, brickred dust on the ground. The grass is pale and brittle here and there. We make our way through the camps, stepping carefully to avoid the pegs and guy lines that reach about the tents. Old people, imperturbable, are lying down on cots and benches in the shadows. Smoke hangs in the air. We smell hamburgers, popcorn, gunpowder. Later there will be fried bread, boiled meat, Indian corn.

Momaday begins the paragraph with the topic sentence, "The celebration is on the north side," and then develops the paragraph spatially as he moves closer to the celebration. He appeals to all five senses—sight, sound, smell, taste, and touch.

Following is a paragraph of exemplification from *A Distant Mirror* by Barbard Tuchman.

Paragraph of Examples

Topic sentence

When I come across a generalization or a general statement in history unsupported by illustration I am instantly on guard; my reaction is, "Show me." If a historian writes that it was raining heavily on the day war was declared, that is a detail corroborating a statement, let us say, that the day was gloomy. But if he writes merely that it was a gloomy day without mentioning the rain, I want to know what is his evidence; what made it gloomy. Or if he writes, "The population was in a belligerent mood," or, "It was a period of great anxiety," he is indulging in general statements which carry no conviction to me if they are not illustrated by some evidence. I write for example that fashionable French society in the 1890s imitated the English in manners and habits. Imagining myself to be my own reader—a complicated fugue that goes on all the time at my desk—my reaction is of course, "Show me." The next sentence does. I write "*Le Grand Steeple* was held at *Auteuil*, le Derby

Example 1

Example 2

Example 3

at Longchamps, unwanted members were *black-boulé* at the Jockey Club, Charles Swann had 'Mr' engraved on his calling cards."

Tuchman states her topic sentence in the first sentence of the paragraph. She develops the paragraph with three examples to support the topic sentence.

Following is a paragraph of comparison and contrast by Bruce Catton in his esssay "Grant and Lee: A Study in Contrasts."

Paragraph of Comparison and Contrast

Topic sentence	So Grant and Lee were in complete contrast, representing two diametrically opposed elements in
Grant	American life. Grant was the modern man emerging; beyond him, ready to come on the stage, was the great age of steel and machinery; of crowded cities
Lee	and a restless burgeoning vitality. Lee might have ridden down from the old age of chivalry, lance in
Clincher	hand, silken banner fluttering over his head. Each
sentence	man was the perfect champion of his cause, drawing both his strengths and his weaknesses from the people he led.

Catton compares and contrasts the two great generals of the War Between the States, Ulysses S. Grant for the North and Robert E. Lee for the South.

Practice. Choose one of the following topics, and write a well-structured, well-developed academic paragraph of 100 words or more. Begin the paragraph with a topic sentence and use a clincher sentence to end it.

Physical Description of a Friend

Narration of an Event at School

Comparison-Contrast of My High School Math Teacher and My College Math Instructor

Definition of a Good Friend

Teachers Who Have Helped Me Develop My Self-Confidence

Reasons I Came to College

How to Make My Favorite Dish

Parts of a Talk Show

The Academic Essay

Of all the many types of writing—for example, fiction or nonfiction, journalistic or legal, informal or formal—the type you are most concerned about in this course and in other college courses in the academic essay. In many of your classes you will be asked to demonstrate your ability to compose an academic essay. According to the assignment, this type of essay may be personal or impersonal, drawn from your experience and knowledge or from research investigation, *expository* (explanatory) or *argumentative* (persuasive). Your primary purpose is to transfer an idea or position from your mind to the minds of your readers through written language (see "The Process of Communicating," p. 10). To accomplish this purpose, you must convince them that you are a *credible* person (knowledgeable in the field of discussion and trustworthy) and that what you say is *valid* (logical or reasonable) and *plausible* (believable). You must also provide sufficient *evidence* (clarifications, details, examples, illustrations) to make your point clearly and convincingly.

STRUCTURE OF THE ACADEMIC ESSAY

The typical structure of the academic essay is *introduction-body-conclusion*, and the movement of thought is from general to specific to general.

1. **Introduction.** The introduction is usually one paragraph that grabs the readers' interest and attention, introduces the general subject, and narrows it to a main idea or thesis. Often the introductory paragraph also states the major points for development in the essay in the order of development. In a sense, the thesis is a one-sentence summary of the essay, and the introductory paragraph is a one-paragraph summary of the essay.

2. **Body.** The body of the essay analyzes the main point and divides it into several subdivisions that you develop with supporting evidence. An academic paragraph begins with a topic sentence (statement of the main idea of the paragraph), states and supports the subdivisions of the topic

sentence, and ends with a clincher or concluding sentence. The academic paragraph is an essay in miniature; that is, it has the same structure (general to specific to general, or topic sentence to developmental details to ending sentence) as the academic essay but on a more restricted basis. As a writer you may divide the thesis into two parts (such as the problem of student parking on campus and a proposed solution), or three parts (such as three major reasons for going to a particular college—social, financial, and academic), or four parts (such as types of students—preppies, nerds, partiers, and gothics). In most cases, for brief (500–1,000 words) essays, two, three, or four subdivisions adequately developed will comprise a satisfactory essay, and each subdivision will be developed in one paragraph.

3. **Conclusion.** The conclusion is the final paragraph that reaffirms the thesis idea and provides a sense of finality for the essay.

RHETORICAL ELEMENTS OF THE ACADEMIC ESSAY

An effective academic essay, as all good writing, has four basic *rhetorical* characteristics; that is, characteristics of effective writing.

Unity means oneness. Everything in the essay relates directly to the idea of the thesis, its subject and slant.

Organization means the ideas, sentences, and paragraphs are arranged in an order that makes sense to the readers. They may be organized in *spatial order* (in the order of location in space, such as right to left or down to up), *chronological order* (in order of occurrence in time), or *logical order* (in the order of idea, such as least important to most important, effect to cause, or problem to solution).

Development means the ideas are adequately developed (explained and supported) to make them clear, understandable, and believable. There are various patterns of development, such as narration, description, example or illustration, enumeration, causes and effects, comparison and contrast, analysis, classification, process, definition, and negation.

Coherence means the ideas, sentences, and paragraphs are connected so that they flow smoothly. The writer has the responsibility to include transitions, signposts, and bridges so that the readers can easily follow the writer's thoughts.

Throughout this course you will study and practice these elements of effective writing.

THE PROCESS OF COMPOSING

Writing or composing is a *process* of steps that are cyclical (repeating and going forward and backward), not linear (going in a straight sequence). The steps include prewriting, writing, and rewriting. You should practice these steps so that they become easy and familiar, and then you may adapt or change them according to your personal preferences.

Prewriting

The prewriting step involves thinking and planning before you write the final paper.

1. Choose a general subject that is of interest to you and your intended readers. Three helpful ways to find something to write about are brainstorming (free association for stimulating a list of ideas), freewriting (writing whatever comes to mind as it comes to mind), and keeping a journal.
2. Restrict or narrow the topic to something that is manageable in the time and space available.
3. State a tentative thesis sentence or main idea to focus your ideas. This sentence should include a restricted subject you want to write about as well as the point that you want to make or the attitude you intend to take. The thesis sentence should be exact, precise, and concise, and it should state just one central idea.

   Example:

Indian blankets are made of wool.	No point of view
Indian blankets are beautiful.	Too vague and unrestricted
Navaho blankets are exquisitely crafted in design, color, and texture.	Satisfactory

   As you write the essay, you may refine the thesis or even discover that you want to change it completely.
4. Gather information relevant to your thesis. You may draw from your memory and experience, or from reading and observation.
5. Organize the information into a logical pattern. You may use a variety of methods to find the best organizational pattern, such as outlining or clustering.

Writing

The next step is putting your ideas down on paper or into a computer. Some writers begin with a discovery draft, but you will save a lot of time and thought if you have an organizational plan before you begin to put your ideas into paragraphs. In the drafting stage, do not worry about checking grammar or spelling or punctuation or about finding the best word or phrasing to express your meaning. Just get your ideas down while they are fresh in your mind.

Rewriting

The final step in writing includes proofreading, revising, and editing your draft. Clean up your writing so that you will communicate what you intend to your readers clearly and effectively.

Proofreading is checking your essay and finding the sections that need to be revised or edited. Proofread your essay several times, and be sure to proofread the final draft carefully.

Revising is making all necessary rhetorical changes to ensure your essay is unified, logically organized, adequately developed, and coherent. This step may include taking out irrelevant statements, rearranging the order of ideas, adding specific details, or adding transitional words and phrases.

Editing is correcting the language skills—spelling, capitalization, punctuation, grammar, sentence structure, word choice—so that they follow the conventions of Standard English.

PREPARING TO WRITE

As you begin your college composition class, you may have problems getting started when you have a writing assignment. You may feel as if you have nothing to say or you may not know where to begin. Here are a few tips to help you get started.

1. Be comfortable. Wear comfortable clothes, sit in a comfortable place, and create the circumstances that make you feel at ease. Maybe you like loud music blaring or perhaps you prefer quiet. Maybe you prefer your

surroundings to be cool or perhaps warm. Maybe you prefer to be alone or perhaps you work best with other people around you. You know yourself and understand under what circumstances you perform best, so set up your situation accordingly.

2. Write at the time best for you. Some writers are morning people, but others have a hard time waking up. Some people prefer to write in the afternoon, whereas others are tired by two or three o'clock and want a break or a nap. Some people write best at night when the house is quiet and all the chores of the day are completed, but others fall asleep after ten o'clock. If you don't know when you can concentrate best, try writing at various times of the day until you can establish a time that works for you. Then arrange your other activities so that you can write at your best time.

3. Write in a special place. Use one place as your writing corner so that when you go there, your mind will be ready to get to work. Your place may be an isolated spot in the college library, the computer lab, a desk in your bedroom, or the kitchen table at home. Whatever spot you choose, you should have room for all your books, paper, pens and pencils, computer, and other supplies.

4. Reduce distractions. Get up in the morning before your family or roommates do, or wait until after they have gone to bed. Turn on the telephone answering machine and turn off your cell phone. Let the people around you know that you have serious work to do and do not want to be disturbed.

5. Establish a ritual. Find and follow a routine that gets you in the mood for writing. Get a glass of water or a cup of coffee, turn off the television, put in your favorite CD, gather all of the books and notes you will need, turn on the computer and check the printer, turn on your lamp, and move off your desk anything that is not related to the job you are working on.

Above all, be serious about your job of writing and stick to it. Budget your time so that you can complete the assignment without rushing.

EXAMPLE OF THE ACADEMIC ESSAY

Professional writers often use the characteristics of the academic essay in their writings. Following is an annotated example by Stephen King, who writes horror novels.

Why We Crave Horror Movies

Stephen King

Introduction

Thesis

Q & A
Asks why
Reason #1

Transition
Reason #2

What?
Don't un-
derstand.
See ¶11.

1   I think that we're all mentally ill; those of us outside the asylums only hide it a little better—and maybe not all that much better, after all. We've all known people who talk to themselves, people who sometimes squinch their faces into horrible grimaces when they believe no one is watching, people who have some hysterical fear—of snakes, the dark, the tight place, the long drop . . . and, of course, those final worms and grubs that are waiting so patiently underground.

2   When we pay our four or five bucks and seat ourselves at tenth-row center in a theater showing a horror movie, we are daring the nightmare.

3   Why? Some of the reasons are simple and obvious. To show that we can, that we are not afraid, that we can ride this roller coaster. Which is not to say that a really good horror movie may not surprise a scream out of us at some point, the way we may scream when the roller coaster twists through a complete 360 or plows through a lake at the bottom of the drop. And horror movies, like roller coasters, have always been the special province of the young; by the time one turns forty or fifty, one's appetite for double twists or 360-degree loops may be considerably depleted.

4   We also go to reestablish our feelings of essential normality; the horror movie is innately conservative, even reactionary. Freda Jackson as the horrible melting woman in *Die, Monster, Die!* confirms for us that no matter how far we may be removed from the beauty of a Robert Redford or a Diana Ross, we are still light-years from true ugliness.

Cause &
Effect
Essay →
Reasons or
Causes

Attention
Getter:
with
examples

Reason #1

Comparison
& contrast

Reason #2

Comparison
& contrast

Transition

5   And we go to have fun.

Reason #3

6   (Ah, but this is where) the ground starts to slope away, isn't it? Because this is a very peculiar sort of fun indeed. The fun comes from

oh, yes!

seeing others menaced—sometimes killed. One critic suggested that if pro football has become the **voyeur's** version of combat, then the hor-

Comparison and contrast

Spectator

ror film has become the modern version of the public lynching.

7   It is true that the (mythic), "fairy-tale"

Usually for children and with happy ending

Defined as a recurring story with a theme that appeals to a group of people because it expresses deep common emotions or feelings

horror film intends to take away the shades of gray. . . . It urges us to put away our more civilized and adult penchant for analysis and to become children again, seeing things in pure blacks and whites. It may be that horror movies provide psychic relief on this level because this invitation to lapse into simplicity, irrationality, and even outright madness is extended so rarely. We are told we may allow our emotions a free rein . . . or no rein at all.

That's civilized behavior!?

Transition

8   (If) we are all insane, (then) sanity becomes a matter of degree. If your insanity leads you to carve up women like Jack the Ripper or the Cleveland Torso Murderer, we clap you away in the funny farm (but neither of those two

Examples

Tone!

amateur-night surgeons was ever caught, heh-heh-heh); if, on the other hand, (your) insanity leads you only to talk to yourself when you're under stress or to pick your nose on your morning bus, then you are left alone to go about

Shifts to you to bring reader

Sarcastic tone again

your business . . . though it is doubtful that you will ever be invited to the best parties.

9   The potential lyncher is in almost all of us (excluding saints, past and present; but then, most saints have been crazy in their own ways), and every now and then, he has to be let loose

Agree?

to scream and roll around in the grass. Our emotions and our fears form their own body, and we recognize that it demands its own

C & C - Metaphor

exercise to maintain proper muscle tone. Certain of these emotional muscles are accepted—even exalted—in civilized society; they are of course, the emotions that tend to maintain the status quo of civilization itself. Love, friendship, loyalty, kindness—these are all the emotions that we applaud, emotions that have been immortalized in the couplets of Hallmark cards and in the verses (I don't dare call it poetry) of Leonard Nimoy.

Civilized emotions

Tone again
Snide

Transition

Cause & Effect

10 When we exhibit (these emotions,) society showers us with positive reinforcement; we learn this even before we get out of diapers. When, as children, we hug our rotten little puke of a sister and give her a kiss, all the aunts and uncles smile and twit and cry, "Isn't he the sweetest little thing?" Such coveted treats as chocolate-covered graham crackers often follow. But if we deliberately slam the rotten little puke of a sister's fingers in the door, sanctions follow—angry **remonstrance** from parents, aunts, and uncles; instead of a chocolate-covered graham cracker, a spanking.

Examples

Tone!
Sarcasm

Look up.

11 (But) anticivilization emotions don't go away, and they demand periodic exercise. We have such "sick" jokes as "What's the difference between a truckload of bowling balls and a truckload of dead babies" (You can't unload the truckload of bowling balls with a pitchfork . . . a joke, by the way, that I heard originally from a ten-year-old.) Such a joke may surprise a laugh or a grin out of us even as we recoil, a possibility that confirms the (thesis;) if we share a brotherhood of man, then we also share an insanity of man. None of which is intended as a defense of either the sick joke or insanity but merely as an explanation of [how] the best horror films, like the best fairy tales, manage to be reactionary,

Transition

Example

Effective use of fragment

*IMP.***

C & C

His argu-
ment is not
easy to
follow.

anarchistic, and revolutionary all at the same
time.   See ¶4

12   The mythic horror movie, like the sick joke,
has a dirty job to do. It deliberately appeals to   Summary &
all that is worst in us. It is morbidity unchained,   Conclusion

Our lowest,
animalistic,
violent
urges

our most (base) instincts let free, our nastiest fantasies realized ... and it all happens, fittingly
enough, in the dark. For those reasons, good
liberals often shy away from horror films. For
myself, I like to see the most aggressive of
them—*Dawn of the Dead*, for instance—as

Examples
of Activi-
ties

lifting a trapdoor in the civilized forebrain and
throwing a basket of raw meat to the hungry
alligators swimming around in that subter-
ranean river beneath.   Simile

13   (Why) bother? Because it keeps them from
getting out, man, it keeps them down there
and me up here. It was Lennon and McCartney   oh, Yeah!
who said that (all you need is love,) and I would
agree with that.

Good
Ending

14   As long as you keep the gators fed.   Tone

Structure/Organization

Introduction	-	¶1-2
Body	-	¶3-11
Reason #1	-	¶3
Reason #2	-	¶4
Reason #3	-	¶5-11
Conclusion	-	¶12-14

Reason #3—developed more fully because it is
the most important!

ANNOTATED DRAFTS OF A STUDENT ACADEMIC ESSAY

On the following pages are three drafts of a student essay. The first draft was the
diagnostic essay written in class at the beginning of a college composition class.
The assignment was an extemporaneous writing for which Delores Staudt
chose one of several topics provided by her instructor. She chose the topic
"Why Students Should or Should Not Go to College Immediately After High
School."

tests are a lot easier ~~when you have been studying~~ _soon after_ ~~and taking high school courses.~~ Much of what you   *Leave*

learn in your ~~freshman~~ year at college is a

refresher of classes you had in high school. The

longer you put off school, the more knowledge of   *S-V Agreement*

math, grammar, and study skills get dumped from   *S-V Agreement*

your brain, and in its place comes financial   *S-V Agreement*

worries, bills, and family.

Good transition & TS for ¶

The third, and in my mind, most compelling, reason

to go to college right out of high school is the fact   *No C*

that you still have your youth. There is so much

time left in your life to be bogged down with

Need to be more specific

"grown-up" issues, it seems almost insane not to take

advantage of the opportunities that are out there

to go to college right away.

In the meantime, you can build relationships with

friends, take time to get to know what you really   *Be specific!*

want to be when you "grow up", and not be forced

to work at a dead end job just to make ends meet.

dg mod

~~Speaking from experience,~~ 35 is not the optimal

time to start college.

Shift in person

You will be hard pressed to find anyone my age who   *no C*

is just starting back to school who will say "I am   *no C*   *C*

so glad I waited!" If life were that great without a

those of us over 30

college degree, ~~we~~ would not be sitting in this class.

Not clear. Restate

There are some benefits to going to college late in

life, but if you do not go immediately out of high

school it is likely you will learn those benefits on

your own.   *Wordy & Vague Pro Ref*

Draft #1

indent for ¶ → If a high school student were to approach me

today and ask my opinion on whether (he/she)

should go immediately to college upon graduation,

SP
I would definately tell that person to go to college

why that GR
as soon as possible. There are many reasons ~~that I~~ *Dic*

Vague Pro Ref & WDY
feel ~~this is beneficial,~~ to go immediately rather

to go immediately is beneficial, *is beneficial,*
  to
~~than wait,~~ but the three most important reasons

Good!
Shift in person → are time, knowledge, and youth.

indent for ¶ → When (you) are 18 years old, you believe time is on

Need transition & topic sentence for ¶.
your side. You tend to put off today what you

feel you can do tomorrow. Before you realize it, a

few years will have passed and the money you

are making at your current job has helped you

get a car, maybe an apartment. The prospects of

what your life would be like if you were to commit

need example
your life to studying do not look so great now. Over

time, relationshipsdeepen and you may even have

marital and family obligations; *Examples needed*
a child or two. Now you are faced with ~~the~~

becomes a distant memory.
~~realization that~~ school ~~comes last on your list of~~

OK. leave sentence in.
~~priorities. It is hard to even imagine how you could~~

~~fit college into an 80 hour work week.~~

Need this sentence for trans & T S. ~~Another plus on your side at 18 is~~

Immediately after high school, provided you made it to class most

of the time, you have gained knowledge that is useful in college.

~~knowledge.~~ The SAT's and placement

Draft #2

At 17 years of age, I knew everything there was to know about life. The road to fortune and success had been laid out in my mind; the mode in which I was to get to that destination was not remotely a concern. I had drawn a blueprint for my life at a very early age; there was no reason to believe this journey would not take place—after all, I had practiced its course many times.

As young as 5 years old, I recall picking dandelions in the field behind our barn. I would don my veil, (an old lace tablecloth,) and would proceed to have each of my stuffed animals line the perimeter of the chicken coop. With all of my "guests" watching, I would practice walking up the ramp of the coop to an imaginary priest awaiting my arrival beside my imaginary soon-to-be husband. I would play the wedding march in my head, (dum-dum-tadum; dum-dum-**ta**-dum...) carefully contemplating my steps up the "isle", neither going too fast nor too slow. My fiancé would stand at the entrance of the coop—a faceless man with a huge grin, who was prepared to offer me his love and admiration. He would lift my veil and give me a kiss that would seal his promise of everlasting devotion. Later, in the afternoon, after throwing my bouquet of dandelions, I would climb up to the hayloft, (which doubled as a stage) and with our "baby" in my arms (time flies when one pretends) watch my husband accept his doctor's degree. He would tell everyone that he could never have done it without his wonderful wife and I would stand up and wave to the audience of pigs and cows, while bouncing my crying stuffed animal over my shoulder. Oddly enough, even at 17 years of age, I truly believed this was how my life would begin and end: in love, with 2 kids and a white picket fence...then I grew up.   *Add specifics*

evident? Through a series of <u>unfortunate events</u>, it became quite my fairy tale ending would not happen the way I had planned; somehow, the script became tainted with evil villains, witches, and reality. I found myself <u>facing</u> a life of welfare, <u>raising</u> two sons on my own, and <u>had</u> no map to navigate myself out of the forest of darkness we had been led into. *Parallel*   It was then that my fairy godmother appeared. My older sister, who had often watched in amusement (and a twinge of sadness) as I played out my pretend life, offered to allow my sons and me to live with her and her family while I finished my degree. Now, at 35, I am doing what should have been done *P* (at 18,) obtaining my college degree—not depending on a mate to fulfill my dreams of success.> *Specify*

   dg
   Looking back, things may have been very different, if 30 years ago in that hayloft, *I* had been the one to accept that *P* "doctor's degree". Thankfully, we are all able to write and rewrite our own script for life: (some just) take longer than others to figure out that *happily-ever-after* begins *Agr &* with finding (yourself) before anyone else.   *shift*

In this in-class composition, Staudt wrote a satisfactory but rather formulaic and uninteresting introduction, but in the essay she had problems transferring her ideas from her mind to the minds of her readers. First, she had rhetorical problems with coherence, especially transitions between paragraphs, and with development, especially lack of specific details and examples to support her generalizations. These two deficiencies caused weak paragraph construction. In addition, she had language skills problems, particularly with pronoun use and wordiness.

Later in the semester she revised her essay and wrote the second draft out of class. She wrote this draft after she had studied unity, organization, development, and coherence; had reviewed language skills and conventions for Standard English; and had practiced proofreading, revising, and editing. She also used the "Checklist for Revising and Editing" at the end of this chapter to help her strengthen her writing.

This draft of Staudt's essay was much livelier and much more well developed with specific words, details, and examples. She *showed* her readers what was happening; she did not just tell them in a vague manner. The essay was also more coherent than her first attempt because she provided more signposts, bridges, and transitions to guide her readers through her ideas. However, in this draft Staudt became too personal for an academic essay and still needed to develop the expository section of her ideas more specifically. She needed to gain more distance from her experience, to draw back and anticipate what her readers would think and question as they read her paper. Upon reflection, she asked for more feedback from her instructor and revised her essay again. This time she combined the first and the second drafts, using her experiences to establish her credibility as one who can give advice on this subject and to introduce her analytical, expository ideas.

The third draft is her final polished, revised version of the essay. It exhibits what she learned in her composition class. As you read this final draft, ask yourself if this were your paper, would you change anything else before turning it in for evaluation?

Draft #3
The Best Time to Go to College
Delores Staudt

At 17 I knew everything there was to know about life. I had laid out my road to fortune and fame in my mind. However, I didn't know the mode through which I was to get to that destination; in fact, it was not remotely a concern to me. I had drawn a blueprint for my life at a very early age. There was no reason for me to believe this journey would not take place—after all, I had practiced its course many times.

As young as 5 years old, I would pick dandelions in the field behind our barn and make myself a beautiful bouquet. I would don my veil (an old lace tablecloth) and would proceed to have each of my stuffed animals line the perimeter of the chicken coop. With all of my "guests" watching, I would practice walking up the ramp of the coop to an imaginary priest awaiting my arrival beside my imaginary soon-to-be husband. I would play the wedding march in my head *(dum-dum-tadum; dum-dum-**ta**-dum)*, carefully contemplating my steps up the aisle, neither going too fast nor too slow. My fiancé would stand at the entrance of the coop—a faceless man with a huge grin, who was prepared to offer me his love and admiration. He would lift my veil and give me a kiss that would seal his promise of everlasting devotion. Later in the afternoon, after throwing my bouquet of dandelions to my guests, I would climb up to the hayloft (which doubled as a stage) and with our "baby" in my arms (time flies when one pretends) watch my husband accept his doctor's degree. He would tell everyone that he could never have done it without his wonderful wife, and I would stand up and wave to the audience of pigs and cows, while bouncing my crying stuffed animal-baby over my shoulder. Oddly enough, even at 17, I truly believed this was how my life would begin and end: in love, with 2 kids and a white picket fence.

Then through a series of unfortunate events I grew up. Because I was foolishly in love and would not listen to my family and friends, I slept with my boyfriend and became pregnant. Feeling that we had to do the "right" thing, we got married before we really knew each other and before he had a job paying enough to support a wife and child. After a healthy boy was born and then 11 months later, a second boy, the stress and responsibility of a family became too much for my husband, so he left me with two infants. It became quite evident my fairy tale ending would not happen the way I had planned: somehow, the script became tainted with evil villains, witches, and reality. I found myself facing a life of welfare, raising two sons on my own in small apartments far away from family and friends, and having no map to navigate myself out of the forest of darkness we were in. I wanted to go to college, and even enrolled one semester, but it was too much for me, so I withdrew. My sons and I struggled as I went from one low-paying job— server, store clerk, cashier—to another until I started working as a home health aid and then in a nursing home and decided I wanted to be a nurse. For several years I kept this dream alive but could not afford to stop work and go to college. Then my fairy godmother appeared. My older sister, who had often watched in amusement (and a twinge of sadness) as I played out my dream life in the barn, offered to allow my sons and me to live with her and her family while I got my RN. Now at 35 I am doing what I wish I had done when I was 18: obtaining my college degree and not depending on a mate to fulfill my dreams of success.

As I look back on my experiences, I realize things could have been very different for me. And if some high school students were to approach me today and ask my opinion on whether they should go immediately to college upon graduation, I would definitely tell them to go to college as soon as possible and not wait several years. There are many reasons that I feel going immediately rather than waiting is beneficial, but the three most important reasons are time, knowledge, and youth.

The first reason I advise young people to go right on to college is time. Usually 18-year-olds believe time is on their side. They tend to put off today what they feel they can do tomorrow. Even though they want to go to college and study engineering or biology or art, they decide to get a job and save some money first. Then before they realize it, a few years have passed and the money they are making has allowed them to buy cars, get their own apartments, buy lots of new clothes, and party and travel when they want to. They seldom think about giving up all this, and if they do, they don't like the prospects of cutting back on their spending and committing themselves to studying. Over time relationships deepen, and they may get married and have children. Now they are faced with marital and family obligations—feeding, clothing, housing, and keeping the family healthy and happy. They find it hard to even imagine how they can fit college into an 80-hour work week plus keep up with home and family obligations. School becomes a distant memory and may even seem like an impossibility. If they had gone to college immediately after high school, time and relationships would probably have worked with them and not against them and their dreams.

The second reason for going to college immediately after high school is knowledge.

Immediately after high school, provided the graduates have attended class most of the time, they have gained knowledge that is useful in college and it is fresh in their minds. The SAT's and placement tests are easier soon after they have been studying and taking high school courses. Much of what they learn in their freshman year of college is a refresher and an extension of what they studied in high school. The longer they put off college, the more knowledge of math, grammar, and study skills gets dumped from their brains, and in its place come bills, financial worries, family problems, and little time for themselves. Thus, if students go immediately to college, they will remember more from high school and will progress more rapidly in college.

The third, and in my mind, most compelling, reason to go to college right out of high school is the fact that they still have their youth. There is so much time left in their lives to be bogged down with grown-up issues that it seems to me almost insane not to take advantage of the opportunities that are out there to go to college right away. Now there are community colleges and universities near the home of most young people. Scholarships and other forms of financial aid, such as BEOG grants and loans, are readily available, and high school as well as college counselors are happy to provide this information for those who ask. While attending college, they can build solid relationships and friendships, take time to know what they really want to be when they grow up, and not be forced to work at a dead-end job just to make ends meet.

From my experiences I have learned that 35 is not the optimal time to start college. Looking back now, I realize that if 30 years ago in that hayloft

I had been the one to accept that "doctor's degree" and if I had made some different decisions when I was young, things may have been very different for me. Anyone would be hard pressed to find a person my age who is just starting back to school who will say, "I am so glad I waited!" If life were that great without a college degree, those of us over 30 would not be sitting in this classroom now. There may be some benefits to going to college late in life, but if an individual does not go immediately to college out of high school, it is likely he or she will learn those benefits the hard way as I have. Nevertheless, thankfully we are all able to write and rewrite our own script for our lives. Some just take longer than others to figure out, as I finally did, that happily-ever-after begins with finding themselves before finding anyone else.

What do you think of Staudt's third draft? Use the following checklist to go through her essay carefully, and then discuss it with your classmates.

Checklist for Revising and Editing

Following is a list of questions to guide you in the process of revising and editing your essays. Use the questions to respond to the essay and to check for any points of needed revision. You may also use it to respond to and evaluate essays by other writers, whether students or professional writers.

1. **Sources:** What sources of information does the author draw upon—experience and memory, observation, reading and research, conversation and interview?

2. **Purpose:** What is the author's purpose in this essay—to narrate, to develop, to explain, to argue or convince, or a combination of these? Does the author accomplish the purpose?

3. **Thesis:** What is the thesis sentence or main point? Does the author state the thesis or imply it? Does the author make the thesis clear?

4. **Unity:** Does the author stick to the thesis? Is every statement in the essay directly relate to the main idea?

5. **Structure and Organization**

   A. **Introduction**
      1) Does the introduction make clear the subject of the essay?
      2) Does the introduction state or imply the thesis sentence clearly?
      3) Does the introduction grab your attention and interest, and make you want to read the essay?

   B. **Body**
      1) What are the major points for development in the essay?
      2) How does the author organize the points of development of the the essay? Is the order of points clear? Why does the author put the points in this order?
      3) Is this order appropriate for the ideas of the essay?
      4) Are there any other points or information that the author should have included? Why?

   C. **Conclusion**
      1) Does the conclusion relate directly to the introduction and to the thesis, as well as to the points in the body of the essay?
      2) Does the conclusion provide a sense of finality or ending to the essay?
      3) Is the conclusion effective?

6. **Development**

   A. What kinds of development does the author use to expand, support, and clarify the general assertions—narration, description, example, process, cause and effect, classification, example, comparison and contrast, definition, negation, statistics, expert opinion?

   B. Does the author provide sufficient evidence to make the subpoints clear and persuasive?

7. **Coherence**

   A. Does the essay flow smoothly from idea to idea? From sentence to sentence? From paragraph to paragraph?

   B. How does the author connect the ideas throughout the essay? What Bridges and signposts does the author use to help the reader navigate through the essay?
      1) What key ideas, words, and phrases does the author repeat?
      2) What pronouns does the author use?

3) What transitional words and phrases does the author use to connect paragraphs? To connect sentences within paragraphs?

8. **Rhetorical Patterns:** What rhetorical patterns does the author use—narration, description, exposition, argument, example or illustration, enumeration, cause, effect, comparison, contrast, analysis, classification, process, definition, problems to solution?

9. **Language Skills and Proofreading**

   A. Has the author proofread and edited the essay carefully for correctness, appropriateness, and effectiveness of language skills?
   - Spelling
   - Capitalization
   - Punctuation
   - Grammar
   - Sentence structure
   - Word choice

   B. What, if anything, should be changed? Why?

10. **Response and Evaluation**

   A. Did the author effectively fulfill the assignment and purpose in the essay?

   B. What is the strongest aspect of the essay? What do you like best? Why?

   C. What could be changed to improve the essay? Why?

At this point you may not understand some of the ideas and procedures discussed in this chapter. Just relax! In this course you will learn to understand them and will have the opportunity to practice them as well as to receive feedback on your application of them in your writings from your classmates and your instructor. The readings in this textbook and the study aids following each selection will help you deepen your comprehension and strengthen your writing.

PART 2

Readings for Writers

CHAPTER FOUR

Home and Family

One can never leave home. One carries the shadows and fears,
the hopes and dreams of home eternally just under the skin.

—MAYA ANGELOU

Suggestions for Journal Entries

Start keeping a composition journal now. You will add entries to it through-out the course. Freewrite for fifteen minutes about one or more of the fol-lowing topics. Keep your journal entries together in a notebook, and date each one. These journal entries will provide you with ideas for discussion and with topics for paragraphs and essays later.

1. Do you agree or disagree with Angelou's comment above? Explain.
2. What does *home* mean to you? Do you have positive or negative memories—or both—of home?
3. What is the difference between a *house* and a *home*?
4. What is your ideal home, the home that you would like to live in?
5. Describe one of the shadows or fears you remember from your childhood home.
6. Describe one of the hopes and dreams you remember from your childhood home.
7. Describe your family. How has it changed since you were a child?
8. Describe a memorable member of your family.
9. What is one of the most important gifts you received as a child? Who gave it to you and under what circumstances? Why is it so significant to you?
10. What is one of the most important decisions you have made about your family?

The Gift

Li-Young Lee

LI-YOUNG LEE was born in Jakarta, Indonesia, of Chinese parents. In 1959, after his father had spent a year in jail as a political prisoner, the family fled Indonesia and came to the United States. Lee attended the University of Pittsburgh, the University of Arizona, and the State University of New York College at Brockport, and now lives in Chicago. Many of his poems are autobiographical, reflecting the two worlds of his Chinese heritage and his American upbringing.

The Gift

To pull the metal splinter from my palm
my father recited a story in a low voice.
I watched his lovely face and not the blade.
Before the story ended he'd removed
the iron sliver I thought I'd die from.   5

I can't remember the tale
but hear his voice still, a well
of dark water, a prayer.
And I recall his hands,
two measures of tenderness   10
he laid against my face,
the flames of discipline
he raised above my head.

Had you entered that afternoon
you would have thought you saw a man   15
planting something in a boy's palm,
a silver tear, a tiny flame.
Had you followed that boy
you would have arrived here,
where I bend over my wife's right hand.   20

Look how I shave her thumbnail down
so carefully she feels no pain.
Watch as I lift the splinter out.
I was seven when my father
took my hand like this,   25

and I did not hold that shard
between my fingers and think,
Metal that will bury me,
christen it Little Assassin,
Ore Going Deep for My Heart.   30
And I did not lift up my wound and cry,
Death visited here!
I did what a child does
When he's given something to keep.
I kissed my father.   35

Comprehension and Discussion

1. What does the *speaker* remember most about the childhood experience? Why?
2. What is the speaker's attitude toward his father? From what specific words and phrases in the poem do you draw your conclusion?
3. Why did the child think he was going to die from the metal splinter in his hand? Is this a typical childish reaction? How did the speaker feel when he realized he was not going to die? What did he do? Why? Is his reaction plausible or believable?
4. Can you remember an event from your childhood that you blew out of proportion, one that you thought you were going to die from, or that someone else was going to die from because of something you had done? Why do you think children have such fears of dying?
5. What does the narrator mean when he says, "Had you followed that boy / you would have arrived here, / where I bend over my wife's right hand" (18–20)? What is the connection between the childhood experience and his experience with his wife?

Language and Technique

1. What does the title "The Gift" mean? What are the connotations or suggestions of the word *gift*? How do the last three lines of the poem relate to the title?
2. What is the difference between *autobiography* and *fiction*? Do you think this poem could be based on an autobiographical event in the poet's childhood? Why or why not? To respond to this question well, you might look up information (in an encyclopedia, a dictionary of biography, or on the Internet) on Lee's life and his relationship with his father. Also, remember that the speaker in a poem is not necessarily the same as the poet.

3. The poet refers to the "splinter" (1), the "iron sliver" (5), and "that shard" (26). Why do you think the poet used three words to describe the foreign object in his hand? Look up the *denotations* or dictionary meanings of these words and write them in your journal. Are the three words synonymous? What are the *connotations* (the suggested meanings) of these words? Write the connotations of the words in your journal as well. Then discuss Lee's use of these three words with your classmates.

4. Lee uses *metaphors* or implied comparisons effectively in the poem. Explain the meaning of each of the following metaphors:

   "his voice still, a well / of dark water" (7–8)

   "the flames of discipline / he raised above my head" (12–13)

   "a silver tear, a tiny flame" (17)

Suggestions for Writing

1. **Sentence.** Construct two metaphors that describe a person you know well or that describe the person's actions. The person may be your father or another relative or a friend.

2. **Paragraph.** Write a paragraph or poem about a memorable gift that you received.

3. **Essay.** Write an essay about a gift you received that has had a lasting impact upon you, one that you have carried with you, possibly one that has shaped your personality. Describe the gift precisely, tell how and why you received it, and explain how it has influenced you.

4. **Essay.** Think of someone with whom you had a deep relationship (positive or negative) when you were a child. The person may be a family member, a friend, a teacher, or a religious mentor. Write an essay about a memorable incident from your childhood that illustrates this individual's personality and your relationship with him or her.

5. **Essay.** Compare and contrast Lee's gift from his father with the gifts Linda Hogan received from her family ("Heritage," p. 55).

Heritage

Linda Hogan

LINDA HOGAN was born in Oklahoma and teaches creative writing in Colorado. A member of the Chickasaw tribe, she values her Native American heritage. In the poem "Heritage" she catalogs the gifts she has received from various older members of her family, not the objects she has been given but the knowledge and feelings.

Heritage

From my mother, the antique mirror
where I watch my face take on her lines.
She left me the smell of baking bread
to warm fine hairs in my nostrils,
she left the large white breasts that weigh down   5
my body.

From my father I take his brown eyes,
the plague of locusts that leveled our crops,
they flew in formation like buzzards.

From my uncle the whittled wood   10
that rattles like bones
and is white
and smells like all our old houses
that are no longer there. He was the man
who sang old chants to me, the words   15
my father was told not to remember.

From my grandfather who never spoke
I learned to fear silence.
I learned to kill a snake
when you're begging for rain.   20

And grandmother, blue-eyed woman
whose skin was brown,
she used snuff.
When her coffee can full of black saliva
spilled on me   25
it was like the brown cloud of grasshoppers
that leveled her fields.

It was the brown stain
that covered my white shirt,
my whiteness a shame.   30
That sweet black liquid like the food
she chewed up and spit into my father's mouth

when he was an infant.
It was the brown earth of Oklahoma
stained with oil.   35
She said tobacco would purge your body of poisons.

It has more medicine than stones and knives
against your enemies.

That tobacco is the dark night that covers me.
She said it is wise to eat the flesh of deer   40
so you will be swift and travel over many miles.
She told me how our tribe has always followed a stick
that pointed west
that pointed east.

From my family I have learned the secrets   45
of never having a home.

Comprehension and Discussion

1. How many members of the speaker's family are included in the poem?
   What has the speaker received from each of these members of her family? Why do you think Hogan chooses to include these family members? Discuss the possible reasons with your classmates. (Remember that
   the poet and the speaker in a poem are not necessarily the same. As
   Emily Dickinson, nineteenth-century American poet, said, the speaker
   may be "a supposed person"; that is, an assumed or fictitious role.)
2. Why does Hogan provide more detail on the gifts from her grandmother (21–44)?
3. What does the speaker mean when she states she "learned to fear silence" (18) from her grandfather? Why did she learn this from him?
   Discuss the possible reasons with your classmates.
4. Why is the speaker's "whiteness a shame" (30)?
5. What does the ending mean: "From my family I have learned the
   secrets / of never having a home" (45–46)? In your journal, write what
   you think this sentence means, and then discuss it with your classmates.
   Do all of you get the same meaning from these lines of the poem? Why
   or why not?

Language and Technique

1. What is the meaning of the title of this poem, "Heritage"? What is the heritage of the speaker in the poem? What is your heritage? *Compare* (explain the similarities) and *contrast* (explain the differences) your heritage with that of the speaker in the poem, and also with that of some of your classmates.

2. Hogan uses *parallel structure* (a technique in which a writer emphasizes the equal value of two or more ideas by expressing them in the same grammatical form) to introduce the gifts from the speaker's family: "From my mother" (1), "From my father" (7), "From my uncle" (10), "From my grandfather" (17). She breaks the parallelism for the grandmother—"And grandmother" (21)—but then returns to the parallel pattern for the summary: "From my family" (45). What is the effect of the parallelism? Why do you think she breaks the pattern for the grandmother?

3. Find some other examples of parallelism in Hogan's poem, and write them in your journal. Share these with your classmates, and record in your journal any additional examples that they point out to you.

4. Hogan uses several *sensory images or details* (words and phrases that describe how things look, smell, sound, taste, or feel) in the poem. Find at least one example of each of the following sensory details in the poem: sight, smell, sound, taste, and touch. Record the images in your journal. Share these with your classmates, and record in your journal any additional ones that they point out to you.

Suggestions for Writing

1. **Sentence.** Using parallel structure, write a sentence about two members of your family.

2. **Paragraph.** Write a paragraph or poem in which you describe or list gifts you have received from various family members. You cannot include everything, so choose carefully, and be specific in your description of each gift. Be prepared to read your paragraph to your classmates and be able to explain why you included each of the gifts.

3. **Essay.** During your lifetime you have received a variety of gifts, some *tangible* (a necklace, a sweater, a book, a car) and some *intangible* (love, understanding, time, a trip, a lesson). Think about all of the gifts you have received, and choose one special gift that was most memorable. Write an essay about that gift—what it was, who gave it to you, why he or she gave it to you, and what it meant to you.

4. **Essay.** Write an essay in which you compare and contrast your life today with the life of one of your parents or grandparents.

5. **Essay.** Did your family have any home remedies, such as what the speaker's grandmother says about tobacco (36–38) or eating the flesh of deer (41–42)? Did your family have any old sayings or beliefs, such as the speaker's grandfather killing a snake to bring rain (19–20)? Write an essay about the home remedies or beliefs or superstitions that have been passed down to you from your family.

What Is a Family?

Helen Bottel

HELEN BOTTEL is a journalist who often writes humorous pieces about family and home. In this essay she uses precise examples to define a family.

Vocabulary Study

hectic (1)	whales (4)
grounded (3, 8)	go-cart (4)

What Is a Family?

1   A family is a group of close relatives who go through all sorts of hectic things together.

2   A family is when the bills pile sky-high and Mom and Dad are worried sick, but you still get that beautiful gown you wanted for the senior prom.

3   A family is when Mom yells at you to get your dirty socks out of the closet. Or when you pay your sister $5 to clean your room—and *you* get grounded because *she* did such a lousy job!

4   A family is when Dad whales into your brother for getting his new screwdriver stuck in the bedroom wall. (He was trying to make a socket to plug in his radio next to the bed.) Or when Mom finds out that he used her best saucepan to mix gasoline and oil for his homemade go-cart.

5   A family is when you ruin your $25 shoes and Mom swears she won't *ever* buy you any more, but the very next day she comes home with another pair *and* a super skirt and sweater. (She'll tell you she got them on sale, but she really didn't.)

6   A family is when you meet your first love and everyone "helps." Your sister makes a dress that fits in all the wrong places, but you tell her it's beautiful. Then Dad slips you money to "buy something special." Little Sis gets the giggles when you introduce "him," and Mom is so fluttery beforehand

you'd think it was *her* first date. But somehow he feels right at home and Dad ends up talking football to him—while you wait 15 minutes.

7   A family is when Mom gives you a home permanent to save you money—and doesn't follow directions and it turns to frizz. In the end it costs more than twice as much to have it professionally straightened, but nobody says "I told you so" out loud.

8   A family is when the kids get threatened with long-term grounding because they ate Mom's beautiful creation for the bridge club, which they "found loose in the refrigerator." But you're all laughing about it next week.

9   A family is when the neighbors call the police because you're pillow-fighting on the front lawn at 1:30 A.M.

10   A family is when everybody laughs, cries and loves together. Once in a while they're hard to live with, but you couldn't live without them.

Comprehension and Discussion

1. What is the relationship among the members of this family? How do they feel toward one another? How would you describe their relationship? Would you like to be a member of this family? What do you consider the ideal family? Write a journal entry about your definition of the ideal family, and share it with your classmates.

2. Compare and contrast your family with the one Bottel's speaker describes in this essay. Write a journal entry of the similarities and differences, and discuss these with your classmates.

3. Few families are as ideal as the one Bottel describes. In fact, some sociologists today claim that family life, especially family values, has disintegrated or gotten worse in the last fifty years. Do you agree? If so, what are some of the things that have contributed to this disintegration? Discuss this idea with an older member of your family or with an older person with whom you work. Take notes in your journal. Then participate in a class discussion of this issue.

4. Which of Bottel's definitions of *family* do you like best? Which do you like least? Which ones seem most realistic? Do any seem to be exaggerated? Participate in a class discussion of your preferences and dislikes, and be able to explain why you have the opinions you do.

5. Who is the speaker in this essay? What is the speaker's attitude toward the family? What specific words, phrases, and details in the essay lead you to your conclusion? Discuss the speaker's role in the family with your classmates.

Language and Technique

1. Below is an analysis of the structure of Bottel's essay:

   Paragraph 1   **Introduction** that states the thesis sentence or main idea of the essay

   Paragraphs 2–9 **Body** that presents eight specific examples that define a family

   Paragraph 10   **Conclusion** that reaffirms the thesis and ends the essay

   Analyze the introduction-body-conclusion structure of Dickey's essay "He Caught the Dream" (pp. 62). Which paragraphs make up each part of Dickey's essay? Take notes in your journal as you study. Then, referring to both the Bottel essay and the Dickey essay, participate in a class discussion of this typical academic structure of writings—introduction, body, conclusion.

2. Which of the happenings in Bottel's essay are humorous? What words and details does the author use to make these events humorous? With your classmates, discuss the techniques that Bottel uses to achieve humor.

3. Not only are some of the details in Bottel's essay humorous, but also a thread of warmth runs through the essay. What words and details does she use to convey this warmth and love that the members of this family have for each other? Discuss this technique with your classmates.

4. In paragraphs 2–10, Bottel uses parallel structure to define a family. Each paragraph begins with "A family is when. . . ." Some grammarians do not consider "is when" proper grammar. Check a grammar handbook to see what the writers say about this grammatical structure. Why do you think Bottel uses this unconventional written grammatical structure repeatedly in her essay? Participate in a discussion with your instructor and your classmates on this usage.

Suggestions for Writing

1. **Sentence.** Writers often define by example rather than by abstraction or generalization, as Bottel does in this essay. For instance, in the comic strip "Peanuts" Charles Schultz defined love as a warm puppy, and a children's rhyme says little girls are made of sugar and spice and everything nice, but little boys are made of snakes and snails and puppy dog tails. Choose five of the following words, and then write a sentence

for each in which you define the word by using a specific example, not an abstract, vague term: *puppy, kitten, baby, little boy, little girl, brother, sister, mother, father, grandmother, grandfather, friend, girlfriend, wife, boyfriend, husband, football* (or other sport) *player, teacher, musician, education, college, test, exercise, dieting, love, jealousy, dishonesty*, or another word that you choose. Write your sentences in your journal, and share them with your classmates.

2. **Paragraph.** Write a paragraph (100 or more words) in which you describe a member of your family. Include physical characteristics, personality traits, attitudes, activities, and goals.

3. **Essay.** Using the technique of Bottel and Schultz, write a definition of your family.

4. **Essay.** Using one of the definition sentences that you wrote in question 1, think of five to ten more examples to define the word you chose, and then write a complete essay of definition, similar to the essay by Bottel defining *family*. Structure your essay as Bottel structured hers: introductory paragraph, body paragraphs of examples, and concluding paragraph.

5. **Essay.** Write an essay on one of the following topics. Use specific examples from your own experience and knowledge to support your thesis.

   - Talk with some older members of your family or older friends or acquaintances to discover specific examples of life thirty years ago. Write an essay in which you explain and exemplify how family life has changed in the last thirty years and what has caused these changes.
   - Write an essay in which you analyze and exemplify the causes of the disintegration of family life *or* of family values, *or* write an essay in which you defend today's family values, taking the stance that not all families have changed in a negative way and using specific examples from your experience and knowledge to defend the modern family.
   - Write an essay in which you enumerate, explain, and exemplify the key values that parents should teach their children and how they can teach children these important lessons of life.

He Caught the Dream

Bronwen Dickey

BRONWEN DICKEY is the daughter of poet and novelist James Dickey. She wrote this reminiscence of her dad soon after his death in 1997. As you read, notice how she shifts between the events surrounding his death and her memories of their relationship as she was growing up.

Vocabulary Study

Betadine (4)

lose-lose situation (5)

image (5)

sycophants (7)

mentor (7)

sonnet (9)

He Caught the Dream

And if the earthly has forgotten thee,

Say to the silent, "I am living."

To the running water, say, "I am."

1   My father always said that when it comes to writing, write what you want to say. The questioning, the changing, the editing . . . that all comes later. "Use the freedom," he said. I have just watched my father die. His life, which was reduced in the end to pulses on a dusty screen, has ended. And, if I can find the strength, this is what I want to say.

2   You could say that the day had been a tough one. As much as the grieving family tried to prepare me, I was horrified by what I saw waiting at the hospital. I did not recognize the man before me. That man was not talkative and vibrant. That man was not determined and strong. That man had given up. And, perhaps, it was time to. He was nothing more than a pained skeleton, and his chest heaved as though every breath was a last valiant effort. His fingers were purple from lack of oxygen, though it was being forced into his lungs in liters. My father was not physically recognizable, but his essence was still strong in the room. His books were strategically arranged nearby, and he still wore two watches, his Citizen Wingman and his Ironman Triathlon. Funny, he always had to be on time.

3   I can't remember exactly what I said to him—I think I was talking about boys and school and other trivia—but I remember him looking up at me through all the tubes and the plastic with tears in his eyes. He did not have the strength to cry, but I think he knew it would be the last time we saw each other. All I could do was burst into tears and flee from the room. Here was the man that changed my diapers, made me peanut-butter sandwiches (with the crusts cut off), showed me how to throw knives and to shoot a bow, read me poetry, stayed up with me all night when I was sick, taught me to play chess, came to all my recitals, braided my hair,

watched movies with me, checked my homework . . . and he was dying. Dying. And where was the pride in his death? Where was the glory in being the human part of an oxygen tank?

4   I forced myself to stop the tears and returned to the room. I sat down in the chair beside his bed and held his hand, which was covered in a mix of blood and Betadine from the IVs. "Come on, Dad," I tried to say with a smile. "I need you, OK?" And what he said, the last words he ever said to me, were, "I've always needed you." God, I loved my father. I squeezed his hand and told him that I loved him, and he nodded. Weary and dazed, I left the hospital with the hope that he would just hold on through the night, but he couldn't.

5   I was awakened at 11:18 PM, Sunday, January 19, with the news that my father had died. In a way, it was a relief. I didn't want him to hurt anymore. He should have been paddling down some wild river in a canoe, or playing bluegrass ballads on his guitar, or tapping away at a typewriter, not straining for breath in some sterile hospital room. I got dressed and drove to the hospital with no tears, and I saw that the door to his room was partially open. Seeing the person you love more than anything in the world dead is one of those lose-lose situations. I figured I either would see him that last time and have that image burned into my memory forever, or I would always wonder and wish I had. My father told me never to look at him dead, and I should have listened. It was the most horrible thing I have ever seen.

6   I never thought there could be such a dramatic difference in a person who is very ill and one who's dead, but the difference was incredible. The lights were off, and there was an eerie backlight behind the bed. My father . . . My father's body was propped up, but his head had fallen back and his mouth was open. He looked like he was in pain. A lot of pain. Did I have to see him gasping for air the last time I ever saw him? I screamed. I didn't know what else to do. I just stood there in hysterics. The only person with me was my brother, Kevin. He didn't know what to do, either. We were both kind of floating around in a sea of turmoil and pain. I am still in that sea. There are islands of normality and "okayness," but the existence of the islands does not destroy the existence of the water.

7   There was no time for grieving that week. There was too much to do. Funeral and memorial-service arrangements, cleaning the house (which we had to sell), appraising most of the big items in the house (which we had to sell), changing locks so our house wouldn't get looted, those sorts of

things. And then we had to deal with all the fans and the sycophants. I don't remember when I really did grieve. I think I do every day, because every day I am overwhelmed with the fact that I will never see him, talk to him, ask him questions or listen to the answers again. He was my mentor and the dominant force in my life.

8   So I am left with memories of greatness. Not the greatness of the writer but the greatness of the father and the teacher. One time in the class he taught, my father was reading his poem "Good-bye to Big Daddy," about the death of football player Big Daddy Lipscomb, and this big ox-headed football player in the class started bawling in the middle of the reading. The class was dismissed, and my dad just went over to this guy and held him while he wept like a child, saying, "It's all right, big boy; it's gonna be OK." That is the kind of teacher James Dickey was. There are no words for the kind of father he was.

9   A few of his favorite quotes echo through my mind like steps down an empty hallway. "Live blindly and upon the hour" from a sonnet by Trumbull Stickney; "None of them knew the color of the sky," the opening line of Stephen Crane's "The Open Boat"; "Catch thou the dream in flight," and a line referring to someone's eyes that were "somewhat strangely more than blue."

10   I live blindly and upon the hour. I will catch the dream in flight, though I do not know the color of the sky. And my father's eyes, though they will not see my graduation, my marriage or my children, will always be somewhat strangely more than blue.

Comprehension and Discussion

1. What kind of relationship did Bronwen Dickey have with her father James Dickey? How does this relationship compare and contrast with your relationship with your father or another significant person? Would you like to be a parent similar to James Dickey? With your classmates, discuss the characteristics of an ideal parent. Take notes on this discussion in your journal.

2. Why was his death a relief to Bronwen? Have you ever felt similar relief when someone you loved has died? What other feelings have you felt (such as sadness, grief, pride, guilt, panic) when someone close to you has died? Discuss these feelings and responses with your classmates.

3. The author says that her father told her never to look at him dead, but she did look at him after he died, and said "It was the most horrible thing I have ever seen" (5). Have you ever seen the body of a dead person? Touched a dead person? How did you respond to this experience? Discuss this experience with your classmates. Is your experience the same or different from those of your classmates? Why?

4. Why does the author tell the story about the football player in her father's class (8)? How is this incident relevant to the essay? What does it add to the essay?

5. What was James Dickey's advice about writing (1)? Do you follow his advice when you write? If not, try it, and then discuss the results with your classmates.

Language and Technique

1. Where in the essay does the author refer to the *title*? What does the title mean? Have you ever known anyone about whom you might say, "He [or She] caught the dream"? Discuss such a person with your classmates.

2. Bronwen Dickey uses *visual images* to help the reader see what she saw:

   "pulses on a dusty screen" (1)

   "still wore two watches, his Citizen Wingman and his Ironman Triathlon" (2)

   "the human part of an oxygen tank" (3)

   "his hand, which was covered in a mix of blood and Betadine from the IVs" (4)

   "an eerie backlight behind the bed" (6)

   What does each of these images mean? What does each suggest? How does each make you feel? Find some other images in this essay, and discuss the meanings and suggestions of all with your classmates.

3. Dickey also uses similes and metaphors in the selection.

   Simile: a comparison with the use of *like* or *as.* Examples from the selection include:

   "he wept like a child" (8)

   "A few of his favorite quotes echo through my mind like steps down an empty hallway" (9)

Metaphor: an implied comparison, without the use of *like* or *as.* For example:

"We were both kind of floating around in a sea of turmoil and pain. I am still in that sea. There are islands of normality and 'okayness,' but the existence of the islands does not destroy the existence of the water" (6).

In each of these similes and this metaphor, what two things are compared? Is the comparison effective? Why or why not? What does it make you feel? What does it make you think? Discuss these similes and metaphors and your responses with your classmates. Do all of you react in the same way? Explain.

4. Another language technique that the author uses is *parallel structure:*

"He should have been paddling down some wild river in a canoe, or playing bluegrass ballads on his guitar, or tapping away at a typewriter, not straining for breath in some sterile hospital room" (5).

"I did not recognize the man before me. That man was not talkative and vibrant. That man was not determined and strong. That man had given up" (2).

What grammatical structures does the author parallel in each of these passages—words, phrases, clauses, or sentences? What is the effect of her use of parallelism? Find the parallel structures that Dickey uses in paragraph 3 and in paragraph 7. Then with your classmates discuss what she parallels in each passage and what the effects are.

Suggestions for Writing

1. **Sentence.** Choose one of the following topics. Then in your journal write a sentence using parallel structure with at least three parallel items. Share your sentence with your classmates.

What I Did Last Weekend

What I Do on My Job

Things _____ Did for Me

Preparations for a Big Event (Vacation, Wedding, Ball Game, etc.)

2. **Paragraph.** Using one of the following topic sentences, write a paragraph developed by *one* narrative example, as in paragraph 8. Share your paragraph with your writing group or your entire class.

> I have pleasant or unpleasant memories of _____ (person, place, event).
>
> He/She is an excellent teacher.
>
> I will never forget the summer I spent _____.

3. **Essay.** Write an essay in which you narrate the final illness and death of a loved one, and explain how you have coped with this loss. Be sure to use plenty of specific details and illustrations as Bronwen Dickey uses in her tribute to her father. Some of these details may include memories of things you did together before the illness. Experiment a bit with language, and use some similes and metaphors and parallel structures in your essay. Share your writing with one of your classmates, pointing out your experimentations to him or her. Together, evaluate the use of similes, metaphors, and parallelism in each of your essays and see if you can think of any ways to improve your writings.

4. **Essay.** How do funerals or other rituals of grieving help people deal with the death of a loved one? Write an essay in which you analyze and explain the rituals of grieving in your culture or religion. Be sure to use specific examples to support and explain your comments.

5. **Essay.** Write an essay in which you state and explain the characteristics of the ideal parent. Be sure to give specific examples to support and explain each characteristic.

Some Want Curbs on Military Moms

David Crary

DAVID CRARY is a journalist who writes columns on contemporary issues. In this essay, he sets forth the two sides of the argument on mothers serving in the military and especially on the battlefront.

Vocabulary Study

curb (title)

conservatives (1, 5, 22)

gender equality (1)

deployment (1, 3, 10)

feminist (3, 7)

warranted (5)

repudiate (7)   contingencies (19)

initiatives (8)   think tank (20)

assessment (10)   constituency (23)

morale (17)

Some Want Curbs on Military Moms

With one single mother from the U. S. Army killed in Iraq and another wounded and captured, some conservatives are urging the military to halt its march toward gender equality and restrict the deployment of mothers in war zones.

"Healthy, responsible nations do not send the mothers of small children to or near the front lines—that violates the most basic human instincts," said Allan Carlson, a historian affiliated with the Family Research Council.

For now, the cause has found few champions in Congress or at the Pentagon; politicians and commanders are pleased by the all-volunteer military's performance in Iraq and proud that three ambushed servicewomen became national heroes. But the critics—mostly from groups opposed to the feminist movement—vow to maintain pressure in hopes the Bush administration might one day review deployment policies.

Bush, asked about the matter Thursday, said it will be "up to the generals" to determine if any changes are warranted.

5   Among the fiercest critics of current policy is conservative activist Phyllis Schlafly, president of the Eagle Forum, who recently wrote a commentary titled "Does the Military Have the Nerve to Celebrate Mother's Day?"

She contended that the women caught in the ambush of the 507th Maintenance Company in Iraq—Jessica Lynch, who was rescued by commandos, and single mothers Lori Piestewa, who was killed, and Shoshana Johnson, who was wounded—did not volunteer for the Army with the ambition of serving in combat.

"The reason these sorry things have happened is that the men in our government and in the U. S. military lack the courage to stand up to feminists and repudiate their assault on family and motherhood," Schlafly wrote.

In a telephone interview, Schlafly said she was frustrated that the Bush administration, which she supports on many issues, had made no effort to roll back Clinton administration initiatives allowing women into a greater range of war-zone duties.

"There is no evidence in all of history that you win wars or advance the cause of women by sending women out to fight," Schlafly said.

10   Some critics of current policy hope that the Pentagon's postwar assessment of deployment in Iraq will look in depth at such issues as pregnancy, motherhood and single-parenthood. Carlson, for one, would like the military to exclude mothers with children younger than 3 from any war-zone deployment.

Col. Catherine Abbott, a Defense Department spokeswoman, said any such special treatment would be difficult to implement, especially if mothers were treated differently from fathers.

"Obviously, it's something that tears on the heartstrings," she said.

"But young dads miss their kids as well. People in the military are volunteers. When they raise their hand (to take the oath of service) they know what they're going into."

Rep. Ike Skelton, D-MO, ranking Democrat on the House Armed Services Committee, said he knows of no one on Capitol Hill eager to revisit the issue of women—mothers or not—in combat.

15   Women who have children or expect to have them "don't have to volunteer," Skelton said. "But they do, and they perform their specialties well."

About 210,000 women serve in the active-duty forces, 15 percent of the total force of 1.4 million. As of September [2002], there were about 24,000 single mothers on active duty and 65,000 single fathers.

Lory Manning, an expert on women in the military with the Washington-based Women's Research and Education Institute, said the motherhood issue is being seized upon by critics because they can no longer make headway with claims that uniformed women lower troop performance and morale.

"The stuffing has been knocked out of their old argument," Manning said. "So their new argument is, 'We can't have mothers at war.' It's a very loaded argument' it ignores the fact that there are lots more single dads than single moms."

Though the military doesn't exempt single parents from war duty, it does try to ensure their children's well-being. Holly Gifford of the Army's Family Programs Directorate said single parents must prepare a plan outlining arrangements for their children's care that accounts for financial and medical contingencies. A soldier unable to make adequate plans can be discharged, Gifford said.

20   Linda Chavez, who heads the Center for Equal Opportunity, a conservative think tank, said the military should not equate fatherhood with motherhood.

"As tragic as the death of a father in a young child's life, it simply can't compare to the loss of a mother," she wrote in a recent commentary.

Still, Janice Shaw Crouse of Concerned Women for America, another conservative group, said that with the victory in Iraq still fresh in Americans' minds, it may be too soon for policy-makers to reopen the debate. "It's an issue that will have to be handled very carefully," she said. "I expect the Bush administration will address it, or else be in trouble with some very basic parts of their constituency."

Comprehension and Discussion

1. What are the arguments for women in the military? What are the arguments against women in the military? Should mothers have special consideration in the military? What is Crary's position on this issue? What is your opinion on this issue? Discuss it with your classmates, and be prepared to defend your position.

2. What is your definition of *hero*? Do you consider the three servicewomen who were ambushed in Iraq heroes? Why? Write a journal entry on your definition of hero. Then discuss the idea of heroism with your classmates. Do most of you have a similar concept of heroes and heroism?

3. Review Skelton's comment in paragraph 15. Then write a journal entry answering the following question: Would the issue of women in the military change if the United States did not have volunteer armed services? Then discuss the question with your classmates.

4. Interview someone who has served in the military on the issue of women in the military. Ask him or her to tell you about specific experiences that led him/her to arrive at his/her position. Record notes on your interview in your journal. Then discuss what you learned with your classmates. Compare and contrast what you discovered with the results of your classmates' interviews. [If you have served in the military, you may interview yourself.]

5. What roles have women played in wartime in previous years? Do some research on this subject, take notes in your journal (be sure to include the *source* of the information you find), bring your information to class, and discuss it with your classmates.

Language and Technique

1. Crary uses direct quotations of various people in this essay. Why do you think he does so? What is the effect of his use of direct quotations? Discuss this use with your classmates.

2. Why does Crary use short paragraphs in his article? Who are the audience or readers of his article? Are such paragraphs appropriate for academic writing? Participate in a class discussion of this issue.

3. Crary presents both sides of the issue of women in the military, but he seems to be in agreement with one side. Do you think he is for or against women and mothers in the military? What clues and statements does he provide in the essay to indicate his stance? Why do you think he does not state his position in the beginning of the article? Working with a group of your classmates, analyze the organization of Crary's explanation of this issue. Then discuss the effectiveness of his organization with your classmates.

4. Several of the comments in this article contain highly connotative or suggestive words and phrases, such as "healthy, responsible nations" (2), "these sorry things" (7), and "Obviously, it's something that tears at the heartstrings" (12). Discuss both the *denotative* meaning (dictionary meaning) and the *connotative* meaning (personal or suggested meaning) of of these phrases with your classmates. Working with a group of your classmates, find other examples of loaded connotative language in this essay, record them in your journal, and discuss these with the entire class.

Suggestions for Writing

1. **Sentence.** Crary uses the dash in paragraph 2 and paragraph 14. Review the use of the dash, and discuss these uses of the dash with your classmates. Then write a sentence in which you use the dash, and share it with your classmates. Notice the variations in the uses of the dash in the sentences written by you and your classmates.

2. **Paragraph.** Write a paragraph of 100–150 words in which you summarize this essay. Be sure to use your own words, not the words of the author. [See pp. 18–19 for suggestions on how to write a summary.]

3. **Essay.** Review the comments of the various people whom Crary quotes:

Carlson (2, 10)

Schlafly (5–9)

Abbott (11–13)

Skelton (14–15)

Manning (17–28)

Gifford (19)

Chavez (20–21)

Crouse (22–23)

In your journal, summarize the position or opinion of each speaker. Participate in a class discussion of these various opinions on this issue of women, especially mothers, in the military. Then choose one with whom you agree or disagree, and write an essay explaining why you have the opinion you have and providing specific examples to support your position.

4. **Essay.** Write an essay in which you respond to one or several comments on one controversial subject from an article you have read in a newspaper or magazine or the Internet, or from a news report you have heard on television or radio. In your essay, use several direct quotations, and provide both sides of the issue. Be sure to use proper punctuation for the quotations. If necessary, review punctuation of quotations in the handbook for the course.

5. **Essay.** Sports figures, such as professional football players, are often called *heroes*. Do you consider them heroes? Write an essay in which you take a stand that sports figures are *or* are not heroes. State the reasons for your position, and be sure to provide specific examples to support each reason.

Blue Winds Dancing

Thomas St. Germain Whitecloud

THOMAS ST. GERMAIN WHITECLOUD was born in New York City, but spent much of his childhood on the Lac du Flambeau Indian Reservation in Wisconsin. After earning a degree in medicine from Tulane University, he practiced medicine in Louisiana and Texas. He also served as a consultant for the Texas Commission on Alcoholism and Drug Abuse for Indians. In this short story he writes about the contrast between the Native American way of life and white civilization.

Vocabulary Study

maelstrom (5)   serene (31)

rabid (12)   imperceptibly (33)

radicals (12)

Blue Winds Dancing

1   There is a moon out tonight. Moon and stars and clouds tipped with moonlight. And there is a fall wind blowing in my heart. Ever since this evening, when against a fading sky I saw geese wedge southward. They were going home. . . . Now I try to study, but against the pages I see them again, driving southward. Going home.

Across the valley there are heavy mountains holding up the night sky, and beyond the mountains there is home. Home, and peace, and the beat of drums, and blue winds dancing over snowfields. The Indian lodge will fill with my people, and our gods will come and sit among them. I should be there then. I should be at home.

But home is beyond the mountains, and I am here. Here where fall hides in the valleys, and winter never comes down from the mountains. Here where all the trees grow in rows; the palms stand stiffly by the road-sides, and in the groves the orange trees line in military rows, and endlessly bear fruit. Beautiful, yes: there is always beauty in order, in rows of growing things! But it is the beauty of captivity. A pine fighting for existence on a windy knoll is much more beautiful.

In my Wisconsin, the leaves change before the snows come. In the air there is the smell of wild rice and venison cooking; and when the winds come whispering through the forests, they carry the smell of rotting leaves. In the evenings, the loon calls, lonely; and birds sing their last songs before leaving. Bears dig roots and eat late fall berries, fattening for their long winter sleep. Later, when the first snows fall, one awakens in the morning to find the world white and beautiful and clean. Then one can look back over his trail and see the tracks following. In the woods there are tracks of deer and snowshoe rabbits, and long streaks where partridges slide to alight. Chipmunks make tiny footprints on the limbs and one can hear squirrels busy in hollow trees, sorting acorns. Soft lake waves wash the shores, and sunsets burst each evening over the lakes, and make them look as if they were afire.

5   That land which is my home! Beautiful, calm—where there is no hurry to get anywhere, no driving to keep up in a race that knows no ending and no goal. No classes where men talk and talk and then stop now and then to hear their own words come back to them from the students. No constant peering into the maelstrom of one's mind; no worries about grades and honors; no hysterical preparing for life until that life is half over; no anxiety about one's place in the thing they call Society.

I hear again the ring of axes in deep woods, the crunch of snow beneath my feet. I feel again the smooth velvet of ghost-birch bark. I hear the rhythm of the drums. . . . I am tired. I am weary of trying to keep up this bluff of being civilized. Being civilized means trying to do everything you don't want to, never doing anything you want to. It means dancing to the strings of custom and tradition: it means living in houses and never knowing or caring who is next door. These civilized white men want us to be like them—always dissatisfied—getting a hill and wanting a mountain.

Then again, maybe I am not tired. Maybe I'm licked. Maybe I am just not smart enough to grasp these things that go to make up civilization. Maybe I am just too lazy to think hard enough to keep up.

Still, I know my people have many things that civilization has taken from the whites. They know how to give; how to tear one's piece of meat in two and share it with one's brother. They know how to sing—how to make each man his own songs and sing them; for their music they do not have to listen to other men singing over a radio. They know how to make things with their hands, how to shape beads into design and make a thing of beauty from a piece of birch bark.

But we are inferior. It is terrible to have to feel inferior; to have to read reports of intelligence tests, and learn that one's race is behind. It is terrible to sit in classes and hear men tell you that your people worship sticks of wood—that your gods are all false, that the Manitou forgot your people and did not write them a book.

10   I am tired. I want to walk again among the ghost-birches. I want to see the leaves turn in autumn, the smoke rise from the lodgehouses, and to feel the blue winds. I want to hear the drums; I want to hear the drums and feel the blue whispering winds.

There is a train wailing into the night. The trains go across the mountains. It would be easy to catch a freight. They will say he has gone back to the blanket; I don't care. The dance at Christmas. . . .

A bunch of bums warming at a tiny fire talk politics and women and joke about the Relief and the WPA and smoke cigarettes. These men in caps and overcoats and dirty overalls living on the outskirts of civilization are free, but they pay the price of being free in civilization. They are outcasts, I remember a sociology professor lecturing on adjustment to society; hobos and prostitutes and criminals are individuals who never adjusted, he said. He could learn a lot if he came and listened to a bunch of bums talk. He would learn that work and a woman and a place to hang his hat are all the ordinary man wants. These are all he wants, but other men are not content to let him want only these. He must be taught to want radios and automobiles and a new suit every spring. Progress would stop if he did not want these things. I listen to hear if there is any talk of communism or socialism in the hobo jungles. There is none. At best there is a sort of disgusted philosophy about life. They seem to think there should be a better distribution of wealth, or more work, or something. But they are not rabid about it. The radicals live in the cities.

I find a fellow headed for Albuquerque, and talk road-talk with him. "It is hard to ride fruit cars. Bums break in. Better to wait for a cattle car going back to the Middle West, and ride that." We catch the next eastbound and walk the tops until we find a cattle car. Inside, we crouch near the forward wall, huddle, and try to sleep. I feel peaceful and content at last. I am going home. The cattle car rocks. I sleep.

Morning and the desert. Noon and the Salton Sea, lying more lifeless than a mirage under a somber sun in a pale sky. Skeleton mountains rearing on the skyline, thrusting out of the desert floor, all rock and shadow and edges. Desert. Good country for an Indian reservation. . . .

15   Yuma and the muddy Colorado. Night again, and I wait shivering for the dawn.

Phoenix. Pima country. Mountains that look like cardboard sets on a forgotten stage. Tucson. Papago country. Giant cacti that look like petrified hitchhikers along the highways. Apache country. At El Paso my road-buddy decides to go on to Houston. I leave him, and head north to the mesa country. Las Cruces and the terrible Organ Mountains, jagged peaks that instill fear and wondering. Albuquerque. Pueblos along the Rio Grande. On the boardwalk there are some Indian women in colored sashes selling bits of pottery. The stone age offering its art to the twentieth century. They hold up a piece and fix the tourist with black eyes until, embarrassed, he buys or turns away. I feel suddenly angry that my people should have to do such things for a living. . . .

Santa Fe trains are fast, and they keep them pretty clean of bums. I decide to hurry and ride passenger coaltenders. Hide in the dark, judge the speed of the train as it leaves, and then dash out, and catch it. I hug the cold steel wall of the tender and think of the roaring fire in the engine ahead, and of the passengers back in the dining car reading their papers over hot coffee. Beneath me there is a blur of rails. Death would come quick if my hands should freeze and I fall. Up over the Sangre De Cristo range, around cliffs and through canyons to Denver. Bitter cold here, and I must watch out for Denver Bob. He is a railroad bull who has thrown bums from fast freights. I miss him. It is too cold, I suppose. On north to the Sioux country.

Small towns lit for the coming Christmas. On the streets of one I see a beam-shouldered young farmer gazing into a window filled with shining silver toasters. He is tall and wears a blue shirt buttoned, with no tie. His young wife by his side looks at him hopefully. He wants decorations for his place to hang his hat to please his woman. . . .

Northward again, Minnesota, and great white fields of snow; frozen lakes, and dawn running into dusk without noon. Long forests wearing white. Bitter cold, and one night the northern lights. I am nearing home.

20   I reach Woodruff at midnight. Suddenly I am afraid, now that I am but twenty miles from home. Afraid of what my father will say, afraid of being looked on as a stranger by my own people. I sit by a fire and think about myself and all other young Indians. We just don't seem to fit in anywhere— certainly not among the whites, and not among the older people. I think again about the learned sociology professor and his professing. So many things seem to be clear now that I am away from school and do not have to worry about some man's opinion of my ideas. It is easy to think while looking at dancing flames.

Morning, I spend the day cleaning up, and buying some presents for my family with what is left of my money. Nothing much, but a gift is a gift, if a man buys it with his last quarter. I wait until evening, then start up the track toward home.

Christmas Eve comes in on a north wind. Snow clouds hang over the pines, and the night comes early. Walking along the railroad bed, I feel the calm peace of snow-bound forests on either side of me. I take my time; I am back in a world where time does not mean so much now. I am alone; alone but not nearly so lonely as I was back on the campus at school. Those are never lonely who love the snow and the pines; never lonely when the pines are wearing white shawls and snow crunches coldly under- foot. In the woods I know there are the tracks of deer and rabbit; I know that if I leave the rails and go into the woods I shall find them. I walk along feeling glad because my legs are light and my feet seem to know that they are home. A deer comes out of the woods ahead of me, and stands silhou- etted on the rails. The North, I feel, has welcomed me home. I watch him and am glad that I do not wish for a gun. He goes into the woods quietly, leaving only the design of his tracks in the snow. I walk on. Now and then I pass a field, white under the night sky, with houses at the far end. Smoke comes from the chimneys of the houses, and I try to tell what sort of wood each is burning by the smoke; some burn pine, others aspen, others tama- rack. There is one from which comes black coal smoke that rises lazily and drifts out over the tops of the trees. I like to watch houses and try to imagine what might be happening in them.

Just as a light snow begins to fall I cross the reservation boundary; somehow it seems as though I have stepped into another world. Deep woods in a white-and-black winter night. A faint trail leading to the village.

The railroad on which I stand comes from a city sprawled by a lake—a city with a million people who walk around without seeing one another; a city sucking the life from all the country around; a city with stores and police and intellectuals and criminals and movies and apartment houses; a city with its politics and libraries and zoos.

25   Laughing, I go into the woods. As I cross a frozen lake I begin to hear the drums. Soft in the night the drums beat. It is like the pulse beat of the world. The white line of the lake ends at the black forest, and above the trees the blue winds are dancing.

I come to the outlying houses of the village. Simple box houses, etched black in the night. From one or two windows soft lamplight falls on the snow. Christmas here, too, but it does not mean much; not much in the way of parties and presents. Joe Sky will get drunk. Alex Bodidash will buy his children red mittens and a new sled. Alex is a Carlisle man, and tries to keep his home up to white standards. White standards. Funny that my people should be ever falling farther behind. The more they try to imitate whites the more tragic the result. Yet they want us to be imitation white men. About all we imitate well are their vices.

The village is not a sight to instill pride, yet I am not ashamed; one can never be ashamed of his own people when he knows they have dreams as beautiful as white snow on a tall pine.

Father and my brother and sister are seated around the table as I walk in. Father stares at me for a moment, then I am in his arms, crying on his shoulder. I give them the presents I have brought, and my throat tightens as I watch my sister save carefully bits of red string from the packages. I hide my feelings by wrestling with my brother when he strikes my shoulder in token of affection. Father looks at me, and I know he has many questions, but he seems to know why I have come. He tells me to go alone to the lodge, and he will follow.

I walk the trail to the lodge, watching the northern lights forming in the heavens. White waving ribbons that seem to pulsate with the rhythm of the drums. Clean snow creaks beneath my feet, and a soft wind sighs through the trees, singing to me. Everything seems to say, "Be happy! You are home now—you are free. You are among friends—we are your friends;

we, the trees, and the snow, and the lights." I follow the trail to the lodge. My feet are light, my heart seems to sing to the music, and I hold my head high. Across white snow fields blue winds are dancing.

³⁰ Before the lodge door I stop, afraid, I wonder if my people will remember me. I wonder—"Am I Indian, or am I white?" I stand before the door a long time. I hear the ice groan on the lake, and remember the story of the old woman under the ice, trying to get out, so she can punish some runaway lovers. I think to myself, "If I am white I will not believe that story; If I am Indian, I will know that there is an old woman under the ice." I listen for a while, and I know that there is an old woman under the ice. I look again at the lights, and go in.

Inside the lodge there are many Indians. Some sit on benches around the walls, others dance in the center of the floor around a drum. Nobody seems to notice me. It seems as though I were among a people I have never seen before. Heavy women with long hair. Women with children on their knees—small children that watch with intent black eyes the movements of the dancers, whose small faces are solemn and serene. The faces of the old people are serene, too, and their eyes are merry and bright. I look at the old men. Straight, dressed in dark trousers and beaded velvet vests, wearing soft moccasins. Dark, lined faces intent on the music. I wonder if I am at all like them. They dance on, lifting their feet to the rhythm of the drums swaying lightly, looking upward. I look at their eyes, and am startled at the rapt attention to the rhythm of the music.

The dance stops. The men walk back to the walls, and talk in low tones or with their hands. There is little conversation, yet everyone seems to be sharing some secret. A woman looks at a small boy wandering away, and he comes back to her.

Strange, I think and then remember. These people are not sharing words—they are sharing a mood. Everyone is happy. I am so used to white people that it seems strange so many people could be together without someone talking. These Indians are happy because they are together, and because the night is beautiful outside, and the music is beautiful. I try hard to forget school and white people, and be one of these—my people. I try to forget everything but the night, and it is a part of me that I am one with my people and we are all a part of something universal. I watch eyes, and see now that the old people are speaking to me. They nod slightly, imperceptibly, and their eyes laugh into mine. I look around the room. All the eyes are friendly; they all laugh. No one questions my being here. The drums begin to beat again, and I catch the invitation in the eyes of the old men. My feet begin to lift to the rhythm, and I look out beyond the walls into the night and see the lights. I am happy. It is beautiful. I am home.

Glossary

Manitou (9)—a spirit or force of nature, either good or bad, deified in the region of the Algonquian Indians who live in the eastern part of the United States and Canada

the Relief and the WPA (12)—special projects set up during the Depression of the 1930s to distribute federal funds to the poor

Salton Sea (14)—a lake in southeastern California

Comprehension and Discussion

1. What is the speaker's conflict? What things does he contrast throughout this short story? How does he characterize each? Point out specific passages in the story that exemplify the contrasts and illustrate his conflict.

2. How does the speaker define *society* and *civilization*? What is his attitude toward civilization?

3. What is the speaker's idea of beauty? In what does he find beauty? Find some specific examples in the essay, and note them in your journal. Then list some of the things in which you find beauty. What does the author mean by "the beauty of captivity" (3)? What examples does he use? Think of other examples of the beauty of captivity from your experience, and note them in your journal. Participate in a class discussion of the concept of beauty and examples of beauty. Does everyone in your class have the same idea of beauty? Why or why not?

4. In paragraph 27, the narrator states that he is not ashamed of the village that is his home and adds that "one can never be ashamed of his own people." Why is he not ashamed? How might he feel if one of his college acquaintances or professors were there with him? Have you ever felt ashamed of where you lived, or of a member of your family? If so, how did you deal with the shame?

5. In paragraph 33, the speaker says that the Indians inside the lodge are communicating without words, that they are "sharing a mood." Have you ever had an experience in which you communicated with someone without words? If so, write a journal entry of this experience.

Language and Technique

1. What is the meaning of the title of this story, "Blue Winds Dancing"? How many times does the narrator refer to this title in the essay? Find and note all of the references, and discuss them with your classmates.

2. Whitecloud often uses *sensory images*—images of sight, smell, sound, taste, and touch. In paragraph 4 he uses several such descriptive images. With a small group of your classmates, reread this paragraph carefully and discuss the impact of the images on you—what you see, what you think, how you feel. Record your responses in your journal.

3. Whitecloud often uses precise verbs to convey visual images. For example, instead of saying "the geese fly," he writes "geese wedge southward" (1). Note some other examples:

    "mountains holding up the night sky" (2)

    "blue winds dancing" (2)

    "fall hides in the valleys" (3)

    "winter never comes down from the mountains" (3)

    "the palms stand stiffly" (3)

    "the orange trees line in military rows" (3)

    "partridges slide to alight" (4)

    Working with a group of your classmates, discuss the meaning of these images, and then find other examples in the story and note them in your journal.

4. Which of the following words best describes the overall tone of this story: *somber, serious, melancholy, nostalgic, depressed, homesick, happy, unhappy, wistful, dissatisfied, regretful, ashamed, reflective*? Can you think of a word that fits better? Discuss the tone of this story with your classmates.

Suggestions for Writing

1. **Sentence.** Write a sentence in which you describe each of the following senses (total of five sentences):

    something that you see

    a smell

    a sound

    a taste

    something that you touch

2. **Paragraph.** In paragraph 3, Whitecloud describes precisely a scene that has great significance to the speaker. Write a paragraph describing a place and a time that is significant to you.

3. **Essay.** Write an essay about a time when you returned home (or another place of importance to you) after having been away for a while. How did you feel as you prepared to return and during the trip back? How did you feel when you arrived? How did the people there react to your returning? How were you treated?

4. **Essay.** Think of a place from your childhood that you visited later in life. Compare and contrast how you remembered the place with how it was when you revisited it. The place may be a house, a school, a stadium, a church or synagogue, a town—any place of importance to you. In your essay, use some of the descriptive techniques that Whitecloud uses in his story, such as exact verbs or visual images.

5. **Essay.** Have you ever felt conflict between two groups of people with whom you have been associated (such as your family or the people with whom you grew up and the people you associate with now, or between two groups in high school or at work or in the armed services) or between two cultures (such as rural and urban, or small town and large city, or two cities or countries or two ethnic groups)? Write an essay in which you explain the conflict you felt, how it affected you, and how you resolved the conflict.

I Wish I'd Been There

David W. Lipscomb

DAVID W. LIPSCOMB was a student in a college composition course when he wrote this essay. The assignment was to write an essay of personal reminiscence in which he used *narration*, *description*, and *exposition* (explanation and interpretation of the experience) to relate a decision or experience that had a great impact on his life.

I Wish I'd Been There

1   You just never know. You can't predict the twists and turns life throws your way. Flitting through our daily routine, we give nary a thought to how quickly change can be thrust upon us. Blind-sided and dazed, we slowly realize that all is not as it should be or was. As we come to terms with sudden change, it is then that second thoughts and regrets begin to assert themselves.

2   Aunt Marianne, my mother's older and slightly spoiled sister, did as my mother did: she married an American GI, moved to the United States, and lived on various Air Force bases through the early 1960's. Aunt Marianne and Uncle Bill were stationed for much of that time in Iowa, a place very different from the pine-filled forests of Bavaria, my aunt and mother's home state in southern Germany.

3   In 1966, whether by accident or design, Aunt Marianne and Uncle Bill Bryant moved into a house on the same street, only a few houses down, from my parents' home, the one I grew up in, on Darlington Drive. After a stint in Viet Nam, Uncle Bill retired from the Air Force; thus began for him the slow, downward spiral that is alcoholism. Years of heavy drinking led to his death from cirrhosis, a severe liver ailment, typically brought on by excessive alcohol consumption, in 1975. During this time, their daughter, Brenda, began the journey into her own private hell: thirty years of drug addiction and misery, culminating in her death in 2001 from a heroin overdose.

4   Aunt Marianne spent much time at our house, where life was more serene. My aunt and I grew closer, as she was a pleasant alternative to my mother, who set rules; Aunt Marianne did not. I enjoyed daily trips to her house, being towed in my little red wagon (I was a small boy, and not a particularly heavy load).

5   In the warmth of the afternoon sun, we would sit on her somewhat de-hydrated lawn and play. As she sprinkled grass into my hair she would sing "Raindrops Keep Falling Your [sic] Head," the hit made famous by singer B.J. Thomas. I would giggle, loving these moments immensely. Or I would crash into her bedroom in the early morning and just lie there in the bed with her until she decided to rise, usually sometime after noon on her days off.

6   The arrival of grandson Christopher in 1974 changed the equation somewhat. He and I developed something akin to a sibling rivalry, vying for the attention of his grandmother, my aunt. As Christopher's mother was off in her world of the drug and party scene, Aunt Marianne became the de facto mother to Christopher until his high school graduation in 1993. My aunt and I did grow apart somewhat during this time, because of the presence of her grandson, but largely due to my growth into the pre-teen and teenage years. That drift is almost inevitable, as at that age our priorities and attachments are significantly altered through peer pressure and other factors.

7   In the early 1980's my aunt became involved in a "partnership" (an in-nocuous term, compared to the alternative, "relationship") with an older man living in the house next door. "Partnership" is probably the more

correct term, as their eventual cohabitation was largely brought on by financial considerations. Don became a surrogate father to Christopher in those years, encouraging the athletically-gifted boy to develop his baseball skills (left-handed pitchers being a hot commodity). Aunt Marianne and Don never married, but they did develop a close friendship and a mutually-beneficial partnership lasting well beyond Christopher's high school graduation and drafting by the Chicago Cubs organization. Christopher enjoyed a successful minor-league career until a series of injuries and judgment errors brought an end to his promising career. Words were never spoken, but I've always thought that Don was silently heartbroken over this. His health declined during this time; he passed away in October 1998.

8   Aunt Marianne, by now having dealt with the death of a husband, a daughter whose addictions forced her into a life of deception and thievery, and the final blow, the death of a companion of over fifteen years, could not be faulted for seeking solace in her own way. While she could never be labeled an "alcoholic," being pure German, beer-drinking is done for more than thirst-quenching: it is part of the national identity. It is a vehicle through which much social interaction takes place. Again, while not a drunk herself by any stretch, she continued to imbibe, even after her doctors told her not to. I know. I enabled her, by sneaking the contraband product to her, as she would drink on the sly. In retrospect, regrets become quite potent, as I ask myself why wasn't I stronger, determined to just say no. She was good at coercion, but I still could have exercised greater resolve.

9   As a child, my aunt had suffered a bout of hepatitis, a viral-induced inflammation of the liver. This was of great concern to the doctors, who noticed the return of the inflamed liver in the early 1990's, and thus strongly recommended abstinence from alcohol. While her liver function was monitored closely, no significant changes were detected for several years; her covert exploits continued.

10   After Don's death (I never referred to him as "uncle," feeling the title was somewhat unnecessary), I took over responsibility of providing my aunt with the only outside activity she enjoyed: daily breakfast at the local Bob Evans restaurant. This was less meal and more social event. She enjoyed the daily conversations with servers, cooks, and hostesses, who had all come to love Aunt Marianne and Don greatly. Again, in hindsight, that daily intake of eggs and bacon was probably not a good idea either, even though she did eventually switch to Egg Beaters, a lower-cholesterol egg substitute. But it was what she loved, and I did not want to take that away from her.

[11] In early March 2000, Aunt Marianne was experiencing health problems beyond what could be attributed to simple diabetes, and COPD, an inflammation in the chest which causes breathing difficulties. In early March we were able to get an emergency visit with her doctor, who, after a brief test, did agree that other factors were at work. He ordered her admission into Brandon Regional Hospital, where several days later terminal cancer of the liver was diagnosed. In the doctor's own words, she could "go any time." My mother especially was devastated, while I tried to maintain something of a stoic nature. We brought her home, and with the indispensable assistance of LifeCare Hospice, began the vigil; it amounted to a deathwatch.

[12] I was unemployed at the time, having been recently laid off from a job. I was able to provide some measure of care for Aunt Marianne, giving her food and liquids, and helping her to the toilet as needed. A nurse came in several times a week to check and monitor her vitals. For the first ten days or so, my aunt was in good spirits and alert. One day, while we were alone, she asked me to bring over to her the Merlin snow globes that were part of her knick-knack collection. As the tinny sounds of the wind-up music boxes played, she told me they were her favorite pieces. I have those globes now: they serve as pleasant reminders.

[13] Family came and went, an endless stream of sympathy-wishers. Brenda attempted a small measure of reconciliation with her mother, an effort to alleviate years of hurt. On the second Friday after Aunt Marianne came home, she became delirious; we all thought it was about time. I was not as faithfully religious as I should have been, but I remembered what I had been taught, and knowing what she had been taught in catechism classes, I prayed with her, asking forgiveness for sins, and asking to be "received." She pulled through this episode, but the end had begun.

[14] The days progressed, the house enveloped in preternatural silence: the only sound beyond reverent, hushed whispers was that of the respirator, producing pure oxygen to assist my aunt's labored breaths. Conversation with her had come to an end, as she was never awake or lucid long enough to hold up her end. Resignation set in for all of us: the metronomic ticking of some subconscious clock could be heard by all.

[15] On Thursday, March 23, 2000, with no change in my aunt's condition beyond deep sleep and slow, shallow breaths, my mother and I decided to go home, take a break, and allow Christopher and Amy, his girlfriend, a chance for some quiet time with his grandmother. We left Aunt Marianne's house about 8 P.M., planning to return in the early morning.

[16]   Shortly after 9 P.M., I received a call from Christopher strongly suggesting that my mother and I return immediately: Amy, as a licenced practical nurse, had noticed an ominous change in my aunt's condition. Five minutes later, we were back at her house. Christopher met us outside, and informed us that the ordeal had ended. My mother broke down; I held it together at least for a few minutes, succumbing to the emotions later in a moment of solitude. It was then that I realized: I had missed the opportunity to say goodbye. She could not have reciprocated, but I'm sure she would have been aware of what was said.

[17]   My family and I made it through the funeral with all the stoicism we could muster. I filed past the open casket at the conclusion of the service, kissed my Aunt Marianne's forehead, and whispered a half-hearted farewell. It could not take the place of what would have been said earlier. At the end of her life, I wish I'd been there: this is the essence of regret.

Checklist for Revising and Editing

Following is a list of questions to guide you in the process of revising and editing your essays. Use the questions to respond to the essay and to check for any point of needed revision. You may also use it to respond to and evaluate essays by other writers, whether students or professional writers.

1. **Sources:** What sources of information does the author draw upon—experience and memory, observation, reading and research, conversation and interview?

2. **Purpose:** What is the author's purpose in this essay—to narrate, to describe, to explain, to argue or convince, or a combination of these? Does the author accomplish the purpose?

3. **Thesis:** What is the thesis sentence or main point? Where does the author state the thesis or imply it? Does the author make the thesis clear?

4. **Unity:** Does the author stick to the thesis? Is every statement in the essay directly related to the main idea?

5. **Structure and Organization:**

   A. **Introduction**
      1) Does the introduction make clear the subject of the essay?
      2) Does the introduction state or imply the thesis sentence clearly?

    3) Does the introduction grab your attention and interest, and make you want to read the essay?

B. **Body**
    1) What are the major points for development in the essay?
    2) How does the author organize the points of development of the essay? Is the order of points clear? Why does the author put the points in this order?
    3) Is this order appropriate for the ideas of the essay?
    4) Are there any other points or information that the author should have included? Why?

C. **Conclusion**
    1) Does the conclusion relate directly to the introduction and to the thesis, as well as to the points in the body of the essay?
    2) Does the conclusion provide a sense of finality or ending to the essay?
    3) Is the conclusion effective?

6. **Development**
   A. What kinds of development does the author use to expand, support, and clarify the general assertions—narration, description, example, process, cause and effect, classification, analysis, comparison and contrast, definition, negation, statistics, expert opinion?

   B. Does the author provide sufficient evidence to make the subpoints clear and persuasive?

7. **Coherence**
   A. Does the essay flow smoothly from idea to idea? From sentence to sentence? From paragraph to paragraph?

   B. How does the author connect the ideas throughout the essay? What bridges and signposts does the author use to help the reader navigate through the essay?
    1) What key ideas, words, and phrases does the author repeat?
    2) What pronouns does the author use?
    3) What transitional words and phrases does the author use to connect paragraphs? To connect sentences within paragraphs?

8. **Rhetorical Patterns:** What rhetorical patterns does the author use—narration, description, exposition, argument, example or illustration, enumeration, cause, effect, comparison, contrast, analysis, classification, process, definition, problem to solution?

9. **Language Skills and Proofreading**

    A. Has the author proofread and edited the essay carefully for correctness, appropriateness, and effectiveness of language skills?

      - Spelling
      - Capitalization
      - Punctuation
      - Grammar
      - Sentence structure
      - Word choice

    B. What, if anything, should be changed? Why?

10. **Response and Evaluation**

    A. Did the author effectively fulfill the purpose and/or assignment in the essay?

    B. What is the strongest aspect of the essay? What do you like best? Why?

    C. What could be changed to improve the essay? Why?

CHAPTER FIVE

Youth and Age

The complete life, the perfect pattern, includes old age as well as youth and maturity. The beauty of the morning and the radiance of noon are good, but it would be a very silly person who drew the curtains and turned on the light in order to shut out the tranquility of the evening. Old age has its pleasures, which, though different, are not less than the pleasures of youth.

—W. SOMERSET MAUGHAM

Suggestions for Journal Entries

1. Respond to Maugham's comment above. Do you agree with what he says?
2. What has been the favorite year of your life so far?
3. What has been the worst year of your life?
4. Recall one of your best birthdays.
5. Do you look forward to growing older? Do you fear aging? Why?
6. What are some of the pleasures of youth?
7. What are some of the pleasures of aging?
8. What age do you think is the age of maturity? In other words, when does a person mature?
9. What are some of the excitements of growing up?
10. What are some of the things that cause anxiety for you?
11. Think of an older family member, friend, or acquaintance. How is this person different from you?

The Fury of Overshoes

Anne Sexton

ANNE SEXTON (1928–1975) grew up in Wellesley, Massachusetts, and married at twenty. After she had a mental breakdown, her therapist suggested she write poetry. She studied with the poet Robert Lowell at Boston University in the 1950s, but did not receive a college degree. Her third book of poetry *Live or Die* (1967) was awarded the Pulitzer Prize. Much of her poetry is *confessional poetry*—poetry that describes the personal affairs of the writer—in which the speaker and the poet are the same.

The Fury of Overshoes

They sit in a row
outside the kindergarten,
black, red, brown, all
with those brass buckles.
Remember when you couldn't   5
buckle your own
overshoe
or tie your own
shoe
or cut your own meat   10
and the tears
running down like mud
because you fell off your
tricycle?
Remember, big fish,   15
when you couldn't swim
and simply slipped under
like a stone frog?
The world wasn't
yours.   20
It belonged to
the big people.
Under your bed
sat the wolf
and he made a shadow   25
when cars passed by

at night.
They made you give up
your nightlight
and your teddy   30
and your thumb.
Oh overshoes,
don't you
remember me,
pushing you up and down   35
in the winter snow?
Oh thumb,
I want a drink,
it is dark,
where are the big people,   40
when will I get there,
taking giant steps
all day,
each day
and thinking   45
nothing of it?

Comprehension and Discussion

1. What does the title of the poem mean?
2. What is the meaning of "The world wasn't / yours" (19–20)?
3. The speaker was afraid of the wolf under her bed (23–27). What were
   you afraid of when you were a child? Were these things real or imaginary? How did they affect you? Write a journal entry about your childhood fears, and share it with your classmates.
4. In line 28, who is *they*? What did they make the speaker give up? Why?
   As you grew up, what specific things do you remember having to give
   up? Who made you give them up? Why?
5. In your journal, *paraphrase* (express in your own words) the last five
   lines of the poem (41–46). Why do children want to grow up so
   much? What, if anything, do we lose as we grow older? Is there anything about childhood that you wish you could hold on to or return
   to? Share your paraphase and your thoughts about childhood with your
   classmates.

Language and Technique

1. Reread the descriptive *image* of the overshoes (1–4). What do you see in your mind as you read this image? Where are the overshoes sitting? What is around the overshoes? Why are the children wearing overshoes? Find other images that Sexton uses, and discuss their meaning (*denotative* or literal and *connotative* or suggestive) with your classmates.

2. Sexton uses the overshoes as a *symbol*, a tangible or concrete object that represents an idea or feeling. What do the overshoes represent? Does the poet use any other symbols in this poem? Discuss these with your classmates.

3. Sexton uses the word *remember* three times in this poem (5, 15, 34). Why does she repeat this word? Is the repetition effective?

4. Is the *point of view* (the vantage point from which a story is told) of the speaker in the poem that of a child or of an adult looking back and remembering her childhood? What evidence in the poem leads you to this conclusion? How would the poem be different if it were written from a different point of view? With a small group of your classmates, rewrite part of this poem from a different point of view, and discuss the difference with the group.

Suggestions for Writing

1. **Sentence.** In your journal, write a sentence specifically describing one item you remember from your childhood, similar to the description of the overshoes (1–4). Share your sentence with your classmates; then discuss the different things all of you remember.

2. **Paragraph.** In your journal, *brainstorm* a list of the most vivid things (specific items) you remember from your childhood. Then use the items in your list to write a paragraph or a poem. Perhaps you remember scenes from your kindergarten, or a place where you lived, or items in your bedroom, or playing with your kitten. Be specific so that your readers can clearly see what you remember.

3. **Essay.** Write an essay about several of the things you were most afraid of when you were a child. Perhaps you, like the speaker in this poem, were afraid of the wolf under your bed or may be you were afraid of the boogy man in the basement. For each one, explain your fear, how it originated, why you were afraid of this thing, and how the fear made you feel.

4. **Essay.** Write an essay about several things you had to give up as you grew up. Explain why you had to give up each thing and how giving it up made you feel.

5. **Essay.** Why do children want to grow up so much? What, if anything, do we lose as we grow older? Is there anything about childhood that you wish you could hold on to or return to? Write an essay about these things and why they are valuable to you.

On Aging

Maya Angelou

MAYA ANGELOU is one of the most well-respected voices of contemporary literature. She is multitalented—a writer, poet, educator, historian, actress, playwright, producer and director, and civil rights activist. Her best known publication is the first volume of her autobiography, *I Know Why the Caged Bird Sings*. Her writings extend beyond race to the *universal* (that which is applicable to all people).

On Aging

When you see me sitting quietly,
Like a sack left on the shelf,
Don't think I need your chattering.
I'm listening to myself.
Hold! Stop! Don't pity me!   5
Hold! Stop your sympathy!
Understanding if you got it,
Otherwise I'll do without it!

When my bones are stiff and aching,
And my feet won't climb the stair,   10
I will only ask one favor:
Don't bring me no rocking chair.

When you see me walking, stumbling,
Don't study and get it wrong.
'Cause tired don't mean lazy   15
And every goodbye ain't gone.
I'm the same person I was back then,
A little less hair, a little less chin,
A lot less lungs and much less wind.
But ain't I lucky I can still breathe in.   20

Comprehension and Discussion

1. In what situation is the speaker in the poem? How does the speaker react to this situation? What words would you use to describe the personality of the person who is speaking in this poem?
2. What does the speaker want? Do these things surprise you? Do you think these things are what the speaker usually receives from other people? How does the speaker suggest that other people treat him or her? Is this the way elderly people are often treated? Why?
3. What does the last line of the poem mean? What is the speaker's tone in this line?
4. How old is a person who is considered "elderly"? Write a journal entry on your answer to this question, and then discuss it with your classmates. How do your opinions differ? Why?
5. Do you know a person whom you consider elderly? In your journal, describe the appearance and personality of this person. Share your journal entry with your classmates.

Language and Technique

1. Who is the *speaker* in this poem? Is the speaker male or female? Why?
2. Who is the *you* in this poem? Whom is the speaker addressing? What words would you use to describe this person?
3. What *visual images* does Angelou use in this poem?
4. In line 2, the poet uses a *simile*: "Like a sack left on the shelf." What does this line suggest? How would a person left like a sack on the shelf probably feel and react?

Suggestions for Writing

1. **Sentence.** Write a sentence in which you use a *simile* to describe yourself, similar to the one the speaker uses in line 2 of the poem—"Like a sack left on the shelf."
2. **Paragraph.** Using your journal entry in response to question 5 under Comprehension and Discussion, write a well-structured paragraph describing an elderly person whom you know. Use (1) a *topic sentence*, (2) *body* (major characteristics of the person and supporting details), and (3) a *clincher or concluding sentence*. Be sure that the topic sentence is general and precise enough to summarize and unify all the details you include in the paragraph. Before you write the body, arrange the details in

the order of the least important to the most important. As you write, add transitional words and phrases to connect the ideas and sentences in the paragraph. Finally, proofread the paragraph carefully.

3. **Essay.** Interview someone of an older generation on what life was like when he or she was younger and how he or she is adjusting or coping with growing older. Write an essay reporting what you discover.

4. **Essay.** Are children responsible for taking care of elderly parents? What do you think? This is one of the most significant issues in our society today. Take a stand on this issue, and write an argument supporting your position. You may want to do some reading or talk to some people of your parents' and your grandparents' generations in order to arrive at your position and to gather information to add to your own experiences.

5. **Essay.** What are some of the services available for elderly people in your area? With your writing group, research what is available, and then write a group essay reporting your findings.

The Door

Gabriel Horn, White Deer of Autumn

GABRIEL HORN, WHITE DEER OF AUTUMN, is a well-known Native American writer and teacher. He writes to preserve the true history of this land and to keep the spirit of his ancestors strong and enduring. The following selection is from *Native Heart*, a collection of autobiographical reflections.

Vocabulary Study

dappled (2)	ebony (9)
sustenances (3)	indiscriminate (12)
taut (7)	inadvertently (16)

The Door

¹ I stood momentarily on the steps of Mrs. Basic's old, wood-framed house and watched the morning star pulsating in the dawn sky. It seemed so big to me. It swelled as it approached and shrank as it faded back. It twinkled and twirled and danced in the deep blue. In my young boy's mind, the very idea of stars stirred a sense of yearning and wonder in me that has never waned. Stars are like islands in the void. Islands of light in the endless dark ocean of space.

2   Like the vitality of stars in the dusk of twilight, the grove-dappled shoreline where I once lived came alive each dawn. On the trail to the beach, palms swayed and pines whistled above the colorful citrus groves in the cool morning wind, and birds of many kinds helped bring a new day to life again. They winged and darted among the trees, whistling, singing, chirping, cawing, crying, and filled me with a sense of balance and beauty. Their sounds proclaimed the morning's birth, and made me aware of the struggles there are to live in this great Circle of Life, in this great Wheel of Life. Among the dunes, sea oats, bent heavy with summer sun, glowed golden yellow in the first rays of early light.

3   I didn't know what to call all this that I loved then. I didn't know the name, Mother Earth, and I didn't know that the forces that kept the balance within her and the universe were all a part of something whole. In my young boy's mind, I didn't know that it was Mother Earth I was admiring. Nurturing, loving, teaching, and beautiful, she was the mother who would always be there for me. Whether I would one day find her in another foster parent's backyard or in a city park as an older man, in my heart she was always there, and it was from being close to her that my ideas about life would shape and form. And it was Mother Earth that would provide me the sustenances for living—love and strength in times of need. She was my real mother even then when I was a boy and didn't know enough with my head to call her so.

4   Living in a childhood paradise with Mrs. Basic, I got to see every day how everything around my world rim was somehow connected. I got to lay out with my older sister Angela and watch the stars at night. What connected me to the stars, and to the spirits who dwell among them, was another feeling I did not have words for then. I didn't know the words to call this sense of oneness I felt with the stars, with nature, and the land, this connection I had to all things, The Great Holy Mystery. For the young will often have the old sacred feelings that are passed on in the blood; it's only later in life when they meet the teachers and the wisdomkeepers that they are given the words to give meaning to the feelings.

5   At the end of the trail winding away from Mrs. Basic's house, just beyond the beach, small waves broke in the offshore breeze, and long lines of pelicans glided out over the water. That's how Mrs. Basic taught me to count, watching pelicans. "One time," I would tell my children many years later with a great sense of accomplishment still sounding in my voice, "I remember counting up to thirty-seven in one long swooping curve."

6   On this particular morning, though, I didn't have time to count.

⁷   I was nine years old that July, and could make fast tracks in the fine white sand when I had a mind to, and on that day, that's exactly what I did . . . until I reached the water's edge. Then I paused, still and taut like a fawn, and contemplated the island.

⁸   I'm gonna be there . . . soon, I thought.

⁹   The island. It was a jewel gleaming in the Gulf, a serpentine stone set in a turquoise sea. It seemed suspended there. Like the earth in the ebony ocean of space, the island's beauty beckoned the spirit in me as the earth must beckon the spirits who dwell among the stars. Mysterious and beautiful, always it pulled me, tugging at my child's sense of curiosity. The island. On this day I would finally be able to touch its green and wild world.

¹⁰   Growing up on the beach, I learned early that the Gulf is a giver of gifts, and the day before I was to be taken away from this boyhood paradise, I discovered that the Gulf had left behind a big door. It lay in a tide pool, wide and long and smooth, and reddish brown, like the summer color of my skin.

¹¹   Such a door could have come from a big boat, perhaps a yacht, maybe a fishing vessel, or even a sunken Spanish ship. There were many of them out there. Sudden storms could descend upon a rich man's day of cruising the sea or a fisherman taking home his big catch. Just like that, it could blow them away like they never mattered at all.

¹²   The Spaniards and the ships of their great armada were not exempt from the indiscriminate forces of nature either, nor from the forces of Calusa Indians who used to live here. In one battle with the Spaniards, not far from the mouth of Tampa Bay, there's evidence that the Calusa sank eighty fiery vessels, the sea swallowing them whole. Nearly an entire Spanish fleet of battle ships heavy with cannons, and merchant haulers filled with Indian gold, were burned and sunk with their stolen booty by the Calusa. And though these brave natives could defend their country fiercely, they could not defend themselves against disease. The remnants of the Calusa people, and the other tribes who flourished in Florida, would live on, but only in the blood of other nations, like the Seminole, the Creek, and the Cherokee. They would live on in the hearts of others as well. And perhaps that's why I've always felt especially connected here, to the oaks and the palms, to the sea, and to the sun.

¹³   For days that spring, I had watched curiously as divers struggled against seasonal storms and fought off attacks by sharks in order to scavenge the area for lost fortunes. Their struggles against the elements seemed to be my first awareness of the "men against nature" mentality. And though it was

common knowledge that most things of value were already taken from the old ships, these divers still searched, day after day after day.

14   My treasures, however, I took in the Indian way, from what the earth and the sea had provided. One of my greatest finds had washed up on the shore on the day the disappointed divers returned to the mainland. What I found wasn't Indian gold or a priceless gem or a shark's tooth or painted dolphins on a pottery shard taken from a burial mound; it was an old, cracked oar that was slowly turning to driftwood. Even though I had nothing to row with it, I listened to my inner voice and buried that oar just the same.

15   The hiding place I picked was where the anoles lived among the morning glory leaves that wound between the dunes and stretched out towards the beach. Anoles are lizards native to Florida that can change shades of green to camouflage themselves on leaves to hide from hungry birds and snakes. They're in danger of extinction now, but back then a whole long vine of various shades of green could move with a twitch of motion. It was only when I squatted real low that I could see the little creatures.

16   While I dug around the oar, they leapt and scurried about for shelter. One inadvertently landed on my arm and froze there. I watched as the creature's chartreuse, scaly skin quickly turned deep, dark emerald green, blending with the smooth brown of me. But while I was being awed by him, a sea gull suddenly swept down and snatched another smaller one right in front of me. The tiny creature was just too slow to change, or couldn't. I felt bad thinking I caused the death, but I also knew that the sea gull had to live too. I learned early that there must be death for things to live. It's part of the balance and the beauty in the Wheel. And it's The Way when it's done like this.

17   When I placed the anole on my arm down on a wide, round leaf, I didn't have to wait long at all before I saw the tiny lizard change colors again. Though other gulls scoured above, they could not see him. Nature was teaching me something about when to be visible and when not to be. I resumed the work of digging up the rest of the oar, careful not to tear the leafy green vine that provided refuge for the rest of the anoles.

18   When I finally pulled the oar out, I noticed that though half of the paddle part was broken off, it wasn't as badly damaged as I had imagined, and I figured it could still work.

19   I dragged the door into the water carrying the oar. It floated real nice, and I hopped on and started paddling, With the mainland behind me and the island ahead, I was a young boy riding away on the womb of Mother Earth, in the ocean of the Mystery, on a door. I was riding on a door towards the island I had contemplated since I could remember, contemplated in the

same manner I had the stars. I even imagined that I was a star-traveler sailing to another world. I imagined that I was like a dolphin in the wild, free in the waters of life, free from the dangers of the white man's school . . . free, I imagined, like an Indian should be.

Glossary

wisdomkeepers (4)—the elders of Native Americans who have retained the traditional Indian worldview; they pass the wisdom and history of the people to new generations by talking and teaching

Circle of Life (2)—symbolizes the natural cycles of life and also represents the inter-relationship that all things share, not only on the earth but also within the universe

Wheel of Life (2, 16)—another way of expressing the Circle of Life concept. Note that Native Americans do not use wheels for labor

Mother Earth (3, 19)—a living cosmic being because the earth gives life; the mother of all life in this world

The Great Holy Mystery (4)—the incomprehensible totality that always was and always will be; the first cause

Calusa (12)—an indigenous extinct American Indian tribe who lived in southern Florida

Seminole, Creek, and Cherokee (12)—North American Indian tribes. The Seminoles came into existence out of resistance. They consisted of the Creek who would not negotiate their Native lands in northern Florida, Georgia, and Alabama away to the United States, and some Cherokee who resisted occupation and surrender. There were also escaped African slaves who joined with these people. Some of these people intermarried with the fragmented survivors of the indigenous populations of Florida and combined forces to form the Seminole Nation which never formally surrendered to the United States

"man against nature" mentality (13)—the Western idea that nature is against humanity and that humanity must struggle to control and suppress natural forces. Westerners have thus separated themselves from nature, rather than the Native American concept that humans are a part of nature and work cooperatively

The Indian Way, The Way (14, 16)—that Mother Earth is not violated to acquire something for human use; no one stealing or destroying any part of Mother Earth for selfish use or gain. Native Americans also believe that the earth or any part of it does not belong to people, that we cannot individually or collectively own it

Comprehension and Discussion

1. In this reminiscence of childhood, what is the meaning of the title of this selection "The Door"? What does a door symbolize? Of what significance is it to the young Horn? How and why does he consider the door as well

as the oar a gift? Who gave him this gift? (See paragraph 10.) When the boy hops on the door out on the water (19), how does he feel? Why?

2. Why does Horn want to go to the island?

3. Horn refers to several major principles of Native American beliefs. Refer to the glossary terms on p. 99 for a brief explanation of these principles. How have these principles shaped Horn? You will probably have to do some reading or talk to a Native American to understand these concepts.

> Circle of Life (2)
>
> Wheel of Life (2, 16)
>
> Mother Earth (3, 19)
>
> The Great Holy Mystery (4)
>
> "man against nature" mentality (13)
>
> the Indian Way, The Way (14, 16)
>
> the Mystery (19)

4. Horn calls this place a "boyhood paradise" (10). What is a *paradise*? Why does he consider this place a paradise? What specific details does he use to convey this sense of paradise? The child narrator indicates that he is to be taken away from this paradise the next day (10). How does that thought make him feel? When you were a child, did you have a place that you considered paradise? How did you feel when you had to leave it? Write a journal entry on your childhood paradise, and share it with your classmates.

5. The author ends the passage with an emphasis on the desire for freedom. Do you think the boy is free? Does he feel free? Why?

Language and Technique

1. The point of view that Horn uses is that of an adult looking back on childhood, remembering and interpreting what happened to him. At times he writes in the voice of a child, and at other times in the voice of an adult. Find examples of both voices in the selection. Note the differences in vocabulary of the two voices. Why do you think the author does not write the piece entirely in the voice of a child, or entirely in the voice of an adult?

2. Horn is a master of description. We the readers can see what he saw because of his vivid descriptions. Go through the essay again, looking for the descriptive passages, mark them, and note the details that you consider

most effective. Be able to explain to your classmates why you choose them to be especially effective.

3. Study paragraph 2 as an example of focused description. The first sentence expresses the topic sentence: "the grove-dappled shoreline . . . came alive each dawn." Then each of following four sentences provides specific details of the beginning of the day. Working with a small group of classmates, analyze this paragraph, and see if you can find other paragraphs that have a similar structure of topic sentence followed by specific descriptive or narrative details supporting the topic sentence.

4. Notice how Horn uses *participles*—descriptive *–ing* or past-tense verbs used as adjectives—following nouns instead of before nouns as is most common.

the morning star pulsating (1)

birds of many kinds . . . whistling, singing, chirping, cawing, crying (2)

sea oats, bent heavy (2)

Working with a group of your classmates, find other examples of this technique later in the essay.

Suggestions for Writing

1. **Sentence.** Write a descriptive sentence in which you use a participle following a noun, as you studied in question 4 under Language and Technique. Share your sentence with your classmates, and discuss with them the variations of the sentences which you and your classmates write.

2. **Paragraph.** Write a paragraph of focused description of a specific place and time, similar to paragraph 2. Begin your paragraph with a clear, precise topic sentence. Then develop the paragraph with four or more descriptive details so the readers will see, hear, and smell what you describe.

3. **Essay.** Write an essay about an event or situation from your childhood that you did not understand when it happened. Use your voice as a child to narrate what happened and then shift to your voice as an adult to explain and interpret the meaning that you now perceive. Remember, when you write as a child, use the vocabulary, sentence structure, and observations of the child. When you write as an adult, use the vocabulary, sentence structure, and explanations of the adult. Share a draft with a small group of classmates, and ask them if your use of voice is effective.

4. **Essay.** To Native Americans, wisdomkeepers have retained the Native American worldview; they are the wise elders who interpret the mysteries

of the universe for other people and who teach others to help them understand and cope with life. Write an essay about a wise older person who has helped you understand and cope with life. You may write about only one major piece of advice or about two or three items of advice. Be sure to include specific examples to illustrate how this person has helped you.

5. **Essay.** Horn is proud of his heritage as a Native American. Write an essay about your heritage. First explain what it is, then explain what it means to you, and finally explain how it has influenced and shaped you.

The Anxiety Button

Kitty Oliver

KITTY OLIVER, born and raised in Jacksonville, Florida, was one of the first African Americans to integrate the University of Florida in the 1960s. After graduation, she worked for the *Miami Herald* for nineteen years and is now Writer in Residence at Florida Atlantic University. *Multicolored Memories of a Black Southern Girl* is the story of her coming of age in a single-parent family and her crossing from an all-black to a predominantly white world. In the following section from her autobiography, Oliver recalls the relationship between her mother and her when she was a child.

Vocabulary Study

veneer (2)	improvise (4)
wax nostalgically (2)	surly (6)
innate (2)	chided (6)
plausible (2)	dispassionately (8)
skewed (2)	novelty (8)
aura (3)	counterpart (8)
sedate (3)	

The Anxiety Button

1   The way Mama tells it, she was expecting to deliver me any moment when she woke up thirsty that night in early December and decided to brave the chill of the clapboard house to get a glass of water from the icebox. Slipping her arms into her flowered duster, she pulled the collar

up close over her ears, careful not to snag the thin lace fringe with her wedding ring. The bulge in her stomach stretched. She paused and calmed it with a circular rub of comfort. Her face dimpled like soft brown dough as she smiled and eased her feet into the house shoes by the bed. Linoleum crackled under my mother's heavy footsteps as she walked down the dark hallway past the bedroom of her father and stepmother. Just inside the kitchen doorway she raised an arm to feel for the string dangling overhead and tugged it firmly. The room exploded with light from the bare bulb in the ceiling. Swiftly, something heavy and furry bounced across the tops of her feet, thudded to the floor, and clattered away like tapping fingernails. As the last inch of a long skinny tail disappeared into a hole in the base-board, Mama, frightened, threw up her hands and screamed. As she tells this part of the story, her soft coal eyes swell with surprise, recreating the moment like it happened yesterday. "My heart jumped in my throat and I felt you jump in my stomach," she says. "You were nervous, too. See, we've always been close like that." And so it seemed.

2   I grew up fearing rats, all right, and so much more. A free-floating anx-iety flowed through our household and not only kept our doors locked to strangers but also limited neighbors' visits. Beneath the veneer of tranquil-ity in the old days, about which people wax nostalgically today, lurked a message that was programmed into me early: the world was not safe for a female child. I inherited a lot of things from Mama that I did not ask for and still cannot seem to get rid of—chafing thighs, a thinning hairline, and truck driver arms, to name a few. So, for many years, her explanation that genetics was also the root of some innate anxiety in my nature seemed plausible. Symptoms of this uneasiness had sprouted early. I sucked my thumb past puberty and gnawed my fingernails until they bled. During thunderstorms I hid under the bed. When clouds drifted by on a sunny day, I was the only kid who imagined fat, menacing faces. My perception was definitely skewed.

3   Mama had other stories to back up her claim about my overall tendency toward distress. I hated Halloween, she said, because when I was a toddler on my first trick-or-treat, we stepped off the stoop and bumped into a teenage neighbor in a witch's costume. The prankster startled me, and I cried so hysterically that we had to turn around and go back inside. I played with sparklers instead of fireworks on the Fourth of July because the loud noises jarred my nerves. I fretted and fought sleep when Mama got dressed up to go out at night, because I could not stand for us to be parted, she said, and

she was the only one who knew how to soothe me. Humming in a honey-sweet alto voice, she fluffed her auburn curls and would watch me in the dresser mirror until I started to nod. Once she was absolutely certain that I was asleep, her lips would brush my cheek and she would leave the ceiling light on for comfort as she tiptoed out of the room. This aura of caution around us was magnified in the outside world. Even in public housing during the supposedly sedate late 1950s, the manual for survival included wariness. Our one-bedroom unit was on the second floor—safer from burglars, Mama theorized. Through one window she could keep an eye on the neighborhood; the other window faced the street. But she kept a .32 pistol in the bottom dresser drawer next to our bed, just in case.

4   I wonder now what private fears of her own Mama must have had to wrestle with late at night while I slept peacefully. She had married too young and married wrong, and now she was paying for it. But she was only in her early twenties, and she could still dream about being a housewife and giving me a home with a mom *and* a dad. Yet she woke up every day to a different reality, one in which she lived alone in a place she hated, with a school-aged child to raise and protect and a future she had to improvise day-to-day. She had generous helpings of mother-love and longing stored up, though—love she had once imagined she would get to share with four or five children. Instead, she poured all of it into me and I soaked it up, still longing for more. Occasionally she got off work early and picked me up from grade school before the final bell to go on one of our scheduled movie dates. I made short, fast steps to keep up with her as we headed for the bus stop, holding her hand tightly and feeling proud to have such a young, attractive mother. Soon after we slipped into the darkness of the theater, however, I would hear heavy breathing, deep and nasal. She was lost in sleep, but she had kept her promise to spend some special time with me.

5   She refused to get welfare like some of her friends, but still bought me play clothes, and church clothes, and two weeks' worth of school clothes every year. If she had an extra quarter, we shared a pint of black walnut ice cream; if she just had a nickel, we bought a dill pickle and took turns taking a bite. She would look at my puffy face and round belly in the mirror of a clothing store and tell me I was actually *cuter* because I was "a little heavy." And when she was not looking, I would sit on the bench in front of her dresser mirror and jab my finger deep into my right cheek, trying to force the skin into a dimple so that my smile would look just like hers.

⁶   At school, I was usually the last or next-to-last student left standing during the Friday spelling bees, and when I won, I got fried chicken, french fries, and sliced tomatoes that night for dinner instead of canned spaghetti. Once in third grade, the teacher sent a note home after one six-week period saying I would be retained if I did not improve in long division, and Mama, who rarely refused me anything, withheld bananas and Jell-O and slapped my fingers, so I knew this was serious. My homework was completed perfectly. If I pouted or answered her in a surly manner, her flash-flood temper would rise with every stroke of the leather belt that stung my bare legs until I cried. "I want you to know how to behave yourself and mind," she chided, "or nobody will want you around. You've got to know how to get along with people." I had learned to stop crying when she left me at a new baby-sitter's. What else did she mean? "You understand, baby?" I lied and said I did.

⁷   Sometimes she pulled out pans of clothing from the refrigerator and we would stay up late beneath the bare-bulb ceiling light in the kitchen as she ironed sadness into the pleats of my dresses. "You're so lucky to have a mother, a good mother," she once intoned, as if needing reassurance. "I never had a real mother to raise me." Dutifully, I replied, "Yes, Mama, I'm really lucky." Another time, sitting at the table beneath that same bare light, hands cradling her face, she cried. "Nobody loves me." I rubbed her back and cried too. "I love you, Mama." But she shook her head, "No, you don't. You're just going to leave someday." She loved me so close, as if she knew that time would soon run out for her to make her mark. "I just want to get you through high school," she often said. She had graduated; her parents and her husband had not. She wanted me to do at least as well as she had done. Beyond that, however, there was no future talk.

⁸   For awhile, I was content in her cocoon. It had plenty of books, neatly stacked in a corner of the bedroom we shared when I was not reading. They were arranged by size and subject matter—animals; cartoons; people; and Archie, Betty, and Veronica. Toys would slip into my life in December for birthdays and Christmases and back out of my life by spring. I watched dispassionately as the garbage truck carted away their remains. "Cindy," with the brown skin and short curly hair, was the first black doll I ever owned; she was a novelty in the late 1950s. And "Blondie," her yellow-haired white counterpart, well, she had lasted the longest. The two slept on our bed during the day, took baths, and cuddled me to sleep at night. Despite several years of my mangling, they survived as my confidantes and playmates, with contorted arms and legs and plucked-chicken hair.

9   When I played outside, I had to stay away from the cluster of apartments where those "rough people" lived, the ones at the center of the neighborhood gossip. Miss A was having her fourth child from yet another father; Miss B sliced her old man's cheek from ear to ear the other night; Miss C's children went around begging and were always getting into trouble. I also had to stay within sight of our apartment door to make sure no one tried to break in—as if an eight-year-old armed with a skate key could stop an intruder. So I played Pitty-Pat and Here-We-Go-Zudeeo with the two girls across the courtyard who did not cut school and did not pick fights. They helped me steady myself as I learned to ride my new bike up and down the walkways without using the training wheels. But at sunset they had to go inside, and, "no, thank you, ma'am," I could not come in. Instead, I climbed on top of the toolbox on their back porch, and the rotting wood pinched my knees as I peered through the window screen at the scene inside. My playmates sat on the living-room floor in front of the television laughing, and I squinted, trying hard to make out the images they were seeing. But there was only a blur. I gave up and pretended to see what they saw so that I could at least laugh along with them. Mama says she saw me sitting there on the box one of those times looking in, and it broke her heart. One day, she came home early and called me upstairs. A tiny-screened black-and-white Sylvania sat on an end table in the living room, bought from a pawn shop and paid on every week. For a long time she took the bus or walked to work instead of hailing cabs. My surprise that day looked like gladness but it was not, at least not at first. The new television meant I was expected to stay inside even more now and would see less of my outside friends. In subtle ways I was already being sorted out socially, although I did not know it then.

10   I do not know exactly when I first realized that Mama and I had become separate entities. The idea just sprouted from bits and pieces of my own childhood memories and ripened with time. Somewhere along the way, the stories began to change; the texture and flavor of them were different, like new seasonings added to an old recipe. *She* was the one who almost had a heart attack when I lurched from behind the front door and shouted "Boo!" one day when she returned home from work. (I was punished with the warning never to frighten her again.) A damp smoldering firecracker had exploded in *her* ear and left her deaf for a few days one Fourth of July when she was a little girl. So, God forbid anything like that should happen to her only child. The anxiety button had been permanently installed.

Comprehension and Discussion

1. The author states, "A free-floating anxiety flowed through our house-hold and not only kept our doors locked to strangers but also limited neighbors' visits" (2), and her mother said that Oliver had an "overall tendency toward distress" (3). What does the word *anxiety* mean? How did this anxiety exhibit itself in the author? What were some of the things she was afraid of? What was the origin of her fears? Compare and contrast her fears with those of Sexton in "The Fury of Overshoes" (p. 90). What were some of your fears when you were younger? Do you know the origin of your fears? Do you still have remnants of any of these fears? Are you afraid of anything now? If so, what? Discuss child-hood fears with your classmates, and then write a journal entry about one of your childhood fears.

2. What were some of the things the author inherited from her mother? What are some of the things you inherited from your mother? Your father? Other relatives?

3. There was very little "future talk" between the author and her mother. The only goal that her mother expressed was to get her daughter through high school. What were some of the goals your parents had for you? Were their goals for you the same as your own goals? Have you achieved any of these goals?

4. The author states, "In subtle ways I was already being sorted out so-cially, although I did not know it then" (9). What does she mean? Have you ever felt that you were being sorted out socially?

5. How did the author's relationship with her mother change? When and how did you realize that your relationship with your mother or father or other significant person was changing and that you were growing up?

Language and Technique

1. What is Oliver's *thesis* or main idea? Does she state it explicitly, or does she imply it?

2. Sometimes Oliver uses *figurative language*—writing meant to be under-stood imaginatively instead of literally, such as similes and metaphors—to make her writing vivid and specific. Study the examples below. Determine what is compared in each, and be prepared to discuss the meaning and the effectiveness of each. Can you find other examples of figurative language in the essay? Discuss with your classmates how fig-urative language goes beyond the literal meaning of the words.

Simile	"clattered away like tapping fingernails" (1)
	"Somewhere along the way, the stories began to change; the texture and flavor of them were different, like new seasonings added to an old recipe" (10)
Metaphor	"flash-flood temper" (5)
	"she ironed sadness into the pleats of my dresses" (7)
	"For awhile, I was content in her cocoon" (8)
	"The idea just sprouted . . . and ripened" (10)

3. Notice how Oliver uses the *dash*. In paragraphs 3 and 4 she uses it to indicate that something will follow to explain what has preceded. In paragraphs 2 and 8 she uses the dash to indicate that a list or catalog will follow to make what has preceded specific. In these sentences, why do you think the author uses the dash instead of the comma? The colon? Are these uses of the dash effective?

4. One of the most effective methods of developing a paragraph is to use specific examples. Study Oliver's use of examples to develop the topic sentence in paragraphs 3 and 7. For each of these paragraphs, what is the topic sentence? Is it stated or implied? Count the number of specific examples she uses in each paragraph. Are the examples effective? Can you think of other examples she might have used? Discuss these paragraphs with your classmates.

Suggestions for Writing

1. **Sentence.** Referring to question 3 under Language and Technique, write two sentences in which you use the dash, and share your sentences with a small group of classmates.

2. **Paragraph.** Write a paragraph in which you develop the topic sentence by examples, similar to paragraphs 3 and 7 in Oliver's essay. State the topic sentence at the beginning of the paragraph, and use at least five specific examples for development. You may use one of the following topic sentences or one of your own.

   [Name of a person] had/has a manual for survival. (See paragraph 3.)

   I remember the special quality time that my [specific relative] spent with me.

I remember the treats and rewards I received when I was good as a child.

I remember the ways I was punished when I misbehaved as a child.

[Name of a person] taught me some valuable lessons.

[Name of a person] showed/shows love for me in various ways.

Share your paragraph with your classmates.

3. **Essay.** Write an autobiographical narrative of one specific memorable event from your childhood or of a series of events (similar to Oliver's essay). Include an introductory paragraph, several body paragraphs, and a concluding paragraph. Be sure your essay has a *thesis* or main idea and that all the narrative details are relevant to the main idea.

4. **Essay.** Write an essay in which you explain why and how children should be punished.

5. **Essay.** Write an essay on how your parents' goals and dreams for you are/were similar to and different from your own.

Teenagers Are Not Becoming More Violent

Mike Males

MIKE MALES is a journalist who often investigates and writes about various aspects of the younger generation. His interests are evident in the titles of two of his books: *The Scapegoat Generation: America's War on Adolescents* and *Framing Youth: 10 Myths About the Next Generation.* In the following selection, first published in the *Los Angeles Times* in 1999, he defends teenagers as a group against what he considers false accusations.

Vocabulary Study

cited (2)	inexplicable (6)
apocalyptic (2)	dire (7)
demonizing (4)	angst-ridden (9)
pathology (4)	aberrations (10)
paradox (5)	draconian (11)
pastoral (5)	nostrums (12)

Teenagers Are Not Becoming More Violent

1   Two weeks after the school massacre in Littleton, Colorado, anguished parents in a California suburb where murder is also rare found such tragedy "can happen here." A 39-year-old man drove his Cadillac into a crowded preschool playground in Costa Mesa, killing a 3-year-old and a 4-year-old, leaving two small children in critical condition and injuring two more toddlers and an adult aide. His motive seemed to be incomprehensible rage: The driver was quoted by police as remorselessly seeking to execute "innocent children" because of a former girlfriend's rejection.

2   But while the shootings in Littleton and schools around the nation have been cited as a horrific sign of America's social breakdown, Costa Mesa's tragedy was not used as a metaphor for apocalyptic social collapse by political leaders and scholarly authorities.

3   Why? Because, like other adults who commit mass killings, the Costa Mesa killer is viewed as an individual psychopath, representative only of his isolated rage. The commentators who magnify a teenage gunman into a poster child for "youth culture" gone terribly awry do not similarly portray a grown-up who commits atrocity as reflecting a diseased "middle-age-culture."

4   As another White House summit on youth and school violence starts, the reasons for the national panic over kids killing kids, versus the virtual ignoring of the far-more-common phenomenon of adults killing kids, raise sobering questions about the attitudes of authorities—and Americans, in general—toward young people. Why do occasional killings by students generate commentary demonizing a generation of young people, when the more prevalent killings by adults draw no similar fears of widespread grown-up pathology?

5   Here is the baffling paradox: While student shootings remain rare, rage killings by middle-aged adults, a group criminologists insist has mellowed out of its violent years, are epidemic. [Since 1997] in Southern California alone, seemingly solid, middle-class, midlife adults committed a dozen massacres—a bus yard of workers raked with assault-rifle barrage, an office filled with semi-automatic pistol fire, children gunned as they fled down a pastoral suburban lane—that left 40 dead, including 16 children.

6   Recent trends provide ample reason to view this inexplicable blood spilling by middle-aged adults of comfortable background as part of a larger, alarming reality. Drug abuse, family violence and breakup, felony arrest and imprisonment have exploded among adults age 30 to 50, the parent generation whose values are extolled by many. Defying every crime

theory, felony arrests of white adults older than 30, California's fastest-rising criminal and prisoner population, have tripled, from 31,000 in 1975 to 106,000 in 1997.

7   This raises a second paradox: Today's middle-class and suburban teenagers are better behaved than kids of the past. Regardless of what dire theory of societal unraveling experts use to explain why two suburban Colorado teens went on a murderous rampage, a major fact is overlooked: The best evidence shows that rates of murder, school violence, drug abuse, criminal arrest, violent death and gun fatality among middle- and upper-class teenagers have declined over the last 15 to 30 years.

8   This is especially true in California. Compared with their counterparts of the 1970s, white teenagers of the late 1990s show sharply lower per-person rates of gun deaths (down 25%), suicide (down 30%), murder arrest (down 30%), criminal arrest (down 50%), drug abuse (overdose deaths down 80%) and violent fatality of all kinds (down an incredible 45% in the last decade). Nationally, surveys show 90% of today's teens are happy and feel good about themselves; 80% get along well with their parents and other adults; more young people volunteer for charities and services than ever; and parents, religion and teachers are the biggest influences on youth.

9   With such statistics, it is hard to justify the widespread belief that today's adolescents are alienated, angst-ridden and troubled. If pop culture, music, video games and Internet images affect teenagers, we should credit them for the fact that young people are behaving better. In fact, it may be that young people's bewildering array of informal, "alternative familes"—ravers, Goths, posses, 'zine cultures, Internet forums, gay and lesbian groups, skateboarders, gay and lesbian skateboarder 'zinesters—help insulate them from the difficulties of increasingly chaotic biological families and account for the surprising good health of youths who should be most at risk.

10   The shootings in Littleton and other schools are not part of a larger trend toward more student and school violence, but tragic aberrations. The political and professional theorists whose explanations for Littleton flooded the media and policy forums displayed a singular failure to get a grip. Twenty-five million teenagers attend 20,000 schools nationwide. Ten students in seven schools committed the widely-publicized shootings of the past 18 months. Teenage gunners are not representatives of all teens, even alienated, outcast ones, but are rare, extremely disturbed individuals. There is no evidence that adolescents are more troubled than adults or any more disturbed today than they ever were. As psychologist Laura Berk's 1997 text, "Child Development," notes, "the overall rate of severe

psychological disturbance rises only slightly (by 2%) from childhood to adolescence, when it is the same as in the adult population—about 15% or 20%."

[11]   But to say that murderous rage is rare and declining among middle-class and affluent youth does not mean its prevalence is zero. Teenagers are subject to the same environments and pressures that drive some adults to violence, and teens inhabit the same adult society whose infestation of superlethal firearms too easily converts anger into slaughter. Exaggerating rare instances of teenage rage into some kind of generation-wide craziness not only inflicts unwarranted paranoia, blanket surveillance, draconian restrictions and harmful interference with normal growing up on a generally healthy generation of young people, it also severely hampers investigation into identifying and forestalling the narrow, individual psychoses that produce rage killers of all ages.

[12]   The baseless panic about young people inflamed by so many politicians, leading psychologists, pundits and institutional scholars is more damaging to our social fabric than the isolated teenage murders they seize upon. Ignoring clear statistics and research, authorities seem to lie in wait for suburban youth killings, months and thousands of miles apart, to validate a false hypothesis of generational disease, even as they ignore more compelling evidence of deteriorating adult behavior. This subversion of health and safety goals to politically warped, crowd-pleasing nostrums about "saving our kids" endangers kids in reality and helps perpetuate America's dismal reputation as the deadliest, most bullet riddled, unhealthiest nation in the Western world.

Glossary

Littleton, Colorado (1)—suburb of Denver and the location of Columbine High School, where in 1999 two male students killed fourteen students and a teacher and wounded others. It has become a national symbol of teenage violence

Comprehension and Discussion

1. What is Males's thesis sentence or main idea, his stance or position concerning violence in society today? In your journal, write out his thesis sentence so that you are prepared to discuss it with your classmates.
2. Males presents an argument to support his position. What evidence, specific details, and examples does he present to support his position? Is his evidence sufficient to convince you to agree with him?

3. Look up the word *paradox* in the dictionary and write it in your journal. What two paradoxes does Males set forth? Discuss these with your classmates.

4. What specific differences does Males point out between the adult population and the teenage population?

5. What specific evidence does Males present to support his contention that today's teenagers are better behaved than those of the past? Do you agree or disagree with the author? What observations from your own experience, knowledge, and reading can you use to support your opinion? Note these in your journal and then discuss them with your classmates. Add to your journal notes additional information from your classmates.

Language and Technique

1. Males uses a relatively high level of language or vocabulary. In your journal, list the words that you think a general reader might not be familiar with, look up the definition of any words that are unfamiliar to you, and write the definitions in your journal. What does this formal level of language tell you about Males's intended *audience* or readers? In other words, for what group of people is he writing?

2. An *introduction* is supposed to accomplish three purposes: (1) to get the reader's attention and interest; (2) to introduce the general subject; and (3) to state or imply the thesis or main idea. Paragraphs 1–3 comprise the introduction of Males's essay. Analyze the introduction and determine if Males achieves these three purposes in his introduction. Discuss your opinion with your classmates.

3. In the last sentence of paragraph 4 Males uses a *rhetorical question*—that is, a question that he does not answer but to which the answer is explicit or known. Is this an effective device at this point in this essay? Why or why not?

4. Throughout the essay Males uses statistics to support his position. Are these statistics convincing to you? Why or why not? Discuss this technique with your classmates.

Suggestions for Writing

1. **Sentence.** In one sentence, express Males's thesis idea in your own words.

2. **Paragraph.** Find an article in a newspaper, or a radio or television report about teenagers in your area, and then write a paragraph summarizing the

report. Share your report with your classmates, and note the variety of information that you and your classmates find.

3. **Essay.** Write an argumentative essay in which you agree or disagree with Males's thesis. Use your own evidence from your reading and experience to support your position.

4. **Essay.** Males presents one way in which he believes teenagers are misunderstood. Write an essay in which you state, explain, and provide examples of another way in which you think teenagers are misunderstood.

5. **Essay.** Write an essay in which you explain the message that one of the following television programs presents to the audience and the effect this program has on its audience: *American Idol, Survivor, Fear Factor, Miss America Pageant, Law and Order, Friends, The Jerry Springer Show, Judge Judy, Oprah,* or one of your choice that your instructor approves.

A Clean, Well-Lighted Place

Ernest Hemingway

ERNEST HEMINGWAY, a favorite American writer, was born in Illinois and had a home in Key West, Florida. Hemingway traveled extensively throughout Europe and Africa, where he gathered material for many of his stories and novels. This story is set in Spain.

Vocabulary Study

despair (4)   syntax (46)

A Clean, Well-Lighted Place

[1] It was late and every one had left the café an old man who sat in the shadow the leaves of the tree made against the electric light. In the day time the street was dusty, but at night the dew settled the dust and the old man liked to sit late because he was deaf and now at night it was quiet and he felt the difference. The two waiters inside the café knew that the old man was a little drunk, and while he was a good client they knew that if he became too drunk he would leave without paying, so they kept watch on him.

"Last week he tried to commit suicide," one waiter said.

"Why?"

"He was in despair."

5   "What about?"

"Nothing."

"How do you know it was nothing?"

"He has plenty of money."

They sat together at a table that was close against the wall near the door of the café and looked at the terrace where the tables were all empty except where the old man sat in the shadow of the leaves of the tree that moved slightly in the wind. A girl and a soldier went by in the street. The street light shone on the brass number on his collar. The girl wore no head covering and hurried beside him.

10   "The guard will pick him up," one waiter said.

"What does it matter if he gets what he's after?"

"He had better get off the street now. The guard will get him. They went by five minutes ago."

The old man sitting in the shadow rapped on his saucer with his glass. The younger waiter went over to him.

"What do you want?"

15   The old man looked at him. "Another brandy," he said.

"You'll be drunk," the waiter said. The old man looked at him. The waiter went away.

"He'll stay all night," he said to his colleague. "I'm sleepy now. I never get into bed before three o'clock. He should have killed himself last week."

The waiter took the brandy bottle and another saucer from the counter inside the café and marched out to the old man's table. He put down the saucer and poured the glass full of brandy.

"You should have killed yourself last week," he said to the deaf man. The old man motioned with his finger. "A little more," he said. The waiter poured on into the glass so that the brandy slopped over and ran down the stem into the top saucer of the pile. "Thank you," the old man said. The waiter took the bottle back inside the café. He sat down at the table with his colleague again.

20   "He's drunk now," he said.

"He's drunk every night."

"What did he want to kill himself for?"

"How should I know."

"How did he do it?"

25   "He hung himself with a rope."

"Who cut him down?"

"His niece."

"Why did they do it?"

"Fear for his soul."

30   "How much money has he got?"

"He's got plenty."

"He must be eighty years old."

"Anyway I should say he was eighty."

"I wish he would go home. I never get to bed before three o'clock. What kind of hour is that to go to bed?"

35   "He stays up because he likes it."

"He's lonely. I'm not lonely. I have a wife waiting in bed for me."

"He had a wife once too."

"A wife would be no good to him now."

"You can't tell. He might be better with a wife."

40   "His niece looks after him. You said she cut him down."

"I know."

"I wouldn't want to be that old. An old man is a nasty thing."

"Not always. This old man is clean. He drinks without spilling. Even now, drunk. Look at him."

"I don't want to look at him. I wish he would go home. He has no regard for those who must work."

45   The old man looked from his glass across the square, then over at the waiters.

"Another brandy," he said, pointing to his glass. The waiter who was in a hurry came over.

"Finished," he said, speaking with that omission of syntax stupid people employ when talking to drunken people or foreigners. "No more tonight. Close now."

"Another," said the old man.

"No. Finished." The waiter wiped the edge of the table with a towel and shook his head.

50   The old man stood up, slowly counted the saucers, took a leather coin purse from his pocket and paid for the drinks, leaving half a peseta tip.

The waiter watched him go down the street, a very old man walking unsteadily but with dignity.

"Why didn't you let him stay and drink?" the unhurried waiter asked. They were putting up the shutters. "It is not half-past two."

"I want to go home to bed."

"What is an hour?"

55 "More to me than to him."

"An hour is the same."

"You talk like an old man yourself. He can buy a bottle and drink at home."

"It's not the same."

"No, it is not," agreed the waiter with a wife. He did not wish to be unjust. He was only in a hurry.

60 "And you? You have no fear of going home before your usual hour?"

"Are you trying to insult me?"

"No, hombre, only to make a joke."

"No," the waiter who was in a hurry said, rising from pulling down the metal shutters. "I have confidence. I am all confidence."

"You have youth, confidence, and a job," the older waiter said. "You have everything."

65 "And what do you lack?"

"Everything but work."

"You have everything I have."

"No. I have never had confidence and I am not young."

"Come on. Stop talking nonsense and lock up."

70 "I am of those who like to stay late at the café," the older waiter said. "With all those who do not want to go to bed. With all those who need a light for the night."

"I want to go home and into bed."

"We are of two different kinds," the older waiter said. He was now dressed to go home. "It is not only a question of youth and confidence although those things are very beautiful. Each night I am reluctant to close up because there may be some one who needs the café."

"Hombre, there are bodegas open all night long."

"You do not understand. This is a clean and pleasant café. It is well lighted. The light is very good and also, now, there are shadows of the leaves."

75 "Good night," said the younger waiter.

"Good night," the other said. Turning off the electric light he continued the conversation with himself. It is the light of course but it is necessary that the place be clean and pleasant. You do not want music. Certainly you do not want music. Nor can you stand before a bar with dignity although that is all that is provided for these hours. What did he fear? It was not fear or dread. It was a nothing that he knew too well. It was all a nothing and a man was nothing too. It was only that and light was all it needed and a certain cleanness and order. Some lived in it and never felt it but he knew it all was nada y pues nada y nada y pues nada. Our nada who art in nada, nada be thy name thy kingdom nada thy will be nada in nada as it is in nada. Give us this nada our daily nada and nada us our nada as we nada our nadas and nada us not into nada but deliver us from nada; pues nada. Hail nothing full of nothing, nothing is with thee. He smiled and stood before a bar with a shining steam pressure coffee machine.

"What's yours?" asked the barman.

"Nada."

"Otro loco mas," said the barman and turned away.

80   "A little cup," said the waiter.

The barman poured it for him.

"The light is very bright and pleasant but the bar is unpolished," the waiter said.

The barman looked at him but did not answer. It was too late at night for conversation.

"You want another copita?" the barman asked.

85   "No, thank you," said the waiter and went out. He disliked bars and bodegas. A clean, well-lighted café was a very different thing. Now, without thinking further, he would go home to his room. He would lie in the bed and finally, with daylight, he would go to sleep. After all, he said to himself, it is probably only insomnia. Many must have it.

Glossary

counted the saucers (50)—Every time patrons in Spanish cafés received a drink, they were given a saucer. When they were ready to pay, they counted the number of saucers in the pile to know how many drinks they had had and how much they should pay.

peseta (50)—a Spanish coin of little value

hombre (62)—man

bodegas (73)—houses of prostitution

nada y pues nada (76)—nothing and then nothing

Otro loco mas (79)—one more nut or crazy person

copita (84)—small drink

Comprehension and Discussion

1. The older waiter characterizes himself with several important state-ments in paragraphs 63–68, 70, 72, 74, 76, and 85. Reread these passages carefully; then in your journal make a list of the characteristics of the older waiter. Compare your list with that of your classmates.
2. The older waiter says to the younger waiter, "We are of two different kinds" (72). In what ways are the two waiters different? In your journal, make a list of the differences. Then compare your list with the lists of your classmates. Discuss with your classmates whether the differences are typical or nontypical of the differences between older and younger people.
3. The old man who is drinking at the café represents a third generation. How is he different from the two waiters? How is the old man similar to the older waiter? Do you agree with the younger waiter's opinion of the old man or with the opinion of the older waiter? Why?
4. What is the meaning of the title of the story? How many times is the title referred to in the story?
5. What is the meaning of the last sentence, "Many must have it"?

Language and Technique

1. What effect does Hemingway's sprinkling of Spanish words throughout the story have on you? Ask your classmates if they have the same reaction as you.
2. Hemingway uses various *images* of light and dark throughout the story. Working with a small group of your classmates, find the references to light and the references to dark.
3. What do light and cleanliness *symbolize* (represent) in this story? In contrast, what do dark and uncleanliness symbolize? How do these symbols add depth of meaning to the story?
4. Who is the main character of this story? Why?

Suggestions for Writing

1. **Sentence.** Review the use of *quotation marks* and how to punctuate quotations. Then, with your classmates, study and discuss how Hemingway uses *dialogue.* When you understand the use of quotation marks, record at least five sentences of a conversation that you overhear, and be sure to

punctuate the sentences correctly. With one of your classmates, check the punctuation of your sentences and of his or her sentences.

2. **Paragraph.** Write a paragraph describing a place, using either images of light *or* images of dark. Share your paragraph with a small group of classmates, and then discuss with them the tone or emotional attitude or atmosphere that is produced by the images of light and dark.

3. **Essay.** Write an essay in which you compare and contrast the younger waiter and the older waiter. Support your assertions with specific references and quotations from the story.

4. **Essay.** Write an essay in which you compare and contrast yourself to someone with whom you have worked, who is of a different generation— either older or younger than you.

5. **Essay.** Depression and despair are common psychological problems today. Do some reading on depression, what it is and how it affects a person. Perhaps talk with someone who has experienced depression and find out how it affected him or her. Then write an essay on the common causes or effects of depression.

It's Not Just a Phase

Katherine E. Zondlo

KATHERINE E. ZONDLO was a teenager when she wrote this essay. It was published in the "My View" column of *Newsweek*. In this selection she explains one of her pet peeves.

It's Not Just a Phase

1   A Few weeks ago my mother invited a friend and her son, a 5-year-old named Joseph, to dinner at our house. Very mature and intelligent for his age, Joseph seemed to have an endless supply of comments that, when spoken in his earnest little voice, kept most of our dinner guests in stitches. Sitting at the table, I was suddenly visited by a flood of childhood memories—memories of having been laughed at for speaking my mind, often using "big words" as Joseph was. I remembered the shame and humiliation I felt, worrying that I had said something wrong or stupid. What a mixed message: adults using sophisticated words around kids and then laughing when they experiment with them. Suddenly, my heart went out to the little boy sitting next to me, looking at us with wide eyes like video cameras, capturing all of our responses on tape to be played over and over

again. For all I know, the footage that Joseph gathered at dinner that night could stay with him forever, a reminder that sometimes, even if you speak the truth and do so sincerely, someone may laugh at you.

2   The adults did not mean to diminish a child's self-esteem or scar him for life. They just wanted to have pleasant conversation. Unfortunately, it was at Joseph's expense. They were suffering from the "how cute" syndrome: adults making light of kids' opinions. They can't effectively put themselves in young people's shoes. As a result, many do not know how to treat us with respect.

3   Another nasty symptom of the "how cute" syndrome is making an unnecessary issue of young people's age. Many magazines and newspapers print a young person's age after a letter in the reader-response section. This suggests to children that adults don't care what kids have to say. Adults just think it's charming that they would write in at all, cute that they have opinions on world issues, adorable that they think of the world past their own backyards. If questioned, the adults would likely say they're simply recognizing and respecting the fact that a young person took the time to write a letter, an act that deserves notice. But publishing a young person's age makes it the central issue and deflects from the writer's point of view.

4   "How cute" is an easy put-down adults use for children. For teens who've grown beyond the cute stage, there's the "it's just a phase" brushoff. "It's just a phase" is a belittling and harmful remark, but one that adolescents hear almost every day to dismiss behavior that adults simply don't (want to) understand. And there are many different ways of saying it. When I got my nose pierced in November, for instance, my parents' first remark was "*When* you decide to take that thing out, will the hole close up?" It didn't occur to them that I might not ever take it out. When I chose to become vegetarian, I heard, "You'll give this up as soon as you get hungry for a pepperoni pizza."

5   As a young person, I am very excited about the world, my future and the endless possibilities both offer. I want to make a positive difference, live a happy life and be true to myself. In college, I'd like to major in women's studies and use this knowledge to improve the status of women and girls in our society. I'm saddened by adults who say "it's just a phase" when I speak of my hopes and dreams. They smile wryly, thinking, "Just wait, young lady, when you enter the real world you'll wake up and realize that one person can't make that much difference." The adults I am drawn to are those who have not completely forgotten their adolescence and its

open-mindedness. They believe in me and my abilities, and encourage me to attain my goals.

6   Adults can learn a lot from young people. Children are born with a clean slate, free from hatred, racism, sexism, homophobia and all of their nasty cousins. Kids cooperate and share, skills requiring attitudes that many nations today seem to be lacking. Maybe the United Nations should watch a few episodes of "Sesame Street" and "Mister Rogers' Neighborhood" at their next meeting. From teens, adults can learn to renew their radical ideas and activist thoughts lost through life and their experiences. They can learn it is never too late to switch gears. They can learn that stubbornness and conviction are actually admirable qualities when compared with being passive and unquestioning.

7   Perhaps if kids and teens took over the government, or at least if we had a voice, the quality of life in this country might well begin to improve. Don't laugh or dismiss this as nonsense. Just think about it.

8   I know I'm not perfect. As a teen, I have already lost much of the innocence and open-mindedness of my childhood. So, in a sense, I'm already jaded. But I'm determined not to lose sight of my future plans. I'm going to cherish my hopes and dreams, hang on to my enthusiasm and keep my belief in the possibilities life has to offer. I'm determined I'll not trade in my idealism for a good job, a fat paycheck and a nice house.

9   Some adults surprise and inspire me. It heartens me when I see them switching gears in middle age, choosing a job or lifestyle that they genuinely enjoy. My mother, for example, decided to return to college when I was 5 to pursue her dream of becoming a physician. Teachers can be a source of motivation, too, especially those who enjoy their career and teach their classes with energy and innovation. Unfortunately, they are few and far between.

10   Little Joseph made an impact on me that night at dinner because his lively conversation was free of inhibitions. The adults at the party were not so spontaneous, and I realized that I, too, will probably soon be watching my words. Adults can still realize their dreams of adolescence if their present path makes them unhappy. Dreams are important to keep and work on. Grown-ups should make themselves look at young people—and that's what we are, young people—in a new light. Respect and try to understand us, love and learn from us. As Robert Frost said, "I go to school to youth to learn the future."

11   And by the way, if you're interested in my age, just leave it to your imagination.

Checklist for Revising and Editing

Following is a list of questions to guide you in the process of revising and editing your essays. Use the questions to respond to the essay and to check for any point of needed revision. You may also use it to respond to and evaluate essays by other writers, whether students or professional writers.

1. **Sources:** What sources of information does the author draw upon—experience and memory, observation, reading and research, conversation and interview?

2. **Purpose:** What is the author's purpose in this essay—to narrate, to develop, to explain, to argue or convince, or a combination of these? Does the author accomplish the purpose?

3. **Thesis:** What is the thesis sentence or main point? Does the author state the thesis or imply it? Does the author make the thesis clear?

4. **Unity:** Does the author stick to the thesis? Is every statement in the essay directly relate to the main idea?

5. **Structure and Organization:**

   A. **Introduction**
      1) Does the introduction make clear the subject of the essay?
      2) Does the introduction state or imply the thesis sentence clearly?
      3) Does the introduction grab your attention and interest, and make you want to read the essay?

   B. **Body**
      1) What are the major points for development in the essay?
      2) How does the author organize the points of development of the the essay? Is the order of points clear? Why does the author put the points in this order?
      3) Is this order appropriate for the ideas of the essay?
      4) Are there any other points or information that the author should have included? Why?

   C. **Conclusion**
      1) Does the conclusion relate directly to the introduction and to the thesis, as well as to the points in the body of the essay?

    2) Does the conclusion provide a sense of finality or ending to the essay?

    3) Is the conclusion effective?

6. **Development**

    A. What kinds of development does the author use to expand, support, and clarify the general assertions—narration, description, example, process, cause and effect, classification, example, comparison and contrast, definition, negation, statistics, expert opinion?

    B. Does the author provide sufficient evidence to make the subpoints clear and persuasive?

7. **Coherence**

    A. Does the essay flow smoothly from idea to idea? From sentence to sentence? From paragraph to paragraph?

    B. How does the author connect the ideas throughout the essay? What Bridges and signposts does the author use to help the reader navigate through the essay?

      1) What key ideas, words, and phrases does the author repeat?

      2) What pronouns does the author use?

      3) What transitional words and phrases does the author use to connect paragraphs? To connect sentences within paragraphs?

8. **Rhetorical Patterns:** What rhetorical patterns does the author use— narration, description, exposition, argument, example or illustration, enumeration, cause, effect, comparison, contrast, analysis, classification, process, definition, problems to solution?

9. **Language Skills and Proofreading**

    A. Has the author proofread and edited the essay carefully for correctness, appropriateness, and effectiveness of language skills?

- Spelling
- Capitalization
- Punctuation
- Grammar
- Sentence structure
- Word choice

    B. What, if anything, should be changed? Why?

10. **Response and Evaluation**

    A. Did the author effectively fulfill the assignment and purpose in the essay?

    B. What is the strongest aspect of the essay? What do you like best? Why?

    C. What could be changed to improve the essay? Why?

CHAPTER SIX

Education

*If a nation expects to be ignorant and free, in a state
of civilization, it expects what never was and never
will be.*

—THOMAS JEFFERSON

Suggestions for Journal Entries

1. What does Jefferson's comment above mean? Do you agree?
2. What does education mean to you?
3. What is the difference between formal education and informal education?
4. What other types of education can you think of?
5. Tell about a pleasant educational experience.
6. Tell about an unpleasant educational experience.
7. What responsibility for a child's development does a teacher have? A parent?
8. Why are you in college now?
9. How do you learn best?
10. How do you write? What is your process or procedure for writing?
11. What subject in school do you enjoy most? Why?

Theme for English B

Langston Hughes

LANGSTON HUGHES was born in Joplin, Missouri, and graduated from Lincoln University. A correspondent, columnist, dramatist, novelist, and poet, Hughes was a major figure in the Harlem Renaissance, the intellectual and literary movement of African American artists and writers in the 1920s.

Theme for English B

The instructor said,

Go home and write
a page tonight,
And let that page come out of you—
Then, it will be true.   5

I wonder if it's that simple?
I am twenty-two, colored, born in Winston-Salem,
I went to school there, then Durham, then here
to this college on the hill above Harlem.
I am the only colored student in my class.   10
The steps from the hill lead down into Harlem,
through a park, then I cross St. Nicholas,
Eighth Avenue, Seventh, and I come to the Y,
the Harlem Branch Y, where I take the elevator
up to my room, sit down, and write this page.   15

It's not easy to know what is true for you or me
at twenty-two, my age. But I guess I'm what
I feel and see and hear, Harlem, I hear you:
hear you, hear me—we two—you, me, talk on this page.
(I hear New York, too.) Me—who?   20

Well, I like to eat, sleep, drink, and be in love.
I like to work, read, learn, and understand life.
I like a pipe for a Christmas present,
or records—Bessie, bop, or Bach.
I guess being colored doesn't make me not like   25
the same things other folks like who are other races.

So will my page be colored that I write?
Being me, it will not be white.
But it will be
a part of you, instructor.
You are white—   30
yet a part of me, as I am a part of you.
That's American.
Sometimes perhaps you don't want to be a part of me.
Nor do I often want to be a part of you.   35
But we are, that's true!
As I learn from you,
I guess you learn from me—
Although you're older—and white—
And somewhat more free.   40

This is my page for English B.

Glossary

College (9)—Columbia University, a university in New York City

Bessie (24)—Bessie Smith, famous African American blues singer

Comprehension and Discussion

1. How does the speaker respond to the English instructor's homework assignment? What does he do? How does he feel? Why? Have you ever been given an assignment similar to the one the speaker of the poem was given? How did you react? Do you think the instructor is a good teacher? Why? What is the relationship between the speaker in the poem and the instructor? How do you think the instructor will react to the way the speaker responds to the assignment?

2. How do you think being the only African American student in the class makes the speaker of the poem feel? What two other characteristics set him apart from the rest of the class? Remember a time when you were set apart from a group, and write a journal entry on the experience. Then share it with your classmates.

3. The speaker says, "It's not easy to know what is true for you or me / at twenty-two, my age" (16–17). Do you agree with him? Do you think knowing what is true is easier when an individual is older? Why or why not? Discuss this comment with your classmates.

4. The speaker continues, "I guess I'm what / I feel and see and hear" (17–18). Do you think that statement is a good definition of *self*? What does he feel? What does he see? What does he hear? What does he like to do? How do you define yourself? Write a journal entry on your definition of yourself.

5. What does the speaker mean when he says that he is a part of the instructor and the instructor is a part of him (28–31)?

Language and Technique

1. Hughes writes this poem partially as an internal *dialogue* of the speaker with himself and partially as a *dialogue* with the speaker's instructor. Why do you think he uses this technique? Is it effective?

2. Hughes uses several *allusions* (references to persons, events, objects, or writings) in the poem, references that he assumes will be familiar to readers: Winston-Salem (7), Durham (8), college on the hill (9), Harlem (9), St. Nicholas (12), the Y (13), Bessie (24), bop (24), Bach (24). What do these allusions tell you about Hughes's concept of his audience for this poem? Do you know what these references mean? Does not knowing some of them interfere with your understanding the poem? In a dictionary or an encyclopedia, look up the meanings of the ones with which you are unfamiliar and write them in your journal. Then discuss the denotative and connotative meanings of these references with your classmates to help you understand the poem better.

4. The *dash* has two major uses. One is to indicate that something is to follow that will explain or illustrate what has preceded; it is like an arrow pointing to and emphasizing what comes after the dash. The other use is similar to using a pair of commas or parentheses; it is to set off an appositive or phrase that renames or restates the word or statement that it follows. Notice Hughes's use of the dash in lines 4, 19, 20, 24, 30, 38, and 39. How is each of these dashes used? Is each one effective? Discuss the poet's use of punctuation with your classmates.

Suggestions for Writing

1. **Sentence.** In one sentence, make an assignment that you think would be effective for this class. Share your assignment with your classmates and your instructor.

2. **Paragraph.** Freewrite a paragraph or more in which you carry on a conversation with yourself. Be as realistic as possible, and try to record

every thought that you have on a subject for at least ten minutes. Choose one of the following subjects: an assignment you have been given, this class, another course you are taking, a teacher you have had, a movie, a troublesome automobile, a song, a favorite pet.

3. **Essay.** Write an essay or a poem in response to the assignment that the speaker's instructor gave him: Go home and write a page about yourself and let that page be honest and true. Share your writing with your classmates.

4. **Essay.** Write an essay narrating an experience in which you felt set apart from the other people in a group, as the speaker felt in his English class. Be sure to identify why you felt separated or isolated and how you responded. Use your journal entry on question 2 in Comprehension and Discussion as a springboard for your essay.

5. **Essay.** Write an essay in which you recall a memorable—positive or negative—assignment, class, or teacher.

To Yrik: Of Popcorn and Unicorns

Sylvia Hicks

SYLVIA HICKS is an English professor and writer who has published poems, articles, reviews, and books. Her major interests are education and related social issues. In this poem she writes about the relationship between a teacher and a student.

Vocabulary Study

academe (5)   unicorns (6)
rhetoricians (5)

To Yrik: Of Popcorn and Unicorns

You came into my life   a bright sparkling
Intelligence in your eyes happy faces
On your ears dinosaurs on your clothes nothing
On your toes   to learn the rules
Of academe, the words of rhetoricians and of deans,   5
The worlds of writers   and of unicorns

You came into my life   searching
Your sophisticated charm   concealing
Innocence

As if we had world enough and time   10
We shared late sunny afternoon words
And laughter   poetry and popcorn
Lightlysaltedhotandgreasy
We solved the world's problems
                                    somewhat unwisely   15
Saving our own for other times—

        Hurry up, please, it's time . . .
        Time for walruses and wands
        And unicorns
        Mr. Kurtz   he dead   20
        The Queen cut off his head

As you leave this phase of life still searching
Remember unicorns
And popcorn
Lightlysaltedhotandgreasy   25

Comprehension and Discussion

1. Who is the *speaker* in the poem? What kind of person is the speaker?
   Who is the person spoken to? What characteristics does this person have?
   What kind of relationship do the two people in the poem have? In your
   journal, make a list of the characteristics of these two people and describe
   their relationship. Identify specific words and phrases in the poem to support your responses. Discuss your interpretation with your classmates.

2. Have you ever had a similar relationship to a teacher or an older person
   who was your mentor and guide, someone who you went to for information and advice? Or have you ever acted as a mentor for a person
   younger than you? Write a journal entry on either type of relationship,
   and share it with your classmates.

3. What are "the rules of academe" (4–5)? What are "the words of rhetoricians and of deans" (5)? What are the "worlds of writers" (6)? What are
   the worlds of unicorns (6)? Why did Yrik want to learn these things?
   How would they be of value to him? Do you know the rules of academe, the words of rhetoricians and deans? Are you familiar with the
   worlds of writers and the worlds of unicorns? Discuss these ideas and
   their value with your classmates.

4. In your journal, *paraphrase* the following lines; that is, express the meaning in your own words. Compare your paraphrase with the paraphrases of your classmates.

   We solved the world's problems/somewhat unwisely/Saving our own
       for other times—(14–16)
   As you leave this phase of life still searching/Remember unicorns/And
       popcorn/Lightlysaltedhotandgreasy (22–25)

5. What is a unicorn? What do unicorns symbolize? Look up the symbolism of unicorns in a specialized dictionary of symbols or of mythology. Write a journal entry on what you discover, and discuss the information with your classmates. How does this symbolism add to the meaning of the poem?

Language and Technique

1. What *visual images* does the poet use to describe the young person?
2. The poet uses several *literary allusions* or references to enhance the meaning of the poem.

   "As if we had world enough and time" (10) – an allusion to "To
       His Coy Mistress" by Andrew Marvel, a poem about how the
       time of life is short and fleeting

   "Hurry up, please, it's time" (17), "time for walruses" (18), and "The
       Queen cut off his head" 21) – allusions to "Alice in Wonder-
       land" by Lewis Carroll, a novel of magic and fantasy and dreams

   "Mr. Kurtz he dead" (20) – an allusion to the novel *Heart of Darkness*
       by Joseph Conrad, a novel about the journey of life and the
       search for truth and understanding of humanity. The character
       Kurtz symbolizes the darkness, evil, and corruption in man.

   What do these references mean in this poem? Discuss the meaning with your classmates.

3. Notice the spacing within the lines in the poem. Why do you think the poet leaves gaps between words on some lines (1, 4, 6, 7, 8, 12, 20) and omits the usual spaces between words on other lines (14, 25)? What is the effect of these techniques?

4. Study the punctuation in the poem: no periods, few commas (two on line 5 and two in the quote in line 20), one dash (16), and ellipsis points (17). What effect does this lack of punctuation, especially end punctuation (such as periods and semicolons), have on the meaning of the poem?

Suggestions for Writing

1. **Sentence.** In two or three sentences, describe how you remember someone when you first met him or her. Begin your first sentence the way Hicks begins this poem, "You came into my life" (1). Share your description with your classmates.

2. **Paragraph.** Review why the person addressed as "you" came into the speaker's life (4–7), and discuss these reasons as well as your reasons for coming to college with your classmates. Then write a paragraph on why you came to college. What did you come to learn? What are you searching for? Share your paragraph with your classmates.

3. **Essay.** Using your journal entry from Question 2 under Comprehension and Discussion, write an essay about an important teacher or mentor or counselor in your life. Explain the relationship you had with this person and what you learned from her or him.

4. **Essay.** Does most education occur in the classroom or outside the classroom? Write an essay on how your relationship with someone outside the classroom taught you one or more valuable lessons.

5. **Essay.** Is it important to believe in magic and dreams and fantasy, or is such belief harmful? Take a stance on the value or lack of value of magic, and write an essay explaining and supporting your position.

A Painful Bashfulness

George McGovern

GEORGE McGOVERN was born in 1922 in Avon, South Dakota. He served as a bomber pilot in World War II, and later became a history professor, a U.S. senator, and a candidate for U.S. president in 1972. McGovern also served as a U.S. ambassador to the United Nations. In the following excerpt from his autobiography, McGovern writes about his shyness as a child and how he overcame it.

Vocabulary Study

implication (2)	coherent (6)
repressing (4)	latent (6)
refute (6)	extemporaneously (7)

A Painful Bashfulness

1   When I was small, my most serious handicap was a painful bashfulness in the presence of strangers. My first year in school was a nightmare. Although I had learned to read prior to the first grade, I refused to participate in the oral reading exercises. The teacher promptly placed me in the circle of the poorest readers. I remained with that group for the balance of the year, sitting red-faced and silent when it came my turn to read. Nor did I recite in class, or volunteer answers, or ever raise a hand for recognition. I desperately wanted to go unnoticed and to remain silent.

2   Somehow my teacher sensed, perhaps from my written work, that I was not totally stupid and she passed me "on condition" to the second grade. There I encountered a determined young instructor who first started the process of loosening my tongue. She did it by a rather direct implication that I would either recite in class or be bounced out of school. But this message was given to me in private after school and she kept me with her in these after-school sessions for several days, forcing me to read and recite to her. She was firm and, indeed, insistent, but the slightest stammering response on my part brought words of strong assurance. The shyness continued, but I did begin to participate, however reluctantly, in class recitations. And I was impressed with that concerned, youthful teacher.

3   Then, in third grade, I came under the influence of Grace Cooley—a self-confident, witty, dedicated woman who enlivened her courses with stories of her experience in international travel. I desperately wanted to please her, and I believe she detected a few possible indications of intelligence in me.

4   There were setbacks from time to time in the struggle against shyness. One embarrassing experience occurred in the second grade when I had been postponing a visit to the rest room rather than raise my hand and ask to be excused. After a painful hour of repressing the forces of nature, a trickle appeared on the floor below my desk. This brought an excited shriek from Dorothy Nash, a girl with a high-pitched voice who sat next to me: "Oh, look what he's doing!" I have never been closer to total heart failure.

5   Looking back to the committed teachers of the Mitchell public-school system, I am convinced that good teachers may be as important in the development of a child as good parents. It was two high school teachers who steered me onto a course that explains much of my subsequent development.

6   As a high school sophomore I took a course in English composition from Miss Rose Hopfner. She was the first teacher to single me out for high praise combined with specific advice. She told me one day that I had a sensitivity and clarity of expression that was rare for a sophomore. Then she

urged me to talk with Bob Pearson, the history teacher and debating coach, about participation in the extracurricular debate program. A few days later I stood up at an evening meeting of the debate squad to refute the proposition "Resolved that the several States should adopt a unicameral legislature." The speech was a disaster. It was supposed to take ten minutes. I spoke for two minutes in barely coherent terms and then sat down humiliated and filled with a sense of failure. But Bob Pearson was soon on his feet giving a serious critique of what I had said and assuring me that it was an adequate first effort. No other person did more to strengthen my confidence and draw out my latent powers of expression than Bob Pearson.

7   Competitive high school debate literally transformed my personality and my approach to life. I learned to organize my thoughts, to buttress my ideas with evidence and to speak extemporaneously. The practice of debating both the affirmative and negative side of each year's debate proposition forced me into the complexities of major public questions.

Comprehension and Discussion

1. Why was McGovern placed in the poor readers' circle? Was he a poor reader? How did he respond? Did his being placed in this circle change him? Were you ever singled out for your behavior in school? What happened? How did you feel? If this happened to you, write a journal entry on the experience.

2. How did his second-grade teacher help him? His third-grade teacher Grace Cooley? His high school English teacher Rose Hopfner? His high school history teacher and debate coach Bob Pearson? In what specific ways did each teacher draw him out? How did each provide positive reinforcement? Why does McGovern call the teachers of the Mitchell public schools "committed"? What does he mean? Do you know any committed teachers? How do they exhibit their commitment to teaching and to students?

3. Do you think McGovern's being able to overcome his bashfulness and become a history professor and respected politician—two occupations that require assertiveness and public speaking—is unusual? Explain.

4. Do you consider bashfulness a disability? Why? What are some other disabilities or problems children may face as they grow up? Write a journal entry enumerating some of these common problems.

5. Do you think that many students are afraid of being called on in class as McGovern was? Why? How does this fear affect their learning? What are some of the tricks students use to avoid being called on in class? Do

college students still use some of these tricks? What can students do to overcome this fear?

Language and Technique

1. What is McGovern's thesis or main idea in this autobiographical selection? Where does he state the thesis? Why does he state it here?
2. McGovern uses a series of *anecdotes* (short, entertaining accounts of events; narrative illustrations) to illustrate his experiences in school because of his bashfulness. How many anecdotes does he use? Why does he choose to include these experiences?
3. As discussed in Chapter 3, there are three types of *organization* or order in writing: *spatial* (organization according to location in space), *chronological* (organization according to time), and *logical* (organization according to idea, such as least important to most important). Which type of organization does McGovern use? Is it appropriate for his essay? Why or why not?
4. Is McGovern's point of view that of the bashful child or that of the adult who has overcome his bashfulness looking back on his childhood? What specifics in the essay lead you to this conclusion? Is this point of view appropriate for this essay? Explain.

Suggestions for Writing

1. **Sentence.** McGovern begins his essay with the sentence "When I was small, my most serious handicap was a painful bashfulness in the presence of strangers." Write a sentence that begins, "When I was small . . ."
2. **Paragraph.** Narrate and describe an incident in your life that was as embarrassing to you as McGovern's encounter with Dorothy Nash was to him (4).
3. **Essay.** Explain how several teachers, counselors, or relatives worked with you to help you overcome a problem that you had in school. Use chronological order for a series of anecdotes, and use vivid specific narrative and descriptive details for support as McGovern does.
4. **Essay.** Think of someone you know who has overcome or learned to cope with a severe disability. Explain the individual's problem and how he or she has dealt with it.
5. **Essay.** Write an essay in which you advise teachers on what they can do to help students develop confidence and thus help them to learn. You may include what they should *not* do as well as what they should do.

Relationships 101

From Time Magazine

This article from *Time*, published in 2003, provides an up-to-date discussion on the issue of whether love can be learned and if love should be taught. As you read, see if the magazine staff writers agree with Buscaglia in the essay on pages 173–183.

Vocabulary Study

polarized (4)   imprimatur (6)
euphoric (5)   secular (7)

Relationships 101

2   Is a classroom the place to learn about love? Some college and high school students are finding out. "O.K. now I'm going to show you how to complain," says Marline Pearson to a class of 15 unusually attentive college students. Pearson, a sociologist, is teaching a course called Couples Relationships at Madison Area Technical College in Madison, Wis. When one of her students mentions that her boyfriend is always, like, falling asleep when they're supposed to do stuff, Pearson seizes what feels like a teachable moment. She suggests the student zero in on a specific time when her boyfriend dozed off and tell him how it made her feel. "Stay away from 'You always' and 'You never,'" she advises. "Even if you think the person does it always."

3   This new breed of romantic counseling—equal parts sex ed, social science and Dear Abby—is now being offered as formal courses at colleges and high schools across the country. Over two weekends, Pearson's students learn methods developed by researchers at the University of Denver and used for marital counseling in churches and in the military. They watch videos of fighting couples and discuss how conflicts can spiral out of control. They learn tidy formulas for success and failure in love: the three characteristics of successful couples (one is a man who can accept influence from a woman), the four behaviors that spell doom (constant criticism is a biggie). Each time Pearson rattles off a list of rules, her students start furiously taking notes, not because they'll be tested—they won't—but because they're truly dying to know.

4   "There's a great hunger for understanding relationships, not just body parts," says Sarah Brown, president of the National Campaign to Prevent

Teen Pregnancy. "Young people tell us they're almost drowning in information about AIDS, condoms, pregnancy. But they want to know, 'How do I break up with my boyfriend without hurting his feelings?'" One recent study of college students' use of counseling services at Kansas State University showed that the percentage of students seeking help for relationship problems rose from 34% in 1989 to 60% in 2001. School counselors say courses like Pearson's—as well as more than half a dozen national relationship-curriculum programs in high schools—are filling a void. They offer healthy models of love for children of divorce and a middle ground in the wake of the culture wars that polarized sex education in the 1980s, with emotionless biology classes at one end and preachy abstinence lectures at the other.

5   Young love has always been traumatic. But the anxious, euphoric stage these programs address used to be a lot shorter. In 1960 the average age of first marriage was 20 for women, 23 for men; today, it's 25 for women, 27 for men. With dating starting at around 15, says David Popenoe of the National Marriage Project at Rutgers University, "now you have 10 or 15 years of figuring out what to do with the opposite sex when marriage isn't uppermost in your mind." It may take them longer to get there, but most high school seniors—65% of girls and 58% of boys, according to a University of Michigan study—still say it's "very likely" they will stay married to the same person for life, numbers that are up slightly from 15 years ago.

6   Of course there's no guarantee that taking a course will help teens and young adults achieve the kind of relationships they say they ultimately want. The last time the U.S. threw itself into teaching young people about love was in the 1950s, when social scientists at colleges offered marriage education. By the '60s, many of those classes were being laughed off campuses as rigid and sexist, or as faulty attempts to stamp the mysteries of emotion with the imprimatur of science. "There's always going to be this sense of the imponderables," says Beth Bailey, author of From Front Porch to Back Seat: Courtship in 20th Century America. "People fall in love. It's not something where you can go down a checklist and match people up by scientific formulas."

7   There are reasons to expect that this movement may be different, however. It's more flexible about the roles of men and women and, at least in some secular classes, it makes room for homosexual relationships. Each course is unique, but the emphasis today is more on developing communication skills and less on establishing moral absolutes. "If we have the right tools, then maybe we'll have a better shot of making our relationships work," says Rebecca Olson, 22, who took Pearson's course last winter with

her boyfriend, Aaron Edge, 23, to help her avoid repeating the mistakes her divorced parents had made. Last month Olson and Edge got engaged.
8   Pearson has decided that teenagers need to get the message before they hit college. So she's publishing a curriculum for high school students. "All their experience tells these young people to be cynical," she says. "And yet part of their spirit says, 'I want it to be different for me.'" You don't have to be an incurable romantic to hope they succeed.

Glossary

Dear Abby (2)—a well-known advice column, especially on relationships

Comprehension and Discussion

1. This essay is about male–female, boyfriend–girlfriend relationships. What other types of relationships with other people do you have in your life? Write a journal entry about the various kinds of relationships in which you are involved.

2. Sex education has long been taught in school. How does relationship education differ from sex education? Is one more valuable than the other? Are both useful?

3. This article advises that when you are talking with your boyfriend or girlfriend, you should not use the phrases "You always" and "You never." Why? Is this good advice for all relationships, not just boyfriend–girlfriend relationships?

4. In a University of Michigan survey of high school seniors, 65 percent of girls and 58 percent of boys say it is very likely that they will stay married to the same person for life. Do you think you will stay married to the same person for life? Write a journal entry answering this question.

5. If the course Relationships 101 were offered at your college, would you take the course? Why or why not? Should such a course be offered at most colleges? Should it be a required course? Should it be offered in high schools also? Write a journal entry explaining your answers to these questions.

Language and Technique

1. This article begins with a question. Is this introduction effective? Explain. With your classmates, discuss this technique as a way to begin an essay. What other ways can you use to begin an essay? Look through the essays

in this textbook, and discuss them with your classmates. Make a list of these techniques in your journal so that you can refer to them as you write your essays.

2. The author of the essay uses various statistics as evidence. With a small group of classmates, study and analyze how the statistics are used, how they are incorporated into the text (including the correct punctuation), and what they add to the essay.

3. The author of the essay uses quotations as evidence. With a small group of classmates, study and analyze how the quotations are used, how they are incorporated into the text (including the correct punctuation), and what they add to the essay.

4. How does the author of the essay connect the paragraphs? With a small group of classmates, analyze the *transition* words and phrases that the author uses to make the paragraphs and thus the essay coherent.

Suggestions for Writing

1. **Sentence.** Discuss with a small group of your classmates how the author of this article uses statistics and incorporates them into the text. Refer to question 2 under Language and Technique. Then in a newspaper or magazine article, find some statistics that interest you. Write a sentence in which you use the statistics, and share your sentence with your classmates. Be sure to punctuate your sentence correctly. Then you and your classmates check one another's sentences.

2. **Paragraph.** Write a *classification* paragraph (one in which you divide, sort, and name items in a group) on the types of relationships you are involved in today. Begin your paragraph with a topic sentence on the types of relationships, and develop your paragraph by stating, explaining, and illustrating three to five types of relationships in your life now.

3. **Essay.** Write an essay answering the question at the opening of this essay, "Is a classroom the place to learn about love?" Review your journal entries and your notes from class discussion on the questions in Comprehension and Discussion to help you get started.

4. **Essay.** Write an essay explaining why you think or do not think that you will stay married to the same person for life. Refer to your journal entry in response to question 4 under Comprehension and Discussion. In your essay, state and explain the reasons for your belief.

5. **Essay.** Write an essay in which you narrate and explain a situation in which you broke up with someone you had been dating or someone to whom you were married. Include why you broke up, the other person's response, and how you felt. If you have never broken up or divorced, you might write an essay on how you have successfully stayed with one person.

To Educate One's Children in the Rules of Race

Clarence Page

CLARENCE PAGE is a journalist who has worked for various newspapers, including the *Chicago Tribune*. He often writes columns about racism and inequality in the United States. In this essay Page uses an experience with his own son as the springboard for his reflections.

Vocabulary Study

dilemmas (1)	pernicious (7)
definitive (3)	subliminal (7)
universal (3)	imbue (12)
catechism (4)	guise (12)
uncannily (4)	unsolicited (13)
trauma (6)	apprehensive (14)
averted (6)	daunting (15)
commiserating (7)	

To Educate One's Children in the Rules of Race

1   A few years ago, after talking to black friends who were raising teenage boys, I realized that I was about to face dilemmas not unlike those my parents faced. My son was turning three years old. Everyone was telling me that he was quite cute, and since he was the spitting image of his dad, I was the last to argue.

2   But it occurred to me that in another decade he would be not three but thirteen. If all goes well, somewhere along the way he is going to turn almost overnight from someone who is perceived as cute and innocent into someone who is perceived as a menace, the most feared creature on

America's urban streets today, *a young black male*. Before he, like me when I was barred from a childhood amusement park, would have a chance to let others get to know him, he would be judged not by the content of his character, but by the color of his skin.

3   When our son was four years old he arrived home from his day care center to announce to his mother, "I want to be a white policeman." Mom was somewhat shaken by this proclamation, she told me later. Where had he picked this up? We had dutifully stripped our conversations of all talk of race in his presence. When it couldn't be avoided, we spelled out the words ("Is she b-l-a-c-k . . . ?") as if discussing an X-rated movie. She was incapable of responding to his announcement other than to ask "Why?" He did not have a definitive answer. He simply thought it would be "cool," the kids' universal stamp of approval.

4   I quietly inched over to a bookshelf and brought down a copy of a book by two black psychiatrists on raising black children. Like a black parental catechism, it quickly offered up a question uncannily similar to our own—*What do you do when a four-year-old says he wants to be white?*—and an answer: *Relax*.

5   Don't panic, the book said. It is quite normal for children to begin to notice color at age four, but they don't attach the same meaning to it that we, their older folks, do. They are looking for role models, people they like enough to want to be like, until someone tells them otherwise. It is not limited to blacks, the book said. Sometimes young white children want to be brown or black like their favorite sports heroes.

6   There, I assured my wife. It is normal. As my parents used to say, it's a phase. Let the lad work it out. If we didn't make a big deal out of it, we figured, neither would he. Still, we did not forget it. A week or so later at a local outdoor folk festival, his mother introduced our son to a police officer who happened to be quite visibly a brown-skinned black man. He cheerfully presented our son with his own "junior officer" badge. Our son never again said he wanted to be a white police officer. He didn't say he wanted to be a black police officer, either. He didn't say anything but "Thank you." Still, his mother and I were relieved. Another little life-warping trauma seemed to be averted. For now.

7   Perhaps we make too much of these little concerns, but we are not alone. We find ourselves commiserating earnestly with other middle-class black parents about issues other parents almost never confront. *(Are white media feeding the ancient and pernicious rules of race to our child through subliminal messages? Did Disney have to give cackling black and Latino voices*

to the lazy, shiftless, and still extremely dangerous hyenas in The Lion King? *Does it matter that the noblest voice, that of the father king lion, happens to be that of an African American, James Earl Jones, Hollywood's favorite voice of God? Does it matter that he also voiced the baddest bad guy in outer space, Darth Vader? Why were there no black people in the first* Star Wars? *What happens to black people in white people's future?)*

8   To educate one's children, who tirelessly produce "Why?" questions about everything, in the rules of race *(Is a little enough? Is more too much?)* is to try to make sense out of nonsense. I quickly gained a new appreciation for what my parents went through when my son, at age five, blurted out while we were on a family drive, "Mom, why do you call your-self black? You look white. Dad looks black."

9   "It's a figure of speech," I said calmly, keeping my eyes on the road, as though I were not the least bit rattled. "Black means your family can be traced back to Africa."

10   Pause.

11   "Do you remember where Africa is?" I asked.

12   Silence. Perhaps our exchange suddenly was sounding too much like academic work. Yet, once again, he got me to thinking. Children do not imbue race with much meaning, and they remind us, however briefly, that we adults shouldn't either. Instead, we adults pass on our prejudices to our children under the guise of setting them straight. Rather than teaching them that different is not necessarily better or worse, we teach them how to make difference the basis for abuse, privilege, and exclusion.

13   His kindergarten classmate Eddy offered an unsolicited example. We were driving to an indoor playground called the Discovery Zone, a national chain where for a few dollars children have an opportunity to wear them-selves out and spend their parents' money on coin-operated amusement machines and great mouthfuls of popcorn, cotton candy, ice cream, and pizza. Eddy, who happens to be black and the child of a struggling single mom, had never been to this little corner of children's paradise. As I was driving us to it, he asked somewhat skeptically, "Do they have any black people at this place?"

14   I assured him that they would. I understood his concern. Even adults are apprehensive of unfamiliar places, and almost every place in the world still was unfamiliar to young Eddy. Even at age five, he already was feeling the impulse that causes many of us African Americans, whenever we walk into a strange roomful of people, to look around and see how many other black people are there.

15 I felt obliged to help liberate Eddy from his racial anxieties, to help him get over the daunting hump of hesitation that causes black people to avoid integrated situations out of fear of some ominous possibility of racial hurt. It's a daunting task, but someone has to do it, for the sake (as James Baldwin once wrote) of our future generations and the bills they must pay.

Glossary

James Baldwin (15)—twentieth-century African American writer of novels and short stories

Comprehension and Discussion

1. What is a *dilemma*? What dilemmas did Page's parents face? What dilemma did he face? What are some of the dilemmas you face in your life? In your journal, list some of dilemmas you face in your life, and discuss them with your classmates. Are your dilemmas similar to or different from their dilemmas? Why?

2. Do you agree with Page that a young black male is the most feared creature on America's urban streets today? Why are young black men often judged not by the content of their character but by the color of their skin? What characteristics of appearance other than skin color often stereotype people? Why should we not rely on our first impressions of others?

3. Page makes several significant observations about race. Think about the meaning of the following statements, and in your journal *paraphrase* (express in your own words) each one. Then participate in a class discussion of these statements.

   - "It is quite normal for children to begin to notice color at age four, but they don't attach the same meaning to it that we, their older folks, do" (4).
   - "To educate one's children, who tirelessly produce 'Why?' questions about everything, in the rules of race *(Is a little enough? Is more too much?)* is to try to make sense out of nonsense" (8).
   - "Children do not imbue race with much meaning, and they remind us, however briefly, that we adults shouldn't either" (12).
   - "Instead, we adults pass on our prejudices to our children under the guise of setting them straight" (12).
   - "Even adults are apprehensive of unfamiliar places"(14).

- "It's a daunting task, but someone has to do it, for the sake (as James Baldwin once wrote) of our future generations and the bills they must pay" (15).

4. Often when people are unsure of the situation in which they find themselves, they will do as Page and his wife decided to do when their son said he wanted to be a white police officer: "If we didn't make a big deal out of it, we figured, neither would he" (6). Think of some situations in your life in which you decided not to "make a big deal" out of them. Jot these in your journal, and participate in a class discussion of this behavior.

5. What is the thesis or main idea of Page's essay? Does he state it or imply it?

Language and Technique

1. Page uses four *anecdotes*, or narrative illustrations, in his essay. Find each, and discuss with your classmates why and how he uses each.

2. In paragraph 9, what does Page mean when he tells his son that "It's a figure of speech"? What is a *figure of speech*? Find some other figures of speech and share them with your writing group.

3. There are three *levels of language—formal, informal,* and *colloquial.* The language in Page's essay is colloquial; that is, it is conversational, as if he is talking with the readers. Examine his word choice and sentence structure to determine the colloquial characteristics of his writing. Discuss these with your classmates.

4. Page uses italics in paragraphs 2, 4, 7, and 8. Look up the uses of italics as punctuation marks. Then discuss with your classmates why Page uses italics where he does.

Suggestions for Writing

1. **Sentence.** After studying and discussing Page's use of italics, write a sentence in which you use italics correctly. Share your sentence with a small group of classmates and explain why you used the italics as you did.

2. **Paragraph.** Choose one of the dilemmas you face (from the list in your journal in response to question 1 under Discussion and Comprehension), and write a well-structured paragraph. Begin with a topic sentence that unifies the paragraph, include specific details and examples to clarify and support the body of the paragraph, and end with a clincher sentence.

3. **Essay.** Think of a prejudice you now have or one you once had. Write an essay in which you explain how you developed this prejudice and the effects it had on you and those around you.

4. **Essay.** Page claims that even adults are apprehensive (anxious, uneasy) about unfamiliar places and situations. Write an essay in which you narrate a situation in which you felt apprehensive.

5. **Essay.** Write an essay in which you examine the major cause or causes of prejudice. Explain and provide specific examples of each cause.

Charles

Shirley Jackson

SHIRLEY JACKSON is a well-known novelist and short story writer. Many of her works are psychological horror stories with surprise endings. Jackson's most famous story is "The Lottery," a favorite among high school and college students. It tells of a village that stones one of its residents each year. The following story is not a tale of horror, but it does contain a surprise ending.

Vocabulary Study

renounced (1)	institution (41)
raucous (2)	reformation (42)
insolently (3)	incredulously (45)
fresh (9)	cynically (48)
deprived (20)	haggard (63)
passionately (31)	primly (68)
elaborately (39)	

Charles

1   The day my son Laurie started kindergarten he renounced corduroy overalls with bibs and began wearing blue jeans with a belt; I watched him go off the first morning with the older girl next door, seeing clearly that an era of my life was ended, my sweet-voiced nursery-school tot replaced by a long-trousered, swaggering character who forgot to stop at the corner and wave good-bye to me.

2   He came home the same way, the front door slamming open, his cap on the floor, and the voice suddenly become raucous shouting, "Isn't anybody here?"

3   At lunch he spoke insolently to his father, spilled his baby sister's milk, and remarked that his teacher said we were not to take the name of the Lord in vain.

4   "How *was* school today?" I asked, elaborately casual.

5   "All right," he said.

6   "Did you learn anything?" his father asked.

7   Laurie regarded his father coldly. "I didn't learn nothing," he said.

8   "Anything," I said. "Didn't learn anything."

9   "The teacher spanked a boy, though," Laurie said, addressing his bread and butter. "For being fresh," he added, with his mouth full.

10   "What did he do?" I asked. "Who was it?"

11   Laurie thought. "It was Charles," he said. "He was fresh. The teacher spanked him and made him stand in a corner. He was awfully fresh."

12   "What did he do?" I asked again, but Laurie slid off his chair, took a cookie, and left, while his father was still saying, "See here, young man."

13   The next day Laurie remarked at lunch, as soon as he sat down, "Well, Charles was bad again today." He grinned enormously and said, "Today Charles hit the teacher."

14   "Good heavens," I said, mindful of the Lord's name, "I suppose he got spanked again?"

15   "He sure did," Laurie said. "Look up," he said to his father.

16   "What?" his father said, looking up.

17   "Look down," Laurie said. "Look at my thumb. Gee, you're dumb." He began to laugh insanely.

18   "Why did Charles hit the teacher?" I asked quickly.

19   "Because she tried to make him color with red crayons," Laurie said. "Charles wanted to color with green crayons so he hit the teacher and she spanked him and said nobody play with Charles but everybody did."

20   The third day—it was Wednesday of the first week—Charles bounced a see-saw onto the head of a little girl and made her bleed, and the teacher made him stay inside all during recess. Thursday Charles had to stand in a corner during story-time because he kept pounding his feet on the floor. Friday Charles was deprived of blackboard privileges because he threw chalk.

21   On Saturday I remarked to my husband, "Do you think kindergarten is too unsettling for Laurie? All this toughness, and bad grammar, and this Charles boy sounds like such a bad influence."

22   "It'll be all right," my husband said reassuringly. "Bound to be people like Charles in the world. Might as well meet them now as later."

23   On Monday Laurie came home late, full of news. "Charles," he shouted as he came up the hill; I was waiting anxiously on the front steps. "Charles," Laurie yelled all the way up the hill, "Charles was bad again."

24   "Come right in," I said, as soon as he came close enough. "Lunch is waiting."

25   "You know what Charles did?" he demanded, following me through the door. "Charles yelled so in school they sent a boy in from first grade to tell the teacher she had to make Charles keep quiet, and so Charles had to stay after school. And so all the children stayed to watch him."

26   "What did he do?" I asked.

27   "He just sat there," Laurie said, climbing into his chair at the table. "Hi, Pop, y'old dust mop."

28   "Charles had to stay after school today," I told my husband. "Everyone stayed with him."

29   "What does this Charles look like?" my husband asked Laurie. "What's his other name?"

30   He's bigger than me," Laurie said. "And he doesn't have any rubbers and he doesn't ever wear a jacket."

31   Monday night was the first Parent-Teachers meeting, and only the fact that the baby had a cold kept me from going; I wanted passionately to meet Charles's mother. On Tuesday Laurie remarked suddenly, "Our teacher had a friend come to see us in school today."

32   "Charles's mother?" my husband and I asked simultaneously.

33   Naaah," Laurie said scornfully. "It was a man who came and made us do exercises, we had to touch our toes. Look." He climbed down from his chair and squatted down and touched his toes. "Like this," he said. He got solemnly back into his chair and said, picking up his fork, "Charles didn't even *do* exercises."

34   "That's fine," I said heartily. "Didn't Charles want to do exercises?"

35   "Naaah," Laurie said. "Charles was so fresh to the teacher's friend he wasn't *let* do exercises."

36   "Fresh again?" I said.

37   "He kicked the teacher's friend," Laurie said. "The teacher's friend told Charles to touch his toes like I just did and Charles kicked him."

38   "What are they going to do about Charles, do you suppose?" Laurie's father asked him.

39   Laurie shrugged elaborately. "Throw him out of school, I guess," he said.

40   Wednesday and Thursday were routine; Charles yelled during story hour and hit a boy in the stomach and made him cry. On Friday Charles stayed after school again and so did all the other children.

41   With the third week of kindergarten Charles was an institution in our family; the baby was being a Charles when she cried all afternoon; Laurie did a Charles when he filled his wagon full of mud and pulled it through the kitchen; even my husband, when he caught his elbow in the telephone cord and pulled telephone, ashtray, and a bowl of flowers off the table, said, after the first minute, "Looks like Charles."

42   During the third and fourth weeks it looked like a reformation in Charles; Laurie reported grimly at lunch on Thursday of the third week, "Charles was so good today the teacher gave him an apple."

43   "What?" I said, and my husband added warily, "You mean Charles?"

44   "Charles," Laurie said. "He gave the crayons around and he picked up the books afterward and the teacher said he was her helper."

45   "What happened?" I asked incredulously.

46   "He was her helper, that's all," Laurie said, and shrugged.

47   "Can this be true, about Charles?" I asked my husband that night. "Can something like this happen?"

48   "Wait and see," my husband said cynically. "When you've got a Charles to deal with, this may mean he's only plotting."

49   He seemed to be wrong. For over a week Charles was the teacher's helper; each day he handed things out and he picked things up; no one had to stay after school.

50   "The P.T.A. meeting's next week again," I told my husband one evening. "I'm going to find Charles's mother there."

51   "Ask her what happened to Charles," my husband said. "I'd like to know."

52   "I'd like to know myself," I said.

53   On Friday of that week things were back to normal. "You know what Charles did today?" Laurie demanded at the lunch table, in a voice slightly awed. "He told a little girl to say a word and she said it and the teacher washed her mouth out with soap and Charles laughed."

54   "What word?" his father asked unwisely, and Laurie said, "I'll have to whisper it to you, it's so bad." He got down off his chair and went around to his father. His father bent his head down and Laurie whispered joyfully. His father's eyes widened.

55   "Did Charles tell the little girl to say *that*?" he asked respectfully.

56   "She said it *twice*," Laurie said. "Charles told her to say it *twice*."

57   "What happened to Charles?" my husband asked.

58   "Nothing," Laurie said. "He was passing out the crayons."

59   Monday morning Charles abandoned the little girl and said the evil word himself three or four times, getting his mouth washed out with soap each time. He also threw chalk.

60   My husband came to the door with me that evening as I set out for the P.T.A. meeting. "Invite her over for a cup of tea after the meeting," he said. "I want to get a look at her."

61   "If only she's there," I said prayerfully.

62   "She'll be there," my husband said. "I don't see how they could hold a P.T.A. meeting without Charles's mother."

63   At the meeting I sat restlessly, scanning each comfortable matronly face, trying to determine which one hid the secret of Charles. None of them looked to me haggard enough. No one stood up in the meeting and apologized for the way her son had been acting. No one mentioned Charles.

64   After the meeting I identified and sought out Laurie's kindergarten teacher. She had a plate with a cup of tea and a piece of chocolate cake; I had a plate with a cup of tea and a piece of marshmallow cake. We maneuvered up to one another cautiously, and smiled.

65   "I've been so anxious to meet you," I said. "I'm Laurie's mother."

66   "We're all so interested in Laurie," she said.

67   "Well, he certainly likes kindergarten," I said. "He talks about it all the time."

68   "We had a little trouble adjusting, the first week or so," she said primly, "but now he's a fine little helper. With occasional lapses, of course."

69   "Laurie usually adjusts very quickly," I said. "I suppose this time it's Charles's influence."

70   "Charles?"

71   "Yes," I said, laughing, "you must have your hands full in that kindergarten, with Charles."

72   "Charles?" she said. "We don't have any Charles in the kindergarten."

Comprehension and Discussion

1. Who is the *narrator* of the short story? What is the *point of view* of the story? How would the story be different if it were told from the point of view of Laurie, the boy? Discuss this difference with your classmates.

2. How do you describe the character Laurie in the story? Is he a *plausible* or believable character? Why or why not? Identify specific descriptions,

actions, and dialogue that make him believable or unbelievable. In your journal, write a paragraph on whether you think he is believable and why. Share your paragraph with your classmates, and be prepared to defend your position.

3. What causes Laurie to act as he does in kindergarten? Why does he do what he does? Is he a bad little boy (like a bad seed) who lies and misbehaves, or is he just an imaginative, overactive, playful little boy (you know, boys will be boys)? Discuss these questions with your classmates, and then in your journal, defend your position.

4. What is the *surprise ending* of the story? Although it is a surprise, is the ending plausible? What clues does Jackson present to *foreshadow* or prepare the reader for this ending? Working with a small group of your classmates, go through this story and identify the clues that prepare the readers for the ending of the story. Record these clues in your journal.

5. Do you know other authors who use surprise endings in their fiction? Are you familiar with any television shows or movies that use surprise endings? If so, make a note of them in your journal. How do such endings affect readers and viewers? Do you like surprise endings? Why or why not? Discuss with your classmates why you do or do not like surprise endings.

Language and Technique

1. Jackson is known for *realism* (presenting or portraying people and things as they really are) in her fiction. Working with a small group of your classmates, identify specific details in the story that help make the characters and the events in this short story realistic—that is, true to life and believable.

2. Working with a small group of your classmates, identify some of the humorous elements in this short story. Then participate in a class discussion of why Jackson includes humor in this realistic story.

3. Analyze Jackson's use of dialogue in this story. Are the characters' comments *plausible* (that is, believable)? Explain.

4. *Irony* is an event or result that is the opposite of what is expected. In paragraph 21 the narrator makes the ironic statement, "this Charles boy sounds like a bad influence." How is this statement ironic? Are there other ironic statements in the story? Is the ending ironic? Discuss the irony in the story with your classmates.

Suggestions for Writing

1. **Sentence.** Paragraph 41 is one long sentence of seventy-four words. The sentence is composed of four independent clauses joined by semi-colons. In your journal, write a sentence with at least three independent clauses joined by semicolons. Then, working with a small group of classmates, share and proofread one another's sentences.

2. **Paragraph.** Listen carefully to a conversation that you overhear, and in your journal take careful notes on it. Then write out the conversation as close to the original as possible. Remember to start a new paragraph each time the speaker changes. Be sure to use quotation marks and other marks of punctuation correctly.

3. **Essay.** Write an essay in which you narrate a series of events from your childhood school days.

4. **Essay.** Write a narrative about an interesting individual you have known.

5. **Essay.** Write an essay in which you analyze and illustrate with specific examples why children misbehave.

Advice to A High School Sophomore

Emily Rubino

EMILY RUBINO was a first-year student in college when she wrote this essay. The in-class writing assignment was to choose a topic and write an essay drawing from her own experience. At the end of her first semester, she reflected on her experiences in college and high school and decided that what she had learned might be helpful to other students.

Advice to A High School Sophomore

1   When a student enters high school, he or she is faced with many new challenges and responsibilities. As a freshman, a student is just finding his or her way around and learning the rules and expectations. When a student reaches sophomore status, however, it is time for that student to step up and really become involved with his or her high school and begin to plan for the future. Through my own experiences, I have found that it is crucial to become involved, take high level courses, and plan for college early!

2   In high school, there are many various classes, clubs, and extracurricular activities for a student to become involved with. Although the teenager's choosing a class or club can be quite overwhelming, these courses or

groups can truly benefit his or her high school career. My advice is to choose as many clubs or classes as possible. Throughout high school, I was involved with Fellowship of Christian Athletes, National Honor Society, and Jay-Teens, which is a community service club. These clubs not only boosted my credentials on my college applications, but also got me involved with my community as well. Painting windows, doing roadside cleanups, or running a field day for elementary students made me feel good about myself and gave me time to bond with my friends, as well as form new friendships. In addition, I recommend that a student take classes involving his or her interests or even classes that just sound interesting as well as the required courses. Unfortunately, I didn't decide to do this until my senior year when I chose classes such as law studies, philosophy, and modern history. These classes not only educated me in what's going on in today's world, but also introduced me to teachers who truly loved their jobs. I also took classes my senior year which not only helped me make lifelong friendships, but also helped me decide what I'd like to work with my entire life: music. A high school student, especially a sophomore, should become involved because these clubs and classes can truly benefit his or her high school experience.

3   Another piece of advice I would like to give a sophomore concerns choice of courses. When a student reaches sophomore status, most schools will allow him or her to take advanced placement courses. I cannot stress the importance of these courses enough! AP classes not only prepare a student for college workloads and exams, but passing these courses can give him or her college credit. Taking AP classes in high school has saved me time and money and has allowed me to skip certain classes, such as early American history and a few science courses. If a student does not want to take these courses, then I recommend honors courses. These classes, which are a bit more challenging and faster-paced than regular classes, look better on college applications and can even give the student a few extra points to boost his or her GPA. Honors courses also give the student an opportunity to be a part of National Honors Society, which is a valuable accomplishment! I especially advise a sophomore not to just "take it easy" because the student thinks he or she can wait until junior or senior year to really get serious. Colleges look at courses taken all the way back in freshman year. Not only is waiting more stressful, but it is also unwise if the student plans to attend college.

4   Lastly, and in my opinion most importantly, is for the student to prepare for college early. In sophomore year in high school, a student should take the PSAT. This test helps him or her to prepare for the real SAT and gives the student an idea of what his or her weaknesses are. If possible, I

even recommend taking the SAT or ACT sophomore year. I unwisely waited until almost the end of my senior year to take the ACT. I luckily did well, but if I had not, I may not have received a score high enough to receive the Bright Futures Scholarship, which my family and I needed if I was going to attend college. Taking these tests early can't hurt. In fact, the tests only leave room for improvement. I also want to stress that sophomores should begin to look for scholarships early. The high school guidance office offers some information on scholarships, and the Internet can reveal thousands of scholarships that a student may be available for. I, once again, waited until the last minute to search for scholarships. My high school guidance office was anything but helpful. Most of the scholarships I found there were for other races or had already expired. The information on the Internet was confusing and overwhelming! Most states offer scholarships for high school students who meet certain qualifications, but I still feel it is best to begin the search early. If a student is uncertain about the career path he or she would like to follow, I recommend taking a career aptitude test. Even if the career chosen is not what a student would like to do (trust me: I have had everything from truck driver to firefighter to armed forces), these tests may still possibly show where a student's interests lie. Being prepared early is a key to becoming well prepared for college.

5   High school can be an overwhelming and exciting time for a student. If a sophomore has a plan, works hard, and gets involved, he or she will have a lot less stress in the long run and will be prepared for whatever lies ahead after high school.

Checklist for Revising and Editing

Following is a list of questions to guide you in the process of revising and editing your essays. Use the questions to respond to the essay and to check for any point of needed revision. You may also use it to respond to and evaluate essays by other writers, whether students or professional writers.

1. **Sources:** What sources of information does the author draw upon—experience and memory, observation, reading and research, conversation and interview?

2. **Purpose:** What is the author's purpose in this essay—to narrate, to develop, to explain, to argue or convince, or a combination of these? Does the author accomplish the purpose?

3. **Thesis:** What is the thesis sentence or main point? Does the author state the thesis or imply it? Does the author make the thesis clear?

4. **Unity:** Does the author stick to the thesis? Is every statement in the essay directly relate to the main idea?

5. **Structure and Organization**

   A. **Introduction**
      1) Does the introduction make clear the subject of the essay?
      2) Does the introduction state or imply the thesis sentence clearly?
      3) Does the introduction grab your attention and interest, and make you want to read the essay?

   B. **Body**
      1) What are the major points for development in the essay?
      2) How does the author organize the points of development of the the essay? Is the order of points clear? Why does the author put the points in this order?
      3) Is this order appropriate for the ideas of the essay?
      4) Are there any other points or information that the author should have included? Why?

   C. **Conclusion**
      1) Does the conclusion relate directly to the introduction and to the thesis, as well as to the points in the body of the essay?
      2) Does the conclusion provide a sense of finality or ending to the essay?
      3) Is the conclusion effective?

6. **Development**

   A. What kinds of development does the author use to expand, support, and clarify the general assertions—narration, description, example, process, cause and effect, classification, example, comparison and contrast, definition, negation, statistics, expert opinion?

   B. Does the author provide sufficient evidence to make the subpoints clear and persuasive?

7. **Coherence**

   A. Does the essay flow smoothly from idea to idea? From sentence to sentence? From paragraph to paragraph?

B. How does the author connect the ideas throughout the essay? What Bridges and signposts does the author use to help the reader navigate through the essay?

1) What key ideas, words, and phrases does the author repeat?

2) What pronouns does the author use?

3) What transitional words and phrases does the author use to connect paragraphs? To connect sentences within paragraphs?

8. **Rhetorical Patterns:** What rhetorical patterns does the author use— narration, description, exposition, argument, example or illustration, enumeration, cause, effect, comparison, contrast, analysis, classification, process, definition, problems to solution?

9. **Language Skills and Proofreading**

A. Has the author proofread and edited the essay carefully for correctness, appropriateness, and effectiveness of language skills?

- Spelling
- Capitalization
- Punctuation
- Grammar
- Sentence structure
- Word choice

B. What, if anything, should be changed? Why?

10. **Response and Evaluation**

A. Did the author effectively fulfill the assignment and purpose in the essay?

B. What is the strongest aspect of the essay? What do you like best? Why?

C. What could be changed to improve the essay? Why?

CHAPTER SEVEN

Gender Roles and Relationships

Everyone admits that love is wonderful and necessary, yet no one agrees on just what it is.

—DIANE ACKERMAN

Suggestions for Journal Entries

1. Do you agree or disagree with Ackerman's comment above? Explain.
2. What are the various kinds of relationships you have—family, friends, coworkers, classmates, and so on?
3. What is a friend?
4. How have gender roles changed in the last thirty years?
5. How has dating changed in the last thirty years?
6. What does marriage mean to you?
7. Why has the divorce rate increased in recent years?
8. What are the effects of divorce on the partners? On the children?
9. Is love innate (born in an individual) or learned?
10. Should there be a course in how to get along with the opposite sex?
11. Should prospective parents be licensed?

Permanently

Kenneth Koch

KENNETH KOCH is a contemporary American poet. In this poem he compares the language of grammar to the language of love, a rather unusual comparison.

Permanently

One day the Nouns were clustered in the street.
An Adjective walked by, with her dark beauty.
The Nouns were struck, moved, changed.
The next day a Verb drove up, and created the Sentence.

Each Sentence says one thing—for example, "Although it was   5
    a dark rainy day when the Adjective walked by, I shall
    remember the pure and sweet expression on her face until
    the day I perish from the green, effective earth."
Or, "Will you please close the window, Andrew?"
Or, for example, "Thank you, the pink pot of flowers on   10
    the window sill has changed color recently to a light yel-
    low, due to the heat from the boiler factory which exists
    nearby."

In the springtime the Sentences and the Nouns lay silently on
    the grass.   15
A lonely Conjunction here and there would call, "And! But!"
But the Adjective did not emerge.

As the Adjective is lost in the sentence,
    So I am lost in your eyes, ears, nose, and throat—
    You have enchanted me with a single kiss   20
    Which can never be undone
    Until the destruction of language.

Comprehension and Discussion

1. Koch uses *personification*—giving human characteristics to nonhuman concepts—in his poem. With a small group of classmates, discuss how Koch characterizes each of the following:

    Noun

    Adjective

Verb

Conjunction

Sentence

2. How do the nouns, adjectives, verbs, and conjunctions interact with and influence each other?

3. What is the meaning of the phrase "the green, effective earth" (8)?

4. What does "the Adjective is lost in the sentence" (18) mean?

5. Poets do not choose words or examples at random; rather, they have a reason or purpose for their choices. Why do you think Koch chose the three sentences in lines 5–13 as examples? What do they mean?

Language and Technique

1. Traditional textbooks and handbooks cite eight *parts of speech: noun, pronoun, verb, adjective, adverb, preposition, conjunction,* and *interjection.* These parts of speech are combined in numerous ways to form sentences. Look up the meaning and function of each of the eight parts of speech. What job or function does each part of speech have in a sentence? In other words, how is each part of speech used in a sentence? In your journal, record what you discover about parts of speech, and record three to five examples of each part of speech. Remember that the part of speech of a word may change according to its use in a sentence. Discuss the functions and your examples of speech with your classmates.

2. In the poem Koch refers to only four of the eight parts of speech. Which ones does he omit? With a small group of classmates, discuss why the poet does not include all eight parts of speech in the poem.

3. Working with a small group of your classmates, identify the nouns, verbs, and adjectives in the three example sentences in lines 5–13.

4. Study the punctuation in lines 5–13—comma, dash, period, question mark, and quotation marks. With your classmates discuss why Koch uses each punctuation mark where he does. What is the purpose or function of each punctuation mark in these lines?

Suggestions for Writing

1. **Sentence.** Write an original sentence in which you illustrate the use of each of the eight parts of speech (a total of eight sentences, one for each part of speech). Underline and label each part of speech.

2. **Paragraph.** Write a paragraph in which you *paraphrase* the poem; that is, express the meaning of the poem, line by line, in your own words.

Do not insert any of your own opinions or interpretations. Record the paragraph in your journal, and share it with your classmates. Where in the poem is the main point or main idea? Compare your paraphrase with those of a small group of classmates. If all of you did not get the same main idea, discuss the poem until all of you can agree.

3. **Essay.** Grammar—including the parts of speech, their uses, and sentence construction—is taught continously from elementary school through high school. However, when students enter college, many do not know or understand the grammar of the English language although they have used it for years in speaking and writing. What is grammar? Is knowledge of the grammar of a language necessary to write well? Write an essay in which you explain why you think so few students understand English grammar well. Also explain what you think should be done so that more students will better comprehend the grammar of their own language and use it to communicate more effectively.

4. **Essay.** Write an essay in which you retell a positive or negative experience you had learning the grammar of English or of another language.

5. **Essay.** Write an essay in which you retell a romantic experience as memorable as the kiss the speaker received.

Neutral Tones

Thomas Hardy

THOMAS HARDY, born in Dorset, England, in 1840, began a career as an architect before he began writing. He published more than a dozen novels, but after writing *Jude the Obscure* he received much negative criticism and devoted himself to poetry for the last twenty years of his life. His poetic themes and techniques are more modern than the Victorian works of his time.

Neutral Tones

We stood by a pond that winter day,
And the sun was white, as though chidden of God,
And a few leaves lay on the starving sod;
　　—They had fallen from an ash, and were gray.

Your eyes on me were as eyes that rove　　　　　　5
Over tedious riddles of years ago;
And some words played between us to and fro
　　On which lost the more by our love.

The smile on your mouth was the deadest thing
Alive enough to have strength to die; 10
And a grin of bitterness swept there by
    Like an ominous bird a-wing . . . . .

Since then, keen lessons that love deceives,
And wrings with wrong, have shaped to me
Your face, and the God-curst sun, and a tree, 15
    And a pond edged with grayish leaves.

Glossary

chidden (2)—scolded or reprimanded

Comprehension and Discussion

1. What is this poem about? Who is the speaker? Who is "we"? Who is "you"? What is the situation in which they find themselves?
2. What is the meaning of line 2, "And the sun was white, as though chidden of God"? Have you ever seen the sun white? If you remember seeing the sun when it was white, write your experience in your journal, and share the experience with your classmates.
3. What does Hardy mean by the phrase "tedious riddles of years ago" (6)?
4. Reread lines 7–8. With a small group of classmates, think of some specific comments the couple might say to each other. Why does the poet speak generally instead of specifically in these lines?
5. Reread the last verse of the poem. Why is this scene etched in the speaker's memory so vividly?

Language and Technique

1. How does this poem make you feel? Record your feelings in your journal. What specific words and images create this feeling in you? *Tone* is the emotional attitude or atmosphere in a piece of writing; it is the emotional feeling that a writer conveys to the readers through words, images, and ideas. Share your journal entry with a small group of classmates, and work together to find one word or phrase that describes the tone of this poem. What other sights or experiences make you feel this way? Discuss them with your classmates.

2. What are the connotations and symbolism of the season of winter? Why did Hardy choose winter as the setting for the poem? How would the poem have been different if the setting were spring or summer?
3. With a small group of classmates, find and mark the visual images or descriptions in the poem. Which do you think is most effective? Why?
4. In line 12, Hardy uses ellipsis points. Look up this punctuation mark and its uses, and record what you discover in your journal. Then discuss with your classmates why Hardy uses ellipsis points in line 12.

Suggestions for Writing

1. **Sentence.** Write a sentence that contains a visual image.
2. **Paragraph.** Write a paragraph in which you describe a scene that you remember vividly.
3. **Essay.** Write an essay in which you narrate the end of a romance or the end of a friendship.
4. **Essay.** Write an essay in which you explain the main reasons love dies and couples break up.
5. **Essay.** Write an essay in which you compare and contrast the love between the couple in "Permanently" by Kenneth Koch (p. 154) and the couple in "Neutral Tones."

Friends, Good Friends—and Such Good Friends

Judith Viorst

JUDITH VIORST is a contemporary nonfiction writer who has published articles and light verse in popular magazines. She writes on topics of interest to today's readers. In this essay she classifies her friends.

Vocabulary Study

forge (18)	context (23)
dormant (19)	calibrated (29)

Friends, Good Friends—and Such Good Friends

1   Women are friends, I once would have said, when they totally love and support and trust each other, and bare to each other the secrets of their souls, and run—no questions asked—to help each other, and tell harsh truths to each other (no, you can't wear that dress unless you lose ten pounds first) when harsh truths must be told.

[2] Women are friends, I once would have said, when they share the same affection for Ingmar Bergman, plus train rides, cats, warm rain, charades, Camus, and hate with equal ardor Newark and Brussels sprouts and Lawrence Welk and camping.

[3] In other words, I once would have said that a friend is a friend all the way, but now I believe that's a narrow point of view. For the friendships I have and the friendships I see are conducted at many levels of intensity, serve many different functions, meet different needs and range from those as all-the-way as the friendship of the soul sisters mentioned above to that of the most nonchalant and casual playmates.

[4] Consider these varieties of friendship:

[5] 1. Convenience friends. These are women with whom, if our paths weren't crossing all the time, we'd have no particular reason to be friends: a next-door neighbor, a woman in our car pool, the mother of one of our children's closest friends or maybe some mommy with whom we serve juice and cookies each week at the Glenwood Co-op Nursery.

[6] Convenience friends are convenient indeed. They'll lend us their cups and silverware for a party. They'll drive our kids to soccer when we're sick. They'll take us to pick up our car when we need a lift to the garage. They'll even take our cats when we go on vacation. As we will for them.

[7] But we don't, with convenience friends, ever come too close or tell too much; we maintain our public face and emotional distance. "Which means," says Elaine, "that I'll talk about being overweight but not about being depressed. Which means I'll admit being mad but not blind with rage. Which means that I might say that we're pinched this month but never that I'm worried sick over money."

[8] But which doesn't mean that there isn't sufficient value to be found in these friendships of mutual aid, in convenience friends.

[9] 2. Special-interest friends. These friendships aren't intimate, and they needn't involve kids or silverware or cats. Their value lies in some interest jointly shared. And so we may have an office friend or a yoga friend or a tennis friend or a friend from the Women's Democratic Club.

[10] "I've got one woman friend," says Joyce, "who likes, as I do, to take psychology courses. Which makes it nice for me—and nice for her. It's fun to go with someone you know and it's fun to discuss what you've learned, driving back from the classes." And for the most part, she says, that's all they discuss.

[11] "I'd say that what we're doing is *doing* together, not being together," Suzanne says of her Tuesday-doubles friends. "It's mainly a tennis relationship,

but we play together well. And I guess we all need to have a couple of playmates."

12 I agree.

13 My playmate is a shopping friend, a woman of marvelous taste, a woman who knows exactly *where* to buy *what*, and furthermore is a woman who always knows beyond a doubt what one ought to be buying. I don't have the time to keep up with what's new in eyeshadow, hemlines and shoes and whether the smock look is in or finished already. But since (oh, shame!) I care a lot about eye-shadow, hemlines and shoes, and since I don't *want* to wear smocks if the smock look is finished, I'm very glad to have a shopping friend.

14 3. Historical friends. We all have a friend who knew us when . . . maybe way back in Miss Meltzer's second grade, when our family lived in that three-room flat in Brooklyn, when our dad was out of work for seven months, when our brother Allie got in that fight where they had to call the police, when our sister married the endodontist from Yonkers and when, the morning after we lost our virginity, she was the first, the only, friend we told.

15 The years have gone by and we've gone separate ways and we've little in common now, but we're still an intimate part of each other's past. And so whenever we go to Detroit we always go to visit this friend of our girl-hood. Who knows how we looked before our teeth were straightened. Who knows how we talked before our voice got un-Brooklyned. Who knows what we ate before we learned about artichokes. And who, by her presence, puts us in touch with an earlier part of ourself, a part of ourself it's important never to lose.

16 "What this friend means to me and what I mean to her," says Grace, "is having a sister without sibling rivalry. We know the texture of each other's lives. She remembers my grandmother's cabbage soup. I remember the way her uncle played the piano. There's simply no other friend who remembers those things."

17 4. Crossroads friends. Like historical friends, our crossroads friends are important for *what was*—for the friendship we shared at a crucial, now past, time of life. A time, perhaps, when we roomed in college together; or worked as eager young singles in the Big City together; or went together, as my friend Elizabeth and I did, through pregnancy, birth and that scary first year of new motherhood.

18 Crossroads friends forge powerful links, links strong enough to endure with not much more contact than once-a-year letters at Christmas. And out of respect for those crossroad years, for those dramas and dreams we once shared, we will always be friends.

[19] 5. Cross-generational friends. Historical friends and crossroads friends seem to maintain a special kind of intimacy—dormant but always ready to be revived—and though we may rarely meet, whenever we do connect, it's personal and intense. Another kind of intimacy exists in the friendships that form across generations in what one woman calls her daughter-mother and her mother-daughter relationships.

[20] Evelyn's friend is her mother's age—"but I share so much more than I ever could with my mother"—a woman she talks to of music, of books and of life. "What I get from her is the benefit of her experience. What she gets—and enjoys—from me is a youthful perspective. It's a pleasure for both of us."

[21] I have in my own life a precious friend, a woman of 65 who has lived very hard, who is wise, who listens well; who has been where I am and can help me understand it; and who represents not only an ultimate ideal mother to me but also the person I'd like to be when I grow up.

[22] In our daughter role we tend to do more than our share of self-revelation; in our mother role we tend to receive what's revealed. It's another kind of pleasure—playing wise mother to a questing younger person. It's another very lovely kind of friendship.

[23] 6. Part-of-a-couple friends. Some of the women we call our friends we never see alone—we see them as part of a couple at couples' parties. And though we share interests in many things and respect each other's views, we aren't moved to deepen the relationship. Whatever the reason, a lack of time or—and this is more likely—a lack of chemistry, our friendship remains in the context of a group. But the fact that our feeling on seeing each other is always, "I'm *so* glad she's here" and the fact that we spend half the evening talking together says that this too, in its own way, counts as a friendship.

[24] (Other part-of-a-couple friends are the friends that came with the marriage, and some of these are friends we could live without. But sometimes, alas, she married our husband's best friend; and sometimes, alas, she *is* our husband's best friend. And so we find ourself dealing with her, somewhat against our will, in a spirit of what I'll call *reluctant* friendship.)

[25] 7. Men who are friends. I wanted to write just of women friends, but the women I've talked to won't let me—they say I must mention man-woman friendships too. For these friendships can be just as close and as dear as those that we form with women. Listen to Lucy's description of one such friendship:

[26] "We've found we have things to talk about that are different from what he talks about with my husband and different from what I talk about with his wife. So sometimes we call on the phone or meet for lunch. There

are similar intellectual interests—we always pass on to each other the books that we love—but there's also something tender and caring too."

27 In a couple of crises, Lucy says, "he offered himself for talking and for helping. And when someone died in his family he wanted me there. The sexual, flirty part of our friendship is very small, but *some*—just enough to make it fun and different." She thinks—and I agree—that the sexual part, though small, is always *some*, is always there when a man and a woman are friends.

28 It's only in the past few years that I've made friends with men, in the sense of a friendship that's *mine*, not just part of two couples. And achieving with them the ease and the trust I've found with women friends has value indeed. Under the dryer at home last week, putting on mascara and rouge, I comfortably sat and talked with a fellow named Peter. Peter, I finally decided, could handle the shock of me minus mascara under the dryer. Because we care for each other. Because we're friends.

29 8. There are medium friends, and pretty good friends, and very good friends indeed, and these friendships are defined by their level of intimacy. And what we'll reveal at each of these levels of intimacy is calibrated with care. We might tell a medium friend, for example, that yesterday we had a fight with our husband. And we might tell a pretty good friend that this fight with our husband made us so mad that we slept on the couch. And we might tell a very good friend that the reason we got so mad in that fight that we slept on the couch had something to do with that girl that works in his office. But it's only to our very best friends that we're willing to tell all, to tell what's going on with that girl in his office.

30 The best of friends, I still believe, totally love and support and trust each other, and bare to each other the secrets of their souls, and run—no questions asked—to help each other, and tell harsh truths to each other when they must be told.

31 But we needn't agree about everything (only 12-year-old girl friends agree about *everything*) to tolerate each other's point of view. To accept without judgment. To give and to take without ever keeping score. And to *be* there, as I am for them and as they are for me, to comfort our sorrows, to celebrate our joys.

Glossary

Ingmar Bergman (2)—a Swedish film producer of psychological films

Camus (2)—a French existential author of novels and short stories

Newark (2)—a city in northeast New Jersey near New York City

Lawrence Welk (2)—an orchestra leader of popular music in the 50s and 60s

Comprehension and Discussion

1. Viorst writes a *classification* essay in which she analyzes and labels her friends and names eight types of friends, but within the eight sections about these types of friends she adds several other types of friends. In your journal, list and briefly define all the types of friends she identifies. Then by each type, write the name of a friend of yours who is this type of friend to you. Would you use the same categories to classify your friends, or would you use different types? What?

2. This essay was written by a woman for other women and was published in *Redbook*, a woman's magazine. Do the types of friends she discusses apply to male friendships as well? That is, are they *universal* types (applicable to all people at all times in all places)? Do male friendships differ from female friendships? If you believe so, how?

3. How has Viorst's attitude toward friends changed?

4. Suzanne says of special-interest friends, "I'd say that what we're doing is *doing* together, not being together" (11). What does this statement mean? Do you have any friends who are similar to Suzanne's tennis friend or Viorst's shopping friend?

5. The author states that with convenience friends, "we maintain our public face and emotional distance" (7). What does this statement mean? In what ways do we put on a public face or mask? Why do we do so?

Language and Technique

1. One of the rhetorical techniques in Viorst's essay is the use of *parallel* sentences and phrases, in which the author repeats a significant phrase for emphasis. With a small group of classmates, study and discuss the following parallel constructions:

"I once would have said" (1–3)

"Which means" (7)

"a friend" (9)

"a woman" (13)

"when . . . (14)

"Who knows" (15)

Now find other examples of parallel construction in paragraphs 17, 21, 24, 28, and 31 (and any others that you can find in the essay). Discuss them with the group.

2. In Viorst's *informal style* she often uses *sentence fragments*—phrases or clauses that do not express a complete thought but have been punctuated as if they did. One example is the following passage from paragraph 7:

> "Which means," says Elaine, "that I'll talk about being overweight but not about being depressed. Which means I'll admit being mad but not blind with rage. Which means that I might say that we're pinched this month but never that I'm worried sick over money."

Why are the constructions beginning with "which" fragments? Working with a small group of classmates, find other examples of fragments in the essay. Then participate in a class discussion on when fragments are appropriate in writing. Is the use of fragments appropriate in formal writing (such as legal documents or medical research studies)? Is the use of fragments appropriate in academic writing? In fiction? In dialogue?

3. Viorst sometimes uses *italics*, as in paragraphs 11, 13, 17, 24, 27, 28, and 31. Why does she use italics in these passages? Some critics consider such use of italics as adolescent, a sign of immature thinking and writing. Do you agree? Are Viorst's italics necessary for meaning?

4. In the *informal style*, Viorst uses sentences of various lengths, some long, and some short—even very short. Paragraph 12 is composed of one short sentence: "I agree." Why do you think the author uses such a short paragraph here? What effect does it have on readers? Discuss this effect with a small group of classmates.

Suggestions for Writing

1. **Sentence.** In paragraph 14, Viorst writes one long sentence (seventy-eight words) with six *subordinate or dependent* clauses beginning with the word "when." Write a similar sentence in which you use at least three parallel subordinate clauses.

2. **Paragraph.** Write a paragraph in *informal style* and then one in *formal style* on one of the topics below. In both paragraphs, provide plenty of specific details. Share your paragraphs with a small group of classmates.

A Party I Attended

My Bedroom

A Football Game

Cheerleading

Studying

My Favorite Restaurant

My Car

3. **Essay.** Write an essay about a friend who fits one of Viorst's types. Refer to your journal entry for question 1 under Comprehension and Discussion. State the type your friend fits, according to Viorst, and provide specific examples as evidence.

4. **Essay.** Write an essay on the similarities and the differences between female and male friends.

5. **Essay.** Write an essay on types of friends, using your own classification system.

Will You Go Out with Me?

Laura Ullman

LAURA ULLMAN is a freelance writer from California. In this essay, written when she was a student at the University of California at Berkeley, she discusses one way in which relationships between males and females are changing.

Vocabulary Study

muster (2)   stereotypical (3)

Will You Go Out with Me?

1   Every day I anxiously wait for you to get to class. I can't wait for us to smile at each other and say good morning. Some days, when you arrive only seconds before the lecture begins, I'm incredibly impatient. Instead of reading the *Daily Cal*, I anticipate your footsteps from behind and listen for your voice. Today is one of your late days. But I don't mind, because after a month of desperately desiring to ask you out, today I'm going to. Encourage me, because letting you know I like you seems as risky to me as skydiving into the sea.

2   I know that dating has changed dramatically in the past few years, and for many women, asking men out is not at all daring. But I was raised in a traditional European household where simply the thought of my asking you out spells naughty. Growing up, I learned that men call, ask, and pay for the date. During my three years at Berkeley, I have learned otherwise. Many Berkeley women have brightened their social lives by taking the initiative with men. My girlfriends insist that it's essential for women to participate more in the dating process. "I can't sit around and wait anymore," my former roommate once blurted out. "Hard as it is, I have to ask guys out—if I want to date at all!" Wonderful. More women are inviting men out, and men say they are delighted, often relieved, that dating no longer solely depends on their willingness and courage to take the first step. Then why am I digging my nails into my hand trying to muster up courage?

3   I keep telling myself to relax, since dating is less stereotypical and more casual today. A college date means anything from studying together to sex. Most of my peers prefer casual dating anyway because it's cheaper and more comfortable. Students have fewer anxiety attacks when they ask somebody to play tennis than when they plan a formal dinner date. They enjoy last-minute "let's make dinner together" dates because they not only avoid hassling with attire and transportation but also don't have time to agonize.

4   Casual dating also encourages people to form healthy friendships prior to starting relationships. My roommate and her boyfriend were friends for four months before their chemistries clicked. They went to movies and meals and often got together with mutual friends. They alternated paying the dinner check. "He was like a girlfriend," my roommate once laughed—blushing. Men and women relax and get to know each other more easily through such friendships. Another friend of mine believes that casual dating is improving people's social lives. When she wants to let a guy know she is interested, she'll say, "Hey, let's go get a yogurt."

5   Who pays for it? My past dates have taught me some things: you don't know if I'll get the wrong idea if you treat me for dinner, and I don't know if I'll deny you pleasure or offend you by insisting on paying for myself. John whipped out his wallet on our first date before I could suggest we go Dutch. During our after-dinner stroll he told me he was interested in dating me on a steady basis. After I explained I was more interested in a friendship, he told me he would have understood had I paid

for my dinner. "I've practically stopped treating women on dates," he said defensively. "It's safer and more comfortable when we each pay for ourselves." John had assumed that because I graciously accepted his treat, I was in love. He was mad at himself for treating me, and I regretted allowing him to.

6   Larry, on the other hand, blushed when I offered to pay for my meal on our first date. I unzipped my purse and flung out my wallet, and he looked at me as if I had addressed him in a foreign language. Hesitant, I asked politely, "How much do I owe you?" Larry muttered, "Uh, uh, you really don't owe my anything, but if you insist . . ." Insist, I thought, I only offered. To Larry, my gesture was a suggestion of rejection.

7   Men and women alike are confused about who should ask whom out and who should pay. While I treasure my femininity, adore gentlemen, and delight in a traditional formal date, I also believe in equality. I am grateful for casual dating because it has improved my social life immensely by making me an active participant in the process. Now I can not only receive roses but can also give them. Casual dating is a worthwhile adventure because it works. No magic formula guarantees "he" will say yes. I just have to relax, be Laura, and ask him out in an unthreatening manner. If my friends are right, he'll be flattered.

8   Sliding into his desk, he taps my shoulder and says, "Hi, Laura, what's up?"

9   "Good morning," I answer with nervous chills. "Hey, how would you like to have lunch after class on Friday?"

10   "You mean after the midterm?" he says encouragingly. "I'd love to go to lunch with you."

11   "We have a date," I smile.

Comprehension and Discussion

1. What is casual dating? What are its advantages? What is its one big disadvantage? How is casual dating different from traditional or more formal dating? Do you, like the author, prefer casual dating?

2. How does Ullman's family's attitude toward dating differ from the attitude of her girlfriends? How does the attitude of your parents or your children differ from your attitude toward dating?

3. According to Ullman, why are men glad that women are now asking them out? Do you agree with the author?

4. How are men and women confused about the new dating customs?

5. Why is the author hesitant to ask out her male classmate? How does she feel? Have you felt similarly when trying to decide to ask someone out?

Language and Technique

1. With a small group of classmates, analyze the introduction (1) and conclusion (8–10). How does Ullman begin the essay? How does she end it? How does the ending tie in with the beginning? Are the introduction and conclusion effective?
2. What does the author mean when she says "letting you know I like you seems as risky to me as skydiving into the sea" (1)? Is this an effective *simile* or comparison? Why?
3. In paragraphs 5 and 6, Ullman contrasts her date with John to her date with Larry. How do these two differ? What does Ullman use these two dates to illustrate?
4. Ullman's style in this essay is *informal*, almost conversational. With a small group of classmates, discuss what makes her style informal. What words make her essay informal? Which sentences contribute to the informality? How does the pronoun use (*I* and *you*) add to the informal level of language? Are there other informal elements in the essay?

Suggestions for Writing

1. **Sentence.** Using the informal style, write a sentence about dating. Then, using the formal style, writing a sentence about dating. Share your sentences with a small group of classmates.
2. **Paragraph.** Paragraph 2 is a paragraph of contrast in which Ullman contrasts the traditional European attitude toward dating to the attitude of college students today. Notice the transitional words that she uses to indicate contrast: *but, otherwise, no longer.* Write a paragraph of contrast on one of the following topics. Underline the transitional words that you use. In preparation for this writing, you may want to talk to your parents or grandparents or another older person.

   Marriage

   Living with Someone of the Opposite Sex Before Marriage

   Divorce

Raising Children

College

Music

Movies

3. **Essay.** Write a narrative essay in which you relate how you wanted to date someone but were nervous about it, how you finally got to go out with the person, what you did on the date and how you felt, and what the results of going out were.

4. **Essay.** Write an essay in which you compare and contrast two dates you have had. Your *thesis* for your essay should be more than "Two dates I have had were different." How were they different? Why were they different? What effect did the differences have upon you?

5. **Essay.** Compare and contrast your parents' attitudes toward dating with your own. Your *thesis* for the essay should be more than "My parents' attitudes toward dating are different from mine." Perhaps you might consider why the attitudes are different, or what the results of the different attitudes are.

Love As A Learned Phenomenon

Leo Buscaglia

LEO BUSCAGLIA was a much respected writer, speaker, and professor of education at the university of Southern California. He designed and taught one of the earliest college courses in love and relationships. From what he and his students learned in this course, he wrote the book *Love* in which he shares his views about love, a very complicated and much misunderstood emotion. In this selection Buscaglia sets forth the view that love is learned.

Vocabulary Study

phenomenon (title, 9)	infringe (17)
taboos (3)	static (24)
mores (3)	assimilated (24)
folkways (3)	coerced (25)
dogmatic (5)	devoid (27)
premises (7)	exploited (30)
complied (17)	

Love As A Learned Phenomenon

1   At the turn of the century a child was found in the forests of a small village in France. The child had been abandoned for dead by his parents. By some miracle he did not die to the forest. He survived, not as a child, even though he was physically a human being, but rather as an animal. He walked on all fours, made his home in a hole in the ground, had no meaningful language above an animal cry, knew ho close relationships, cared about no one or no thing except survival.

2   Cases such as this—that of Kumala, the Indian girl, for instance—have been reported from the beginning of time. They have in common the fact that if man is raised as an animal he will behave as an animal, for man "learns" to be human. Just as man learns to be a human being, so he learns to feel as a human being, to love as a human being.

3   Psychologists, psychiatrists, sociologists, anthropologists and educators have suggested in countless studies and numerous research papers that love is a "learned response, a learned emotion." How man learns to love seems to be directly related to his ability to learn, those in his environment who will teach him, as well as the type, extent and sophistication of his culture. Family structure, courtship practices, marriage laws, sex taboos, for instance, all vary according to where one lives. The mores and folkways involved in love, sex, marriage and the family are different, for instance, in Bali than they are in New York City. In Bali, for instance, the family structure is close; in Manhattan, it is loose and less structured. In Bali, marriage is polygamous; in Manhattan, at least for legal purposes, monogamous.

4   These facts concerning the effects of learning upon behavior appear self-evident when stated. Yet, they seem to have little, if any, effect upon the majority of people when applied to love. Most of us continue to behave as though love is not learned but lies dormant in each human being and simply awaits some mystical age of awareness to emerge in full bloom. Many wait for this age forever. We seem to refuse to face the obvious fact that most of us spend our lives trying to find love, trying to live in it, and dying without ever truly discovering it.

5   There are those who will dismiss love as a naive and romantic construct of our culture. Others will wax poetic and tell you that "love is all," "love is the bird call and the glint in a young girl's eyes on summer night." Some will be dogmatic and tell you emphatically that "God is Love." And some, according to their own unique experience, will tell us, "Love is a strong, emotional attachment to another . . ." etc. In some cases you will

find that people have never thought of questioning love, much less defining it, and object violently even to the suggestion that they think about it. To them love is not to be pondered, it is simply to be experienced. It is true that to some degree all of these statements are correct, but to assume that any one is best or all there is to love, is rather simple. So each man lives love in his limited fashion and does not seem to relate the resultant confusion and loneliness to this lack of knowledge about love.

6 If he desired to know about automobiles, he would, without question, study diligently about automobiles. If his wife desired to be a gourmet cook, she'd certainly study the art of cooking, perhaps even attend a cooking class. Yet, it never seems as obvious to him that if he wants to live in love, he must spend at least as much time as the auto mechanic or the gourmet in studying love. No mechanic or cook would ever believe that by "willing" the knowledge in his field, he'd ever become an expert in it.

7 In discussing love, it would be well to consider the following premises:

> One cannot give what he does not possess.
>   To give love you must possess love.
> One cannot teach what he does not understand.
>   To teach love you must comprehend love.
> One cannot know what he does not study.
>   To study love you must live in love.
> One cannot appreciate what he does not
>   recognize. To recognize love you must
>   be receptive to love.
> One cannot have doubt about that which he
>   wishes to trust. To trust love you must
>   be convinced of love.
> One cannot admit what he does not yield to.
>   To yield to love you must be vulnerable
>   to love.
> One cannot live what he does not dedicate
>   himself to. To dedicate yourself to love
>   you must be forever growing in love.

8 A human child, newly born, knows nothing of love. He is totally helpless, mostly ignorant, dependent and vulnerable. If left alone, uncared for for any time before he is six or seven years of age, he will most likely die. He will

take longer to learn independence than any living creature. And, it seems that, as societies become more complicated and sophisticated, the time before independence is attained is extended to the point to which the individual remains dependent, if not economically, emotionally, until his death.

9   As the human child grows, the world which surrounds him, the people interacting in his world, will teach him what love means. At first, it may mean that when he is hungry, lonely, in pain or discomfort, he cries out. His cry may bring a response, usually someone who will feed him so he'll no longer feel hunger pains; hold him so he'll no longer feel lonely; remove or eliminate the source of his pain so he'll again feel comfort. These will be the first interactions which will teach him to identify with another being. He is still not able to relate this source of comfort to a human role, like mother, father, servant, female governess, grandmother. It is likely that if a wolf—which has been known to serve this purpose for a child—were to fulfill his basic needs, he would form an attachment of need to the wolf. But it's not yet love, simply a need attachment. No matter. It is this first reaction-interaction, onesided and simple though it may seem, that eventually will lead to the complicated, multi-faceted phenomenon, love.

10   At this point, the attitude of the object upon whom the child depends and reacts plays an important role. The object, too, has needs. According to his needs, so will he respond to the child. The reinforcement for a mother's rising in the night and caring for the child or doing the thousand different chores required of the 20th century mother, for example, may be simply the feeling of fulfillment in having created life or the smile of the child or the warmth of the child against her body. But, nevertheless, she'll need the reinforcement or she will abandon the child. According to how these acts meet her needs, so she will respond in kind. It has been noted that in mothers of autistic, totally non-responsive infants, the mothers tend to pull away, to hold the child less, fondle and caress him less, and generally respond to him less.

11   As the child grows, so does his world and so do his attachments. His world of love is still limited, usually to his family; his father, his brothers, his sisters, but mostly his mother. Each family member in his turn will play a role in reaching the child something of love. He will do this by how he handles the child, how he plays or speaks with him, how he reacts to him. Certainly, no family member has ever set out deliberately to "teach" love to a child. Love is an emotion, that is true. But it is also a "response" to an emotion and, therefore, an "active" expression of what is felt. Love is not learned by osmosis. It is actually acted out and acted upon.

[12] In turn, each family member can teach only what he knows of love. The child will more and more act out what he's learning. Those positive elements he expresses which are approved and reinforced according to the family's feelings and beliefs will be adopted as part of his behavior. Those elements of his expressed behavior of which his family disapproves and which are not reinforced, which may even be punished, will not become a part of his behavorial repertory. For example, if the family is a demonstrative group where affection is outwardly expressed, the child will be reinforced by a positive response when he expresses this. The child leaps into his father's arms and plants a kiss on his mouth, full and juicy. The father returns this in kind, joyfully, verbally, tenderly, smilingly, approvingly. He is teaching the child that this outward expression of love is a good one. On the other hand, a child may spontaneously leap upon his father who may be equally loving, but whose expression of love does not include demonstrative acting out of affection. This father may tenderly hold the child away from him and smilingly say, "Big men don't hug and kiss each other." This father has taught his child that it is well to love, but that an outward show of love is not approved in his environment. The French philosopher, Jean-Paul Sartre, has said, "Long before birth, even before we are conceived, our parents have decided who we shall be."

[13] Aside from the immediate family, there are other influences which teach love. The effect of these influences can be strong. One of these is the individual's culture. It is this culture which, in many cases, has raught the family its responses to love. So it will serve to further reinforce the child's actions.

[14] A French child, for example, born and raised in a Chinese society by Chinese parents, will grow up as a Chinese child with the Chinese child's games, his responses, his manners, his reactions, his likes and dislikes, his language, his aspirations and dreams.

[15] On the other hand, this same French child raised in a Chinese culture by French parents will become a French child in a Chinese society—holding on to those aspects of the French culture he is being taught by his parents and adapting them as he grows up in order to live in a Chinese society. He will then develop those French characteristics common to French children, but will have, also, to adjust them to the Chinese culture.

[16] No person can be totally free of cultural pressures and influences. To become a "socially approved" person, one must always give up some of himself. A Robinson Crusoe can be totally free on his island, but he pays for his freedom with isolation. When Friday, a second person, appears, he has a choice. He can either co-habit with him and make him one like himself

which would involve changing his habits and participating in a democratic interchange, or he can make Friday his slave. This decision will require little or no change of Crusoe's personality and life except that he keep a continual, forceful, watchful eye on Friday, his slave.

17   In the fall of 1970, I had an interesting experience in social living. I enjoy fall leaves, the colors, the sound of the leaves as you walk on them. For this reason, I allow them freely to collect on my path and on the walk that runs before my home. They become like a crackling, multi-colored sound carpet under my feet. One day, I was at home with some students and responded to a knock on the front door. It was a group of neighbors who had come to complain about the accumulation of what they saw as a neighborhood "eyesore." They asked if I would clean up the leaves and they also politely offered to do it for me. I quickly agreed to comply with their request, much to the disillusionment of the students who felt that I had "copped out" and should have told them to which layer of Dante's Hell they might go. I explained that we could reach a mutually satisfactory solution if they'd help me to rake the leaves into the baskets. They complied questioningly and begrudgingly, cursing the "hung-up" culture that would infringe upon an individual's rights. The leaves finally collected, I gathered up the baskets and poured the leaves over my living room floor. Now the neighbors would have a more acceptable scene to gaze upon and I would have my wondrous fall color world to crackle beneath my feet to my heart's content. (It was such a simple thing to sweep and vacuum when I so desired.) I had yielded to the culture, for I enjoy and need neighbors, but I also met my own needs. I enjoy and need fall leaves.

18   It is possible that when we choose to give up one freedom of a lower order, we achieve a freedom of a still higher order. (By sweeping the leaves I still have neighbors who care. A man never knows when he will need a cup of flour.) The culture and society has the power, then, if we choose to be a member of it, to affect our thoughts, limit our choices, mold our behavior, teach us its definition of adjustment and show us what it means by love.

19   How you learn love, then, will be somewhat determined by the culture in which you grow.

20   The unique family and the individual's culture may, at times, come into conflict. My parents and family, a large, warm, demonstrative, highly emotional Italian one, with strong personal ties and attachments, taught me an outward expression of love. But going to school and hugging and kissing the children and teachers was soon taught out of me as immature, effeminate and, to say the least, disruptive. I can recall the confusion in my mind

when one of my classmates' mothers came to my home and explained to my confused parents that I was not a suitable playmate for their children, that I was too "physical." But it no longer became a conflict when it was explained, and I was able to understand, that when I was in our home and homes like ours there was a correct way of expressing our affection but in other homes it might be different. I was to observe and respond accordingly, using my own judgment. By this time of course I was convinced that a handshake or even a warm smile could never mean as much pleasure for me as a warm embrace or a tender kiss. (I still believe it's true.)

21   The child, so far, is continually at the mercy of his teachers—the environment in which he lives and those individuals (human persons) with whom he'll come into contact. They are responsible for teaching him to love. His parents, of course, will be his foremost teachers. They will have the strongest impact upon him and will teach him only the kind of love they've learned and only to the degree to which they've learned it. For they, too, have been at the mercy of their teachers and their culture. Teachers can only teach what they hare learned. If the love they've learned is immature, confused, possessive, destructive, exclusive, then that is what they'll pass on and teach to their young. If, on the other hand, they know a love that is growing, free, mature, they'll teach this to their children. The child cannot resist his teachers. He has little of no power to do so. In order to exist at some level of comfort, he must accept what is offered, often without question. In fact, he has few questions for he has little knowledge and nothing to compare it to. He is spoon-fed his world, handed the tools to meet its requirement and the symbols with which to organize it. He is even taught what things are significant, what sounds to listen for and what they mean, and what is valueless. In other words, he is taught to be a particular type of human lover. To be loved in return, he need but listen, see and respond as others do. It is a simple matter but the cost to his individuality is great.

22   Language is the main means by which we transfer knowledge, attitudes, prejudices, feelings and those aspects which make personality and culture unique. Language is taught and learned in and through the family and society. Any normal child has the biological, mental and physical equipment to learn any of the world's languages. He can execute, as an infant, all the sounds of the Universal Phonetic Alphabet. Although he will never be formally taught, by the time he is three or four years of age, he will be speaking, intelligibly, the language of his culture. He'll learn the system of the language and the color and tone of that language. The words

he'll use and what they mean will be decided by those in his immediate world who will be teaching him. He's unable to read, of course, and therefore he'll learn his language orally. He is unaware that the language he learns will determine who he is, how he will see the world, how he will organize the world and how he will present his world to others.

23   All words have an intellectual content. We could have little difficulty defining, for instance, a "table" or a "home." But each word also has an emotional content. It becomes a very different thing when you are asked to define a "home" as opposed to telling about the "first home" you can remember. We all know rhe superficial meaning of the word "free." But if we were to try to define freedom in terms of ourselves in our present milieu, we would be hard-pressed.

24   Timothy Leary, when he was doing his interesting work in language and awareness, called words: "The imprint (the freezing) of external awareness." He explained that each time a parent or society teaches a child a new symbol he is given both an intellectual and an emotional content for the symbol. The content is limited by the attitudes and feelings of his parents and society. This process begins too early for the child to have much to say about what words will mean for him. Once "frozen," the attitudes and feelings toward the objects or person to which the words refer become very stable, in many cases irreversible. Through words, then, the child is given not only content but attitude. His attitudes of love are so formed. A sort of map is set up, Leary continues, which is static and upon which all subsequent learning of attitudes and awareness take place. The child's "map" will be determined by how closely the symbols resemble the facts and how they are taken in, assimilated, analyzed and reinforced through experience. The important language for establishing behavior, relationships, action, attitudes, empathy, responsibility, trust, caring, joy, response—the language of love, in other words, will thus be set.

25   From this point the child is still at the mercy of his teachers. He has been coerced, due to lack of experience and through his dependence, to trust his teachers and to accepting the love world they offer him as reality.

26   At about this time he goes to school. Great hope lies in education. Through education he's offered his first possible escape—broad, new worlds to discover, full of different, exceptional and exciting attitudes and definitions of life and love. But he's soon disillusioned. In place of freeing him to pursue his own world, he is now in a new environment often even less flexible than his home. Charles Reich makes this point dramatically in *The Greening of America:* "While the school's authority is lawless, school is

nevertheless an experience made compulsory by the full power of the law, including criminal penalties. (The option to go to private school does exist for families that can afford it, but this is not the students' own option, and it is obviously available only to a few.) School has no prison bars, or locked doors like an insane asylum, but the student is no more free to leave it than a prisoner is free to leave the penitentiary."

27   With the child thus imprisoned, formal education assumes as its major task the process of passing on the "accumulated knowledge of the past," usually at the expense of the present and the future. It is a "feeding in" rather than a "leading out." Everything is taught but seemingly what is necessary for the growing individual's knowledge of self, of the relationship of his self to others. He finds many of his teachers lifeless individuals, devoid of enthusiasm, hope or joy. Erich Fromm said, "Living is the process of continuous rebirth. The tragedy in the life of most of us is that we die before we are fully born." Modern education does little to guide the child from death to rebirth.

28   Neither the love of self—what educators call self-respect—not love of others—responsibility and love for his fellow man—can ever be taught in our present educational system. Teachers are too busy "managing" to be "creating." As Albert Einstein said, "It is nothing short of a miracle that instruction today has not strangled the holy curiosity of inquiry. For this delicate little plant lies mostly in need of freedom without which it will fall into rack and ruin and die without fail."

29   So the individual, now fully grown, leaves our schools confused, lonely, alienated, lost, angry, but with a mind full of isolated, meaningless facts which together are laughingly called an education. He knows neither who he is, where he is or how he got there. He has no concept of where he's going, how to arrive there nor what he'll do when he gets there. He has no idea what he has, what he wants, nor how to develop it. In essence, he's a type of robot—old before his time, living in the past, confused by the present, frightened by the future, much like the teachers who made him.

30   Nowhere along the way has he been directly exposed to love as a learned phenomenon. What he has learned of love he has come upon indirectly, by chance or by trial and error. His greatest exposure and often his only teaching has been through the commercial mass media which has always exploited love for its own ends. Frustrated poets with the aid of Metro-Goldwyn-Mayer and 20th Century Fox created Romantic Love for the world market. Their concept of love usually goes no deeper than boy meets girl, girl hassles boy (or vice-versa), boy loses girl, girl and boy gain

insight through some magical stroke of fate, boy gets girl, and they live "happily ever after." All this with variation.

31   A classic case in point was the success of Rock Hudson-Doris Day films. Rock meets Doris. Rock woos Doris with attention; gifts, flowers, kind words, wild chases and special manners. Doris keeps running from Rock's advances for six reels. At last, Doris can resist no longer, she yields and gives herself to Rock. Rock carries Doris across the threshold. Fade out.

32   What would be most interesting would be to see what happens after the fade. Most certainly, any girl such as the character Doris portrays, who has run from a man for six reels, is frigid and any man who has put up with that kind of nonsense is impotent. They deserve each other.

33   Still, it's this example and countless others that create for us the notion of what love is.

34   Deodorant ads, cigarette commercials, cosmetic companies play an additional role in strengthening this insane notion of love. You are assured that love means running together through a meadow, lighting two cigarettes in the dark or applying a deodorant daily. You are given the idea that love just "happens," and usually at first sight. You don't have to work at love—love requires no teacher—you just fall into love—if you follow the right rules, and play the "game" correctly.

35   I would not want to form a partnership with an architect who has only a little knowledge of building or a broker who has a limited knowledge of the stock market. Still, we form what we hope to be permanent relationships in love with people who have hardly my knowledge of what love is. They equate love with sex, attraction, need, security, romance, attention and a thousand similar things. Certainly, love is all of these and yet no one of these things. Someone in love class once said, "I wish she could love me more and need me less."

36   So most of us never learn to love at all. We play at love, imitate lovers, treat love as a game. Is it any wonder so many of us are dying of loneliness, feel anxious and unfulfilled, even in seemingly close relationships, and are always looking elsewhere for something more which we feel must certainly be there? "Is that all there is?" the song asks.

37   There is something else. It's simply this—the limitless potential of love within each person eager to be recognized, waiting to be developed, yearning to grow.

38   It's a never too late to learn anything for which you have a potential. If you want to learn to love, then you must start the process of finding out what it is, What qualities make up a loving person and how these are

developed. Each person has the potential for love. But potential is never realized without work. This does not mean pain. Love, especially, is learned best in wonder, in joy, in peace, in living.

Glossary

Jean-Paul Sartre (12)—a French existentialist novelist

Robinson Crusoe (16)—the protagonist of the Defoe novel who is shipwrecked on a deserted island

Friday (16)—Robinson Crusoe's companion on the island

Dante's Hell (17)—9 circles of severe punishment in *The Divine Comedy*

Universal Phonetic Alphabet (22)—the sounds of pronunciation used in many Latin-based or Romance languages

Timothy Leary (24)—a professor, linguist, and psychologist, who became famous in the 1960s for his experiments with LSD

Charles Reich, *The Greening of America* (26)—Yale law professor who wrote *Greening* in 1970, in which he called for social and economic reform by democratic means and urged careful use of natural resources

The "accumulated knowledge of the past" (27)—a phrase from Victorian essayist and poet Matthew Arnold, picked up by William Bennett and others to express their recommendations for the knowledge necessary to be an educated and ethical person

Erich Fromm (27)—psychologist and writer of the 1960s and 1970s

Albert Einstein (28)—a famous physicist of the 1900s who developed theories of relativity to explain the space-time continuum

Metro-Goldwyn-Mayer and 20th Century Fox (30)—the two major film studios during the 1950s and 1960s

Rock Hudson-Doris Day films (31)—a series of romantic films of the 1950s in which these two co-starred and in which the romance ended happily

Comprehension and Discussion

1. To what three things is man's ability to love directly related? What evidence does Buscaglia provide to support, explain, and clarify each of these three?

2. What 7 premises are helpful in understanding love? Why are these premises important? Do you agree with Buscaglia on these 7 statements? Why?

3. Buscaglia asserts that an individual learns love from 1) family, 2) cultural group, and 3) mass media (such as movies and advertising). How does an

individual learn about love from each of these groups? Review Paragraphs 8–35, and with a small group of classmates, trace the education
in love of an individual from birth to adulthood. According to the author, what is the result of this process? Do you agree with him? Why?

4. Throughout the essay, Buscaglia discusses the influence of an individual's
culture upon the individual. Look up the definition of "culture" and of
"society" in a dictionary and an encyclopedia, and write a journal entry
on what you discover. Identify the name and date of publication of the
dictionary and the encyclopedia you use. Share your journal entry with
a small group of classmates.

5. In Paragraphs 30–35, Buscaglia discusses Romantic Love and indicates
his attitude toward it. What does he mean by Romantic Love? What is
the origin of this type of love? How is it evident in movies? In advertising? Think of some specific current movies, television shows, and ads
that exemplify this type of love, and discuss them with your classmates.

Language and Technique

1. The first two paragraphs comprise the introduction to the essay. An
effective introduction should do three things: 1) get the reader's attention and interest; 2) introduce the general subject; 3) state the thesis or
main idea. How does Buscaglia accomplish these three tasks? Where
does he state his thesis? How is the conclusion (36) related to the
introduction?

2. Is this essay *exposition* (explanation of an idea), or *argument* (attempt to
convince the reader of the author's stance, or position), or both? Discuss
this question with a small group of classmates. If you decide both, is one
or the other dominant?

3. In a recent, college-level desk dictionary and in an encyclopedia, look
up the word "educate" and its variations (educated, education, educational, educator). In your journal, record the etymology (origin) and
definitions of these words and of the word "educe." Also, record the
name and the date of publication of the dictionary and encyclopedia
you use. Participate in a class discussion of what you discover. The word
"educate" is from the Latin "educare," and the word "educe" is from the
Latin "educere," with the prefix "e" (for "ex") meaning "out." Thus,
both words originate from the idea of drawing out or bringing out.
How does the origin "educate" relate to Buscaglia's comment, "It [formal
education] is a 'feeding in' rather than a 'leading out'"? What does he

mean by this statement? Do you agree with the author? What experiences have you had that support your position?

4. Buscaglia often develops a paragraph by *example* or illustration. Study Paragraphs 12, 17, 20, and 23. The author constructs each of these paragraphs beginning with a topic sentence and then providing one or more examples to support the topic sentence idea. In Paragraph 12, he ends with a clincher sentence, but he does not use a clincher in the other three paragraphs. With a small group of classmates, analyze the structure, the number of examples, and the transitions in each of these four paragraphs. Then working with the group, find additional paragraphs in Buscaglia's essay developed by example, and discuss the structure of these paragraphs.

Suggestions for Writing

1. **Sentence.** In a handbook of English grammar and punctuation, look up the *dash* and *parentheses* and their uses as marks of punctuation. Record what you discover in your journal. With a small group of classmates, study Buscaglia's use of the dash (2, 9, 15, 21, 24, 26, 28, 29, 34, and 37) and of parenthesis (17, 18, 20, 21, 26, 30). Then write one sentence in which you use the dash and one in which you use parentheses. Working with classmates in a small group, check the correctness and effectiveness of one another's sentences.

2. **Paragraph.** Referring to your notes from your study and discussion in Question #4 under Language and Technique above, write a paragraph developed by one sustained example (17), examples of comparison and contrast (12, 23), *or* a series of examples (20). Begin your paragraph with a clear topic sentence, and stick to your topic sentence to provide unity in the paragraph. Also, use transition words and phrases, similar to those Buscaglia uses, to connect the ideas and sentences and provide coherence within the paragraph. Underline the transitions you use.

3. **Essay.** With your classmates, discuss the meaning and suggestions of the 7 premises of understanding love (7) and of the following statements from the essay. Then choose one of these statements (or another statement from the essay which your instructor approves), and write an essay in which you agree or disagree and explain why. Use specific examples or illustrations from your own experience to develop your essay.

> Long before birth, even before we are conceived, our parents have decided who we shall be. —Sartre (12)

To become a "socially approved" person, one must always give up some of himself. (16)

The unique family and the individual's culture may, at times, come into conflict. (20)

Teachers are too busy "managing" to be "creating." (28)

I wish she [he] could love me more and need me less. (35)

It's never too late to learn anything for which you have a potential. (38)

4. **Essay.** Write an essay in which you state your own concept of love, and explain how you learned love. What specific people, experiences, discussions, films, TV shows, and/or readings have influenced how you define and exhibit love at this point in your life?

5. **Essay.** Write an essay in which yon explain the message or messages that we receive today from movies and television programs. The messages may be about love or about war or violence or crime or the future or government or any other subject of interest to you. Refer to specific titles of movies or TV programs, and explain the message that each presents and how it conveys that message to viewers.

The Chaser

John Collier

JOHN COLLIER was born, raised, and started his career as a writer in England, but moved to the United States in 1935. In Hollywood he wrote a number of screenplays, novels, and short stories. This story is typical of his short fiction—brief and *ironic* with a surprising twist.

Vocabulary Study

obscurely (1)

imperceptible (7, 23)

oblige (17, 23)

scorn (23)

siren (33, 35)

The Chaser

1   Alan Austen, as nervous as a kitten, went up certain dark and creaky stairs in the neighborhood of Pell Street, and peered about for a long time on the dim landing before he found the name he wanted written obscurely on one of the doors.

2   He pushed open this door, as he had been told to do, and found himself in a tiny room, which contained no furniture but a plain kitchen table, a rocking-chair, and an ordinary chair. On one of the dirty buff-coloured walls were a couple of shelves, containing in all perhaps a dozen bottles and jars.

3   An old man sat in the rocking-chair, reading a newspaper. Alan, without a word, handed him the card he had been given. "Sit down, Mr. Austen," said the old man very politely, "I am glad to make your acquaintance."

4   "Is it true," asked Alan, "that you have a certain mixture that has—er—quite extraordinary effects?"

5   "My dear sir," replied the old man, "my stock in trade is not very large—I don't deal in laxatives and teething mixtures—but such as it is, it is varied. I think nothing I sell has effects which could be precisely described as ordinary."

6   "Well, the fact is . . ." began Alan.

"Here, for example," interrupted the old man, reaching for a bottle from the shelf.

7   "Here is a liquid as colourless as water, almost tasteless, quite imperceptible in coffee, wine, or any other beverage. It is also imperceptible to any known method of autopsy."

8   "Do you mean it is a poison?" cried Alan, very much horrified.

9   "Call it a glove-cleaner if you like," said the old man indifferently. "Maybe it will clean gloves. I have never tried. One might call it a life-cleaner. Lives need cleaning sometimes."

10   "I want nothing of that sort," said Alan.

11   "Probably it is just as well," said the old man. "Do you know the price of this? For one teaspoonful, which is sufficient, I ask five thousand dollars. Never less. Not a penny less."

12   "I hope all your mixtures are not as expensive," said Alan apprehensively.

13   "Oh dear, no," said the old man. "It would be no good charging that sort of price for a love potion, for example. Young people who need a love potion very seldom have five thousand dollars. Otherwise they would not need a love potion."

14   "I am glad to hear that," said Alan.

15   "I look at it like this," said the old man. "Please a customer with one article, and he will come back when he needs another. Even if it *is* more costly. He will save up for it, if necessary."

16   "So," said Alan, "you really do sell love potions?"

17   "If I did not sell love potions," said the old man, reaching for another bottle, "I should not have mentioned the other matter to you. It is

only when one is in a position to oblige that one can afford to be so confidential."

18   "And these potions," said Alan. "They are not just—just—er—"

19   "Oh, no," said the old man. "Their effects are permanent, and extended far beyond the mere casual impulse. But they include it. Oh, yes, they include it. Bountifully, insistently. Everlastingly."

20   "Dear me!" said Alan, attempting a look of scientific detachment. "How very interesting!"

21   "But consider the spiritual side," said the old man.

22   "I do, indeed," said Alan.

23   "For indifference," said the old man, "they substitute devotion. For scorn, adoration. Give one tiny measure of this to the young lady—its flavour is imperceptible in orange juice, soup, or cocktails—and however gay and giddy she is, she will change altogether. She will want nothing but solitude and you."

24   "I can hardly believe it," said Alan. "She is so fond of parties."

25   "She will not like them any more," said the old man. "She will be afraid of the pretty girls you may meet."

26   "She will actually be jealous?" cried Alan in a rapture. "Of me?"

27   "Yes, she will want to be everything to you."

28   "She is, already. Only she doesn't care about it."

29   "She will, when she has taken this. She will care intensely. You will be her sole interest in life."

30   "Wonderful!" cried Alan.

31   "She will want to know all you do," said the old man. "All that has happened to you during the day. Every word of it. She will want to know what you are thinking about, why you smile suddenly, why you are looking sad."

32   "That is love!" cried Alan.

33   "Yes," said the old man. "How carefully she will look after you! She will never allow you to be tired, to sit in a draught, to neglect your food. If you are an hour late, she will be terrified. She will think you are killed, or that some siren has caught you."

34   "I can hardly imagine Diana like that!" cried Alan, overwhelmed with joy.

35   "You will not have to use your imagination," said the old man. "And, by the way, since there are always sirens, if by any chance you *should*, later on, slip a little, you need not worry. She will forgive you, in the end. She will be terribly hurt, of course, but she will forgive you—in the end."

36   "That will not happen," said Alan fervently.

37 "Of course not," said the old man. "But, if it did, you need not worry. She would never divorce you. Oh, no! And, of course, she will never give you the least, the very least, grounds for—uneasiness."

38 "And how much," said Alan, "is this wonderful mixture?"

39 "It is not as dear," said the old man, "as the glove-cleaner, or life-cleaner, as I sometimes call it. No. That is five thousand dollars, never a penny less. One has to be older than you are, to indulge in that sort of thing. One has to save up for it."

40 "But the love potion?" said Alan.

41 "Oh, that," said the old man, opening the drawer in the kitchen table, and taking out a tiny, rather dirty-looking phial. "That is just a dollar."

42 "I can't tell you how grateful I am," said Alan, watching him fill it.

43 "I like to oblige," said the old man. "Then customers come back, later in life, when they are better off, and want more expensive things. Here you are. You will find it very effective."

44 "Thank you again," said Alan. "Good-bye."

45 "Au revoir," said the old man.

Glossary

draught (33)—draft

au revoir (45)—French for I'll see you again

Comprehension and Discussion

1. What is a love potion? What is a love potion supposed to do? Why does Alan Austen want a love potion? What does he think it will do? What does the old man say it will do? Do you believe such potions really exist and will work?

2. What is Alan's definition of love as described by the old man (32)? What is your definition of love? Write a journal entry on what love means to you, and then participate in a class discussion on the meaning of love.

3. What is a "glove-cleaner" (9)? Why is it also a "life-cleaner"? Why does the old man think that Alan will want a glove-cleaner later? How is the ending of the story *ironic* (a difference between appearance and reality)?

4. In paragraph 35, what is the meaning of the phrase "in the end"? Why does the old man repeat this phrase?

5. What does the title "The Chaser" mean? Does "chaser" have pleasant or unpleasant connotations?

Language and Technique

1. In the first two paragraphs Collier presents the *setting* for the story—the time and place in which the events occur along with descriptive details. With a small group of classmates, review these two paragraphs and determine the *mood* (emotion created in the reader, or atmosphere) that is established by the setting.
2. Why does the author not give the old man a name? Why is he always referred to as "the old man"?
3. *Foreshadowing* is a series of clues that an author uses to prepare the reader for the ending of the story. One bit of foreshadowing in this story is the discussion of the glove-cleaner (4–7). Working with a small group of classmates, find other elements of foreshadowing in the story.
4. Notice Collier's use of *dialogue*. When the speaker shifts, the author begins a new paragraph. Discuss with your classmates why dialogue is usually written this way.

Suggestions for Writing

1. **Sentence.** Write one sentence in which you state a theme or main point of this short story. A *theme* is a central idea or universal meaning of a literary selection. It is the author's observation about human nature or the human condition, meaning that is applicable to current readers of the story. Most pieces of literature have more than one theme. At the beginning of your sentence identify the title and author of the story; then precisely and concisely state the author's slant toward the topic. For example:

   In "The Chaser" by John Collier, one of the themes is that (state a dependent clause that states the main subject of the story and summarizes the author's attitude toward that subject).

   Here is a specific example:

   Vague: In "The Chrysanthemums" by John Steinbeck the theme is loneliness. (Does not tell how loneliness affects people in the story.)

   Precise: In "The Chrysanthemums" by John Steinbeck one of the major themes is that people often find ways to compensate for loneliness.

   Share your statement of theme with your classmates. Do all of you have the same statement of theme? Why or why not?

2. **Paragraph:** Write a paragraph in which you describe the *setting* of one of the following. Select the details and the words for your paragraph to convey the mood or atmosphere you wish to convey to your readers. Share your paragraph with a small group of classmates, and see if they can identify the *mood* you intended to create. If not, ask them how you can revise your paragraph to create the intended mood.

> A Fast-Food Restaurant
>
> Your Bedroom
>
> The Classroom You Are Now In
>
> The Place Where You Worship
>
> The Mall the Day after Christmas
>
> A Gymnasium during a Basketball Game
>
> A Deserted House
>
> The Beach at Midnight

3. **Essay.** One way of interpreting the *title* of a piece of writing is to analyze its parts:

   a. the *literal meaning*—its *denotative* and *connotative* meanings.
   b. the *psychological or character meaning*—the meaning to the main characters.
   c. the *thematic or universal meaning*—the implied meaning that is applicable to all people in all places at all times; thus, its meaning to readers today.

   Write an essay in which you analyze the title "The Chaser" according to its three levels of meaning.

4. **Essay.** Copy a brief conversation or dialogue between two people, one which you overhear. If you have trouble writing as fast as you need to, use a tape recorder and then transcribe the conversation. Once you have written out the dialogue, write an essay in which you quote the conversation, your interpretations, and the conclusions that you draw about the people talking, judging from their comments and the way in which they speak. Use the correct punctuation for the quotations from the speakers, and start a new paragraph when the speaker changes.

5. **Essay.** Write an essay in which you describe your ideal mate. What characteristics would he or she have? How would these character traits be exhibited in his or her speech, actions, and attitudes?

"Until Death Do Us Part," or *"Until Our Feelings Change"*?

Lindy Cleland

LINDY CLELAND was a college student when she wrote this essay. The assignment in her composition class was to write an essay of cause and effect. She chose the general topic of divorce and restricted her topic to the major causes of divorce.

"Until Death Do Us Part," or "Until Our Feelings Change"?

1   Society's increased tolerance and acceptance of divorce over recent decades has lessened the stigma attached to marriage dissolution. This change in society coupled with the self-perpetuating nature of divorce has seen the expectancy of a marriage in the United States of America to last 'til death' drop to just 50%. A person who has an ex-husband or ex-wife in his or her resume will provide innumerable reasons for his or her divorce, and he or she will usually be reduced to telling the cause of the divorce in a 'he said, she said' blame and justification style. Looking beyond the fine details of these individual stories, I say there are just two causes for divorce: people's defective decisions to marry in the first place; and couples' willingness to renege on the contract they made at the altar on their wedding days. Men and women with just one marriage certificate to their names and no divorce papers to match would possibly argue that the only possible cause of divorce is the latter.

2   Many young men and women walk zombie-like down the aisle on their wedding day; they simply see marriage as the next logical step in their lives. This unquestioning waltz toward marriage is often the cause for divorce later in life. These young couples have typically graduated from high school, graduated from college, enjoyed a year or so of work in their career, and been dating their sweetheart for a couple of years or more. When they ask themselves "What next?" they see marriage and children are the subsequent scripted life events. At this precise point in time when these couples could have chosen to take the time to expand their horizons and travel or explore the realms of their own adult personalities, they choose to follow the road laid down by society. By choosing the road of marriage at this stage in life, these young couples cut their years of youthful, free spirited, adventure short. Instead of taking off and trekking in Nepal, hiking across Spain, or following their hearts' desires, these couples

are inviting the next phase of responsibility into their lives. They get married today, they have a mortgage tomorrow, and the top tier of their wedding cake is in the freezer awaiting baby number one's arrival. These couples have no idea what it is that really makes them happy. A decade or two later with a mound of laundry in front of them, a stack of bills beside them, three kids who need collecting and depositing from various activities, it is inevitable that one or the other of these spouses will catch a glimpse of the unknown world. He or she will realize the absolute need for some active decision-making and freedom in life. I'll give you one guess at what the first active decision that spouse makes will be.

3   Further examples of defective decision-making are shotgun weddings and rushed romances; both are almost guaranteed to cause divorce. A good Catholic friend of mine married when she was six months pregnant at the age of 21; the same good friend was divorced by the age of 22 when her baby was 15 months old. In rushing down the aisle to please the church and her family, Kirsty failed to recognize that she would not be able to tolerate living with a dope-smoking 21-year-old whose total life interests were limited to playing video games and flicking through car magazines. Had Kirsty never married Danny, then she would never have divorced Danny either. Dana, another friend of mine, met her husband John while she was vacationing in Bermuda. Neither she nor he had felt a love so strong before. By complete coincidence they both had dogs named Sam, uncles named George, and tattoos on their right shoulder blades. These *amazing* coincidences sealed their love and confirmed to them that someone up above wanted them to be together. They married within three months of meeting each other. During their three-month courtship, Dana did not realize that John indulged in the barbaric pastime of hunting small furry animals, and eighteen months later the two were divorced. The marriage of two people who barely know each other usually has a predictable, if not programmed, ending.

4   The "He will do. He will change in time" attitude is another classic cause of divorce. This attitude is held mostly by women whose biological clocks are ticking faster than their heart-beats. These women fall into the trap of hastily choosing a husband who, by their standards, is second-rate. Driven by unseen biological forces, these women marry whoever comes along and then go about the molding process: "Must you watch every football game aired?" "Close your mouth when you chew your food!" "Can't you be a little more outgoing for a change?" "Wouldn't it be a good idea if you washed the car and mowed the lawn on the weekend?" "Take that sweater off, and we'll go shopping for some new clothes for you

tomorrow." These men may not realize it, but they are expected to undergo personality transplants once the certificate of marriage has been notarized. Failure to conform to their wives' expectations puts these men at risk of being disposed of faster than a dirty diaper once their use has expired—once they have sired the desired number of children. These women view their husbands as pliable figures who provide the elements necessary for them to fulfill their own life goals. In this type of marriage, the husband's inability to gratify the wife beyond her primal needs causes the pair to divorce. Either the wife leaves in disgust when she realizes she does not have the power to change her husband's personality, or the husband finds his self-esteem and shoots out the door to find someone who loves him as he is. The only hope for a marriage like this is a visit to the Dr. Phil show with a lot of follow-up counseling.

5   "Until death do us part." If these words were spoken with integrity during the ceremony of marriage, then the causes divorce discussed above would not have any merit. The undeniable cause of all divorce, over and above defective decision-making, is the fact that 50% of marriages contain at least one partner who is willing to marry just until the going gets tough. The existence of prenuptial agreements is testimony to the tongue-in-cheek nature of wedding vows; some marrying couples have no vision whatsoever of choosing a nursing home together. Although many people may intend to be true to their vows, societal acceptance and the near-endorsement of divorce through pop-psychology television shows have made the decision to divorce a much simpler road to follow than the rocky track of saving a failing marriage.

6   In some cultures, divorce may only be instigated by the man, and in societies where government assistance and child support laws are absent, divorce is a financial impossibility for many people. In my opinion, the people of the United States of America at large are lucky to have the luxury of calling reasons such as those listed above as causes of divorce. They are lucky to have the rights and the means to void their commitments and learn from their mistakes instead of having to live with them like jail sentences until death.

Checklist for Revising and Editing

Following is a list of questions to guide you in the process of revising and editing your essays. Use the following questions to respond to the essay and to check for any point of needed revision. You may also use it to respond to and evaluate essays by other writers, whether students or professional writers.

1. **Sources:** What sources of information does the author draw upon—experience and memory, observation, reading and research, conversation and interview?

2. **Purpose:** What is the author's purpose in this essay—to narrate, to develop, to explain, to argue or convince, or a combination of these? Does the author accomplish the purpose?

3. **Thesis:** What is the thesis sentence or main point? Does the author state the thesis or imply it? Does the author make the thesis clear?

4. **Unity:** Does the author stick to the thesis? Is every statement in the essay directly relate to the main idea?

5. **Structure and Organization:**
   A. **Introduction**
      1) Does the introduction make clear the subject of the essay?
      2) Does the introduction state or imply the thesis sentence clearly?
      3) Does the introduction grab your attention and interest, and make you want to read the essay?
   B. **Body**
      1) What are the major points for development in the essay?
      2) How does the author organize the points of development of the essay? Is the order of points clear? Why does the author put the points in this order?
      3) Is this order appropriate for the ideas of the essay?
      4) Are there any other points or information that the author should have included? Why?
   C. **Conclusion**
      1) Does the conclusion relate directly to the introduction and to the thesis, as well as to the points in the body of the essay?
      2) Does the conclusion provide a sense of finality or ending to the essay?
      3) Is the conclusion effective?

6. **Development**
   A. What kinds of development does the author use to expand, support, and clarify the general assertions—narration, description, example,

process, cause and effect, classification, example, comparison and contrast, definition, negation, statistics, expert opinion?

B. Does the author provide sufficient evidence to make the subpoints clear and persuasive?

7. **Coherence**

   A. Does the essay flow smoothly from idea to idea? From sentence to sentence? From paragraph to paragraph?

   B. How does the author connect the ideas throughout the essay? What Bridges and signposts does the author use to help the reader navigate through the essay?

   1) What key ideas, words, and phrases does the author repeat?

   2) What pronouns does the author use?

   3) What transitional words and phrases does the author use to connect paragraphs? To connect sentences within paragraphs?

8. **Rhetorical Patterns:** What rhetorical patterns does the author use— narration, description, exposition, argument, example or illustration, enumeration, cause, effect, comparison, contrast, analysis, classification, process, definition, problems to solution?

9. **Language Skills and Proofreading**

   A. Has the author proofread and edited the essay carefully for correctness, appropriateness, and effectiveness of language skills?

   • Spelling
   • Capitalization
   • Punctuation
   • Grammar
   • Sentence structure
   • Word choice

   B. What, if anything, should be changed? Why?

10. **Response and Evaluation**

   A. Does the author effectively fulfill the purpose and/or assignment in the essay?

   B. What is the strongest aspect of the essay? What do you like best? Why?

   C. What could be changed to improve the essay? Why?

CHAPTER EIGHT

Dreams, Goals, Decisions

I love the challenge of doing things people say can't be done.
The minute somebody says, "That can't be done," I respond
by thinking it would be interesting, exciting and fulfilling to
prove it can be done.

—RUDY GIULIANI

Suggestions for Journal Entries

1. How do you respond to Giuliani's statement above? Do you agree with him?
2. What dreams for the future do you have? How do you imagine yourself ten years from now?
3. What is the difference between goals and dreams?
4. What is the difference between short-term and long-term goals? Why are short-term goals necessary?
5. How do you go about making a decision?
6. How has an important decision change your life?
7. How do you feel when one of your dreams or goals is not fulfilled?
8. What has been one of the greatest disappointments of your life?
9. How much control of your own future, of your destiny, do you think you have?
10. What are some of the roadblocks that have kept you from achieving some of your dreams or goals?
11. Do you have someone in your life who keeps encouraging you to keep trying and not give up hope?

The Road Not Taken

Robert Frost

ROBERT FROST is one of the most popular poets in America. His choice of familiar topics, his use of natural settings, and his use of common language appeal to a wide audience. In this poem he effectively expresses a dilemma felt by most of us at some point in our lives.

The Road Not Taken

Two roads diverged in a yellow wood,
And sorry I could not travel both
And be one traveler, long I stood
And looked down one as far as I could
To where it bent in the undergrowth;   5

Then took the other, as just as fair,
And having perhaps the better claim,
Because it was grassy and wanted wear;
Though as for that the passing there
Had worn them really about the same,   10

And both that morning equally lay
In leaves no step had trodden black.
Oh, I kept the first for another day!
Yet knowing how way leads on to way,
I doubted if I should ever come back.   15

I shall be telling this with a sigh
Somewhere ages and ages hence:
Two roads diverged in a wood, and I—
I took the one less traveled by,
And that has made all the difference.   20

Comprehension and Discussion

1. How does the poem open? What season of the year is it? How do you know? How is the image of coming to the forks in a road *symbolic*? What is it symbolic of? What is the *mood* that is established in the first few lines of the poem?

2. What is the decision that the speaker has to make? What does he choose? What is the result of his choice?
3. What does the speaker mean when he states that he took the road "less traveled by" (19)? How did that choice affect his life? Write a journal entry on a time in your life when you took the road less traveled by.
4. What are some of the important decisions that you have had to make in your life? How have these decisions affected your life? List some of these decisions in your journal, and then discuss them with your classmates.
5. Does the speaker regret the choice that he made earlier in life? Looking back on his life, what is his attitude toward his decision? Do you regret any decisions that you have made?

Language and Technique

1. Frost uses several natural *images* to establish the setting of the speaker's experience. There are two in the first verse. Find them and discuss them with a small group of classmates. Then, working with the group, find other images of nature in the rest of the poem.
2. Who is the *speaker* of the poem? Remember, the speaker is not necessarily the poet; the speaker may be and usually is an imaginary person, similar to the characters in a short story, novel, or movie. What kind of person is the speaker? In your journal, make a list of adjectives describing the speaker, and compare your list with that of your classmates. Be prepared to defend each of the descriptive words on your list.
3. The poem has regular *rhyme*. Working with a small group of classmates, analyze and identify which lines in the poem rhyme.
4. The poem also has regular *rhythm—iambic tetrameter*. *Iambic* means a beat of two syllables, an unstressed syllable followed by a stressed or emphasized syllable. *Tetrameter* means four beats to a line. The first verse of the poem is scanned or analyzed for rhythm below. Study this example, and then work with your small group of classmates to scan the three other verses of the poem.

>   -   /   -   /   - - / -   /
>   Two roads di-verged in a yel-low wood,
>   -   / - / -   - / -   /
>   And sor-ry I could not tra-vel both
>   -   / - / - - / - /
>   And be one tra-vel-er, long I stood

```
    -     /    -    /  - / - -   /
And looked down one as far as I could
    -   /  -  /  - -   /   -    /
To where it bent in the un-der-growth;
```

Suggestions for Writing

1. **Sentence.** Write several sentences describing a natural scene to set a *mood*. Choose the words and images carefully in order to convey the mood to your readers. Share your sentences with a small group of your classmates, and see if they can determine the mood you intended in your passage.

2. **Paragraph.** Write a paragraph in which you paraphrase the poem. To *paraphrase* means to express the meaning in your own words. Then share your paraphrase with a small group of classmates. Compare and contrast the paraphrases of all members of your group.

3. **Essay.** Take your journal entry from question 3 under Comprehension and Discussion, and expand it into an essay in which you explain a time in your life when you took a road less traveled by, why you chose this path, and how your choice affected you.

4. **Essay.** The steps involved in the *creative problem-solving process* may be identified as:

   a. Identify the problem. State it clearly and precisely.
   b. Analyze and explain why it is a problem.
   c. Identify possible solutions, and briefly explain each.
   d. Choose the best solutions (usually three or four). Avoid choosing only two in order to prevent illogical either-or thinking.
   e. Gather information to support all the best solutions, and identify the advantages and disadvantages of each.
   f. Choose one solution that will work best for you, and explain why.

   Choose one of the following problems or one of your own choice that your instructor approves, and apply the steps of the problem-solving process to your problem. Then write an essay explaining the process you have gone through.

   Buying a Sound System, a Vehicle, or a House

   Deciding Which College to Attend

   Deciding What to Name a Child or Pet

   Choosing a College Major

Deciding What Gift to Give Someone Close to You

Deciding How You Will Spend Your Time on Your Day Off

Solving a Problem on Your Job

5. **Essay.** Think of an important decision that has affected your community, city, state, or country, or the world in the last three to five years. Write an essay in which you clearly state and explain the decision, why it was made, and the effects of the decision. If any of your classmates choose the same decision, discuss the causes and effects with them before you write your essay.

Dead My Old Fine Hopes

Anonymous Haiku

HAIKU is an ancient form of Japanese poetry that compresses words and ideas into a very brief package. It is a brief unrhymed poem that traditionally presents a visual image of some aspect of nature plus a reflection or comment on the image. Sam Hamill says, "A great haiku presents—through imagery drawn from intensely careful observation—a web of associated ideas requiring an active mind on the part of the listener [or reader]." In its strictest form, the haiku consists of seventeen syllables, either in four lines of 5-5-2-5, or in three lines, usually 5-7-5. However, modern poets do not follow this rigid form. This poem is an example of the 5-5-2-5 form of haiku.

Dead My Old Fine Hopes

Dead my old fine hopes
And dry my dreaming,
But still,
Iris blue each spring.

Comprehension and Discussion

1. What does this poem mean? *Paraphrase* the poem in your journal; that is, express the meaning in your own words, line by line. Then share your paraphrase with a small group of classmates, and compare your paraphrase to theirs.

2. What does the iris *symbolize*? Explain.

3. The seasons of the year—spring, summer, fall, winter—have stock or established *symbolism*. If you do not know the meaning of these seasonal

symbols, look them up and write them in your journal. Why is spring the appropriate season for this haiku?

4. In a book or on the Internet, find another example of a haiku—ancient or contemporary—and copy it in your journal. Share the haiku with your classmates. Which haiku shared by classmates do you like best? Why?

5. Find another poem in this textbook that you like, or bring to class a copy of another poem that you like. Share it with your classmates, and explain to them how is it similar to and different from this haiku.

Language and Technique

1. Which is a more appropriate and effective medium to express the meaning of this poem—*prose* or *poetry*? Why? What would be lost in translation through paraphrasing in prose?

2. Read the haiku aloud and scan the *rhythm* of the poem.

3. Poetry, as all literary forms, is difficult to define and categorize, but one definition is that *poetry* is language under pressure. How does this definition apply to this poem?

4. If possible, bring some Japanese painting or Japanese music to class to share and discuss with your classmates. What similar characteristics do you find in the haiku and the other forms of Japanese art?

Suggestions for Writing

1. **Sentence.** Try your hand at writing a *haiku* according to the definition in the headnote.

2. **Paragraph.** Rewrite the paraphrase of this poem in your journal (question 1 under Comprehension and Discussion) in a well-structured paragraph, beginning with a topic sentence and then quoting and explaining the meaning line by line with appropriate transitional words to connect the ideas.

3. **Essay.** Write an essay in which you compare and contrast a Japanese poem with a British or American poem.

4. **Essay.** Many people consider song *lyrics* as forms of poetry. Choose the lyrics of one of your favorite songs, and write an essay in which you defend the position that the lyrics are meaningful and poetic.

5. **Essay.** In a dictionary of literature, look up the definition of *poetry.* Then write an essay in which you define and illustrate the definition.

I Want to Be Miss América

Julia Alvarez

JULIA ALVAREZ was born in the Dominican Republic, but after her father par-ticipated in a failed coup against the dictator Rafael Trujillo, the family moved to the Bronx in New York City. Now a professor of English at Middlebury College in Vermont, Alvarez has published novels, poetry, and essays. Much of her writing deals with her growing up in two cultures and her attempting to adjust to life in America.

Vocabulary Study

sallow (9)	inane (17)
Nair (10)	sappy (19)
gangrenous (10)	ethnic (20)
sashayed (14)	quintessential (20)
ritual (16)	diaphanous (20)
coveted (16)	exotic (20)

I Want to Be Miss América

1   As young teenagers in our new country, my three sisters and I searched for clues on how to look as if we belonged here. We collected magazines, studied our classmates and our new TV, which was where we discovered the Miss America contest.

2   Watching the pageant became an annual event in our family. Once a year, we all plopped down in our parents' bedroom, with Mami and Papi presiding from their bed. In our nightgowns, we watched the fifty young women who had the American look we longed for.

3   The beginning was always the best part—all fifty contestants came on for one and only one appearance. In alphabetical order, they stepped for-ward and enthusiastically introduced themselves by name and state. "Hi! I'm! Susie! Martin! Miss! Alaska!" Their voices rang with false cheer. You could hear, not far off, years of high-school cheerleading, pom-poms, bleachers full of moon-eyed boys, and moms on phones, signing them up for all manner of lessons and making dentist appointments.

4   There they stood, fifty puzzle pieces forming the pretty face of America, so we thought, though most of the color had been left out, except for one, or possibly two, light-skinned black girls. If there was a "Hispanic," she

usually looked all-American, and only the last name, López or Rodríguez, often mispronounced, showed a trace of a great-great-grandfather with a dark, curled mustache and a sombrero charging the Alamo. During the initial roll-call, what most amazed us was that some contestants were ever picked in the first place. There were homely girls with cross-eyed smiles or chipmunk cheeks. My mother would inevitably shake her head and say, "The truth is, these Americans believe in democracy—even in looks."

5   We were beginning to feel at home. Our acute homesickness had passed, and now we were like people recovered from a shipwreck, looking around at our new country, glad to be here. "I want to be in America," my mother hummed after we'd gone to see *West Side Story,* and her four daughters chorused, "OK by me in America." We bought a house in Queens, New York, in a neighborhood that was mostly German and Irish, where we were the only "Hispanics." Actually, no one ever called us that. Our teachers and classmates at the local Catholic schools referred to us as "Porto Ricans" or "Spanish." No one knew where the Dominican Republic was on the map. "South of Florida," I explained, "in the same general vicinity as Bermuda and Jamaica." I could just as well have said west of Puerto Rico or east of Cuba or right next to Haiti, but I wanted us to sound like a vacation spot, not a Third World country, a place they would look down on.

6   Although we wanted to look like we belonged here, the four sisters, our looks didn't seem to fit in. We complained about how short we were, about how our hair frizzed, how our figures didn't curve like those of the bathing beauties we'd seen on TV.

7   "The grass always grows on the other side of the fence," my mother scolded. Her daughters looked fine just the way they were.

8   But how could we trust her opinion about what looked good when she couldn't even get the sayings of our new country right? No, we knew better. We would have to translate our looks into English, iron and tweeze them out, straighten them, mold them into Made-in-the-U.S.A. beauty.

9   So we painstakingly rolled our long, curly hair round and round, using our heads as giant rollers, ironing it until we had long, shining shanks, like our classmates and the contestants, only darker. Our skin was diagnosed by beauty consultants in department stores as sallow; we definitely needed a strong foundation to tone down that olive. We wore tights even in the summer to hide the legs Mami would not let us shave. We begged for permission, dreaming of the contestants' long, silky limbs. We were ten, fourteen, fifteen, and sixteen—merely children, Mami explained. We had long lives ahead of us in which to shave.

10   We defied her. Giggly and red-faced, we all pitched in to buy a big tube of Nair at the local drugstore. We acted as if we were purchasing contraceptives. That night we crowded into the bathroom, and I, the most courageous along these lines, offered one of my legs as a guinea pig. When it didn't become gangrenous or fall off as Mami had predicted, we creamed the other seven legs. We beamed at each other; we were one step closer to that runway, those flashing cameras, those oohs and ahhs from the audience.

11   Mami didn't even notice our Naired legs; she was too busy disapproving of the other changes. Our clothes, for one, "You're going to wear *that* in public!" She'd gawk, as if to say, What will the Americans think of us?

12   "This *is* what the Americans wear," we would argue back.

13   But the dresses we had picked out made us look cheap, she said, like bad, fast girls—gringas without vergüenza, without shame. She preferred her choices: fuchsia skirts with matching vests, flowered dresses with bows at the neck or gathers where you wanted to look slim, everything bright and busy, like something someone might wear in a foreign country.

14   Our father didn't really notice our new look at all but, if called upon to comment, would say absently that we looked beautiful. "Like Marilina Monroe." Still, during the pageant, he would offer insights into what he thought made a winner. "Personality, Mami," my father would say from his post at the head of the bed, "Personality is the key," though his favorite contestants, whom he always championed in the name of personality, tended to be the fuller girls with big breasts who gushed shamelessly at Bert Parks. "Ay, Papi," we would groan, rolling our eyes at each other. Sometimes, as the girl sashayed back down the aisle, Papi would break out in a little Dominican song that he sang whenever a girl had a lot of swing in her walk:

> Yo no tumbo caña,
> Que la tumba el viento,
> Que la tumba Dora
> Con su movimiento!

> ("I don't have to cut the cane,
> The wind knocks it down,
> The wind of Dora's movement
> As she walks downtown.")

My father would stop on a New York City street when a young woman swung by and sing this song out loud to the great embarrassment of his daughters. We were sure that one day when we weren't around to make him look like the respectable father of four girls, he would be arrested.

15   My mother never seemed to have a favorite contestant. She was an ex-beauty herself, and no one seemed to measure up to her high standards. She liked the good girls who had common sense and talked about their education and about how they owed everything to their mothers. "Tell that to my daughters," my mother would address the screen, as if none of us were there to hear her. If we challenged her—how exactly did we *not* appreciate her?—she'd maintain a wounded silence for the rest of the evening. Until the very end of the show, that is, when all our disagreements were forgotten and we waited anxiously to see which of the two finalists holding hands on that near-empty stage would be the next reigning queen of beauty. How can they hold hands? I always wondered. Don't they secretly wish the other person would, well, die?

16   My sisters and I always had plenty of commentary on all the contestants. We were hardly strangers to this ritual of picking the beauty. In our own family, we had a running competition as to who was the prettiest of the four girls. We coveted one another's best feature: the oldest's dark, almond-shaped eyes, the youngest's great mane of hair, the third oldest's height and figure. I didn't have a preferred feature, but I was often voted the cutest, though my oldest sister liked to remind me that I had the kind of looks that wouldn't age well. Although she was only eleven months older than I was, she seemed years older, ages wiser. She bragged about the new kind of math she was learning in high school, called algebra, which she said I would never be able to figure out. I believed her. Dumb and ex-cute, that's what I would grow up to be.

17   As for the prettiest Miss America, we sisters kept our choices secret until the very end. The range was limited—pretty white women who all *really* wanted to be wives and mothers. But even the small and inane set of options these girls represented seemed boundless compared with what we were used to. We were being groomed to go from being dutiful daughters to being dutiful wives with hymens intact. No stops along the way that might endanger the latter; no careers, no colleges, no shared apartments with girlfriends, no boyfriends, no social lives. But the young women on-screen, who were being held up as models in this new country, were in college, or at least headed there. They wanted to do this, they were going to do that with their lives. Everything in our native culture had instructed us otherwise: girls were to have no aspirations beyond being good wives and mothers.

18   Sometimes there would even be a contestant headed for law school or medical school. "I wouldn't mind having an office visit with her," my father would say, smirking. The women who caught my attention were the prodigies who bounded onstage and danced to tapes of themselves playing original compositions on the piano, always dressed in costumes they had sewn, with a backdrop of easels holding paintings they'd painted. "Overkill," my older sister insisted. But if one good thing came out of our watching this yearly parade of American beauties, it was that subtle permission we all felt as a family: a girl could excel outside the home and still be a winner.

19   Every year, the queen came down the runway in her long gown with a sash like an old-world general's belt of ammunition. Down the walkway she paraded, smiling and waving while Bert sang his sappy song that made our eyes fill with tears. When she stopped at the very end of the stage and the camera zoomed in on her misty-eyed beauty and the credits began to appear on the screen, I always felt let down. I knew I would never be one of those girls, ever. It wasn't just the blond, blue-eyed looks or the beautiful, leggy figure. It was who she was—an American—and we were not. We were foreigners, dark-haired and dark-eyed with olive skin that could never, no matter the sun blocks or foundation makeup, be made into peaches and cream.

20   Had we been able to see into the future, beyond our noses, which we thought weren't the right shape; beyond our curly hair, which we wanted to be straight; and beyond the screen, which inspired us with a limited vision of what was considered beautiful in America, we would have been able to see the late sixties coming. Soon, ethnic looks would in. Even Barbie, that quintessential white girl, would suddenly be available in different shades of skin color with bright, colorful outfits that looked like the ones Mami had picked out for us. Our classmates in college wore long braids like Native Americans and embroidered shawls and peasant blouses from South America, and long, diaphanous skirts and dangly earrings from India. They wanted to look exotic—they wanted to look like us.

21   We felt then a gratifying sense of inclusion, but it had unfortunately come too late. We had already acquired the habit of doubting ourselves as well as the place we came from. To this day, after three decades of living in America, I feel like a stranger in what I now consider my own country. I am still that young teenager sitting in front of the black-and-white TV in my parents' bedroom, knowing in my bones I will never be the beauty queen. There she is, Miss America, but even in my up-to-date, enlightened dreams, she never wears my face.

Glossary

West Side Story (5)—a popular Broadway musical and motion picture of the 1960s.

gringas (13)—American girls

Bert Parks (14)—the emcee of the Miss America pageant for years

Comprehension and Discussion

1. How did watching the Miss America pageant affect Alvarez and her family? How did each member of the family react to the television show? How does this program still affect the author today? Why? How do you respond when you watch this pageant?

2. How were the Alvarez sisters different from the Miss America contestants? How did these differences make the Alvarez sisters feel?

3. How did the futures of the Miss America contestants seem to be different from the futures of Alvarez and her sisters? Why?

4. Why does Alvarez still feel like a stranger in the United States which has now become her home country? Have you ever felt like a stranger in a place where you were supposed to belong?

5. Look up the meaning of the word *Hispanic* in a dictionary or an encyclopedia. In your journal, write down the origin and the meaning of the word. Discuss the meaning and the misuses of the word with your classmates. What is the difference between *Hispanic* and *Latino/Latina?* What are the differences among *Hispanic, Spanish*, and *Puerto Rican?* Talk with some Hispanic classmates, friends, or acquaintances, or, if you are Hispanic, some relatives about what it means to be Hispanic in the United States today. How are the experiences of Hispanic people similar to and different from immigrants to the United States from other countries?

Language and Technique

1. Alvarez does not explicitly state the *thesis* of this essay, but implies it in the last paragraph. Discuss with your classmates what the main idea of the essay is. Why does she not state the thesis explicitly in the introduction of the essay?

2. Alvarez often uses *figurative language* (*metaphors, similes, personification*, etc.) to enrich the essay. With your classmates, discuss the meaning and the effectiveness of each of the following phrases:

    "false cheer" (3)

    "fifty puzzle pieces forming the face of America" (4)

"like people recovered from a shipwreck" (5)

"The grass always grows on the other side of the fence" (7)

"Made-in-the-U.S.A. beauty" (8)

"a sash like an old-world general's belt of ammunition" (19)

3. What principle of organization does Alvarez use in the essay? Why is this organization appropriate for this selection?
4. An effective *title* does two things: (1) it grabs the reader's attention and makes him or her want to read the essay; and (2) it suggests the topic or main idea of the selection. How well does the title of this essay fulfill these two functions?

Suggestions for Writing

1. **Sentence.** In the second sentence of paragraph 13, Alvarez uses a *colon* and three *parallel* phrases to describe the clothes her mother wanted her sisters and her to wear. Through her descriptions she also conveys her attitude toward these clothes. Write a similar sentence in which you describe or illustrate a style of clothes that you do not like. Share your sentence with your classmates. Do any of you share the same dislikes in clothes?
2. **Paragraph.** In paragraph 3 the author describes the part of the Miss America pageant that she and her sisters considered the best—the beginning of the pageant. Write a paragraph on your favorite part of one of the following topics:

   A Football Game (or other sports event)

   A Pep Rally

   A Religious Service

   A School Term

   A Concert

   A Shopping Trip

   A Visit to a Favorite Relative

   A Meal at Your Favorite Restaurant

3. **Essay.** Alvarez explains the differences between the options that were traditionally available for female Hispanics in her family and those available to the Miss America contestants (17). How do your goals and

dreams for yourself differ from those your family has or had for you? Write an essay explaining a conflict between your expectations for yourself and the expectations of your family for you.

4. **Essay.** Alvarez wanted to be Miss America but felt that she never could be. Is there some role that you wanted to achieve or some celebrity or hero that you wanted to be like? Write an essay tracing your dream and whether you achieved it.

5. **Essay.** What is the ideal body image for women and men in America today? Where does our society today get its standards of beauty? What influences our ideas of a beautiful woman or a handsome man? Write an essay on these influences and the effects they have on men and women.

Changing the Tapes

Bertice Berry

BERTICE BERRY was born the sixth of seven children in a poor African American family headed by an alcoholic mother. She could not have predicted what the future would hold for her. She overcame all obstacles, earning a PhD and becoming a college professor of sociology. Now she is a successful speaker, singer, stand-up comic, and television personality. The following selection from her autobiography reveals the personal traits and attitudes that helped her reach her goals.

Vocabulary Study

irony (2)   fluke (17)

Changing the Tapes

1   No matter how positive you try to be, things happen. And they will make you angry. This is dangerous because I often get the urge to slap somebody silly, and I don't have some device in my head that says, Yo, Bertice, chill. Don't do that. So I have to use humor when things make me angry. So far, it's worked, but I keep Johnnie Cochran's phone number by my bedside.

2   A lot of comedy comes from conversations I have with myself about all the things in the world that make me angry or despairing. I try to find the irony in life. Alice Walker has said there's a point at which even grief becomes absurd. At that point laughter gushes up to retrieve the sanity. I cultivate that laughter. My humor is not based on hatred; it comes from realizing how stupid other people can be. Not stupid as in Forrest Gump

(by the way, didn't it bother anyone else that he was named after the founder of the Ku Klux Klan?). But stupid as in they haven't read a book in years or talked to anyone who's [*sic*] life doesn't revolve around soap operas or get his news from talk shows.

3   Herein lies the possibility to create change.

4   Now, I usually fly first-class, not because I have a lot of money, but because I fly so often to comedy gigs that I can get upgraded for free. Once when I had just taken a seat on a plane, the flight attendant came up to me and said, "You must be in the wrong seat. Somebody named *Doctor Berry* is supposed to be sitting there." I took a deep breath and fought back the urge to punch her in her implants.

5   I pursed my lips and batted my eyes and said, "Oh, I can understand your mistake. It's because I look so—young." Girlfriend spent the whole flight trying to give me every peanut on the plane.

6   If you hear about racism in one of those serious, angry discussions Americans love to have, you're going to come away with one of two responses. You'll either say, "Like, that happened two hundred years ago. It wasn't me, leave me alone." Or you'll say, "That's right, you the enemy. I'm gonna kill you today."

7   The great thing about humor is that it really does have a lasting impression. Right now, if I told you a joke about a poodle, I could make you laugh. A few months from now, if you saw a poodle, you'd snicker. You might not remember the joke, and you probably wouldn't remember where you heard it. But you'd associate that poodle with the emotion it evoked.

8   By changing the emotions that are evoked, my humor tries to interrupt the tapes in people's heads, the tapes that say that Asians are bad drivers, that African-Americans have rhythm while Whites don't have any. Actually, they do, it's just on the wrong beat. Irish are drunks, and White people smell like dogs when they get wet. Hah! Now most Whites probably never heard that one. But the next time it rains, they'll be checking.

9   A young woman once told me, "Jehovah's Witnesses steal."

10   I really had to say, "Whaaaat?" 'cause in my whole life I had never heard this. I asked her why she thought this, and she said, "Well, when they come to your house, you have to turn out all the lights and hide until they go away."

11   Nobody ever told her this, but she believed it because of her parents' behavior. It was the only way she could make sense of what happened. All right, it wasn't the only way, but she never stopped to think about a new reason once she'd figured this one out.

12   That's the power of what you hear about yourself and other people—it keeps reinforcing itself unless you stop it. Even if you think it's not true, you're still going to wonder the next time the tape starts to run in your head.

13   *I was poor, I was Black, and I was female. It seemed that everything outside of me said that I couldn't make it. But the tiny voice within said that I would.*

14   I'll always remember a character from the Li'l Abner comic strip, Joe *\@#/?. He's the one who was always walking around with the rain cloud over his head. Other people would be standing in the sun, but Joe *\@#/? lived in a perpetual downpour. "We'll never make it" was his trademark whine.

15   If I wanted to live that way, I could have my own personal hurricane.

16   My own mother was the first to tell me I'd never amount to anything. She would curse the day I was born. Then, in the same breath, she'd cry and pray for my success. That was the mother I chose to listen to, a woman who believed that there was a way out, even if she'd lost sight of it.

17   Other people took up the refrain that I'd never make it. When I said that I wanted to go to college, one of my high school teachers predicted that I'd never be accepted, and if by some fluke I did get in, I shouldn't unpack because surely they'd be sending me home.

18   I lived out of my suitcase for the first five weeks of college. And even once I realized I wasn't the victim of some big practical joke, I still worried about making it. Of course, I did graduate and I did get the President's Cup for Most Outstanding Student. And it was presented to me by a two-time Nobel Prize-winner, Linus Pauling. *And* then there is the matter of the master's degree and the Ph.D., thank you very much, Mr. High School Teacher. Nah, nah nah nah nah, nah.

19   All my life I heard that if I walked like, talked like, dressed like, ate like, acted like, and—most important—looked like the people in charge, I would be accepted. I would be, I would be . . . a Huxtable. But I realized that I am never going to look like a White man. Thank you, Jesus.

20   It's not that there's something wrong with looking like a White man. Some of my best friends are White men. But I am a Black woman, and that gives me a beauty and a strength that is unique. We possess a quality that cannot be captured or copied. Sure, plenty of folks are trying to suck our flavor, as the young people say. But all the collagen injections in the world can't give you the kiss of a Black woman's lips.

[21] There is a lot of power in being a Black woman, but most of the world still thinks like James Brown when he sings that song, "It's a Man's World." So, as good as I am, I'm probably just getting up to about 10 percent of my potential.

Comprehension and Discussion

1. How does Berry deal with anger? How do you deal with anger? Does her method work for you? Anger has now been recognized as a major problem in our society, so much so that classes in anger management are now held. Find out what these courses consist of, and discuss anger management with your classmates.

2. Berry states that she tries to find the *irony* in life (2). Examples are the experiences she relates in paragraphs 4–5, 9–11, and 15–18. What does the phrase *the irony in life* mean? Discuss this concept with your classmates. Then write a journal entry on an example of the irony in life.

3. In paragraph 3, Berry says, "Herein lies the possibility to create change." What does she mean by this statement? Where is the possibility to create change? How does she go about the process of creating change?

4. What does the title of the essay "Changing the Tapes" mean? Reread paragraph 12, and then identify the tapes in her head that Berry had to change to be successful. Have you ever thought about the things that other people tell you or that you repeat to yourself as "tapes"? Is it more difficult to change the tapes in your own head or in the heads of other people (like the flight attendant in paragraphs 4–5)?

5. With your classmates, discuss Berry's philosophy of life—the beliefs, principles, and attitudes that guide her decisions and actions. What helped her overcome the obstacles she faced in life? Is she an optimist or a pessimist? Is she a dreamer? What is the difference between dreams and goals? Would you like to know her? Do you think she would be a good friend?

Language and Technique

1. Berry uses several contemporary *allusions* or references to enrich the essay. However, readers who do not know the references miss much of the implied or suggested meaning. With your classmates, discuss the meaning of each of the following allusions and what it adds to the essay:

Johnnie Cochran (1)	Forrest Gump (2)
Alice Walker (2)	Ku Klux Klan (2)

Jehovah's Witnesses (9)   Nobel Prize (18)
Li'l Abner comic strip (14)   Linus Pauling (18)
Joe ★ \ @ # / ? (14)   a Huxtable (19)
the President's Cup (18)   James Brown (21)

2. The author develops paragraphs 7 and 8 by examples. Each begins with the main idea in a topic sentence. In paragraph 7 Berry uses one sustained example and in paragraph 8 she uses four examples. With a small group of classmates, analyze these two paragraphs, and find other paragraphs developed by example in the essay.

3. Berry presents serious thoughts sprinkled with humor. Find some examples of her *humor*—the passages that make you smile or laugh out loud—and discuss them with your classmates.

4. Berry uses *informal* and *colloquial* or conversational language in her essay, creating the effect that she is talking right to you, the reader. One example of her conversational language is "Yo, Bertice, chill" (1). Working with a small group of classmates, find other examples of - *colloquialisms.*

Suggestions for Writing

1. **Sentence.** Write a sentence in which you *summarize* Berry's philosophy of life (that is, the principles, beliefs, and attitudes that she lives by).

2. **Paragraph.** Write a paragraph developed by one sustained example (similar to paragraph 7) or a series of three to five examples (similar to paragraph 8) on the topic of common stereotypes in our society. Begin your paragraph with a clear topic sentence. Share your paragraph with your classmates.

3. **Essay.** Write an essay in which you narrate an experience in which someone—perhaps you—lost his or her temper. Explain the outcome and how the person (or you) coped with or defused the anger.

4. **Essay.** Later in this autobiography Berry advises people to "Take time out to dream." Write an essay on your dreams and goals and how you intend to achieve them.

5. **Essay.** Write an essay on the causes and/or effects of one of the following examples of anger in our society:

Road Rage

Sports Violence

Child/Spouse/Elder Abuse

Boxing

Terrorism

Suicide Bombers

Racism

Hate Crimes

Guts, Grace, and Glory: Face to Face with Rudy Giuliani
Frank Lalli

FRANK LALLI is an award-winning journalist who has served as editor-in-chief of *George* magazine and *Money* magazine. In this selection he interviews Rudy Giuliani, the mayor of New York City on September 11, 2001. The mayor reveals how he learned to fight for what he believes in and how he overcame his worst fear to achieve his goals and to be a successful, much-admired leader.

Vocabulary Study

revitalizing (6)	maniacal (25)
inundated (9)	belligerent (25)
debris (10)	warped (25)
counterproductive (19)	prevail (26)
crystallized (19)	embodied (27)
overcompensating (23)	concentric (30)

Guts, Grace, and Glory: Face to Face with Rudy Giuliani

1 **RD:** What is your first memory?

   Giuliani: In the late '40s, at the height of the rivalry between the New York Yankees and the Brooklyn Dodgers, we lived so close to Ebbets Field that you could hear the fans cheering. But my father was a Yankee fan. Before I had a choice, he began dressing me up in a little Yankee uniform—even my bat had Yankee pinstripes.

2 **RD:** Was it dangerous to go around in a little Yankee uniform?

Giuliani: That's more than a joke. And that experience has something to do with my character and personality. I had to physically defend myself from neighborhood kids who would attack me. Once they put a rope around my neck and tried to hang me from a tree. My grandmother chased them away.

3   **RD:** Why did your father continue sending you out in the uniform?

Giuliani: He thought I would learn how to stand up for what I believed in. And he turned out to be right. There are a thousand ways to teach a child that lesson, and that was his way. My father also taught me how to box, beginning when I was very young. He would sit in a chair, so as I grew up he remained my height. He would have a pair of boxing gloves on, and I would have a pair. And he would tell me to try to hit him. Then he would show me how to defend myself; he would never hit me.

4   **RD:** What did your mother say?

Giuliani: That he was going to make me too violent. So in response, he would always lecture me, saying I shouldn't be a bully, shouldn't be an aggressor and should never fight with anyone smaller than me.

5   **RD:** Did his lessons sink in?

Giuliani: Yes, they did. Let me fast-forward to September 11. All that day, I could hear him saying to me: "In a crisis, when everybody else gets very, very excited, you have to become the calmest person in the room, so you can figure a way out of the situation." He would say that over and over. And on September 11, his voice was in my head.

6   **RD:** Starting with your father making you a Yankee fan in Brooklyn, you have achieved the unachievable—crushing the mob when you were a prosecutor, becoming a Republican mayor of a Democratic stronghold, and then revitalizing the city that experts had written off as the Rotting Apple.

7   **RD:** Did you ever think you were facing something you couldn't beat?

Giuliani: Yes, on September 11. What ignited that feeling was seeing a man jump from Tower One. An aide said people were jumping, but my mind rejected it. Then, as I walked closer to the towers, a police officer told me to look up, keep looking up, so nothing would hit us. Suddenly, I see a man hurl himself from above the 100th floor and come flying down. I followed that from beginning to end. And I grabbed Police Commissioner Bernie Kerik's arm and said, "We're in uncharted territory. We're going to have to invent a way to get through this."

8   **RD:** How did you fight your fears?

Giuliani: The feeling reemerged when the first tower came down. I feared we might be attacked again, maybe later that day. I kept asking the police commissioner: "Have we thought about the Statue of Liberty, the Stock Exchange, the Empire State Building?" And then I started addressing, how am I going to explain this to people? Then, I thought of Winston Churchill. If the people of Britain could get through months of bombing during World War II, we can get through a day or two of this. That comforted me. I said, that's how I'll explain it to the people: This is not unprecedented, people have gotten through it before, and we're just as good as they were. I knew all Americans—not just New Yorkers—would respond to that message.

9   **RD:** During that terrible day, in a sense, you were alone at the national microphone delivering that message. How did that happen?

Giuliani: I was there. I was the mayor of New York. My whole approach as mayor was to be there and to be in charge. If I had not gone on TV, it would have been worse for the city. After the first tower collapsed, my press office was inundated with calls from reporters saying, we understand the mayor is dead.

10   **RD:** Why did the press think that?

Giuliani: We were missing for 20 minutes. Someone saw us go into a building, then that building got hit with debris as the first tower fell, and they never saw us come out. They didn't know we got out on another street. So when I got to the microphones, I was saying, "I'm here and I'm okay, and the city's here and the city's okay." I had to balance being honest and being hopeful. I had to say this is a horrible, awful, terrible thing, but somehow we're going to get through this. Maybe it's similar to Churchill telling his people he had nothing to offer but blood, sweat and tears. If he had said, "The Nazis are bombing us, no problem," his people would have said, "You're crazy. Go smoke one of your cigars; you're retired."

11   **RD:** What gave you hope?

Giuliani: Two things. One was the brave way people were evacuating. They were rushing, but they weren't knocking each other over. Many were stopping to help people. That said to me their spirit hadn't been broken. And the second was when I saw the newspaper photo of the firefighters putting our flag up. It looked like Iwo Jima. That brave act gave me a great sense that the American spirit is as strong as it ever was. The debris was five to seven stories high; the fires were at 2500 to 3000 Fahrenheit. They were standing on top of hell when they put up that flag.

12   **RD:** How long did Ground Zero remain that dangerous?

Giuliani: For weeks. I wanted President Bush to come, and he did on that Friday. But I was very worried. When the President got up with the firemen, he was standing on a mound of debris. I know [laughs] the Secret Service wanted to tackle him and bring him down.

13 **RD:** What were you thinking during the days after the attack?

Giuliani: Many, many times I thought about my last conversation with my father, when he was dying of cancer. I wanted to know if he had ever been afraid during his life. He said, "I was always afraid." And then he said, "Courage is doing what you have to do even though you are afraid."

14 **RD:** That sounds like Churchill.

Giuliani: Then he added, "If you're not afraid at times, you're crazy."

15 **RD:** And that sounds like a guy from Brooklyn.

Giuliani: And I gave him a hug and gave him a kiss. My father probably had delivered that message about courage to me in other ways for the last ten years. But saying it that way right before he died had a very, very big impact on me. Since then, I've always understood that courage is about the management of fear, not the absence of fear.

16 **RD:** When you were diagnosed with prostate cancer two years ago, what went through your mind?

Giuliani: It made me ask questions about life, death and mortality that ultimately helped me get through September 11. I concluded that everyone lives every day with the possibility of dying. People with cancer just confront it more dramatically.

17 **RD:** Were you ever as frightened?

Giuliani: No. No, no, no, no. Because it's lonely. You have to come to terms with a deadly disease. But during the time I was diagnosed with prostate cancer, incredible numbers of people died of all different things, including the awful tragedy of September 11. Getting cancer is just another way of having to deal with the human situation.

18 **RD:** Soon after you faced your own mortality, the public's response to your leadership on September 11 gave you a measure of immortality.

Giuliani: Right. But it's hard for me to accept that. Sometimes when people wave, yelling, "Rudy, way to go, Rudy," I say to myself, "Why are these people waving at me?

19 **RD:** What do you make of the mass response to the tribute to victims at the Metropolitan Opera?

Giuliani: The head of the Met told me the company wanted to stage a benefit performance on September 22, and asked if I'd speak. When I arrived I realized they had put a giant TV screen in the plaza in front of the opera house, so the public could see the performance. But people were not going out then, so there was concern. If only five people showed up, that could send a counterproductive message: Everybody's scared. At intermission, I walked outside and there were thousands of people. That crystallized something for me. People weren't going out—but not because of fear. They were mourning.

20   **RD:** And you got a standing ovation that went on for five minutes.

Giuliani: Almost as long as Caruso and Plácido Domingo and Luciano Pavarotti—but never as long [laughing]. It was a great experience. It helped me see that the beautiful things in life have to go on. Otherwise, the terrorists win.

21   **RD:** At several 9/11 funerals, you addressed the children of fallen firemen and policemen. You said that in one sense they had gotten a gift. They now knew—and would know forever—that their father was a great man. Now your son, Andrew, and daughter, Caroline, know you are being hailed as a great man too. Do you worry that they might feel pressure to live up to your hero's image?

Giuliani: It's hard for me to think of myself as a great man. I don't accept that. I have never wanted my children to feel they had to live their lives in a particular way—or that they had to compete with me in any way. My mother and father taught me: Find something you enjoy doing, and you will be happy. That's what I tell my children. And not just tell them—I try to conduct myself in a way that allows them to find their own path to happiness.

22   **RD:** Have you talked to Andrew or Caroline about this since 9/11?

Giuliani: [Laughing] No. My son, who is now 16, is much more interested in meeting ballplayers—his real heroes—than talking to me. And while I was mayor, my 12-year-old daughter was most impressed that I met *NSYNC. That's the way kids are, if you don't distort them.

23   **RD:** Perhaps overcompensating for his background, your father insisted that you never cheat, nor lie—to the point where he overdid it. Do you try to avoid overdoing it with your son and daughter?

Giuliani: My father constantly put tremendous pressure on me about being honest about everything. My mother had a different way. You could never meet her expectations. If you came home with a 90, she'd say, how come it's not 95? If you got 100, how come you didn't get all 100s? That was her imperfect way of motivating. So when I see my kids' report cards, I give them positive reinforcement. I don't want to put extraordinary pressure on them. Some parents make their children believe that whatever happens is so crucial, and it really isn't. Children's lives are not determined in their 10th year or 15th year or by whether they get into the right college or have one bad year in school. I think too much pressure is put on kids to be perfect.

24   **RD:** How will New York City react if it is attacked again?

Giuliani: New York is going to be here forever, and the people of the city will do what they have to do to get through whatever happens.

25   **RD:** What makes you so confident?

Giuliani: People who live in freedom are stronger than any terrorists. They are operating out of hatred and maniacal anger that ultimately will destroy them. Hitler did tremendous damage, but he didn't win. Our ideas of freedom and democracy are right. I don't mean this in a belligerent way. I mean it in a moral and philosophical way: We're right, and they're wrong. That doesn't mean all our ideas are right, or that we're always right. But our philosophy is correct; their philosophy is warped. Ultimately, many more people will follow our way of life than theirs.

26   **RD:** Is this generation ready for the challenges ahead?

Giuliani: I remember reading Tom Brokaw's book about the World War II generation [*The Greatest Generation*] and thinking, I'm pretty sure we would have the same strength. But, you don't know—just as you don't know what you might do. But on September 11, I knew we were strong enough. This generation is no different than the one that fought the Second World War because the same set of beliefs—the same core values—motivates us. That's why we'll prevail, as we always have.

27   **RD:** You attended Catholic schools and even thought about becoming a priest. Who was your favorite saint?

Giuliani: St. Francis because of his kindness and humanity. I often think of Father [Mychal] Judge [the Fire Department chaplain who died at Ground Zero]. Sometimes I would see him in his Franciscan robes and sandals, and sometimes in his fireman's uniform. To me, he embodied the ideal blend of spirituality and public service. Growing up, I learned about leadership by reading the biographies of political leaders, like Churchill, and saints, like St. Francis. I have prayed to St. Francis from kindergarten on.

28   **RD:** Did you pray on September 11?

Giuliani: I pray at night when I go to bed—not every night, though maybe I should [laughing]. But during September 11 and after, I found myself praying in the middle of the day, asking God to help me do the right thing. I became intensely religious trying to figure things out. Why did one man live and another die? The building we were in could have been crushed by the first tower. When you contemplate those questions—the mysteries of life—it humbles you. It drives you to your knees.

29 **RD:** You have said that God spared you for a purpose.

Giuliani: God has a plan, even when you don't understand it fully. But you do have a sense of it, and you have a choice. You can conduct yourself in accordance with it, or not. You can either do good, or bad. I am trying to devote my life to as many good purposes as possible.

30 **RD:** How will you do good?

Giuliani: I believe you do good in concentric circles, beginning with the people you support and who support you. I have a very big family [laughing], including all the people who served with me in government and now work with me in our consulting business. I also am spending more time with my children. And September 11 has made me much closer to Judith [his companion, Judith Nathan]. We were close already. And then we went through hell together. In addition, I feel a special responsibility to protect the families of the fallen firemen and policemen through the Twin Towers Fund.

31 **RD:** Will you run for office again?

Giuliani: When I was younger I set my sights on specific jobs, like U.S. Attorney, mayor. But my prostate cancer and September 11 have changed me. I'm going to let that decision come into focus in the next year or two. The possibilities are far more exciting that way. I do see myself in public office. I just don't know where or when.

Arm-in-Arm in an Aisle of Joy

32 The Mayor's father taught him to do funerals. "He was enormously insistent," Rudy Giuliani recalls with a chuckle. "He'd say the family needs you to embrace them now more than at a happy occasion, like a wedding or bar mitzvah."

33 So no one was surprised when the mayor rushed to a Staten Island hospital last August to console the family of a 27-year-old fireman who had just died of a heart attack on the way to a fire. Giuliani soon learned the news was even worse. The fireman's mother, Gail Gorumba, had lost her husband, her father and now her son, all in the past 12 months. Yet, she was the one comforting her family.

34 Giuliani asked her how she could get through so much tragedy with such remarkable grace.

³⁵ "Whenever terrible things happen," she said, "I focus on the good things life gives you. So now, I'm thinking about my daughter Diane's wedding in two weeks. We're going to make it even more joyful."

³⁶ A few days later, Fire Commissioner Thomas Von Essen walked into the mayor's office with a request from Mrs. Gorumba. She wanted to ask for a favor, but only if the mayor was willing to grant it. "There are no men left in her family," Von Essen said, "so would you walk her daughter down the aisle?"

³⁷ Giuliani didn't hesitate: "I would be honored to do it."

The wedding date was Sunday, September 16—as it turned out, only five days after the World Trade Center catastrophe, the worst attack on American soil in history.

³⁸ That week the family asked whether the mayor was still planning to attend the wedding. "I said, 'Not only can I do it, I want to do it,'" Giuliani recalls. "The wedding helped get me through that terrible week. The idea that in the worst times of life, you have to take full advantage of the beautiful things that come along—I think that's what living is all about."

³⁹ The ceremony was in a little country church in Brooklyn's Gerritsen Beach, a determinedly middle-class neighborhood that had lost more than two dozen firefighters, policemen and others at Ground Zero. The pews were packed, and more than 200 people gathered outside waving small American flags as they waited for the mayor.

⁴⁰ Giuliani arrived on time, and in black tie, complete with a white pocket-square and white rose boutonniere. Ordinarily, he hates getting into a tux. "But I thought, we are going to will ourselves to make this a joyous occasion," he said, "because I need it, the family needs it, and the city needs it."

⁴¹ As they came down the aisle arm in arm, the bride beamed under her white flowing veil, the mayor concealed his nervousness—"I thought, don't screw this up, don't fall"—and the crowd burst into a sustained wave of applause.

⁴² Outside, sitting in the shade of a tree, Doris Mendez, whose son Charles was among the missing firemen, told a reporter: "That's a great thing the mayor did. To give us something happy to come and see."

Glossary

Churchill (8)—the leader of Great Britain during World War II

Caruso and Placido Domingo and Luciano Pavarotti (20)—great opera singers who performed at the Metropolitan Opera

Comprehension and Discussion

1. What lessons did Giuliani learn from his father? How did his father teach him these lessons? How did those lessons shape Giuliani into the man who led New York City after the terrorist attacks that caused the Twin Towers to fall and thousands to die? What important lessons have you learned from your father or mother or another important person? How have they helped make you the man or woman you are today? Write a journal entry on these lessons that have shaped your life.

2. What are Giuliani's major achievements? You can get some information on his achievements from this interview, but you may also want to look him up in an encyclopedia or on the Internet, and record the key facts in your journal. Discuss what you discover with your classmates.

3. How did Giuliani fight his fears and get through the days immediately following the 9/11 tragedy? What gave him hope? Overall, is he an optimist or a pessimist?

4. How does Giuliani's father define *courage*? Ernest Hemingway, the novelist and short story writer, defined *courage* as grace under pressure. How do you define *courage*? Is Giuliani courageous? Whom in your life do you consider courageous?

5. How did Giuliani's bout with cancer help him get through 9/11? Does serious illness such as cancer often make the patient stronger? Why?

Language and Technique

1. How does an *interview* differ from the familiar form of *essay*? One difference is that an interview does not have the expected transitions between paragraphs, and it is set up in a question-and-answer format. What are some other differences? Why is an interview different from an essay?

2. What is Lalli's purpose in the interview? How does Lalli organize the questions he asks Giuliani? Why does he put them in the order that he does? Is the order easy to follow?

3. What do the *allusions* or references to Churchill, Hitler, and 9/11 add to the interview?

4. What does the sidebar "Arm-in-Arm in an Aisle of Joy" (printed at the end of the interview) add to the interview and your understanding of Giuliani? Why do you think Lalli did not include it in the interview portion of the selection?

Suggestions for Writing

1. **Sentence.** Write one sentence in which you express your opinion of Rudy Giuliani. Share your sentence with your classmates.

2. **Paragraph.** Write a paragraph in which you define *leadership*, analyze its characteristics, and provide examples.

3. **Essay.** Abraham Lincoln said, "A leader is someone who leads a people to a goal which he can see but they cannot." Write an essay explaining this statement, and providing examples of leaders who fit this definition.

4. **Essay.** Giuliani says that on September 11 he heard the voice of his father in his head saying, "In a crisis, when everybody else gets very, very excited, you have to become the calmest person in the room, so you can figure a way out of the situation." The remembered comment helped him get through the terrible tragedy. Write an essay in which you explain an event in your life in which you heard the words of someone in your head, and how those words helped you get through a difficult situation.

5. **Essay.** Interview someone whom you admire, and write a report of the interview.

   Before the interview:

   a. Prepare specific questions you want to ask, but be flexible and allow the interview to take other directions if they seem valuable.

   b. Make an appointment so that the interviewee and you can set aside sufficient time for the interview. Be on time for the interview.

   c. Take with you your prepared questions, pen and notepad, and tape recorder (if you are using one). If you tape record the interview, first ask the interviewee for permission to tape record his or her comments.

   d. If you are discussing a sensitive subject, ensure the interviewee that his or her identity will not be revealed if that is his or her preference.

   After the interview:

   a. Soon after the interview, transcribe the tape or organize your notes.

   b. Select the questions and answers from the interview that you want to report, and determine the best order for organization.

   c. Make notes of your observations from the interview.

   Write the interview essay:

   a. Introduction: Write a paragraph in which you include the subject of the interview, the interviewee, his or her position, a description of

where you conducted the interview, and why you decided to interview this person.

  b. Body: Arrange the questions and answers from the interview in an
order that helps you achieve your purpose.

  c. Conclusion: Summarize in a paragraph what you learned from the
interview and what you want your readers to take with them.

My Family

Garrison Keillor

GARRISON KEILLOR is a well-known writer and radio personality and the
host of *A Prairie Home Companion*, set in Lake Wobegon, Minnesota. The
radio program generally broadcasts from St. Paul, Minnesota, and can
be heard on National Public Radio (NPR). This narrative poem is from the
"Introduction" to *Leaving Home*, in which Keillor comments about his
family: "We had to stop short of the destination we dreamed of and we
have to look to others to cross those mountains that stopped us and make
the home that we tried so hard to reach."

My Family

Our people aimed for Oregon
When they left Newburyport—
Great-grandma Ruth, her husband John,
But they pulled up in Wobegon,
Two thousand miles short.   5

It wasn't only the dangers ahead
That stopped the pioneer.
My great-grandmother simply said,
"It's been three weeks without a bed.
I'm tired. Let's stay here."   10

He put the horses out to graze
While she set up the tent,
And they sat down beside their blaze
And held each other's hand and gazed
Up at the firmament.   15

"John," she said, "what's on your mind
Besides your restlessness?
You know I'm not the traveling kind,
So tell me what you hope to find
Out there that's not like this?"   20

The fire leaped up bright and high,
The sparks as bright stars shone.
"Mountains," he said. "Another sky.
A green new land where you and I
Can settle down to home.   25

"You are the dearest wife to me.
Though I'm restless, it is true,
And Oregon is where I'd be
And live in mountains by the sea,
But never without you."   30

They stayed a week to rest the team,
Were welcomed and befriended.
The land was good, the grass was green,
And slowly he gave up the dream,
And there the journey ended.   35

They bought a farm just north of town,
A pleasant piece of rolling ground,
A quarter-section, mostly cleared;
He built a house before the fall;
They lived there forty years in all,   40
And by God persevered.

And right up to his dying day
When he was laid to rest,
No one knew—he did not say—
His dream had never gone away,   45
He still looked to the west.

She found it in his cabinet drawer:
A box of pictures, every one

Of mountains by the ocean shore,
The mountains he had headed for   50
In the state of Oregon.

There beside them lay his will.
"I love you, Ruth," the will began,
"and count myself a well-loved man.
Please send my ashes when I die   55
To Oregon, some high green hill,
And bury me and leave me lie
At peace beneath the mountain sky,
Off in that green and lovely land
We dreamed of, you and I."   60

At last she saw her husband clear
Who stayed and labored all those years,
His mountains all uncrossed.
Of dreams postponed and finally lost,
Which one of us can count the cost   65
And not be fill with tears?

And yet how bright those visions are
Of mountains that we sense afar,
The land we never see:
The golden west and golden gate   70
Are visions that illuminate
And give wings to the human heart
Wherever we may be.
That old man by dreams possessed,
By Oregon was truly blessed   75
Who saw it through the eye of faith,
The land of his sweet destiny:
In his eye, more than a state
And something like a star.

I wrote this poem in Oregon,   80
Wanting the leaden words to soar

In memory of my ancestor
And all who lie long the way.
God bless us who struggle on:
We are the life that they longed for,   85
We bear their visions every day.

Comprehension and Discussion

1. Why did Ruth and John stop in Wobegon? Why did they stay there?
2. What are the differences in the attitudes of Ruth and John? Why did John want to go to Oregon? What did Oregon *symbolize* or mean to John? Why did Ruth want to stay in Wobegon?
3. Why did John not tell anyone that he wanted to continue to Oregon?
4. What two things did Ruth find in John's cabinet drawer after he died? What was his last request? What did Ruth realize as a result of her discovery?
5. Reread lines 67–79. How are these lines *symbolic* and *universal* (representative to all people everywhere)? How are they applicable to you today?

Language and Technique

1. This *narrative poem* is a story in poetic form. Why do you think Keillor chose poetry instead of prose to convey his ideas to readers?
2. Keillor uses several familiar *symbols* of dreams and of the pioneer spirit in the United States. With your classmates, discuss the symbolism and the meaning of each of the following:

    "mountains that we sense afar" (68)

    "The golden west" (70)

    "golden gate" (70)

    "wings to the human heart" (72)

    "Oregon" (75)

    "land of his sweet destiny" (77)

    "a star" (79)

3. Why did Keillor write this poem? What is his attitude toward his ancestors? The last verse of the poem and the following quotation from the "Introduction" to *Leaving Home* provide clues to his purpose:

> These stories are not about my family, and yet I hope they carry on our family tradition of storytelling and kitchen talk, the way we talk and what we talk about. I believe in reincarnation only as we may experience it through our children; I hope my parents recognize themselves in me, just as I see myself in the tall young man upstairs playing the blues on his pink electric guitar; and I hope that our old radio show lives on in the homes of a few people who recognized the people in the stories. We had to stop short of the destination we dreamed of and we have to look to others to cross those mountains that stopped us and make the home that we tried so hard to reach.

Discuss his purpose with your classmates.

4. How is this poem *universal*? That is, how is its meaning applicable to people other than Keillor's relatives in Minnesota?

Suggestions for Writing

1. **Sentence.** Write a sentence in which you state where your ancestors came from and why.
2. **Paragraph.** Write a prose paragraph or a narrative poem about a person who was not what he or she seemed to be or someone who had a private secret.
3. **Essay.** Write an essay in which you explain a dream that you voluntarily postponed or gave up as John gave up his dream. Explain why you postponed or gave up the dream, and explain how you felt and how you coped with losing the dream.
4. **Essay.** Write an essay in which you define, explain, and illustrate the pioneer spirit, the call of the West, and the last frontier to American pioneers. How are these concepts related to dreams? You may draw some examples from Western movies, television programs, and books.
5. **Essay.** Write an essay in which you identify, explain, and illustrate some of the frontiers that are still available for exploration today.

The Loss of Dreams

Joseph Geil

JOSEPH GEIL was a college student when he wrote this essay in a composition class in which he had been studying literature. His assignment was to focus on one aspect of two or more plays and to *compare and contrast* how the idea was reflected in the plays. He chose the topic of the loss of one's dreams, and decided to compare and contrast the protagonists in *A Raisin in the Sun* by Lorraine Hansberry and *Death of a Salesman* by Arthur Miller.

The Loss of Dreams

1   Both "Death of a Salesman" by Arthur Miller and "A Raisin in the Sun" by Lorraine Hansberry deal with similar issues inside a family setting. The biggest of these issues deals with the American Dream. Willy Loman of "Death of a Salesman" and Walter Younger of "A Raisin in the Sun" dream of the riches and the power that exist in the world and neither will stop at anything to get it. Although both men share the same dream and work hard in their own ways to achieve it, once the dream is lost, the result for the two men is very different.

2   First off, both Willy and Walter want the same things. Willy wants love, respect, and to be known throughout the New England area. Willy also instills this desire into his two boys. Willy's philosophy is that through recognizability and respect riches and power will follow. In contrast, Walter dreams of living the executive life with the meetings and the plain black Chrysler for himself and the Cadillac convertible for his wife. He imagines his home full of servants and the power and money to send his son to any school his son desires. Therefore in this aspect both Walter and Willy are the same.

3   Secondly, Walter and Willy both strive to make their dreams happen with the same zealous fervor. Willy's way to achieve his dream was through hard work, many hours on the road, staying away from home for long periods of time, and working ten to twelve hours daily. Willy thought this work ethic would lead him to a position as a member of the board in his company, but instead it left him both physically and mentally ill. Although Walter also worked hard to provide for his family, his way was more of a get-rich-quick scheme involving his mother's insurance check for ten thousand dollars. Plenty of thinking, planning, and number-crunching took place toward his investment of opening up a liquor store. When the deal

turned out to be a scam, Walter became a mentally broken man. Although both Walter and Willy used different ways to attempt to achieve their dreams, both ways resulted in failure.

4   This failure leads to the final point. And that is how the loss of the dream affects each person. Willy chose the cowardly way out and killed himself. He used his life insurance policy as an excuse, but he just could not face the fact that he was not made for greatness. Walter's lost dream had a much happier result. He finally realized what was really important in life. He realized that he was surrounded by those who loved and depended on him. And ultimately Walter realized that it was time to stop chasing stars and fulfill his role as head of the household and put the family's needs above his own.

5   In conclusion, Willy and Walter both shared the same dream and strived to obtain it, but when the dream escaped their grasp, the result was vastly different. In both cases though, had the protagonists focused on reality and those things obtainable to bring true happiness, then their lives could have brought the greatness they desired, the greatness resulting in the admiration and love from those that really matter, the family.

Checklist for Revising and Editing

Following is a list of questions to guide you in the process of revising and editing your essays. Use the following questions to respond to the essay and to check for any point of needed revision. You may also use it to respond to and evaluate essays by other writers, whether students or professional writers.

1. **Sources:** What sources of information does the author draw upon—experience and memory, observation, reading and research, conversation and interview?

2. **Purpose:** What is the author's purpose in this essay—to narrate, to develop, to explain, to argue or convince, or a combination of these? Does the author accomplish the purpose?

3. **Thesis:** What is the thesis sentence or main point? Does the author state the thesis or imply it? Does the author make the thesis clear?

4. **Unity:** Does the author stick to the thesis? Is every statement in the essay directly relate to the main idea?

5. **Structure and Organization:**

   A. **Introduction**
      1) Does the introduction make clear the subject of the essay?
      2) Does the introduction state or imply the thesis sentence clearly?
      3) Does the introduction grab your attention and interest, and make you want to read the essay?

   B. **Body**
      1) What are the major points for development in the essay?
      2) How does the author organize the points of development of the the essay? Is the order of points clear? Why does the author put the points in this order?
      3) Is this order appropriate for the ideas of the essay?
      4) Are there any other points or information that the author should have included? Why?

   C. **Conclusion**
      1) Does the conclusion relate directly to the introduction and to the thesis, as well as to the points in the body of the essay?
      2) Does the conclusion provide a sense of finality or ending to the essay?
      3) Is the conclusion effective?

6. **Development**

   A. What kinds of development does the author use to expand, support, and clarify the general assertions—narration, description, example, process, cause and effect, classification, example, comparison and contrast, definition, negation, statistics, expert opinion?

   B. Does the author provide sufficient evidence to make the subpoints clear and persuasive?

7. **Coherence**

   A. Does the essay flow smoothly from idea to idea? From sentence to sentence? From paragraph to paragraph?

   B. How does the author connect the ideas throughout the essay? What Bridges and signposts does the author use to help the reader navigate through the essay?
      1) What key ideas, words, and phrases does the author repeat?
      2) What pronouns does the author use?
      3) What transitional words and phrases does the author use to connect paragraphs? To connect sentences within paragraphs?

8. **Rhetorical Patterns:** What rhetorical patterns does the author use—narration, description, exposition, argument, example or illustration, enumeration, cause, effect, comparison, contrast, analysis, classification, process, definition, problems to solution?

9. **Language Skills and Proofreading**

   A. Has the author proofread and edited the essay carefully for correctness, appropriateness, and effectiveness of language skills?

   - Spelling
   - Capitalization
   - Punctuation
   - Grammar
   - Sentence structure
   - Word choice

   B. What, if anything, should be changed? Why?

10. **Response and Evaluation**

   A. Does the author effectively fulfill the purpose and/or assignment in the essay?

   B. What is the strongest aspect of the essay? What do you like best? Why?

   C. What could be changed to improve the essay? Why?

CHAPTER NINE

Popular Culture

It has become appallingly obvious that our technology has exceeded our humanity.

—ALBERT EINSTEIN

Suggestions for Journal Entries

1. What does the comment by Albert Einstein above mean? Do you agree?
2. What is culture?
3. What culture and subcultures do you live in?
4. What is popular culture? What makes up popular culture?
5. Why is popular culture called "popular"?
6. What parts of popular culture affect you most?
7. Why has popular culture become increasingly violent?
8. How does popular culture affect children?
9. Why do celebrities often allow themselves to be exploited for popularity?
10. What is your suggestion for a new television series?
11. Why is reality TV popular? Is it really realistic?

Indian Movie, New Jersey

Chitra Banerjee Divakaruni

CHITRA BANERJEE DIVAKARUNI is a contemporary writer of poetry and short stories. Most of her writings focus on Indians who have left India to seek a new, better life, but who are disappointed when their dreams and expectations do not come true. In this poem the speaker finds escape from unpleasant reality at the movies.

Indian Movie, New Jersey

Not like the white filmstars, all rib
and gaunt cheekbone, the Indian sex-goddess
smiles plumply from behind a flowery
branch. Below her brief red skirt, her thighs
are satisfying-solid, redeeming   5
as tree trunks. She swings her hips
and the men-viewers whistle. The lover-hero
dances in to a song, his lip-sync
a little off, but no matter, we
know the words already and sing along.   10
It is safe here, the day
golden and cool so no one sweats,
roses on every bush and the Dal Lake
clean again.
       The sex-goddess switches   15
to thickened English to emphasize
a joke. We laugh and clap. Here
we need not be embarrassed by words
dropping like lead pellets into foreign ears.
The flickering movie-light   20
wipes from our faces years of America, sons
who want Mohawks and refuse to run
the family store, daughters who date
on the sly.
       When at the end the hero   25
dies for his friend who also
loves the sex-goddess and now can marry her,
we weep, understanding. Even the men
clear their throats to say, "What *qurbani!*

What *dosti!*" After, we mill around   30
unwilling to leave, exchange greetings
and good news: a new gold chain, a trip
to India. We do not speak
of motel raids, canceled permits, stones
thrown through glass windows, daughters and sons   35
raped by Dotbusters.
        In this dim foyer
we can pull around us the faint, comforting smell
of incense and *pakoras,* can arrange
our children's marriages with hometown boys and girls,   40
open a franchise, win a million
in the mall. We can retire
in India, a yellow two-storied house
with wrought-iron gates, our own
Ambassador car. Or at least   45
move to a rich white suburb, Summerfield
or Fort Lee, with neighbors that will
talk to us. Here while the film-songs still echo
in the corridors and restrooms, we can trust
in movie truths: sacrifice, success, love and luck,   50
the American that was supposed to be.

Glossary

qurbani (29)—sacrifice

dosti (30)—friendship

Dotbusters (36)—anti-Indian gangs in New Jersey

pakoras (39)—fried appetizers

Comprehension and Discussion

1. How does the female Indian filmstar differ from the white filmstar?
2. Why does the speaker in the poem like to go to the Indian movies in New Jersey? Why do you like to go to the movies? Are your reasons similar to those of the speaker? Write a journal entry on why you do or do not like to go to a movie theater.
3. What are the unpleasant aspects of life for the speaker as an immigrant to New Jersey from India? What are the speaker's dreams? How are the speaker's dreams similar to your dreams? How are they different?

4. What are the truths of the Indian movies? Are these the same as the truths that are set forth in lots of Hollywood and television movies? Explain.
5. What does the last line of the poem mean?

Language and Technique

1. What is the *tone*—the attitude or emotion conveyed by the poem? What words and details contribute to this tone? Discuss the tone with your classmates.
2. Working with a small group of classmates, find at least one *sensory image* or description of each of the following: sight, smell, and sound. Record these images in your journal.
3. With a small group of classmates, discuss the meaning of the following *figures of speech:*

   Simile: "words / dropping like lead pellets into foreign ears" (18–19)

   Metaphor: "The flickering movie-light / wipes from our faces years of America" (20–21)

4. What does using several Indian words add to the poem?

Suggestions for Writing

1. **Sentence.** Use a parallel list, similar to the author's list in lines 20–24, to complete one of the following sentences:

   My parents were disappointed in me because

   My parents were pleased with me because

   I am disappointed in my child because

   I am pleased with my child because

   I am disappointed with myself when I

   I am pleased with myself when I

2. **Paragraph.** Write a paragraph in which you narrate and describe a night at the movies or a night of watching television or a videocassette or DVD at home.
3. **Essay.** Write a review and evaluation of a movie that you have seen recently (in the theater, on television, on DVD, or on videocassette). Include the following elements in the essay:

   • An introductory paragraph in which you (a) get the reader's attention and interest, (b) introduce the movie, and (c) state your thesis sentence.

- A *synopsis* of the movie in which you summarize the plot—tell what happens to whom, when, and where.
- An evaluation of the movie in which you judge the effective and ineffective parts of the movie, and explain and support each with specific examples from the movie.
- A concluding paragraph in which you indicate to your readers if you recommend the movie for them to see and briefly explain why.

4. **Essay.** Write a classification essay in which you explain the major types of movies that are popular today and the reasons they are popular. Provide specific examples of each type.
5. **Essay.** Movies have been negatively criticized recently because of so much bad language, sex, violence, and absurdity. Write an essay in which you defend or attack current movies. Include specific examples to support your position.

Watching Television

Robert Bly

ROBERT BLY, born in Minnesota, studied writing at Harvard and the University of Iowa. He is a prolific writer of prose and poetry. His best-known book is the controversial *Iron John: A Book About Men*, and he conducts seminars to help men get in touch with their emotions. In this poem he criticizes the violence on television.

Watching Television

Sounds are heard too high for ears,
From the body cells there is an answering bay;
Soon the inner streets fill with a chorus of barks.

We see the landing craft coming in,
The black car sliding to a stop,   5
The Puritan Killer loosening his guns.

Wild dogs tear off noses and eyes
And run off with them down the street—
The body tears off its own arms and throws them into the air.

The detective draws fifty-five million people into his revolver, 10
Who sleep restlessly as in an air raid in London;
Their backs become curved in the sloping dark.

The filaments of the soul slowly separate;
The spirit breaks, a puff of dust floats up;
Like a house in Nebraska that suddenly explodes. 15

Comprehension and Discussion

1. What kind of television program is the speaker in this poem watching? What happens? Is he writing about one program or a combination of bits and pieces from several programs?
2. What animals are described in stanza 1?
3. Who is the Puritan Killer in line 6?
4. What does the last stanza mean? Whose soul and spirit are breaking apart? The creatures on television? The viewer of television? Modern society? All? (Note that a complex piece of literature may have more than one level of meaning.)
5. What does this poem mean? Write a journal entry on your interpretation of this poem, and discuss your interpretation with your classmates.

Language and Technique

1. Why does Bly organize the details in the poem as he does? Is the organization smooth and easy to follow? Or does it contain surprising shifts that make the poem seem disjointed? Explain.
2. What does the phrase "the Puritan Killer" (6) mean? Look up the meaning of *Puritan* in a dictionary and the history of the Puritans in an encyclopedia. Record what you discover in your journal. Is the phrase *Puritan Killer* an *oxymoron* (that is, two words of opposite meaning joined in a phrase)? Discuss this phrase and its use in the poem with your classmates.
3. What *visual images* are presented in the poem? Are they clear and precise, or vague and indistinct? What is the effect of these images upon the reader? Discuss these images with your classmates.

4. What is the meaning of the two following *similes?* What does each refer to? Do these two comparisons make the poem clearer or more confusing?
   • "sleep restlessly as in an air raid in London" (11)
   • "Like a house in Nebraska that suddenly explodes" (15)

Suggestions for Writing

1. **Sentence.** Write a sentence that contains an *oxymoron.* If you can't think of one, look up this figure of speech on the Internet. Just type the word *oxymoron* into the Search box of your Internet browser. You will find several sites devoted to oxymorons.

2. **Paragraph.** Write a paragraph in which you *paraphrase* the poem (see tips on paraphrasing, pp. 23–25). Do not interpret or comment; just restate in your own words. Then, referring to question 5 under Comprehension and Discussion, write a well-structured paragraph on the meaning of the poem, using quotations and paraphrases from the poem to support your interpretation.

3. **Essay.** Write a *synopsis,* or summary of the plot (see pp. 26–30 for tips on writing a synopsis), of a television program or movie that frightened you. It may be one you saw as a child or one you have seen recently. If you choose one that you have not seen recently, be sure that you can remember the details of the *plot, setting,* and *characters* to include in your essay. Then analyze and explain why you reacted as you did.

4. **Essay.** Violence in media has been negatively criticized in the last decade. Write an essay on the topic of violence in media. First, choose one of the following areas of the media. Then explain the causes *or* the effects of this violence. Cite specific titles, events or scenes, and explanations to support your comments.

   Television Movies

   Television Series

   Television News

   Cartoons

   Music Videos

   Television Talk Shows

   Movies

   Video Games

5. **Essay.** Bly's response to television watching is rather negative and bleak. Write an essay in which you respond to Bly's evaluation, and defend television programming as positive, optimistic, and uplifting.

Sports Hero: Muhammed Ali

Jaime Marcus

JAIME MARCUS wrote this essay in honor of Muhammed Ali to explain why he is a cultural hero to the whole world. It was first published on the Internet by the My Hero Website. My Hero is a not-for-profit educational web project whose mission is "to enlighten and inspire people of all ages with an ever-growing internet archive of hero stories from around the world." The purpose is "to provide a unique educational experience that promotes literacy and creates cultural communication." Everyone is invited to take part in this interactive web project: "By publicly honoring your hero on this award-winning site, you reward those who have made a difference and bring a new hope to this global online community." Visit My Hero at www.myhero.com or email the organization at myhero@myheroproject.org.

Vocabulary Study

prowess (1)	fathom (3)
culture, cultural (2, 9)	presumptuous (3)
status (2)	relinquishing (3)
icon (2)	diminished (3)
humanitarian (2)	vilified (4)
arduous (3)	ferocious (7)
brazen (3)	dynamic (7)
anthem (3)	transcending (7)
maligned (7)	

Sports Hero: Muhammed Ali

1   Was it his physical prowess, his social commentary, his clever, cocky rhymes? Or was it his post boxing, humanitarian endeavors? Maybe it's all of the above for many who have been inspired, uplifted, and touched by the greatest champion of all time, Muhammad Ali.

2   Muhammad Ali has undoubtedly been a fixture in world culture since the 1960's. Seizing the gold medal at the Olympics in 1960, battling

George Foreman in "The Rumble in the Jungle" in Zaire, and going head to head with Joe Frazier in "The Thrilla in Manila" in the Philippines, were highlights of a career that earned Ali the status of world icon. Since his retirement in 1981, Ali has engaged in many humanitarian endeavors, including a 1990 journey to Iraq to negotiate the release of 15 hostages. In the last 20 years, Ali's cultural status has hardly diminished: 3 billion television viewers around the world watched him open the Atlanta Olympics in 1996.

3   Inspiring billions has been an arduous work in progress for Ali. Many Americans were slighted by his brazen "I am the greatest" anthem. White America couldn't fathom a black man being so presumptuous. These same Americans were also enraged by Cassius Clay's insistence on relinquishing what he called his "slave name" for the Muslim name, Muhammad Ali. "I don't have to be what you want me to be; I'm free to be what I want," Ali said of his name change.

4   The relationship did not improve much when Ali spoke out against Vietnam, refusing to join the Army during the war. His short defense "I ain't got no quarrel with them Viet Cong" spoke volumes, but the media vilified him. The government prosecuted him for draft dodging, and the boxing commission took away his license. He was idle for three and a half years during what should have been the peak of his career.

5   Ali's return to boxing was a spectacular one. He regained his title in 1974, knocking out tough guy George Foreman in the eighth round in the famed "Rumble in the Jungle." This widely-publicized fight became a permanent chapter in boxing history.

6   Ali wrote of this fight:

> "'The Rumble in the Jungle' was a fight that made the whole country more conscious. I wanted to establish a relationship between American blacks and Africans. All the time I was there, I'd travel to the jungles, places where there was no radio or television, and people would come up and touch me, and I could touch them. The fight was about racial problems, Vietnam. All of that."

7   Although "The Rumble in the Jungle" could not hold a torch to 1975's "Thrilla in Manila," a battle with Joe Frazier (which Ali also won), "The Rumble in the Jungle" stands out among other sporting events for its social impact and lasting effect on Ali himself. Still ferocious in the ring, Ali's meeting with the people of Africa had added another dynamic to his personality: compassion. Ali has—sometimes anonymously—donated millions of dollars

to a variety of individuals and organizations transcending race and class barriers. Not bad for a man maligned for his religious affiliation.

[8] In 1984, it was revealed that the man the Kentucky Senate has named "the greatest athlete of all time" was stricken with Parkinson's disease. But true to form, Ali hasn't let his illness stop him from being free to do what he wants.

[9] Never has a sports figure inspired so many people in so many different directions. Ali has shown that a sport can be more than entertainment; it can also be a cultural event with the power to change social values. And he has shown that a black man can stand up to social oppression.

Comprehension and Discussion

1. What is Marcus's thesis? Where does he state it?
2. Marcus claims that Muhammed Ali is "the greatest champion of all time" (1). What does the world *champion* mean in this context? What evidence does the author provide to support his statement? Does he provide sufficient evidence? Does his argument convince you? Which of Ali's accomplishment is the most significant to you? Why?
3. What three actions of Ali upset many white Americans?
4. Ali was born in Louisville, Kentucky. How has the Kentucky Senate honored him?
5. What does the word *hero* mean to you? Check the definition in a dictionary or an encyclopedia, and write a journal entry on what you discover. How does this meaning apply to Muhammed Ali? Who are some of the people who are heroes to you? Does an individual have to be publicly known to be considered a hero?

Language and Technique

1. Marcus introduces the essay with two questions and a "maybe" statement. Why do you think he begins the essay in this way? What is the effect on readers?
2. Working with a group of classmates, analyze the structure of this essay. Identify the paragraph(s) in the introduction, the body, and the conclusion. How many sections or subdivisions are in the body?
3. What words and phrases does Marcus use to connect the paragraphs in the essay? Remember, a writer may use familiar transitional words and phrases for *coherence*, but he or she may also use repetition of key words and ideas. Identify these devices for coherence on your own, and then discuss them with your classmates.

4. Paragraphs 2, 3, and 7 are structured beginning with a topic sentence followed by examples. Working with a group of classmates, analyze the structure of and write an outline of each of these paragraphs.

Suggestions for Writing

1. **Sentence:** Marcus often uses parallel structure to connect ideas and to economize expression. One example of his use of parallelism is Sentence 2 in Paragraph 2:

    > Seizing the gold medal at the Olympics in 1960, battling George Foreman in "The Rumble in the Jungle" in Zaire, and going head to head with Joe Frazier in "The Thrilla in Manila" in the Philippines, were highlights of a career that earned Ali the status of world icon.

    The author uses three-*ing gerunds* ("seizing," "battling," "going") as subjects of the verb "were," listing highlights of Ali's career. Write a similar sentence in which you use three or more accomplishments of someone you admire or someone you know. Share your sentence with a small group of your classmates.

2. **Paragraph:** Using Paragraphs 2, 3, and 7 as models, write a paragraph of exemplification. Begin your paragraph with a topic sentence, and use two or more examples to support and develop the topic sentence. You may also add a clincher at the end of the paragraph.

3. **Essay:** Write an essay about someone you consider a hero. This person may be an historical figure, a sports figure, a celebrity, a politician, or someone you know personally. Be sure to include plenty of examples to support your idea and to clarify your stance for your readers. If you want to read other similar essays before you write yours, go to www.myhero.com to read sample essays on heroes from a variety of fields.

4. **Essay:** Write an essay of definition of the word *hero*. Refer to your journal entry and your notes on the class discussion for Question 5 under Comprehension and Discussion above. In your essay, make clear what you think a hero is and is not, and provide examples to support your opinion. Structure your essay with an introduction, body, and conclusion similar to the structure of Marcus's essay on Ali.

5. **Essay:** Write an essay about someone who has had to deal with a dread disease as Ali has coped with Parkinson's disease. Explain the effects of the disease on the individual, and how he or she has dealt with the problem.

Crazy Horse Malt Liquor

Michael Dorris

MICHAEL DORRIS, after earning degrees from Georgetown and Yale Universities, taught Native American studies and anthropology at Dartmouth College. He wrote novels, short stories, and essays, many about the Native American perspective. His best-known book is *The Broken Cord* which details his experiences as a single, adoptive father and his son's struggles because of fetal alcohol syndrome. He married Louise Erdrich who is also a well-known Native American writer. In this essay Dorris criticizes the way the image of American Indians is used in popular culture.

Vocabulary Study

impeccably (1)	relegates (3)
facsimiles (1)	conjures (4)
ethnographically (1)	allusion (5)
ersatz (2)	ethanol (5)
opaque (3)	pomp (7)
impermeable (3)	

Crazy Horse Malt Liquor

1   People of proclaimed good will have the oddest ways of honoring American Indians. Sometimes they dress themselves up in turkey feathers and paint to boogie on fifty-yard lines. Sometimes otherwise impeccably credentialed liberals get so swept up into honoring that they beat fake tom-toms or fashion their forearms and hands into facsimiles of axes European traders used for barter and attempt, unsuccessfully, to chop their way to victory. Presumably they hope that this exuberant if ethnographically questionable display will do their teams more good against opponents than those rituals they imitate and mock did for nineteenth-century Cheyenne or Nez Percé men and women who tried, with desperation and ultimate futility, to defend their homelands from invasion.

2   Everywhere you look such respects are paid: the street names in woodsy, affluent subdivisions, mumbo jumbo in ersatz male-bonding weekends and Boy Scout jamborees, geometric fashion statements, weepy antilittering public service announcements. In the ever popular noble/savage spectrum, red is the hot, safe color.

³   For five hundred years flesh and blood Indians have been assigned the role of a popular culture metaphor. Today, they evoke fuzzy images of Nature, The Past, Plight, or Summer Camp. War-bonneted apparitions pasted to football helmets or baseball caps act as opaque, impermeable curtains, solid walls of white noise that for many citizens block or distort all vision of the nearly two million contemporary Native Americans. And why not? Such honoring relegates Indians to the long ago and thus makes them magically disappear from public consciousness and conscience. What do the three hundred federally recognized tribes—with their various complicated treaties governing land rights and protections, their crippling unemployment, infant mortality, and teenage suicide rates, their often chronic poverty, their manifold health problems—have in common with jolly (or menacing) cartoon caricatures, wistful braves, or raven-tressed Mazola girls?

⁴   Perhaps we should ask the Hornell Brewing Company of Baltimore, manufactures of The Original Crazy Horse Malt Liquor, a product currently distributed in New York with packaging inspired by, according to the text on the back, "the Black Hills of Dakota, *steeped* [my italics] in the History of the American West, home of Proud Indian Nations, a land where imagination conjures up images of blue clad Pony Soldiers and magnificent Native American Warriors."

⁵   Whose imagination? Were these the same blue-clad lads who perpetrated the 1890 massacre of two hundred captured, freezing Lakota at Wounded Knee? Are Pine Ridge and Rosebud, the two reservations closest to the Black Hills and, coincidentally, the two counties in the United States with the lowest per capita incomes, the Proud Nations? Is the "steeping" a bald allusion to the fact that alcohol has long constituted the number one health hazard to Indians? Virtually every other social ill plaguing Native Americans—from disproportionately frequent traffic fatalities to arrest statistics—is related in some tragic respect to ethanol, and many tribes, from Alaska to New Mexico, record the highest percentage in the world of babies born disabled by fetal alcohol syndrome and fetal alcohol effect. One need look no further than the warning label to pregnant women printed in capital letters on every Crazy Horse label to make the connection.

⁶   The facts of history are not hard to ascertain: the Black Hills, the *paha sapa,* the traditional holy place of the Lakota, were illegally seized by the U.S. government, systematically stripped of their mineral wealth—and have still not been returned to their owners. Crazy Horse, in addition to being a patriot to his people, was a mystic and a religious leader murdered after

he voluntarily gave himself up in 1887 to Pony Soldiers at Fort Robinson, Nebraska. What, then, is the pairing of his name with forty ounces of malt liquor supposed to signify?

7   The Hornell brewers helpfully supply a clue. The detail of the logo is focused on the headdress and not the face; it's pomp without circumstance, form without content. Wear the hat, the illustration seems to offer, and in the process fantasize yourself more interesting (or potent or tough or noble) than you are. Play at being a "warrior" from the "land that truly speaks of the spirit that is America."

8   And if some humorless Indians object, just set them straight. Remind them what an honor it is to be used.

Comprehension and Discussion

1. How are American Indians a *popular culture metaphor?* What is popular culture? What is a metaphor? What examples of this metaphor does Dorris cite? Who assigned this metaphor to American Indians? What are the results of Native Americans being assigned this role? Can you and your classmates think of additional examples of this metaphor for Native Americans?

2. Dorris states that American Indians are being used (8). How does he think they are being used? Who is using them? Do you agree?

3. What is the significance of the Hornell Brewing Company's Original Crazy Horse Malt Liquor? How is this malt beverage packaged and advertised? Why does Dorris object to the sales pitch?

4. Can you think of other popular culture metaphors? Find other examples of popular culture metaphors and stereotypes on television programs and in advertising (magazine, radio, TV, online, billboard). List these in your journal, and participate in a class discussion on popular culture metaphors. Do some of them portray other ethnic groups or cultural subgroups and minorities in a negative manner?

5. What is fetal alcohol syndrome (5)? Look up this problem—what it is, what causes it, whom it affects, and its effects. Is there any cure? Any effective treatment? Discuss this disability with your classmates.

Language and Technique

1. What is Dorris's *tone* (emotional attitude conveyed through selection of examples and word choice) in this essay? Discuss his tone with your classmates. Why does he use this tone? Do you think his tone is justified?

2. Dorris briefly (in a word or phrase) mentions several examples of the mistreatment of Native Americans, both contemporary and historical, but he devotes five paragraphs—over half the essay—to the Hornell Brewing Company and Crazy Horse Malt Liquor. Why does he devote so much space to this example? Why does he place the Hornell example at the end of the essay?

3. Dorris, a professor of anthropology and Native American studies, uses several historical *allusions* or references to deepen the meaning of the essay. Discuss the meaning of the following with your classmates. Several of the references you can figure out from the context. If you do not know the historical references, look them up and record them in your journal before the class discussion.

Cheyenne (1)

Nez Percé (1)

Mazola (3)

Lakota (5)

Wounded Knee (5)

the Proud Nations (5)

the Black Hills (6)

Crazy Horse (6)

Pony Soldiers (6)

4. What *ironies* are evident in the comments of the Hornell brewers? What ironic statements does Dorris make?

Suggestions for Writing

1. **Sentence.** In paragraph 4, Dorris uses both *italics* and *brackets* in the quotation from the Hornell text on the back of the malt liquor bottle. The italics for *steeped* emphasize a word that Dorris wants to stress and call attention to its double meaning. The bracketed note [my italics] indicates an addition that is not in the original. Find a one-sentence quotation from an essay in this textbook or from a newspaper article, copy it, place quotation marks around it (with the period inside the quotation marks), and insert italics and brackets in a similar manner.

2. **Paragraph.** Write a paragraph in which you describe an Indian or other ethnic logo, mascot, or motto with which you are familiar.

3. **Essay.** Write an *expository* (explaining) *narrative* (story or experience) about an experience in which either you were called a derogatory

name by someone else or you called someone else by a negative name. Explain the situation and the effects of the event.

4. **Essay.** One of the most controversial issues in recent years has been the use of ethnic (Native American, Hispanic, Arabic, Italian, African, etc.) words and pictures as logos and mascots (such as baseball teams called the Indians or football teams called the Seminoles). Some sports teams have changed their names to try to defuse the situation and to avoid alienating members of the ethnic group. Do you think a sports team or a product should change its name, logo, or mascot for these reasons? Write an essay in which you take a stance on this controversy, and present a logical, credible argument to support your position.

5. **Essay.** *Symbols* are all around us. Participate in a class discussion on some common symbols. Then choose a symbol—religious (such as menorah, crucifix), national (such as the U.S. flag, Statue of Liberty), historical (such as the Confederate flag or the Flying Tigers), organizational (such as the Red Cross), or business (such as the RCA dog or the Taco Bell Chihuahua), and write an essay in which you explain the origin of the symbol and its meaning. You will probably have to do some reading and research to gather the information for your essay.

Families Should Attempt to Live Without Television

Chiori Santiago

CHIORI SANTIAGO contributes regularly to the "Family Matters" column of *Diablo*, a monthly magazine that covers the East Bay area of San Francisco, California. In this column she responds to the annual National TV-Turn-Off-Week, sponsored by a Washington, D.C. based organization named TV-Free America.

Vocabulary Study

ambience (3)	consumerism (5)
intermittent (3)	ambivalent (6)
griot (3)	surreal (9)
revert (4)	mayhem (12)
justifications (5)	insidious (16)
pique (5)	lethargic (17)

Families Should Attempt to Live Without Television

1   If you're the parent of a child in Contra Costa's public schools, you'll soon be receiving an important notice reminding you that April 21–28, 1997, is TV Turn-Off Week. Organized by concerned Orinda, California, mom and political activist Ellen Schwartz, the event is a plea for families to take a vacation from the mayhem and merchandising of television for seven days. It's an important effort, and I urge you to take part.

2   I hope I will be doing the same, but I'm doubting my stamina.

An Addict's Admission

3   I love television. Always have. As I write this, the television is on in the next room, its steady drone of canned laughter and peppy theme music creating a friendly ambience in the empty house, its intermittent flicker as soothing as candlelight. I'm sure that television's resemblance to the hearth fulfills some deep and primitive yearning in the human soul. Take a walk through the neighborhood at night and you sense its ever presence; behind venetian blinds and picture windows the blue glow beckons, asking us to sit hypnotized by dancing light and listen to the lull of the griot's tales—even if they're corrupted by commercials for athletic shoes and panty liners.

4   I admit, I'm an addict. To get me through TV Turn-Off Week I'll need one of those electronic monitors they give to petty criminals. It'll sound an alarm when I rise and sneak through the sleeping house to catch Conan O'Brien's monologue or the revelatory climax of *All About Eve*. "Just a little fix, please," I can hear myself say. I will do my best to maintain a moral steadfastness as long as my kids are awake. I will brightly unplug the set and suggest a game of Scrabble. The minute they're tucked in, though, I'm afraid I'll revert like a skid row junkie in a sea of denial for one little nip at my bottle of electronic comfort.

5   Hypocrites like me have a bagful of justifications. Look at all that's wonderful about television, I say. By what other means can you, in a single evening, take a train ride across Russia or learn about a distant galaxy far, far away? Television can pique the imagination, it's informative, and it's overrated as a fount of evil. Television has never compelled me to corporate consumerism (the only product label I look for is the one that says "50% Off") or to copycat crime. I've seen my sister-in-law do all her high school homework while watching TV, listening to a Walkman and talking on the telephone—simultaneously—and she got straight As.

6 Television isn't so much bad as it is mindless. What bothers me is not the level of distasteful content, but the lack of content. Mainstream programming features three themes: people or animals killing each other, people winning things and people making fools of themselves. I'm amazed that with sixty-four cable channels, there's nothing worth watching on Saturday night. Therefore, I'm pretty ambivalent about the medium; I think TV Turn-Off Week is a great idea—for someone else. But recently, two incidents made me think that Ellen Schwartz has a point.

Two Disturbing Incidents

7 I was in the backyard with my six-year-old son a few weekends ago when we heard someone coughing loudly in another yard. It was an intrusive, rabid kind of cough, to be sure, but nothing out of the ordinary, I thought. My son had a different theory.

8 "I think someone's being murdered," he said.

That upset me. What he said was disturbing enough, but I was really bothered by the way he said it, with an air of nonchalance, as if the sound of someone being murdered two yards over was a sound you'd expect to hear on a quiet Sunday.

9 Why not? Murder, as relayed by television, has been a constant part of my son's environment. He hears about it every night on the six o'clock news, in advertisements for the movie of the week. Cartoon characters spend whole half hours trying to wipe out each other. The horror of death dissolves in the surreal life of television programming. . . . Try as we do to monitor his viewing, restricting him to the Disney channel and Nickelodeon, the violent world intrudes. Murder is just another fact of life for him, no more remarkable than a school lunch.

10 The other incident happened when I called the kid for dinner and he was so absorbed in the tube that he didn't respond. Now, you can talk about how TV rots your brain and leads to smoking, short attention span and obesity, and I'll say, "Pshaw." But let it lead to a kid not listening to his mother and, believe me, TV is in big trouble.

11 So, I went to see Ellen Schwartz. She runs a nonprofit organization called Healing Our Nation from violence out of an office in Walnut Creek, California, that barely holds a very large desk and an even more expansive personality. Schwartz is the kind of person who could make you swallow cod liver oil and love it—not because it's good for you, but because her sheer enthusiasm sweeps you up in the zeal of her crusade.

How Children Respond to TV Violence

12   Schwartz . . . is no temperance fanatic. She, too, grew up in the age of television and loved it as much as I do. She remembers getting up early on beautiful summer days to pour a howl of cereal and hunker down to watch cartoons. "But there's such an important difference between the TV we watched and the TV our kids watch," she says. "We saw the consequences of violence. Now there are no consequences. We don't see the shattered lives and disabilities. Nowadays, comedy is put downs followed by a laugh track. Fifty-two percent of the nightly news is devoted to mayhem: rape, robbery, war. Children don't see compassion. That's when we have anger and alienation."

13   Kids' models of conflict resolution come from these shows, according to Schwartz. A script in which people are shown discussing their feelings and working out problems, won't hold our attention long enough to sell a jar of peanut butter, so television captures attention with a steady rhythm of shootings, seductions or pratfalls. "When this is the predominant model, you're not getting realistic conflict resolution," she says. Hence, an increase in violence, disrespect, apathy and a fixation on instant gratification that everyone from the American Medical Association to the Congress of National Black Churches to the National Association of Elementary School Principals says is leading to a culture in which caring and interaction are outmoded concepts.

14   That realization led Schwartz to create an ad hoc TV turn-off effort in 1987. "When my son was nine we had such battles over what he could and couldn't watch," she explains. "During one of these battles my husband said, 'Fine, let's just get the TV out of the house.' We'd sit on the deck and watch the stars. We dusted off the bikes, and instead of sitting and eating ice cream in front of the tube, we rode into town and bought cones. We spoke to each other!"

15   The TV's back, and Schwartz's husband and son continue to indulge in routine doses of sports programs and cheesy sitcoms. On the other hand, her daughter, now nine, grew up without television's constant presence and isn't dependent on it for entertainment. Reason enough, Schwartz thinks, to put TV in its place and turn attention to alternative entertainment that can bring us together as families.

16   More insidious that violence and twisted values is the way TV separates us from intimacy and interaction. I think of all the times I've used television to buy a little time away from my kids. I've used it, essentially, to ignore them. Should I be surprised when my son uses it to ignore me?

The Perfect Addiction

17 TV is the perfect addiction. There we sit, slack-jawed, pupils dilated, in a suburban version of an opium den, avoiding problems and conversation. "It controls the room," Schwartz says. "No one gets up from the TV refreshed and renewed. Instead, they're disgruntled. They're lethargic. It is hypnotic. Kids will lie to be able to watch TV. And most of all, it's not an addiction you have to admit, because we all have it.

18 "Television robs us of life. Why are we spending so many hours watching other people's lives instead of exploring the gifts of the people we care about?"

19 TV Turn-Off Week is not meant as punishment. The information packet schoolchildren will bring home contains lists of alternative things to do (my favorites: "clean up your room" and "think"), good discussion questions for teachers and convincing arguments for people like me, pointing out that it isn't the black box that's criminal—it's the way we let it control us.

20 "TV Turn-Off Week gives us a break," says Schwartz. "We're all such mysteries; the little hurts and confusions and frustrations often come out when we talk to each other. We need enough quiet time to figure out our passions. Turning off the TV is a promise to be there for your kids. They want time with us more than anything."

21 Will I be able to live one week without Helen Mirren and Dennis Richmond? I'm not sure. I will make a pledge, though. I promise to listen to my son pick his way through *The Foot Book* for the seventeenth time, to pay attention when my husband explains the fine points of a 1-3-1 zone trap in basketball, and to hear the murmurings of the house at night, the little creakings and shiftings that, in the absence of TV, whisper a reminder that this place is a home.

Comprehension and Discussion

1. What is TV Turn-Off Week? Who organized it? What is its purpose? What is the author's opinion of this week? Why does she say that families should attempt to live without television? What is your opinion of such a week? How do you think TV has affected family life? How would you probably respond to a week without television? Write a journal entry about how a week without television would probably affect you. Be sure to include specific examples. Participate in a class discussion on the subject.

2. Santiago and Schwartz say they are addicts (4). What are they addicted to? What does *addict* mean? In your journal, write the dictionary definition

of *addict* along with several examples of addictions with which you are familiar. Do you know anyone who is addicted to television? To soap operas? To the Internet? To video games? Discuss addictions with your classmates. From the class discussion, add other examples of addiction to the list in your journal.

3. What does the author say is good about television? What is not good? What is surreal about television? Do you agree with her? In your journal, write your own examples of what is good about television, what is not good, and what is surreal. Participate in a class discussion of the advantages and the disadvantages of television, and add examples from the class discussion to your journal entry.

4. Ellen Schwartz says that television is different today from when she was a child. How does she claim it is different? Do you think television is different today from when you were a child? Why, or why not? In your journal, write your response to this question, and then discuss it with your classmates.

5. What is conflict resolution? What does Santiago say kids learn from television about conflict resolution?

Language and Technique

1. What is the author's *tone* or attitude in this essay? Mark specific words, phrases, and examples that have led you to conclude what you have about the author's tone in this essay. Be prepared to discuss the author's tone with your classmates.

2. Find several words and phrases that the author uses to describe television. Are any of these descriptions contradictory? Why do you think the author uses such a wide variety of ways to describe television?

3. The *dash* is like a strong comma; it stresses what it sets off more forcefully than a comma. Santiago uses the dash several times in the essay (paragraphs 3, 5, 6, and 19). With your classmates, discuss the various ways she uses the dash, and determine if you think she uses the dash effectively.

4. Notice how Santiago uses dialogue throughout the essay, and how she punctuates the exact quotations from the people to whom she talks. Do you think she uses dialogue effectively? Why?

Suggestions for Writing

1. **Sentence.** Write 2 sentences in which you use the dash. Share your sentences with your classmates.

2. **Paragraph.** Reread Santiago's description of television in paragraph 3. Notice her use of specific details and precise descriptive words. Write a paragraph describing one of the following:

a movie theater	a sports bar
a fast food restaurant	your bedroom
a football game	your car or vehicle
a pep rally	a church service

3. **Essay.** Using your journal entry and notes from the class discussion in response to Question #2 under Comprehension and Discussion above, write an essay about someone you know who is addicted to one of the following (the person may be yourself). Explain and illustrate the person's addiction and how it has affected him or her.

television	chocolate
movies	coffee
the Internet	cigarettes
fast food	alcohol
shopping	a drug (be specific)
video games	a sport (be specific)
soap operas	chat rooms

4. **Essay.** Do you think a national TV Turn-Off Week would be successful? Write an essay in which you explain whether it would be successful or unsuccessful, explain why, and explain how it would affect people. You may use your journal notes and notes from the class discussion on this subject.

5. **Essay.** Write an essay in which you compare and contrast television when you were a child to television today. Be sure to provide specific examples and descriptions of specific programs.

Media Literacy Education Can Address the Problem of Media Violence

Elizabeth Thoman

ELIZABETH THOMAN is founder and director of the Center for Media Literacy, a California-based nonprofit organization that produces teacher training and community education materials designed to promote media literacy. This argument is from her testimony before the US Senate Committee on Commerce, Science, and Transportation, July 12, 1995.

Vocabulary Study

literacy (title)	self-perpetuating (13)
information highway (4)	paranoia (13)
continuum (5)	Good Samaritan ethic (13)
depictions (9)	consensus (17)
diffuse (12)	proliferated (20)
syndrome (13)	

Media Literacy Education Can Address the Problem of Media Violence

1   For 40 years, the American people have been engaged in a "circle of blame" about media violence. Here's how it works:

Viewers, particularly parents, concerned for their children about something they see on television or in the media, blame those who write and create the shows.

Writers/directors say it's the producers who require violence in programs in order to get them financed.

Producers blame *corporate executives* for demanding "action" in order to get ratings.

Corporate executives say competition is brutal and blame the advertisers for pulling out unless a show gets high ratings.

Advertisers say it's all up to the *viewers*!

2   It's time to stop the circle of blame and recognize we all share responsibility for the culture we are creating and passing on to our children. It is very important that we consider a variety of solutions to this issue. *There is no one solution.* But among the efforts being presented here today, I believe that media literacy education is a fresh and valuable contribution to ultimately reducing the depiction of violence on television and in the media.

Defining Media Literacy

3   What is media literacy?

4   Media literacy, as defined in a 1992 report from the Aspen Institute, is the movement "to expand notions of literacy to include the powerful postprint media that dominate our informational landscape." We define the media literate person as one who can "access, understand, analyze, and communicate messages in a variety of forms." Call it "driver's training for

the information highway." In any case, we are talking about a new vision of literacy for the 21st century.

5   The media literacy movement actually encompasses three stages on a continuum of what we might call a "media empowerment movement."

6   The first stage is learning to *balance or manage one's media "diet."* Just as we teach children good eating habits, we must also teach our children good viewing habits that they can take into adulthood and, ultimately, share with their own children. This stage requires parent education, of course, and programs are beginning to be conducted by the parent-teacher association (PTA), parent education programs, churches and others. For many parents, it's also the *motivational training* that will be needed to help them understand that, like it or not, *managing media in their children's lives* is an essential part of parenting today. Such motivational training may also be a necessary step for some parents to purchase and use any kind of blocking or monitoring device.

7   The second stage is learning *specific skills of critical viewing*—that is, learning to analyze and question what is on the screen, how it is constructed and what may have been left out. This is the task of more formal media literacy classes in schools and after-school programs for children and teens as well as in adult education opportunities for grown-ups of all ages.

8   The third stage we call critical or social analysis. It explores deeper issues of how mass media makes meaning in society and drives the consumer economy, that is, who produces the media we experience—and for what purpose? What are the political, economic and social forces that converge to shape the cultural environment in which we live our lives? This stage also questions whether our mass media system can or should be different. This more philosophical stage will not be engaged in by everyone, but is necessary for informed and responsible media activism or what I call "citizenship in a media culture." . . .

9   With that brief overview, let me address specifically how media literacy applies to the current problem we are facing in our media about depictions of violence.

The Wrong Question

10   For those same 40 years the circle of blame I mentioned earlier has been fueled by one unanswerable question: "Does watching violence cause someone to become violent?" Or as the talk shows might put it: Does TV kill?

11   The reason we've gotten nowhere on this issue for 40 years is because this is the wrong question to ask about violence in the media.

¹²   It's a limiting question because it focuses the impact of media only on single individuals rather than a more diffuse impact on larger communities which are, of course, made up of individuals but which also have their own cultural "environment" that is larger than any one individual.

¹³   According to the American Psychological Association's (APA) 1993 report, *Violence and Youth: Psychology's Response*, there are actually four long term effects of viewing violence:

1. Increased aggressiveness and anti-social behavior.
   (This may not just be becoming an ax-murderer. It can also mean increased arrests for domestic violence and child abuse, drunk driving, even an "in your face" attitude about the world.)
2. Increased fear of being or becoming a victim.
   (The "mean world syndrome"/creating a self-perpetuating prison of paranoia)
3. Increased desensitization to violence and victims of violence.
   (Loss of "Good Samaritan" ethic and fundamental principle of democratic societies; building the common good)
4. Increased appetite for more and more violence in entertainment and real life.
   (The ability to tolerate more violent media and to engage in increasingly risky or dangerous behaviors)

¹⁴   If we consider all four effects and reflect on everyday life in current society, we will surely agree with the APA that "Even those who do not themselves increase their violent behaviors are significantly affected by their viewing of violence."

¹⁵   To reduce the issue of media violence to "does TV kill?" trivializes a very complex question that faces our global society on the brink of the 21st century. The real question should be: *What is the long-term impact on our national psyche when millions of children, in their formative years, grow up decade after decade bombarded with very powerful visual and verbal messages demonstrating violence as the way to solve problems?*

The Larger Question

¹⁶   Actually there's even a larger question here than just the question of the portrayal of violent images on TV and in the media.

¹⁷   The much larger question is:

- *What kind of culture, what kind of psychological environment do we want our children to grow up in?*

• And then, when we achieve some consensus on that, we can further decide what is the role and responsibility of mass communications and technology (among many other factors) in contributing to that cultural, that mental environment.

[18]   The Center for Media Literacy believes that to engage this question is to explore a fundamental issue of our time. But we need it to happen not just in political speeches or talk shows or even academic forums. We need to enroll *millions of Americans* in what we might call a "national conversation" to resolve the issue of media violence in their own lives and ultimately in our common society. This is not as difficult as it might seem.

People Want Information

[19]   All across America, every day, and into the night, there are classes in schools and colleges, discussion groups in church basements and public libraries and Rotary clubs. There are after-school programs for teen-agers and elderhostels for senior citizens. People of all ages are hungry for relevant information that can help them cope with the stresses of living today. *I propose that media literacy education is a valuable and critical tool for learning to navigate our way through the sea of information and images that make up our modern media-saturated society.*

[20]   Perhaps violence has proliferated in our mass entertainment culture because citizens haven't had the information they need to make truly informed choices. In the past 20 years, we've learned to make different choices around smoking and cholesterol and buckling up your seatbelt. Media literacy proposes that, with different information, viewers might make different choices or engage in different behaviors.

[21]   There is clear evidence that skills of media literacy can be taught to even young children and they can have an impact on a child's ability to apply critical thinking to a variety of media. Does that mean they will never watch Power Rangers again? Not necessarily. But I guarantee they'll never watch it passively or without thinking again—and that alone can make a huge difference! . . .

The Promise of Media Literacy

[22]   *Media literacy education is, I believe, a fundamental step in the long-term "de-marketing" of violence as a commodity in our culture.*

[23]   I have no doubt that when millions of Americans have the opportunity to examine the many issues around media violence and practice skills of

media advocacy and action, . . . we will see a dramatic increase in the public opinion and strategic actions that will slowly, but surely, yield changes in our media system. Because it is an educational process and not a "quick fix" solution, media literacy may not make the headlines today. But it will influence the media world our children will inherit tomorrow. This is what counts.

Comprehension and Discussion

1. What is the "circle of blame" of media violence? Who does Thoman say is responsible for the culture of violence? Do you agree with her? In your journal write your opinion of who is to blame for media violence. According to the author, what is the solution to the culture of media violence? Do you agree or disagree with her? Why? Write a journal entry on your position, and participate in a class discussion on these issues.

2. What is literacy? What is a literate person? Look up *literacy* in an encyclopedia or on the Internet, and write a journal entry on what you discover. What is media literacy? Who should be responsible for teaching children media literacy? You have studied communications literacy (reading, writing, listening, speaking) and computations literacy (arithmetic, mathematics, algebra, geometry, calculus, probability) in school. Have you been taught media literacy? Do you think media literacy should be included in education? If so, at what level? Discuss this issue with your classmates, and take notes in your journal.

3. What are the three stages of the continuum of a media empowerment movement? Explain and illustrate each stage.

4. What are the four long-term effects of viewing violence, according to the American Psychological Association?

5. What is the real question that we should be asking about media violence?

Language and Technique

1. Working with a small group of classmates, find all the instances in which Thoman uses *italics* in her essay. Mark these in the text or record them by paragraph and sentence in your journal (if you don't want to write in your textbook). What are italics? What are italics used for? Why does Thoman use italics?

2. Thoman uses various formatting techniques to emphasize, highlight, and make clear her comments in the text. One of these techniques is italics

(see Question #1 above.) With your writing group, find examples and discuss her use of these other techniques:

Questions

Numbering

Bullets

3. Thoman also uses various punctuation marks to emphasize her points. With your writing group, find examples of each of the following uses of punctuation, and discuss the use of each. If you need to, review the rules or conventions for use of each of these marks of punctuation.

Parentheses

Dash

Quotation Marks

Colon

Exclamation Mark

Ellipsis Points

4. What is Thoman's thesis sentence in this essay? Where does she state it? Why does she not state it in the introduction to her essay?

Suggestions for Writing

1. **Sentence.** Write a sentence in which you use italics. Share your sentence with your writing group, and explain why you chose to use italics how and where you did.

2. **Paragraph.** Write a definition of communications literacy or computations literacy, similar to the Aspen Institute definition of media literacy in Paragraph 4. You may use some quotations from other sources as Thoman does. If you do, be sure to cite your sources and use quotation marks and other marks of punctuation correctly.

3. **Essay.** Review how Thoman explains the three stages of a media empowerment movement in paragraphs 5–8. Then choose one of the topics below and write a process essay in which you analyze or divide the topic into 3 stages (or more) or parts and explain and illustrate each stage or part. Model your essay on Thoman's mini-essay: Paragraph 1—Introduction; Paragraph 2—Stage One; Paragraph 3—Stage Two; Paragraph 4—Stage Three. You may add a fifth paragraph for concluding your essay.

> Buying a House
> Finding a Job
> Quitting a Job
> Critically Observing a Sport (Identify one specific sport.)
> Planning a Wedding
> Planning a Trip

4. **Essay.** Write an essay in which you argue for including media literacy in the high school curriculum and what you think should be included in such a course.

5. **Essay.** Thoman calls for critical viewing of and critical thinking about media. What is *critical thinking?* What are critical thinking skills? Look up the meaning of critical thinking, and participate in a class discussion of critical thinking and viewing. Then write an essay in which you define and illustrate critical thinking and viewing.

The Portable Phonograph

Walter Van Tilburg Clark

WALTER VAN TILBURG CLARK, professor of English, was born in Maine and grew up in Nevada. He wrote short stories and novels, the most well known of which is *The Ox-Bow Incident* about mob psychology leading to a lynching. His stories are psychological studies, usually with an unexpected twist at the end. In this story he explores life without the technology to which we have become accustomed.

Vocabulary Study

undulations (1)	acrid (3)
rakish (1)	traversed (4)
wuthering (2)	niche (4, 7)
pinions (2)	daubed (4)
plaintive (2)	doddering (6)
protracted (2)	loath (14)
intrenched (3)	delectable (45)
chary (3)	dissonance (45)
petty (3)	resonant (49)

The Portable Phonograph

[1] The red sunset, with narrow, black cloud strips like threats across it, lay on the curved horizon of the prairie. The air was still and cold, and in it settled the mute darkness and greater cold of night. High in the air there was wind, for through the veil of the dusk the clouds could be seen gliding rapidly south and changing shapes. A sensation of torment, of two-sided, unpredictable nature, arose from the stillness of the earth air beneath the violence of the upper air. Out of the sunset, through the dead, matted grass and isolated weed stalks of the prairie, crept the narrow and deeply rutted remains of a road. In the road, in places, there were crusts of shallow, brittle ice. There were little islands of an old oiled pavement in the road too, but most of it was mud, now frozen rigid. The frozen mud still bore the toothed impress of great tanks, and a wanderer on the neighboring undulations might have stumbled, in this light, into large, partially filled-in and weed-grown cavities, their banks channeled and beginning to spread into badlands. These pits were such as might have been made by falling meteors, but they were not. They were the scars of gigantic bombs, their rawness already made a little natural by rain, seed and time. Along the road there were rakish remnants of fence. There was also, just visible, one portion of tangled and multiple barbed wire still erect, behind which was a shelving ditch with small caves, now very quiet and empty, at intervals in its back wall. Otherwise there was no structure or remnant of a structure visible over the dome of the darkling earth, but only, in sheltered hollows, the darker shadows of young trees trying again.

[2] Under the wuthering arch of the high wind a V of wild geese fled south. The rush of their pinions sounded briefly, and the faint, plaintive notes of their expeditionary talk. Then they left a still greater vacancy. There was the smell and expectation of snow, as there is likely to be when the wild geese fly south. From the remote distance, toward the red sky, came faintly the protracted howl and quick yap-yap of a prairie wolf.

[3] North of the road, perhaps a hundred yards, lay the parallel and deeply intrenched course of a small creek, lined with leafless alders and willows. The creek was already silent under ice. Into the bank above it was dug a sort of cell, with a single opening, like the mouth of a mine tunnel. Within the cell there was a little red of fire, which showed dully through the opening, like a reflection or a deception of the imagination. The light came from the chary burning of four blocks of poorly aged peat, which gave off a petty warmth and much acrid smoke. But the precious remnants of wood, old fence posts and timbers from the long deserted dugouts,

had to be saved for the real cold, for the time when a man's breath blew white, the moisture in his nostrils stiffened at once when he stepped out, and the expansive blizzards paraded for days over the vast open, swirling and settling and thickening, till the dawn of the cleared day when the sky was a thin blue-green and the terrible cold, in which a man could not live for three hours unwarmed, lay over the uniformly drifted swell of the plain.

4   Around the smoldering peat four men were seated cross-legged. Behind them, traversed by their shadows, was the earth bench, with two old and dirty army blankets, where the owner of the cell slept. In a niche in the opposite wall were a few tin utensils which caught the glint of the coals. The host was rewrapping in a piece of daubed burlap, four fine, leather-bound books. He worked slowly and very carefully, and at last tied the bundle securely with a piece of grass-woven cord. The other three looked intently upon the process, as if a great significance lay in it. As the host tied the cord, he spoke. He was an old man, his long, matted beard and hair gray to nearly white. The shadows made his brows and cheekbones appear gnarled, his eyes and cheeks deeply sunken. His big hands, rough with frost and swollen by rheumatism, were awkward but gentle at their task. He was like a prehistoric priest performing a fateful ceremonial rite. Also his voice had in it a suitable quality of deep, reverent despair, yet perhaps, at the moment, a sharpness of selfish satisfaction.

5   "When I perceived what was happening," he said, "I told myself, 'It is the end. I cannot take much; I will take these.'

6   "Perhaps I was impractical," he continued. "But for myself, I do not regret, and what do we know of those who will come after us? We are the doddering remnant of a race of mechanical fools. I have saved what I love; the soul of what was good in us here; perhaps the new ones will make a strong enough beginning not to fall behind when they become clever."

7   He rose with slow pain and placed the wrapped volumes in the niche with his utensils. The other watched him with the same ritualistic gaze.

8   "Shakespeare, the Bible, *Moby Dick*, *The Divine Comedy*," one of them said softly. "You might have done worse; much worse."

9   "You will have a little soul left until you die," said another harshly. "That is more than is true of us. My brain becomes thick, like my hands." He held the big, battered hands, with their black nails, in the glow to be seen.

10   "I want paper to write on," he said. "And there is none."

11   The fourth man said nothing. He sat in the shadow farthest from the fire, and sometimes his body jerked in its rags from the cold. Although he

was still young, he was sick, and coughed often. Writing implied a greater future than he now felt able to consider.

12 The old man seated himself laboriously, and reached out, groaning at the movement, to put another block of peat on the fire. With bowed heads and averted eyes, his three guests acknowledged his magnanimity.

13 "We thank you, Doctor Jenkins, for the reading," said the man who had named the books.

14 They seemed then to be waiting for something. Doctor Jenkins understood, but was loath to comply. In an ordinary moment he would have said nothing. But the words of *The Tempest,* which he had been reading, and the religious attention of the three, made this an unusual occasion.

15 "You wish to hear the phonograph," he said grudgingly.

16 The two middle-aged men stared into the fire, unable to formulate and expose the enormity of their desire.

17 The young man, however, said anxiously, between suppressed coughs, "Oh, please," like an excited child.

18 The old man rose again in his difficult way, and went to the back of the cell. He returned and placed tenderly upon the packed floor, where the firelight might fall upon it, an old, portable phonograph in a black case. He smoothed the top with his hand, then opened it. The lovely green-felt covered disk became visible.

19 "I have been using thorns as needles," he said. "But tonight, because we have a musician among us"—he bent his head to the young man, almost invisible in the shadow—"I will use a steel needle. There are only three left."

20 The two middle-aged men stared at him in speechless adoration. The one with the big hands, who wanted to write, moved his lips, but the whisper was not audible.

21 "Oh, don't," cried the young man, as if he were hurt. "The thorns will do beautifully.

22 "No," the old man said. "I have become accustomed to the thorns— but they are not really good. For you, my young friend, we will have good music tonight.

23 "After all," he added generously, and beginning to wind the phonograph, which creaked, "they can't last forever."

24 "No, nor we," the man who needed to write said harshly. "The needle, by all means."

25 "Oh, thanks," said the young man. "Thanks," he said again, in a low, excited voice, and then stifled his coughing with a bowed head.

26 "The records, though," said the old man when he had finished winding, "are a different matter. Already they are very worn. I do not play them more than once a week. One, once a week, that is what I allow myself.

27 "More than a week I cannot stand it; not to hear them," he apologized.

28 "No, how could you?" cried the young man. "And with them here like this."

29 "A man can stand anything," said the man who wanted to write, in his harsh, antagonistic voice.

30 "Please, the music," said the young man.

31 "Only the one," said the old man. "In the long run we will remember more that way."

32 He had a dozen records with luxuriant gold and red seals. Even in that light the others could see that the threads of the records were becoming worn. Slowly he read out the titles, and the tremendous, dead names of the composers and the artists and the orchestras. The three worked upon the names in their minds, carefully. It was difficult to select from such a wealth what they would at once most like to remember. Finally the man who wanted to write named Gershwin's "New York."

33 "Oh, no," cried the sick young man, and then could say nothing more because he had to cough. The others understood him, and the harsh man withdrew his selection and waited for the musician to choose.

34 The musician begged Doctor Jenkins to read the titles again, very slowly, so that he could remember the sounds. While they were read, he lay back against the wall, his eyes closed, his thin, horny hand pulling at his light beard, and listened to the voices and the orchestras and the single instruments in his mind.

35 When the reading was done he spoke despairingly. "I have forgotten," he complained. "I cannot hear them clearly.

36 "There are things missing," he explained.

37 "I know," said Doctor Jenkins. "I thought that I knew all of Shelley by heart. I should have brought Shelley."

38 "That's more soul than we can use," said the harsh man. *"Moby Dick* is better.

39 "By God, we can understand that," he emphasized.

40 The doctor nodded.

41 "Still," said the man who had admired the books, "we need the absolute if we are to keep a grasp on anything.

42 "Anything but these sticks and peat clods and rabbit snares," he said bitterly.

43 "Shelley desired an ultimate absolute," said the harsh man. "It's too much," he said. "It's no good; no earthly good."

44 The musician selected a Debussy nocturne. The others considered and approved. They rose to their knees to watch the doctor prepare for the playing, so that they appeared to be actually in an attitude of worship. The peat glow showed the thinness of their bearded faces, and the deep lines in them, and revealed the condition of their garments. The other two continued to kneel as the old man carefully lowered the needle onto the spinning disk, but the musician suddenly drew back against the wall again, with his knees up, and buried his face in his hands.

45 At the first notes of the piano the listeners were startled. They stared at each other. Even the musician lifted his head in amazement, but then quickly bowed it again, strainingly, as if he were suffering from a pain he might not be able to endure. They were all listening deeply, without movement. The wet, blue-green notes tinkled forth from the old machine, and were individual, delectable presences in the cell. The individual, delectable presences swept into a sudden tide of unbearably beautiful dissonance, and then continued fully the swelling and ebbing of that tide, the dissonant inpourings, and the resolutions, and the diminishments, and the little, quiet wavelets of interlude lapping between. Every sound was piercing and singularly sweet. In all the men except the musician, there occurred rapid sequences of tragically heightened recollection. He heard nothing but what was there. At the final, whispering disappearance, but moving quietly, so that the others would not hear him and look at him, he let his head fall back in agony, as if it were drawn there by the hair, and clenched the fingers of one hand over his teeth. He sat that way while the others were silent, and until they began to breathe again normally. His drawn-up legs were trembling violently.

46 Quickly Doctor Jenkins lifted the needle off, to save it, and not to spoil the recollection with scraping. When he had stopped the whirling of the sacred disk, he courteously left the phonograph open and by the fire, in sight.

47 The others, however, understood. The musician rose last, but then abruptly, and went quickly out at the door without saying anything. The others stopped at the door and gave their thanks in low voices. The doctor nodded magnificently.

48 "Come again," he invited, "in a week. We will have the 'New York.'"

49 When the two had gone together, out toward the rimmed road, he stood in the entrance, peering and listening. At first there was only the resonant boom of the wind overhead, and then, far over the dome of the dead, dark plain, the wolf cry lamenting. In the rifts of clouds the doctor

saw four stars flying. It impressed the doctor that one of them had just been obscured by the beginning of a flying cloud at the very moment he heard what he had been listening for, a sound of suppressed coughing. It was not near by, however. He believed that down against the pale alders he could see the moving shadow.

50   With nervous hands he lowered the piece of canvas which served as his door, and pegged it at the bottom. Then quickly and quietly, looking at the piece of canvas frequently, he slipped the records into the case, snapped the lid shut, and carried the phonograph to his couch. There, pausing often to stare at the canvas and listen, he dug earth from the wall and disclosed a piece of board. Behind this there was a deep hole in the wall, into which he put the phonograph. After a moment's consideration, he went over and reached down his bundle of books and inserted it also. Then, guardedly, he once more sealed up the hole with the board and the earth. He also changed his blankets, and the grass-stuffed sack which served as a pillow, so that he could lie facing the entrance. After carefully placing two more blocks of peat on the fire, he stood for a long time watching the stretched canvas, but it seemed to billow naturally with the first gusts of a lowering wind. At last he prayed, and got in under his blankets, and closed his smoke-smarting eyes. On the inside of the bed, next the wall, he could feel with his hand, the comfortable piece of lead pipe.

Glossary

Moby Dick—a classic 19th century American novel by Herman Melville.

The Divine Comedy—a long poem by Dante, often considered the best of the Italian Renaissance.

Note: All four books that Dr. Jenkins chose to bring with him—Shakespeare, the Bible, *Moby Dick*, and *The Divine Comedy*—explore the nature and motivations of mankind.

The Tempest—Shakespeare's last play, a romantic fantasy of shipwrecked people who with the help of supernatural powers return to a happy, prosperous life.

Phonograph—Early portable phonographs required no electricity and were wound up by hand.

George Gershwin—an American composer who wrote classical jazz.

Percy Bysshe Shelley—an English Romantic poet who wrote poems about the soul, beauty, and mutability or change.

Claude Debussy—a French romantic composer

nocturne—a night piece

Comprehension and Discussion

1. Where are the characters in this short story? What has happened to them? Describe their surroundings.
2. Characterize the speaking characters in the story: Dr. Jenkins, the musician, and the man who wanted to write. What personality traits do they exhibit in the story? How do they react to the situation in which they now find themselves? Why is the fourth man in the group just a shadowy figure? Discuss the characters with your classmates.
3. What has Dr. Jenkins brought with him? How does each character respond to these items?
4. What record do the men choose to hear? Why does the musician not want to listen to Gershwin? How do the men react to Debussy?
5. How does the story end? What does this ending reveal about Dr. Jenkins's character traits? What does Clark suggest about human nature? How is the ending ironic?

Language and Technique

1. What *mood* does Clark establish in the description of the *setting* or time and place (1–3)? With a small group of classmates, go through the beginning of the short story, and find words, phrases, and images that set the mood.
2. Working with a small group of classmates, find the various religious references in the story, and discuss the effect these references have on the meaning of the story.
3. What clues of *foreshadowing* (hints that suggest events that happen later) does Clark provide to prepare you for the ending?
4. Why do you think Clark wrote this short story? What is the theme of the story?

Suggestions for Writing

1. **Sentence.** Write a sentence in which you state the *theme* or main idea of the story.
2. **Paragraph.** Write a paragraph on the *mood* of the story as established in the beginning. Refer to the study and discussion in question 1 under Language and Technique.
3. **Essay.** What do you think happens after the story ends? Why? Write an essay in which you pick up the narration and carry it forward. Explain why you think these events would occur by referring to specifics in the story.

4. **Essay.** If you realized most of your world was being destroyed and you could take only a few items that you could carry with you, what would you take? Books? Music? Pictures? Statues? Why? Write an essay in which you explain what you would take and why.

5. **Essay.** Write an essay on the levels of meaning of the title of the short story:
   a. The literal or dictionary level of meaning
   b. The psychological or character level of meaning; the meaning of the title to the characters in the story
   c. The thematic or universal level of meaning; the author's observations about human nature and our relationship to one another; the meaning applicable to our lives today

Use specific references, paraphrases, and quotations from the story to support your interpretation.

Death by Video Game: Fact or Fiction?

Nathan E. Florand

NATHAN E. FLORAND was a student in a college composition course when he wrote this essay on video games. The assignment was to take a stance on a controversial subject and write an *argument*, presenting evidence to convince the readers to agree with his position. Florand chose to write a defense of video games. As you read his argument, ask yourself if he presents sufficient evidence to convince you that his position is valid.

Death by Video Game: Fact or Fiction?

1   Within the last few years many human atrocities have occurred. Two students rampaged through an unsuspecting high school, another two held a round of target practice near a local highway, planes fell from the sky and crashed into major metropolitan areas, and plague and famine have been sweeping the world. The reason? Why, video games, of course—or at least that's the impression the government, uninformed parents, and local media are trying to make. With the continuous wave of terror sweeping the nation, people, now more than ever, use video games as scapegoats for any and all unfortunate incidents that occur; however, scapegoats are normally based on convenience, not fact.

2   The reason video games receive such negative hype is due in part to many common misconceptions. First are the classic and most prevalent beliefs that video games are pointless and only teach children to kill each other.

Those statements are disputed not only by the opinions of many nonviolent gamers who enjoy playing violent video games but also by the fact that violent crimes have diminished since video games have become widely available. Yet another common misconception about video games is that they rot the mind. While the average gamer may appear comatose during any given session, actually accomplishing anything in modern-day games requires extreme amounts of hand-eye coordination and reaction time for which the gamer must be mentally and physically alert. Reflexes aren't the only aspects gamers exercise during a game though. Many games contain complex puzzles, which require the gamer to exercise complex reasoning and problem-solving skills in order to move on to the next goal. A perfect example comes from the "M"-rated (M stands for mature audiences, and these titles can be sold only to someone seventeen or older) Capcom title *Resident Evil 3: Nemesis*. A certain situation in this game requires a player to use various cranks and valves in order to properly treat a vial of contaminated water. The sheer depth of the puzzle can take an average gamer anywhere from fifteen to forty-five minutes to correctly solve the problem and move on in the game. Solving this problem, though, offers the player a high degree of self-satisfaction, knowing he or she has finally accomplished the goal. Many would also argue that video games are for individuals who do not have many friends, that they are shy recluses who spend unlimited hours alone with their video games. However, actuality contradicts this statement: games today tend to focus on multiplayer and community functions, even including internet capabilities in some games, as opposed to the stand-alone single-player games of the past. Video games have become a medium for meeting and beating new people as well as renewing and building relationships with the ones the gamer already knows.

[3]   With the misconceptions aside, video games still receive incredibly terrible press. Many incidents have occurred in which video games were mentioned and instantly blamed instead of people investigating and finding the real causes of the problems. One illustration of this illogical jumping to conclusions is the case in March 2002 of a woman announcing she would sue Sony because her son committed suicide minutes after playing an immensely popular online game entitled *Ever Quest*. Instantly the woman gained sympathizers for her cause and the assault began. However, the fact that her twenty-one-year old son had been diagnosed with depression and a schizoid personality disorder prior to his playing the game and committing suicide did not surface until much later in the investigation. Maybe the video game was not the cause of his death after all. The Columbine shootings were another incident in which video games received unwarranted

blame and extremely negative press. After the two boys ended their rampage with enough weapons and ammo to supply a small militia, it was discovered that they had played the vastly popular first-person-shooter entitled *Doom*. Instantly the blame was shifted from the parents and the boys themselves to video games and every other form of media imaginable. What was not revealed until about a year after the incident was an excerpt from a journal written by one of the boys that expressed his overall disdain for the world and all the people in it. These shootings were performed under the influence of hate in its purest form, not video games. A short while after the Columbine shootings a sudden surge of crimes involving individuals in their teens and early twenties made a new trend very apparent. The criminals, having seen the reaction from parents and the media, learned that if they could scapegoat a controversial form of media, then the brunt of the attention could be shifted away from them. It seems the American people strongly support the culture of victimization (a term which means that people try to blame others for their problems without having to take any responsibility) moreso than many would like to believe. Another example makes my previous statement painfully obvious. One night two Tennessee teens decided they were bored and the only thing that would cure their boredom would be to go to a local highway and use the passing cars for target practice. The boys were later arrested after they had killed one man and wounded another. When questioned, the boys simply stated Grand Theft Auto, another popular video game, inspired them. No mention was made that the parents purchased the game for the boys despite its "M"-rating, or how the boys managed to procure two firearms; however, the clincher of this incident is that the surviving victims are attempting to sue the creators of the video game—not the boys, the parents, or any other parties directly involved!

4   The majority of people who continuously attack video games have never actually played and are not at all aware of the positive aspects video games offer. One benefit of gaming for many people is that video games offer stress relief. The reason is through video games, especially the more violent ones, a person can release pent up aggression on a virtual opponent instead of beginning a murderous rampage in the middle of a city street. Video games can also prove great exercise. Anti-video game advocates would probably argue that gamers do little more than exercise their thumbs and strain their eyes while playing. Their argument is valid in some instances, but video game companies, seeking to give the gamer a realistic experience, have created games that involve quite a bit of human bodily

interaction. The game *Dance Dance Revolution*, for example, requires a player to continuously step on four arrows (up, down, left, and right) to the tune and beat of different types of music. To the uninformed these movements may not seem like much exercise, but many songs play at three hundred or more beats per minute and require a player to step rapidly in place for long periods of time. This game provides very good exercise for a player's heart, lungs, and muscles. As I have already stated, video games also can be a form of social interaction. The variety of video games available allows gamers to find others who share their interests and further aids by giving them a form of entertainment while they get to know one another. Many games have online capabilities so instead of playing with the same people who live in a gamer's area, a player can now start a game that spans the globe; such gaming helps to close cultural gaps as well. As I also mentioned earlier, video games are also mental stimulus. Scientists are discovering more positive uses video games every day. They have been proven to hone problem-solving skills and hand-eye coordination due to the challenging puzzles or rapid game play contained in most games. Now studies are being performed to see if video games can be used to prevent Alzheimer's disease; this use is quite possible because video games exercise the mind and require undivided attention and concentration constantly while a person plays.

5   Most incidents claimed to involve negative effects of video games have many deeper underlying causes, but too often people accept video games as the bane of humanity instead of trying to discover the real causes. Human beings live in a culture of victimization in which the most common answer is the easy one, so scapegoats, such as video games are used for convenience, not validity.

Checklist for Revising and Editing

Following is a list of questions to guide you in the process of revising and editing your essays. Use the following questions to respond to the essay and to check for any point of needed revision. You may also use it to respond to and evaluate essays by other writers, whether students or professional writers.

1. **Sources:** What sources of information does the author draw upon— experience and memory, observation, reading and research, conversation and interview?

2. **Purpose:** What is the author's purpose in this essay—to narrate, to develop, to explain, to argue or convince, or a combination of these? Does the author accomplish the purpose?

3. **Thesis:** What is the thesis sentence or main point? Does the author state the thesis or imply it? Does the author make the thesis clear?

4. **Unity:** Does the author stick to the thesis? Is every statement in the essay directly relate to the main idea?

5. **Structure and Organization:**

   A. **Introduction**
      1) Does the introduction make clear the subject of the essay?
      2) Does the introduction state or imply the thesis sentence clearly?
      3) Does the introduction grab your attention and interest, and make you want to read the essay?

   B. **Body**
      1) What are the major points for development in the essay?
      2) How does the author organize the points of development of the essay? Is the order of points clear? Why does the author put the points in this order?
      3) Is this order appropriate for the ideas of the essay?
      4) Are there any other points or information that the author should have included? Why?

   C. **Conclusion**
      1) Does the conclusion relate directly to the introduction and to the thesis, as well as to the points in the body of the essay?
      2) Does the conclusion provide a sense of finality or ending to the essay?
      3) Is the conclusion effective?

6. **Development**

   A. What kinds of development does the author use to expand, support, and clarify the general assertions—narration, description, example, process, cause and effect, classification, example, comparison and contrast, definition, negation, statistics, expert opinion?

   B. Does the author provide sufficient evidence to make the subpoints clear and persuasive?

7. **Coherence**

   A. Does the essay flow smoothly from idea to idea? From sentence to sentence? From paragraph to paragraph?

B. How does the author connect the ideas throughout the essay? What Bridges and signposts does the author use to help the reader navigate through the essay?

1) What key ideas, words, and phrases does the author repeat?

2) What pronouns does the author use?

3) What transitional words and phrases does the author use to connect paragraphs? To connect sentences within paragraphs?

8. **Rhetorical Patterns:** What rhetorical patterns does the author use— narration, description, exposition, argument, example or illustration, enumeration, cause, effect, comparison, contrast, analysis, classification, process, definition, problems to solution?

9. **Language Skills and Proofreading**

A. Has the author proofread and edited the essay carefully for correctness, appropriateness, and effectiveness of language skills?

- Spelling
- Capitalization
- Punctuation
- Grammar
- Sentence structure
- Word choice

B. What, if anything, should be changed? Why?

10. **Response and Evaluation**

A. Does the author effectively fulfill the purpose and/or assignment in the essay?

B. What is the strongest aspect of the essay? What do you like best? Why?

C. What could be changed to improve the essay? Why?

CHAPTER TEN

The World of Work

Man today lives a robot life, one in which he is deprived
of his own being and becomes instead a mere role, occupation,
or function.

—CHARLES A. REICH

Suggestions for Journal Entries

1. Do you agree or disagree with Reich's comment above?
2. Do you have a job? What kind of work do you do? Do you enjoy your work?
3. Why do you work? Why do most people work? Do you know anyone who works for the sake of working?
4. What is your work ethic (principles of right conduct)? How did you develop this ethic?
5. Have work ethics and attitudes toward work changed in the last fifty years?
6. What job or task have you done for which you felt "a joy in doing work well"?
7. Is school work?
8. Should housework be considered a job?
9. What are the stresses of working while going to college?
10. Do you know anyone who gets his or her identity from work, who when asked "Who are you?" answers, "I am a doctor (or lawyer, teacher, contractor, musician, etc.)?
11. What was your first job? Did you earn any money doing this work?

To be of use

Marge Piercy

MARGE PIERCY was born in Detroit, Michigan, to a Welsh-English Protestant father who repaired heavy machinery and a Jewish mother of Russian and Lithuanian descent; she left school in the tenth grade to go to work. With the aid of scholarships, Piercy went to college and received her BA from the University of Michigan and her MA from Northwestern. Since then, she has published poems, essays, a novel, and a play. Her working-class background and work ethic are evident in the following poem.

Vocabulary Study

dallying (3)   botched (19)

muck (10)

To be of use

The people I love the best
jump into work head first
without dallying in the shallows
and swim off with sure strokes almost out of sight.
They seem to become natives of that element,   5
the black sleek heads of seals
bouncing like half-submerged balls.

I love people who harness themselves, an ox to a heavy cart,
who pull like water buffalo, with massive patience,
who strain in the mud and the muck to move things forward,   10
who do what has to be done, again and again.

I want to be with people who submerge
in the task, who go into the fields to harvest
and work in a row and pass the bags along,
who are not parlor generals and field deserters   15
but move in a common rhythm
when the food must come in or the fire be put out.

The work of the world is common as mud.
Botched, it smears the hands, crumbles to dust.
But the thing worth doing well done   20

has a shape that satisfies, clean and evident.
Greek amphoras for wine or oil,
Hopi vases that held corn, are put in museums
but you know they were made to be used.
The pitcher cries for water to carry   25
and a person for work that is real.

Comprehension and Discussion

1. What are the characteristics of the workers whom Piercy admires? Why does she admire them? Do you admire workers like these? Do you know any? Are you this type of worker? Do you think an employer would want to hire this type of worker? Why? What other types of workers have you observed? With your classmates, discuss the attitudes of contemporary workers toward their jobs. How are their attitudes related to the way they work? Write a journal entry summarizing the class discussion.

2. What does the author mean by "parlor generals and field deserters" (15) on the job? Do you know any parlor generals? Or perhaps a parlor coach? Would a parlor coach be similar to a Monday-morning quarterback? Do you know a parlor doctor or politician? Do you know any field deserters? Discuss parlor generals and field deserters with your classmates. Write a journal entry of your reactions to the discussion.

3. What is "work that is real" (26)? Isn't all work *real*? What is *unreal* work? Have you ever held a job that was unreal work? How about real and unreal schoolwork? Discuss this notion of real and unreal work with your classmates. Write a journal entry on an unreal job you have had to do.

4. In your journal, *paraphrase* (express the meaning in your own words) the last stanza (18–26). Compare your paraphrase of the poem with those of your classmates.

5. What are some of the common everyday chores or tasks that many people prefer not to do? Discuss with your classmates how to make these tasks more enjoyable.

Language and Technique

1. Piercy uses several animal *metaphors* or comparisons for the workers that she admires: seals (6), an ox (8), and water buffalo (9). What does each of these metaphors mean? What does each suggest? Does each metaphor have a favorable connotation or suggestion?

2. What is Piercy *alluding* or referring to when she says, "when the food must come in or the fire must be put out" (17)?

3. Explain the *simile* "The work of the world is common as mud / Botched, it smears the hands, crumbles to dust" (18–19).

4. Piercy says she "loves" certain types of workers (stanzas 1–2). What does she mean by *love*—what is her *connotation* of *love* in this context? What are some *synonyms* of this meaning of *love*? Do you think her use of *love* in this way is appropriate? Why or why not? Discuss her use of the word *love* with your classmates. Does everybody agree? What are your connotations of *love*?

Suggestions for Writing

1. **Sentence.** Write a sentence in which you express an original animal metaphor for a specific type of work.

2. **Paragraph.** Describe the type of worker you most admire. Be sure to give specific characteristics of the workers, as Piercy does in her poem. Try to use some metaphors and similes also.

3. **Essay.** Think of a job you have had. It may be one that you liked or one that you did not enjoy. List the activities and duties of the work that you did. Then write an essay in which you explain specifically why you liked or disliked the work.

4. **Essay.** Referring to your notes on the discussion in question 1 under Comprehension and Discussion, write an essay on the attitudes of contemporary workers toward work. Use specific examples from your observations to support and clarify each attitude.

5. **Essay.** Write an essay on real and unreal schoolwork, providing specific examples of both.

When the Mind Is At Peace

Layman P'ang

LAYMAN P'ANG (P'ang Yun) was a Chinese Buddhist Zen Master in the eighth century. When he reached middle age, he gave his house to the Buddhists for use as a temple and put all his money and belongings on a boat and sank them in a lake because he thought he was too attached to his material possessions. He destroyed them instead of giving them to other people because he feared they would become as attached to them as he was. After that, he and his family earned their living making and selling bamboo utensils. In this poem he sets forth his attitude toward work and peace of mind.

When the Mind Is At Peace

When the mind is at peace,
the world too is at peace.
Nothing real, nothing absent.
Not holding on to reality,
not getting stuck, in the void,   5
you are neither holy nor wise, just
an ordinary fellow who has completed his work.

Comprehension and Discussion

1. What brings peace to Layman P'ang's mind? What brings peace to your
   mind? Write a journal entry on what makes you feel peaceful.
2. What is P'ang's attitude toward work? Do you agree with him? What is
   your attitude toward work? Is it just a means to an end, or do you find
   pleasure in work as P'ang does? Compare Marge Piercy's attitude toward work (p. 277) with that of P'ang.
3. What is Zen Buddhism? Do some research in an encyclopedia or online on this religion. Record what you discover in your journal. How
   are P'ang's attitudes toward individual peace and work consistent with
   Buddhist beliefs? Participate in a class discussion on Buddhist beliefs.
4. Reread the headnote about the author of this poem. Do you think
   P'ang was wise or foolish to get rid of all his possessions? Why? Catholic
   priests and nuns, Buddhist priests, and other religious leaders take a vow
   of poverty. Do you think you could ever do the same?
5. Work does not always bring money. What kinds of work bring you the
   most pleasure? Your job? Housework? Gardening? Taking care of children? Working on cars? What else? Why? What kinds of work bring you
   the least pleasure? Explain.

Language and Technique

1. This poem has no rhyme or regular rhythm, a poetic technique called
   free verse. Compare and contrast this poem to a poem that rhymes. Do
   you prefer one or the other? Why?
2. Why does the poet repeat the phrase "at peace"? (1–2)
3. Why does the poet repeat various negatives: "nothing" (3), "not" (4–5),
   "neither-nor" (6)?
4. Why does the poet end the poem as he does? Do you think this ending
   is effective?

Suggestions for Writing

1. **Sentence.** Write a one-sentence definition of the word *work*. Compare your sentence to those of your classmates.
2. **Paragraph.** Write a paragraph in which you *paraphrase* the poem. To paraphrase means to express the meaning, line by line, in your own words. (See tips on writing a paraphrase, pp. 23–25.) Share your paraphrase with a small group of classmates. As a group, choose the best paraphrase, and share it with the entire class.
3. **Essay.** Write an essay on the best or worst job you have ever had. Explain why and provide specific examples to clarify your reasons.
4. **Essay.** Write an essay explaining real and unreal school work. Provide examples of each to clarify.
5. **Essay.** Write an essay in which you explain how materialism is evident in our society today, and provide specific explanations and examples to clarify and support your ideas.

From *No Shame in My Game*

Katherine S. Newman

KATHERINE S. NEWMAN, an anthropologist and professor of urban studies at Harvard University, is known for her research on city life and city workers. In this essay she argues that the job of fast-food worker, despite its being considered low status, is actually a high-skill job and should be given more respect.

Vocabulary Study

virtuoso (1)	loath (7)
demeaning (2)	mandated (9)
rudimentary (4)	denuded (9)
norms (4)	placate (13)
ethnic (5)	parlay (13, 16)
admonished (6)	devoid (14)
amalgamation (6)	

From No Shame in My Game

1   Elise has worked the "drive-through" window at Burger Barn for the better part of three years. She is a virtuoso in a role that totally defeated one of my brightest doctoral students, who tried to work alongside her for a

week or two. Her job pays only twenty-five cents above the minimum wage (after five years), but it requires that she listen to orders coming in through a speaker, send out a stream of instructions to co-workers who are preparing the food, pick up and check orders for customers already at the window, and receive money and make change, all more or less simultaneously. She has to make sure she keeps the sequence of orders straight so that the Big Burger goes to the man in the blue Mustang and not the woman right behind him in the red Camaro who has now revised her order for the third time. The memory and information-processing skills required to perform this job at a minimally acceptable level are considerable. Elise makes the operation look easy, but it clearly is a skilled job, as demanding as any of the dozen better-paid positions in the Post Office or the Gap stores where she has tried in vain to find higher-status employment.

2   This is not to suggest that working at Burger Barn is as complex as brain surgery. It is true that the component parts of the ballet, the multiple stations behind the counter, have been broken down into the simplest operations. Yet to make them work together under time pressure while minimizing wastage requires higher-order skills. We can think of these jobs as lowly, repetitive, routinized, and demeaning, or we can recognize that doing them right requires their incumbents to process information, coordinate with others, and track inventory. These valuable competencies are tucked away inside jobs that are popularly characterized as utterly lacking in skill.

3   If coordination were the only task required of these employees, then experience would probably eliminate the difficulty after a while. But there are many unpredictable events in the course of a workday that require some finesse to manage. Chief among them are abrasive encounters with customers, who [. . .] often have nothing better to do than rake a poor working stiff over the coals for a missing catsup packet or a batch of french fries that aren't quite hot enough. One afternoon at a Burger Barn cash register is enough to send most sane people into psychological counseling. It takes patience, forbearance, and an eye for the long-range goal (of holding on to your job, of impressing management with your fortitude) to get through some of these encounters. If ever there was an illustration of "people skills," this would be it.

4   Coping with rude customers and coordinating the many components of the production process are made all the more complex by the fact that in most Harlem Burger Barns, the workers hail from a multitude of countries and speak in a variety of languages. Monolingual Spanish speakers fresh from the Dominican Republic have to figure out orders spoken in Jamaican

English. Puerto Ricans, who are generally bilingual, at least in the second generation, have to cope with the English dialects of African Americans. All of these people have to figure out how to serve customers who may be fresh off the boat from Guyana, West Africa, Honduras. The workplace melting pot bubbles along because people from these divergent groups are able to come together and learn bits and snatches of each other's languages—"workplace Spanish" or street English. They can communicate at a very rudimentary level in several dialects, and they know enough about each other's cultural traditions to be able to interpret actions, practices, dress styles, and gender norms in ways that smooth over what can become major conflicts on the street.

5   In a world where residential segregation is sharp and racial antagonism no laughing matter, it is striking how well workers get along with one another. Friendships develop across lines that have hardened in the streets. Romances are born between African Americans and Puerto Ricans, legendary antagonists in the neighborhoods beyond the workplace. This is even more remarkable when one considers the competition that these groups are locked into in a declining labor market. They know very well that employers are using race- and class-based preferences to decide who gets a job, and that their ability to foster the employment chances of friends and family members may well be compromised by a manager's racial biases. One can hear in their conversations behind the counter complaints about how they cannot get their friends jobs because—they believe—the manager wants to pick immigrants first and leave the native-born jobless. In this context, resentment builds against unfair barriers. Even so workers of different ethnic backgrounds are able to reach across the walls of competition and cultural difference.

6   We are often admonished to remember that the United States is a multicultural society and that the workforce of the future will be increasingly composed of minorities and foreigners. Consultants make thousands of dollars advising companies on "diversity training" in order to manage the process of amalgamation. Burger Barn is a living laboratory of diversity, the ultimate melting pot for the working poor. They live in segregated spaces, but they work side by side with people whom they would rarely encounter on the block. If we regard the ability to work in a multiethnic, multilingual environment as a skill, as the consulting industry argues we should, then there is much to recommend the cultural capital acquired in the low-wage workplaces of the inner city.

7   Restaurant owners are loath to cut their profits by calling in expensive repair services when their equipment breaks down, the plumbing goes out, or the electrical wiring blows. Indeed, general managers are required

to spend time in training centers maintained by Burger Barn's corporate headquarters learning how to disassemble the machinery and rebuild it from scratch. The philosophers in the training centers say this is done to teach managers a "ground-up" appreciation for the equipment they are working with. Any store owner will confess, however, that this knowledge is mainly good for holding labor costs down by making it unnecessary to call a repairman every time a milk shake machine malfunctions. What this means in practice is that managers must teach entry-level workers, especially the men (but women as well), the art of mechanical repair and press them into service when the need strikes. Indeed, in one Harlem restaurant, workers had learned how to replace floor-to-ceiling windows (needed because of some bullet holes), a task they performed for well below the prevailing rates of a skilled glazier.

8   Then, of course, there is the matter of money. Burger Barn cash registers have been reengineered to make it possible for people with limited math abilities to operate them. Buttons on the face of the machine display the names of the items on the menu, and an internal program belts out the prices, adds them up, and figures out how much change is due a customer, all with no more than the push of a finger on the right "pad." Still, the workers who man the registers have to be careful to account for all the money that is in the till. Anything amiss and they are in deep trouble: they must replace any missing cash out of their wages. If money goes missing more than once, they are routinely fired. And money can disappear for a variety of reasons: someone makes a mistake in making change, an unexpected interloper uses the machine when the main register worker has gone into the back for some extra mustard packets, a customer changes her mind and wants to return an item (a transaction that isn't programmed into the machine). Even though much of the calculation involved in handling funds is done by computer chips, modest management skills are still required to keep everything in order.

9   While this is not computer programming, the demands of the job are nonetheless quite real. This becomes all too clear, even to managers who are of the opinion that these are "no-skill" jobs, when key people are missing. Workers who know the secrets of the trade—how to cut corners with the official procedures mandated by the company on food preparation, how to "trick" the cash register into giving the right amount of change when a mistake has been made, how to keep the orders straight when there are twenty people backed up in the drive-through line, how to teach new employees the real methods of food production (as opposed to the

official script), and what to do when a customer throws a screaming fit and disrupts the whole restaurant—keep the complicated ballet of a fast food operation moving smoothly. When "experts" disappear from the shift, nothing works the way it should. When they quit, the whole crew is thrown into a state of near-chaos, a situation that can take weeks to remedy as new people come "on line." If these jobs were truly as denuded of skill as they are popularly believed to be, none of this would matter. In fact, however, they are richer in cognitive complexity and individual responsibility than we acknowledge.

10 This is particularly evident when one watches closely and over time how new people are trained. Burger Barn, like most of its competitors, has prepared training tapes designed to show new workers with limited literacy skills how to operate the equipment, assemble the raw materials, and serve customers courteously. Managers are told to use these tapes to instruct all new crew members. In the real world, though, the tapes go missing, the VCR machine doesn't work, and new workers come on board in the middle of the hamburger rush hour when no one has time to sit them down in front of a TV set for a lesson. They have to be taught the old-fashioned way—person to person—with the more experienced and capable workers serving as teachers.

11 One of my graduate students learned this lesson the hard way. A native of Puerto Rico, Ana Ramos-Zayas made her way to a restaurant in the Dominican neighborhood of upper Harlem and put on an apron in the middle of the peak midday demand. Nobody could find the tapes, so she made do by trying to mimic the workers around her. People were screaming at her that she was doing it all wrong, but they were also moving like greased lightning in the kitchen. Ana couldn't figure out how to place the cheese on the hamburger patty so that it fit properly. She tried it one way and then another—nothing came out right. The experienced workers around her, who were all Spanish-speakers, were not initially inclined to help her out, in part because they mistook her for a white girl—something they had not seen behind the counter before. But when they discovered, quite by accident, that Ana was a Latina (she muttered a Spanish curse upon dropping the fifth bun in a row), they embraced her as a fellow migrant and quickly set about making sure she understood the right way to position the cheese.

12 From that day forward, these workers taught Ana all there was to know about the french fry machine, about how to get a milk shake to come out right, about the difference between cooking a fish sandwich and a chicken sandwich, and about how to forecast demand for each so that

the bins do not overfill and force wastage. Without their help, provided entirely along informal lines, Ana would have been at sea. Her experience is typical in the way it reveals the hidden knowledge locked up inside what appears to surface observers (and to many employees themselves) as a job that requires no thinking, no planning, and no skill.

[13]   As entry-level employment, fast food jobs provide the worker with experience and knowledge that ought to be useful as a platform for advancement in the work world. After all, many white-collar positions require similar talents: memory skills, inventory management, the ability to work with a diverse crowd of employees, and versatility in covering for fellow workers when the demand increases. Most jobs require "soft skills" in people management, and those that involve customer contact almost always require the ability to placate angry clients. With experience of this kind, Burger Barn workers ought to be able to parlay their "human capital" into jobs that will boost their incomes and advance them up the status ladder.

[14]   The fact that this happens so rarely is only partially a function of the diplomas they lack or the mediocre test scores they have to offer employers who use these screening devices. They are equally limited by the popular impression that the jobs they hold now are devoid of value. The fast food industry's reputation for de-skilling its work combines with the low social standing of these inner-city employees to make their skills invisible. Employers with better jobs to offer do recognize that Burger Barn veterans are disciplined: they show up for work on time, they know how to serve the public. Yet if the jobs they are trying to fill require more advanced skills (inventory, the ability to learn new technologies, communication skills), Burger Barn is just about the last place that comes to mind as an appropriate proving ground. A week behind the counter of the average fast food restaurant might convince them otherwise, but employers are not anthropologists out looking for a fresh view of entry-level employment. They operate on the basis of assumptions that are widely shared and have neither the time nor the inclination to seek out the hidden skills that Barn employees have developed.

[15]   Perhaps fast food veterans would do better in the search for good jobs if they could reveal that hidden reservoir of human capital. But they are as much the victims of the poor reputation of their jobs as the employers they now seek to impress. When we asked them to explain the skills involved in their work, they invariably looked at us in surprise: "Any fool could do this job. Are you kidding?" They saw themselves as sitting at the bottom of the job chain and the negative valence of their jobs as more or less justified. A lot of energy goes into living with that "truth" and retaining some sense of

dignity, but that effort does not involve rethinking the reputation of their work as skillfree. Hence they are the last people to try to overturn a stereotype and sell themselves to other employers as workers who qualify for better jobs. [16] I have suggested here that neither the employers nor the job-seekers have got it right. There are competencies involved in these jobs that should be more widely known and more easily built upon as the basis for advancement in the labor market. Yet even if we could work some magic along these lines, the limitations built into the social networks of most low-wage workers in the inner city could make it hard to parlay that new reputation into success.

Comprehension and Discussion

1. In paragraphs 2 and 3, Newman describes the job at Burger Barn. Some of her descriptive words and phrases are "valuable competencies," "coordination," "finesse," "abrasive encounters," "patience," "forebearance," "an eye for the long-range goal," and "fortitude." What does each of these characteristics mean? How is each evident on a job? Are they desirable characteristics for any worker? Why? Discuss these characteristics with your classmates.

2. Newman also discusses the types of work and thinking skills that are necessary for a fast-food worker: "information-processing skills" (1), "higher-order skills" (2), "cognitive complexity" (9), "soft skills" (13). What does each of these phrases mean? Are the connotations positive or negative? Are they the types of skills usually associated with a fast-food worker? Do you agree with Newman that these skills are necessary for a fast-food worker?

3. According to Newman, what is the attitude of most employers toward fast-food workers? What is the attitude of the fast-food workers toward themselves? What does she mean by the phrase "negative valence" (15)? In the author's view, are these attitudes correct? Justified? Write a journal entry on your attitude toward fast-food workers.

4. Newman calls the Burger Barn (representing all fast-food businesses) a "workplace melting pot" (4) and a "living laboratory of diversity, the ultimate melting pot for the working poor" (6). What is a melting pot? What is diversity training (6)? Do you agree that a fast-food establishment is a melting pot of contemporary society? Discuss this concept with your classmates, and explain your response to them.

5. In paragraph 5, Newman states that managers often have managerial biases—race- and class-based preferences and racial biases—by which

they make decisions on whom to hire. Do you agree? Based on your experience, take a stance on this issue, write a journal entry, and then discuss it with your classmates.

Language and Technique

1. Newman's essay is an *argument* in which she takes a stance and defends her position. What is the thesis or main idea of this essay? Where does Newman state this thesis? Where does she repeat it? Trace the evidence that she presents to support her position. One of the most useful techniques in argumentative writing is to present the opposing opinion and then *refute* or tear it down. Where in the essay does Newman refute her opposition? Is her refutation effective? The purpose of argument is to persuade the reader that the position of the author is *feasible* (believable and logical). Does Newman convince you to agree with her position? Discuss the effectiveness of her argument with your classmates, and write a journal entry on your opinion.
2. Another technique the author uses is *narration* (1 and 11), which is a type of writing that tells a story, or describes events, usually in their order of occurrence. Why do you think she narrates these specific events? What is the effect of the narrative episodes?
3. Newman uses *contrast* to show what the fast-food job is not, a technique known as *negation* (explaining what something is not): "not . . . as complex as brain surgery" (2) and "not computer programming" (9). Why do you think she chose these two jobs to contrast with fast-food work?
4. Newman often uses *parallel structure* effectively to list a series of items. She uses this technique in sentence 3, paragraph 9; sentence 1, paragraph 12; sentence 2, paragraph 13; sentence 4, paragraph 14; and sentence 5, paragraph 14. Notice how the author uses the colon in paragraph 13 and parentheses in paragraph 14 with the parallel structures. Discuss each of these constructions with your classmates, and explain what is paralleled and what the effect is.

Suggestions for Writing

1. **Sentence.** Write a sentence in which you use parallel structure to list the parts of a job with which you are familiar or to list the benefits of a job.
2. **Paragraph.** Write a paragraph in which you narrate the duties of a particular job or the activities that are involved in learning a specific job.

3. **Essay.** Have you ever worked as a server in a fast-food or other type of restaurant or as a bartender? Were your experiences similar to the activities Newman discusses, or were they different? Write an essay in which you narrate and explain your experiences.
4. **Essay.** Think of a job with which you are familiar that you consider underrated. List the specific ways that you consider it misunderstood or underrated. Then list the specific benefits of the job. Write an argumentative essay in which you explain your opinion of this job and try to persuade your classmates to agree with your position. In your essay, use some of the writing techniques that Newman uses.
5. **Essay.** Can you recall an incident in which you experienced managerial bias? Write an essay in which you narrate this incident, and explain the effects it had on you.

Flexible Futures

Susan Greenfield

SUSAN GREENFIELD is a professor of pharmacology at Oxford University in England and director of the Royal Institution of Great Britain. In this article written in 2003 for *People Management* she looks to the job market of the future.

Vocabulary Study

encapsulate (2)	deemed (6)
paragons (2)	malleable (7)
virtual (3)	transcendence (8)
agenda (3)	proactive (9)
scenario (4)	base (10)
downtime (4)	void (10)
portfolio careers (4)	derived (10)

Flexible Futures

1   Our jobs define who we are, but the blurring of work and home life could lead our sense of who we are to unravel at the seams.

2   Rightly or wrongly, we are defined by our work. It can give us status, encapsulate our skills and knowledge, and even hint at our predispositions

and emotional make-up. In an ideal world, the not-so-distant-future work-force will consist of flexible, curious, commercially savvy individuals who are fully aware of their strengths and weaknesses. These paragons will take responsibility for planning their own career paths. Everyone will be an expert in something, and on the alert for lifelong retraining.

3   As the corporate context for work changes, we shall start to see an ever-increasing proliferation of alliances of smaller, more virtual units that, although independent, will network with each other. Imagine hundreds of small enterprises on sub-contracts as satellites around a bigger company, creating a galaxy of flexible relationships with suppliers, other subcontractors and users. An immediate result will be a more co-operative culture—yet with less security—involving more frequent change of jobs. Driven by the just-in-time agenda on which small, high-risk businesses thrive, firms will have to bid for "employee time" almost on a day-to-day or piecework basis.

4   This imminent scenario means that, as a workforce, we shall have to come to terms with more downtime and the ever-pressing need to update our skills. By taking "portfolio" careers into our own hands, with little regard for corporate loyalty, there will be a big shift towards personal and communications skills rather than maintaining an expertise based solely on knowledge and intelligence. For most of the next generation, flexibility in learning new skills and promoting or adapting to change will be the major requirement as they work their way through smaller companies (99 per cent of UK businesses in 2001 employed fewer than 50 people).

5   However, there will be some fall-out from this scenario; a significant sector of the population will probably be unable to adopt a perpetual learning mindset. The average employee might feel demoralized, inadequate and old as they compete alongside a younger generation comfortable with change and shifting realities.

6   A critical issue is likely to be the degree of stress involved as everyone tries to learn new skills, anxious that, any day now, their current expertise will be deemed obsolete. Who knows if we would wish to conduct our working lives in such a state of red-alert, or whether we would find the constant change stimulating?

7   For the next generations of workers, the world will be interactive and will be seen as inconstant and malleable. For these "people of the screen," there will no longer be a need to read or write, thanks to voice-activated computers and the trend toward icon manipulation and instant access.

Inevitably, therefore, there will be changes not simply in literacy skills but also in imagination.

[8] Future generations will think differently, will have a much narrower attention span and this will be coupled with a transcendence of space and time frames. All training and development will be highly personalized, even to the point where the traditional education system could collapse. The emphasis may instead be on learning by doing, ie by having an experience rather than studying.

[9] All round, it seems likely that traditional boundaries in our lives will be breaking down—between home and work, work and leisure, work and retirement, one generation and the next and even roles within family units. Until now it has been those very boundaries that have defined us. If, as part of the workforce, we need to constantly change, to become proactive rather than reactive and consistent, then our clear-cut sense of who we are might start to unravel.

[10] As a result, we need to be sure about our definition of human nature—it is not merely the ability to control our base desires, nor can it be rooted in our emotions, most, if not all, of which are present in animals. Instead, our behaviours are based on "metaphorical thinking" (viewing one thing in terms of another) and our sense of self. This, in turn, is realised by our prior experiences. In short, we will need to cope with a void, the loss of a self previously derived from work. We need to use our ingenuity to harness new technologies and use the opportunities of business to generate "learning by doing"—it will be for the advantage of all.

Comprehension and Discussion

1. Is Greenfield optimistic or pessimistic about jobs in the future? Why? What evidence do you find in the essay to support your conclusion? Write a journal entry on your conclusion.

2. The author asserts that today we are defined by our work, our jobs. What does she mean by this statement? Do you agree with her? Then in the future, she adds, we will not be defined by our work. Why? What will be the effect of this change on human beings?

3. How does Greenfield describe the workforce of the future? How will the corporate context for work change in the future?

4. In paragraph 4, the author states that in 2001, 99 percent of businesses in the United Kingdom employed fewer than fifty people. The percentage

of businesses in the United States that employ fewer than fifty people is less than that of the United Kingdom, but it is surprisingly high. Look up this statistic for the United States. Many statistical sources are available in the reference section of the college library and online. Some online sources are FedStats (*www.fedstats.gov/*) which provides statistics from over 100 U.S. federal government agencies; Statistical Abstract of the United States (*www.census.gov/statab*); Bureau of Labor Statistics (*www.bls.gov/*); and Economic Statistics (*www.whitehouse.gov/fsbr/esbr.html*). Record the statistics you find in your journal, and discuss them with your classmates.

5. Greenfield states that the traditional education system could collapse (8). Review her argument, and explain why she thinks such a collapse could happen. What changes in the job market could cause such a collapse?

Language and Technique

1. What is Greenfield's thesis sentence? Where does she state the thesis? How does she reaffirm the thesis idea in the conclusion?

2. The author presents a *chain of causes and effects* to support and clarify her prediction for the future. Working with a small group of classmates, trace the causal chain through the essay.

3. No one can really predict the future, but informed people can draw conclusions based on current facts and trends as to what will probably happen in the future. Does Greenfield provide sufficient evidence to prove her predictions are possible and even probable? Is Greenfield qualified to write about this topic? Is this essay primarily exposition or argument? That is, is her purpose to explain (*exposition*) her prediction for the future or is it to convince readers (*argument*) to accept her prediction and to act on it by preparing themselves for what is going to happen in the world of work? Explain.

4. The author uses several phrases in an unfamiliar sense by combining them in a business context. In your journal, write what you think each of the following phrases means, and then discuss them with your classmates.

> "virtual units" (3)
>
> "high-risk businesses" (3)
>
> "piecework basis" (3)
>
> "a state of red-alert" (6)
>
> "icon manipulation" (7)

"become proactive rather than reactive" (9)

"metaphorical thinking" (10)

Suggestions for Writing

1. **Sentence.** Using what you discovered in your research for question 4 under Comprehension and Discussion, write a sentence in which you contrast the percentage of businesses that employ fewer than 50 people people in the United Kingdom and in the United States.
2. **Paragraph.** Write a paragraph in which you state your major field of study in college and the reasons you have chosen this curricular major. If you have not yet decided what you want to major in, write on a field of study in which you are interested or explain why you have not yet determined a major.
3. **Essay.** Write an essay in which you explain how computers are currently used in a job with which you are familiar and how computers have changed this field.
4. **Essay.** Write an essay in which you identify and explain future job opportunities and conditions in the field of your chosen college major or, if you have not yet chosen a major, in a field in which you are interested. You will have to conduct some research in the library or online to write this essay.
5. **Essay.** Talk with someone who has worked for over twenty years in the field of your major or in a field in which you are interested. Ask what changes he or she has experienced in the field and how these changes have affected the work atmosphere and the individual. As a courtesy to your interviewee, arrange an appointment ahead of time and be prepared with questions. Either take notes or tape record (with permission of the interviewee) the discussion. Then write an essay in which you report what you discover. Be sure to draw a conclusion from the discussion, and use that conclusion or generalization as the thesis to unify your essay.

The Do-It-Yourself Economy

Ellen Goodman

ELLEN GOODMAN is a well-known syndicated op-ed columnist. A graduate of Radcliff College, she has worked at *Newsweek*, the *Detroit Free Press*, and now at the *Boston Globe*. She has won many awards, including the Pulitzer Prize for Distinguished Commentary. She focuses on current events, social change, and emerging shifts in our public and private lives. In this essay she tackles the issue of jobs. As you read, pay particular attention to the *tone* (attitude) of her essay.

Vocabulary Study

outsourcing (3)   annals (8)

benignly (4)   tinker (10)

kiosks (5)   alleged (13)

strategic (7)   dragooned (15)

The Do-It-Yourself Economy

1   Have you seen those economists scratching their heads trying to understand the jobless recovery? Every time they run the numbers, they end up with a question mark: How is it possible that only 1,000 new jobs were created in the past month?

2   Well, maybe it's time we let them in our little secret. The economy has created hundreds of thousands of new jobs. Only they aren't in the manufacturing sector. They aren't even in the service economy. They're in the self-service economy.

3   Companies are coming back to life without inviting employees back to work for one simple reason: They are outsourcing the jobs to us. You and I, my fellow Americans, have become the unpaid laborers of a do-it-yourself economy.

4   It all began benignly enough a generation ago when ATMs replaced bank tellers. The ATM was followed by the self-service gas station. At first in the classic bait and switch, we were offered a discount for being our own gas jockey; now we have to pay a premium to have a person fill 'er up.

5   Now, gradually, we are scanning our own groceries at the supermarket, getting our own boarding passes at airport kiosks and picking up movie tickets from machines that don't call in sick, go on vacation or require a pension.

6   People who used to have secretaries now have Microsoft Word. People who used to have travel agents now have the Internet. People who used to drop off their film to be developed have been lured into buying new cameras for the joy of printing or not printing pictures ourselves.

7   We also serve (ourselves) by having to wait longer for the incredible shrinking support system. When was the last time you called your health

plan? The service consists of a hold button, a list of phone options and the strategic decision that sooner or later, a percentage of us will give up.

[8]   Remember 4-1-1? If you actually want information from a phone company today, you have to pay someone in Omaha to give you the new number of a neighbor in Albany.

[9]   If the phone breaks, you may have to fix-it-yourself. A new chapter in the annals of the self-service economy comes from a friend who was told by Verizon to go find the gray box attached to her house and test the line herself. The e-mail instructions told her merrily: "You don't have to be a telephone technician or an electrical engineer." Next year they'll by telling her to climb the telephone pole.

[10]   Then, of course, there is the world of computers. We have all become our own techie. A Harvard Business School professor actually told a reporter recently that we fix them ourselves because: "There's a real love of technology and people want to get inside and tinker with them." My friends have as much of a desire to tinker with computer insides as to perform amateur appendectomies.

[11]   But tech support has become less reliable than child support checks from an ex-husband. *Consumer Reports* says 8 million people a year contact the tech support lines at software companies and one-third of them don't get any help. These same companies have laid off more than 30,000 support workers and replaced them with messages telling us to fix our "infrastructure migration" by performing an "ipconfig/release" and "ipconfig/renew."

[12]   As for online help? If my Web server were managing 9-1-1, I would still be on the floor somewhere gasping for breath. The only part of the self-help economy that keeps us aloft is a battery of teenagers fed and housed solely because they can get the family system back up.

[13]   Oh, and if we finally find someone to perform a so-called service call, we end up with an alleged appointment for the convenient hour known as "when the cows come home."

[14]   I don't know how much labor has been transferred from the paid to the unpaid economy, by the average American now spends an extraordinary amount of time doing work that once paid someone else's mortgage. The only good news is that the corporations can't export the self-help industry to Bombay. Or maybe that's the bad news.

[15]   People, actual human beings who work and interact, are now a luxury item. The rest of us have been dragooned into a invisible unpaid labor force without even noticing. We scan, we surf, we fix and we rant. To which I can only add the motto of the do-it-yourself economy: Help!

Comprehension and Discussion

1. Goodman asks a question in paragraph 1: "How is it possible that only 1,000 jobs were created in the past month?" Then answers it in her essay. What is her answer? What is her "little secret"? Do you agree with her? With your classmates, discuss her answer and your responses.
2. What is the self-service economy? How is it related to outsourcing jobs to us?
3. Working with a group of classmates, identify and list in your journal all the examples Goodman uses to support her claim about the self-service economy.
4. What jobs in the self-service economy do you now perform? Working with a small group of classmates, see how many examples (other than those in Goodman's essay) you can think of. List these self-help jobs in your journal. Then participate in a discussion on this subject with the entire class. Add any additional examples to your list in your journal.
5. What is Goodman's attitude toward this change in our economy—pro, con, or ambivalent? What in the essay leads you to your conclusion? Do you agree with her?

Language and Technique

1. In what two sentences does Goodman state her thesis? Why does she state it twice?
2. What are some of Goodman's sarcastic and humorous comments? Discuss these comments with your classmates. What do these comments add to the essay? How do they affect the *tone* of the essay?
3. Goodman is known for making complex issues understandable to readers. This essay was first published as a column on the page opposite to the editorial page in the *Boston Globe* and was syndicated in other newspapers throughout the nation. Who do you think she wrote this column for? Who are her *audience* (those she intended to read it)? Why? Discuss her audience with your classmates.
4. Find an editorial or column of interest to you in your local newspaper or a magazine. Share your selection with a small group of classmates, and discuss how your selections *compare* (are similar to) and *contrast* (are different from) Goodman's column. In your journal, make notes on the discussion.

Suggestions for Writing

1. **Sentence.** In sentence 3, paragraph 15, Goodman writes a parallel sentence composed of four brief independent clauses or sentences joined by the conjunction *and*: "We scan, we surf, we fix and we rant." Write a similarly constructed sentence on one of the following topics. If you choose to write about something in the past, be sure to use past tense verbs. Share your sentence with a small group of classmates.

A Class	A Football Game
A Concert	How You Feel Right Before A Big Test
A Religious Service	High School Graduation
A Party	A Family Gathering
Shopping	Using a Computer

2. **Paragraph.** Drawing from the class discussions and your journal entries, write a paragraph in which you agree or disagree with Goodman's position.

3. **Essay.** Write an essay in which you narrate all the do-it-yourself jobs you carry out in a typical week in your life. Be sure that your thesis and your tone reveal your attitude toward these activities.

4. **Essay.** Write a *comparison-contrast* essay about a job that has been affected by the trend toward a do-it-yourself economy. Explain what the duties of the job used to be, and then contrast what the duties are now. If you can't think of any specific job, *brainstorm* (make a list by free association in order to generate a chain of ideas) with your classmates on this topic.

5. **Essay.** What do you think has caused the shift toward a do-it-yourself economy? With your classmates, *brainstorm* the contributing factors. Then write an essay on what you consider to be the main reasons for this shift.

A & P

John Updike

JOHN UPDIKE, after graduation from Harvard, worked briefly for the *New Yorker* magazine, but quickly decided to devote himself exclusively to free-lance writing. Since then, he has become one of America's most productive and most highly regarded writers of both fiction and poetry, winning the Pulitzer Prize in 1981. He often writes about male–female relationships, especially in the workplace.

Vocabulary Study

colony (10)   kingpins (19)

varicose veins (10)   gesture (31)

racy (14)

A & P

1   In walks these three girls in nothing but bathing suits. I'm in the third checkout slot, with my back to the door, so I don't see them until they're over by the bread. The one that caught my eye first was the one in the plaid green two-piece. She was a chunky kid, with a good tan and a sweet broad soft-looking can with those two crescents of white just under it, where the sun never seems to hit, at the top of the backs of her legs. I stood there with my hand on a box of HiHo crackers trying to remember if I rang it up or not. I ring it up again and the customer starts giving me hell. She's one of these cash-register-watchers, a witch about fifty with rouge on her cheekbones and no eyebrows, and I know it made her day to trip me up. She'd been watching cash registers for fifty years and probably never seen a mistake before.

2   By the time I got her feathers smoothed and her goodies into a bag— she gives me a little snort in passing, if she'd been born at the right time they would have burned her over in Salem—by the time I get her on her way the girls had circled around the bread and were coming back, without a pushcart, back my way along the counters, in the aisle between the checkouts and the Special bins. They didn't even have shoes on. There was this chunky one, with the two-piece—it was bright green and the seams on the bra were still sharp and her belly was still pretty pale so I guessed she just got it (the suit)—there was this one, with one of those chubby berry-faces, the lips all bunched together under her nose, this one, and a tall one, with black hair that hadn't quite frizzed right, and one of these sunburns right across under the eyes, and a chin that was too long—you know, the kind of girl other girls think is very "striking" and "attractive" but never quite makes it, as they very well know, which is why they like her so much— and then the third one, that wasn't quite so tall. She was the queen. She kind of led them, the other two peeking around and making their shoulders round. She didn't look around, not this queen, she just walked straight on slowly, on these long white prima-donna legs. She came down a little hard on her heels, as if she didn't walk in her bare feet that much, putting down

her heels and then letting the weight move along to her toes as if she was testing the floor with every step, putting a little deliberate extra action into it. You never know for sure how girls' minds work (do you really think it's a mind in there or just a little buzz like a bee in a glass jar?) but you got the idea she had talked the other two into coming in here with her, and now she was showing them how to do it, walk slow and hold yourself straight.

3   She had on a kind of dirty-pink—beige, maybe, I don't know—bathing suit with a little nubble all over it and, what got me, the straps were down. They were off her shoulders looped loose around the cool tops of her arms, and I guess as a result the suit had slipped a little on her, so all around the top of the cloth there was this shining rim. If it hadn't been there you wouldn't have known there could have been anything whiter than those shoulders. With the straps pushed off, there was nothing between the top of the suit and the top of her head except just *her*, this clean bare plane of the top of her chest down from the shoulder bones like a dented sheet of metal tilted in the light. I mean, it was more than pretty.

4   She had sort of oaky hair that the sun and salt had bleached, done up in a bun that was unraveling, and a kind of prim face. Walking into the A & P with your straps down, I suppose it's the only kind of face you *can* have. She held her head so high her neck, coming up out of those white shoulders, looked kind of stretched, but I didn't mind. The longer her neck was, the more of her there was.

5   She must have felt in the corner of her eye me and over my shoulder Stokesie in the second slot watching, but she didn't tip. Not this queen. She kept her eyes moving across the racks, and stopped, and turned so slow it made my stomach rub the inside of my apron, and buzzed to the other two, who kind of huddled against her for relief, and then they all three of them went up the cat-and-dog-food-breakfast-cereal-macaroni-rice-raisins-seasonings-spreads-spaghetti-soft-drinks-crackers-and-cookies aisle. From the third slot I look straight up this aisle to the meat counter, and I watched them all the way. The fat one with the tan sort of fumbled with the cookies, but on second thought she put the package back. The sheep pushing their carts down the aisle—the girls were walking against the usual traffic (not that we have one-way signs or anything)—were pretty hilarious. You could see them, when Queenie's white shoulders dawned on them, kind of jerk, or hop, or hiccup, but their eyes snapped back to their own baskets and on they pushed. I bet you could set off dynamite in an A & P and the people would by and large keep reaching and checking oatmeal off their lists and muttering "Let me see, there was a third thing, began with A, asparagus, no ah,

yes, applesauce!" or whatever it is they do mutter. But there was no doubt, this jiggled them. A few houseslaves in pin curlers even looked around after pushing their carts past to make sure what they had seen was correct.

6   You know, it's one thing to have a girl in a bathing suit down on the beach, where what with the glare nobody can look at each other much anyway, and another thing in the cool of the A & P, under the fluorescent lights, against all those stacked packages, with her feet paddling along naked over our checkerboard green-and-cream rubber-tile floor.

7   "Oh Daddy," Stokesie said beside me. "I feel so faint."

8   "Darling," I said. "Hold me tight." Stokesie's married, with two babies chalked up on his fuselage already, but as far as I can tell that's the only difference. He's twenty-two, and I was nineteen this April.

9   "Is it done?" he asks, the responsible married man finding his voice. I forgot to say he thinks he's going to be manager some sunny day, maybe in 1990 when it's called the Great Alexandrov and Petrooshki Tea Company or something.

10   What he meant was, our town is five miles from the beach, with a big summer colony out on the Point, but we're right in the middle of town, and the women generally put on a shirt or shorts or something before they get out of the car into the street. And anyway these are usually women with six children and varicose veins mapping their legs and nobody, including them, could care less. As I say, we're right in the middle of town, and if you stand at our front doors you can see two banks and the Congregational church and the newspaper store and three real-estate offices and about twenty-seven old freeloaders tearing up Central Street because the sewer broke again. It's not as if we're on the Cape, we're north of Boston and there's people in this town haven't seen the ocean for twenty years.

11   The girls had reached the meat counter and were asking McMahon something. He pointed, they pointed, and they shuffled out of sight behind a pyramid of Diet Delight peaches. All that was left for us to see was old McMahon patting his mouth and looking after them sizing up their joints. Poor kids, I began to feel sorry for them, they couldn't help it.

12   Now here comes the sad part of the story, at least my family says it's sad, but I don't think it's so sad myself. The store's pretty empty, it being Thursday afternoon, so there was nothing much to do except lean on the register and wait for the girls to show up again. The whole store was like a pinball machine and I didn't know which tunnel they'd come out of. After a while they come around out of far aisle, around the light bulbs, records at discount of the Caribbean Six or Tony Martin Sings or some such gunk you wonder

they waste the wax on, sixpacks of candy bars, and plastic toys done up in cellophane that fall apart when a kid looks at them anyway. Around they come, Queenie still leading the way, and holding a little gray jar in her hand. Slots Three through Seven are unmanned and I could see her wondering between Stokes and me, but Stokesie with his usual luck draws an old party in baggy gray pants who stumbles up with four giant cans of pineapple juice (what do these bums *do* with all that pineapple juice? I've often asked myself) so the girls come to me. Queenie puts down the jar and I take it into my fingers icy cold. Kingfish Fancy Herring Snacks in Pure Sour Cream: 49¢. Now her hands are empty, not a ring or a bracelet, bare as God made them, and I wonder where the money's coming from. Still with that prim look she lifts a folded dollar bill out of the hollow at the center of her nubbed pink top. The jar went heavy in my hand. Really, I thought that was so cute.

13   Then everybody's luck begins to run out. Lengel comes in from haggling with a truck full of cabbages on the lot and is about to scuttle into that door marked MANAGER behind which he hides all day when the girls touch his eye. Lengel's pretty dreary, teaches Sunday school and the rest, but he doesn't miss that much. He comes over and says, "Girls, this isn't the beach."

14   Queenie blushes, though maybe it's just a brush of sunburn I was noticing for the first time, now that she was so close. "My mother asked me to pick up a jar of herring snacks." Her voice kind of startled me, the way voices do when you see the people first, coming out so flat and dumb yet kind of tony, too, the way it ticked over "pick up" and "snacks." All of a sudden I slid right down her voice into her living room. Her father and the other men were standing around in ice-cream coats and bow ties and the women were in sandals picking up herring snacks on toothpicks off a big glass plate and they were all holding drinks the color of water with olives and sprigs of mint in them. When my parents have somebody over they get lemonade and if it's a real racy affair Schlitz in tall glasses with "They'll Do It Every Time" cartoons stenciled on.

15   "That's all right," Lengel said. "But this isn't the beach." His repeating this struck me as funny, as if it had just occurred to him, and he had been thinking all these years the A & P was a great big dune and he was the head lifeguard. He didn't like my smiling—as I say he doesn't miss much—but he concentrates on giving the girls that sad Sunday-school-superintendent stare.

16   Queenie's blush is no sunburn now, and the plump one in plaid, that I liked better from the back—a really sweet can—pipes up, "We weren't doing any shopping. We just came in for the one thing."

17   "That makes no difference," Lengel tells her, and I could see from the way his eyes went that he hadn't noticed she was wearing a two-piece before. "We want you decently dressed when you come in here."

18   "We *are* decent," Queenie says suddenly, her lower lip pushing, getting sore now that she remembers her place, a place from which the crowd that runs the A & P must look pretty crummy. Fancy Herring Snacks flashed in her very blue eyes.

19   "Girls, I don't want to argue with you. After this come in here with your shoulders covered. It's our policy." He turns his back. That's policy for you. Policy is what the kingpins want. What the others want is juvenile delinquency.

20   All this while, the customers had been showing up with their carts but, you know, sheep, seeing a scene, they had all bunched up on Stokesie, who shook open a paper bag as gently as peeling a peach, not wanting to miss a word. I could feel in the silence everybody getting nervous, most of all Lengel, who asks me, "Sammy, have you rung up their purchase?"

21   I thought and said "No" but it wasn't about that I was thinking. I go through the punches, 4, 9, GROC, TOT—it's more complicated than you think, and after you do it often enough, it begins to make a little song, that you hear words to, in my case "Hello (*bang*) there, you (*gung*) hap-py *pee*-pul (*splat*)!"—the *splat* being the drawer flying out. I uncrease the bill, tenderly as you may imagine, it just having come from between the two smoothest scoops of vanilla I had ever known were there, and pass a half and a penny into her narrow pink palm, and nestle the herrings in a bag and twist its neck and hand it over, all the time thinking.

22   The girls, and who'd blame them, are in a hurry to get out, so I say "I quit" to Lengel quick enough for them to hear, hoping they'll stop and watch me, their unsuspected hero. They keep right on going, into the electric eye; the door flies open and they flicker across the lot to their car, Queenie and Plaid and Big Tall Goony-Goony (not that as raw material she was so bad), leaving me with Lengel and a kink in his eyebrow.

23   "Did you say something, Sammy?"

24   "I said I quit."

25   "I thought you did."

26   "You didn't have to embarrass them."

27   "It was they who were embarrassing us."

28   I started to say something that came out "Fiddle-de-doo." It's a saying of my grandmother's, and I know she would have been pleased.

29   "I don't think you know what you're saying," Lengel said.

30   "I know you don't," I said. "But I do." I pull the bow at the back of my apron and start shrugging it off my shoulders. A couple customers that had been heading for my slot begin to knock against each other, like scared pigs in a chute.

31   Lengel sighs and begins to look very patient and old and gray. He's been a friend of my parents for years. "Sammy, you don't want to do this to your Mom and Dad," he tells me. It's true, I don't. But it seems to me that once you begin a gesture it's fatal not to go through with it. I fold the apron, "Sammy" stitched in red on the pocket, and put it on the counter, and drop the bow tie on top of it. The bow tie is theirs, if you've ever wondered. "You'll feel this for the rest of your life," Lengel says, and I know that's true, too, but remembering how he made that pretty girl blush makes me so scrunchy inside I punch the No Sale tab and the machine whirs "pee-pul" and the drawer splats out. One advantage to this scene taking place in summer, I can follow this up with a clean exit, there's no fumbling around getting your coat and galoshes, I just saunter into the electric eye in my white shirt that my mother ironed the night before, and the door heaves itself open, and outside the sunshine is skating around on the asphalt.

32   I took around for my girls, but they're gone, of course. There wasn't anybody but some young married screaming with her children about some candy they didn't get by the door of a powder-blue Falcon station wagon. Looking back in the big windows, over the bags of peat moss and aluminum lawn furniture stacked on the pavement, I could see Lengel in my place in the slot, checking the sheep through. His face was dark gray and his back stiff, as if he'd just had an injection of iron, and my stomach kind of fell as I felt how hard the world was going to be to me hereafter.

Comprehension and Discussion

1. What job does Sammy, the narrator, have at the A & P? What is his relationship to his boss? How does this relationship change? What causes the relationship to change?

2. Have you ever worked in a grocery story or held a similar job? Have you ever had a boss similar to Lengel? What was your relationship to him or her? Write a journal entry on your boss.

3. How does the narrator describe the people in the store? How do the three girls contrast to the other customers? Why does the narrator call one of the girls Queenie? Is that an appropriate name for her? Why does she blush when Lengel speaks to the girls (14, 16)?

4. Updike suggests a class difference between the employees of the grocery store and the girls who come in to buy canned herring snacks. What specific words and phrases provide clues to this class distinction? What do these references to class tell you about Sammy, the narrator?
5. Why does Sammy quit his job? Is his action believable? Is it justified? Is it foolish? Would you have done the same? Take a position on his action stating your position. Write a journal entry and share it with your classmates.

Language and Technique

1. The setting for Updike's story is at the A & P. What is the A & P? Is there an A & P where you live? What stores are you familiar with that are similar to the A & P? What specific details does Updike use to help you visualize the A & P? What is the atmosphere or *mood of* the place? How does the author convey this mood?
2. Some of Updike's *allusions* or references are to items familiar to people in the 1960s when this short story was published: "A & P" (title), "HiHo crackers" (1), "Great Alexandrov and Petrooshki Tea Company" (9), and "Falcon" (32). Do you know what these references mean? If not, discuss them with your classmates or ask an older person you know. Does lack of knowledge of these references interfere with your understanding of the story? Why or why not?
3. In paragraph 12, Updike uses an *analogy* or comparison of the grocery store to a pinball machine. Is it effective? Explain. Find other examples of *figurative comparisons* (*analogies*, *similes*, *metaphors*) in the story, and discuss their meaning and effectiveness with your classmates.
4. Updike uses an *informal conversational level of language* in keeping with the story being told from the point of view of the young man Sammy. Find specific examples of conversational words and phrases. Are they realistic? Are they the expressions you would expect from a young man working in a grocery story?

Suggestions for Writing

1. **Sentence.** In sentence 1 of paragraph 4, Updike describes Queenie's hair: "She had sort of oaky hair that the sun and salt had bleached, done up in a bun that was unraveling." Look around you in one of your classes, at work, or at a restaurant, and find a person with interesting hair and observe it carefully. Then write a sentence in which you describe this person's hair

specifically, similar to Updike's description. Share your sentence with your classmates, and see if they can identify the person you have described.

2. **Paragraph.** Study Updike's description of the three girls in bathing suits in paragraphs 1–5. Notice the *specific details* he includes and the order in which he arranges these details. Then think of a striking person or small group of people with which you are familiar. Make a list of as many specific *visual details* as you can recall (at least ten) and write a paragraph in which you describe the person or group using the specific details. Share your draft with one of your classmates, and ask if he or she can see the person or people clearly. If not, revise the paragraph until the picture is clear. Ask your classmate to give you some specific suggestions to improve your paragraph, and do the same for your classmate.

3. **Essay.** Narrate a memorable experience you have had on a job. It may be a pleasant or an unpleasant experience. Include how you felt as it was happening, and what you did as a result of the event. Use informal conversational language as Updike does in his short story.

4. **Essay.** Write a *character sketch* of a boss you have had. Include a physical description of him or her, personality traits (with specific examples of each), and typical actions and reactions.

5. **Essay.** Write an essay in which you narrate a moment in your life when you suddenly "felt how hard the world was going to be" (32) to you after that.

My Worst Job Ever

Matthew Derek

MATTHEW DEREK wrote this essay as a personal experience essay assignment early in College Composition I. As you read his essay, think about two things: (1) What did he learn from the experience? (2) Have you had a job as bad as this one? Did you learn anything from it? (3) Does Derek agree with Newman's attitude toward fast-food jobs (p. 281)?

My Worst Job Ever

[1] Smoldering it burns with an existence so small and futile. I watch as it slowly fizzles into a mere skeleton of its former self. It has been dejuiced and shrunk. I think about that with a bit of sadness. My boss walks up to me. "Matt, wake up. We're wrapped!" My name is Matt Derek and this was my job.

² I started working at McDonald's when I was in high school. I was at the edge in my household. If I didn't get a job, I would be kicked out of the house. With some hesitation, I got a job at MacD's. My buddy worked there, and he was in tight with management. I hoped that association would work out well for me. I was hired at top pay—a whole six dollars and fifteen cents an hour. I had a job, and my dad was happy. However, this job turned out to be the worst job I have ever had.

³ One of the reasons it was a bad job was the pay. Yes, I was hired at McDonald's for top pay for a cook, but $6.15 was not enough for me to pay my expenses. I worked parttime and started at 20 hours a week, so I made only $123 gross a week or $392 a month. Of course, income tax and social security were taken out, so I was left with only about $78 a week or $312 a month. Out of that I had to pay car insurance, which was over half of my bi-weekly pay. I needed the insurance to drive my father's beat-up old truck to work when I didn't get dropped off and picked up. Also, now that I had a job, my parents expected me to pay something for room and board at home, and they expected $20 a week from me. That took all that I made. I had thought I would have a little money to spend like I wanted to, but that didn't happen, and I still had to ask my dad for money for school.

⁴ Another bad part of this job was my working conditions. My job as a cook was monotonous, just row after row of beef patties. Every once in a while when another worker was absent, I got to move along the assembly line and put the dressings on the bun or even cook french fries. All day long I smelled the grease from the frying, sizzling burgers, and the smell got in my clothes, my nose, and my hair. I saw and smelled so many hamburgers that I still can't eat them—anywhere. And my boss was a real jerk, always on me to work harder and telling me how lucky I was to have this job.

⁵ Another reason that it was such a bad situation was that it interfered with my social life. Between school and work, I had hardly any time to hang out. I did have my own transportation, so my friends liked to go places with me but only when I had enough money for gas and that was not often.

⁶ Things got better for a while because the company built a new store near my home, and they needed experienced workers to go over and train the new employees. The only reason I was sent over was because my buddy—who was to be the boss at the new store—requested it. I was out of school by this time, so he increased my hours to 30 a week. That may sound good, but I was trying to save for a new car—the old truck had stopped running—and I had to save a lot. My friends pretty much disappeared. I had always been the one with the truck, so when I lost it,

everyone went his or her own way. This was my day: I got dropped off at work, worked 10 or more hours a day, got picked up from work, went home, went to bed, and did it again. Only on the days I was off did I even get to watch television.

7 I finally got my car, and guess what? I even got promoted. I got another raise, so I started making seven dollars an hour. I was taking home over four hundred dollars bi-weekly, so I decided to get my own place. Big mistake! Let me put it to you this way: when a nineteen-year-old wants to get his own place, it's not just because he wants to be independent. I would go to work at eight in the morning and stay out partying till four in the morning. When I was at work, I was tired, drowsy, and grumpy. My boss—my good buddy—cut my hours, and I could not support myself anymore. Needless to say, the apartment thing didn't last very long, and I had to move back home with my family.

8 Eventually everything came full circle. I still had the job, I moved back to my parents' home, and everyday I stared at those rows and rows of smoldering meat patties. I felt as beaten and alone as they were. I looked around my workplace thinking to myself, "Is this my life? Is this where I will be forever, a professional burger flipper?" I contemplated my situation and concluded that if I were still flipping burgers at fifty, I'd probably die. So I decided to quit working at McDonald's and to start college so I would be qualified to get a better job. I will say though if I hadn't worked at McDonald's I would have never met my girlfriend. Not to mention that the experience does look good on an application.

Checklist for Revising and Editing

Following is a list of questions to guide you in the process of revising and editing your essays. Use the following questions to respond to the essay and to check for any point of needed revision. You may also use it to respond to and evaluate essays by other writers, whether students or professional writers.

1. **Sources:** What sources of information does the author draw upon—experience and memory, observation, reading and research, conversation and interview?

2. **Purpose:** What is the author's purpose in this essay—to narrate, to develop, to explain, to argue or convince, or a combination of these? Does the author accomplish the purpose?

3. **Thesis:** What is the thesis sentence or main point? Does the author state the thesis or imply it? Does the author make the thesis clear?

4. **Unity:** Does the author stick to the thesis? Is every statement in the essay directly relate to the main idea?

5. **Structure and Organization:**

   A. **Introduction**
      1) Does the introduction make clear the subject of the essay?
      2) Does the introduction state or imply the thesis sentence clearly?
      3) Does the introduction grab your attention and interest, and make you want to read the essay?

   B. **Body**
      1) What are the major points for development in the essay?
      2) How does the author organize the points of development of the essay? Is the order of points clear? Why does the author put the points in this order?
      3) Is this order appropriate for the ideas of the essay?
      4) Are there any other points or information that the author should have included? Why?

   C. **Conclusion**
      1) Does the conclusion relate directly to the introduction and to the thesis, as well as to the points in the body of the essay?
      2) Does the conclusion provide a sense of finality or ending to the essay?
      3) Is the conclusion effective?

6. **Development**

   A. What kinds of development does the author use to expand, support, and clarify the general assertions—narration, description, example, process, cause and effect, classification, example, comparison and contrast, definition, negation, statistics, expert opinion?

   B. Does the author provide sufficient evidence to make the subpoints clear and persuasive?

7. **Coherence**

   A. Does the essay flow smoothly from idea to idea? From sentence to sentence? From paragraph to paragraph?

   B. How does the author connect the ideas throughout the essay? What Bridges and signposts does the author use to help the reader navigate through the essay?

1) What key ideas, words, and phrases does the author repeat?

2) What pronouns does the author use?

3) What transitional words and phrases does the author use to connect paragraphs? To connect sentences within paragraphs?

8. **Rhetorical Patterns:** What rhetorical patterns does the author use—narration, description, exposition, argument, example or illustration, enumeration, cause, effect, comparison, contrast, analysis, classification, process, definition, problems to solution?

9. **Language Skills and Proofreading**

A. Has the author proofread and edited the essay carefully for correctness, appropriateness, and effectiveness of language skills?

- Spelling
- Capitalization
- Punctuation
- Grammar
- Sentence structure
- Word choice

B. What, if anything, should be changed? Why?

10. **Response and Evaluation**

A. Does the author effectively fulfill the purpose and/or assignment in the essay?

B. What is the strongest aspect of the essay? What do you like best? Why?

C. What could be changed to improve the essay? Why?

CHAPTER ELEVEN

Science and Technology

Ours is the age which is proud of machines that think and suspicious of men who try to.

—H. M. JONES

Suggestions for Journal Entries

1. Do you agree with Jones's statement above? Why or why not?
2. What is the most interesting or fascinating area of science to you? Explain.
3. What are the advantages and disadvantages of the new technologies?
4. Do science and humanities conflict?
5. Do science and religion conflict?
6. What technology do you use every day?
7. Our world has moved from the Industrial Age to the Information Age. What will be the next age?
8. Why should people who are not specialists in science and technology keep themselves informed of recent discoveries and developments in these areas?
9. When computers were first in widespread use, experts said that computers would lead to a paperless society? Has this happened?
10. How is science fiction related to real life?
11. What developments in science or technology (health, business, education, travel, personal gadgets, computers, art, etc.) would you like to see?

In Computers

Alan P. Lightman

ALAN P. LIGHTMAN is a professor of English, a specialist in contemporary literature, and a literary critic. He writes articles for academic journals as well as poetry. In the following poem he sets forth a brief view of the future of the world.

In Computers

In the magnets of computers will
  be stored

Blend of sunset over wheat
  fields.
Low thunder of gazelle.   5
Light, sweet wind on high
  ground.
Vacuum stillness spreading from
  a thick snowfall.

Men will sit in rooms   10
  upon the smooth, scrubbed earth
  or stand in tunnels on the moon
  and instruct themselves in how it
  was.
Nothing will be lost.   15
Nothing will be lost.

Comprehension and Discussion

1. What four things does the speaker say will be stored on computers (3–9)? How will they be stored? What do these items represent or symbolize? Write a journal entry on what these items suggest to you. Why do you think the poet chooses these items to highlight? What other information and material is stored on computers? What do you store on your computer hard drive, disks, or CDs? Write a journal entry on what you store in a computer or disk or CD.

2. In this poem what has happened to the world that we know? What evidence in the poem brings you to this conclusion?

3. Who are the men in line 10? What are they doing?

4. What is the meaning of lines 13–14? Paraphrase these lines in your journal.
5. What is the meaning of lines 15–16? Paraphrase these lines in your journal.

Language and Technique

1. What *visual images* do you find in the poem? Working with a small group of classmates, find and discuss the meaning—both *denotative* and *connotative*—of each image.
2. How does the *mood* conveyed by the poem change from stanza 2 to stanza 3? Does the mood change again at the end of the poem? Discuss these mood shifts with your classmates.
3. What is the denotative and the connotative meaning of the word *instruct* in line 13?
4. Why is the sentence "Nothing will be lost" (15–16) repeated at the end of the poem? What is the *irony* in this statement?

Suggestions for Writing

1. **Sentence.** Write a sentence in which you express a visual image of something in the scene around you now.
2. **Paragraph.** Write a paragraph of what you predict for the future of the world. Share your paragraph with your classmates.
3. **Essay.** Write a personal essay about your experiences with computers and what you think and feel about them.
4. **Essay.** Write an essay in which you provide a synopsis of a science fiction novel, short story, or movie that projects the future of the world. Then indicate whether you believe the selection's forecast of the future is plausible or believable, and why.
5. **Essay.** Write an essay in which you explain how information is stored in computers. Your classmates are your audience of readers, a general audience probably unfamiliar with the electronic process.

The Leading Edge

Sylvia Hicks

SYLVIA HICKS is an English professor and writer who has published poems, articles, reviews, and books. Her major interests, reflected in her writings, are education and related social issues. In 1983 the poet attended an international conference on how technology is affecting our lives. Over 6000 people attended the meeting in Vancouver, Canada, but only 6 were in the arts and humanities like the poet; all the other attendees were scientists and engineers. In this poem the poet uses the voice of a speaker reflecting on this conference and on changes in our world and possibilities for the-future. As you read, compare and contrast her view of the future with that of Lightman (p. 311).

The Leading Edge

today we are   on the brink
of a new world
of technology   all around
evidence of changing

the nature of work   5
the process of learning
the way of thinking
the manner of living
what we value
who we are   10

today we are   on the brink
of an unknown world

a world of burnout   fallout   crack
of stimulation   creativity   reality
a world in a race between education and disaster   15

the more things change
the more they stay the same
or so the wise one says

today we are   on the brink

today   we are   20

Comprehension and Discussion

1. What does the title "The Leading Edge" mean? What *connotations* or suggestions do you have of this phrase "leading edge"? What does the word *brink* mean? What are your *connotations* of this word? How does the line "today we are on the brink" relate to the title "The Leading Edge"?

Why do you think the poet used the word *brink* instead of *edge* in the poem? Write a journal entry on the *denotations* and *connotations* of these statements, and discuss the meanings with your classmates.

2. In lines 1–4, the speaker says that today we are on the edge of a new technological world and that there is evidence of change all around us. Then in lines 5–11, the speaker lists 6 examples of change. What are they? Do you agree that these things in our world are changing? Participate in a class discussion of how these changes have and still are affecting our lives and of other changes that are also occurring. In your journal, summarize the discussion.

3. In lines 13–14, the speaker presents two possible future worlds that we may face. Write a journal entry on the meaning of each of these possibilities. Participate in a class discussion comparing and contrasting these two worlds and their implications. Which world do you think is in our future? Why?

4. What does line 15 mean? Participate in a class discussion on the meaning of this statement. Do you agree with this comment?

5. What does the last line (20) mean?

Language and Technique

1. Why does the poet repeat the line "today we are on the brink" three times (1, 11, 19)?

2. Throughout the poem, the writer uses spaces instead of traditional punctuation (such as commas, colons, dashes, or periods) to indicate breaks and pauses in the meaning. In the last line "today   we are" (20), what is the impact of the space between *today* and *we*? Do you think this technique is effective? Why?

3. The poet uses *parallelism* several times in the poem. One example is in lines 11, 13, and 15: "an unknown world," "a world," "a world." What is the impact of the parallel repetition on readers? Working with a small group of your classmates, find other examples of parallelism in this poem, and write them in your journal.

4. What is the *tone* or attitude of this poem? Is the speaker optimistic? Or pessimistic? Or realistic? Or something else? Why?

Suggestions for Writing

1. **Sentence.** Write a sentence in which you use parallel repetition to emphasize an idea.

2. **Paragraph.** With a small group of classmates, discuss the ideas, the worldview, and the tone of this poem and the Lightman poem (p. 311). In your journal, take notes on the discussion. Then write a paragraph in which you compare and contrast this poem to the Lightman poem.

3. **Essay.** Write an essay in which you explain your ideal world for the future. Be sure to state specific characteristics of your world and examples of each characteristic.

4. **Essay.** Write a cause and effect essay in which you identify one or more recent technological changes, and explain how this technological change has affected your life.

5. **Essay.** In line 15, the speaker suggests that education can prevent worldwide disaster? Do you agree or disagree? Write an essay in which you respond to this idea. Be sure to provide specific evidence and examples to support your position.

My Magical Metronome

Lewis Thomas

LEWIS THOMAS was born in New York and educated at Princeton and Harvard. He has worked as a research pathologist and a medical administrator. The writer of several collections of essays about various medical issues, Thomas writes this essay from the point of view of a patient, not a doctor.

Vocabulary Study

metronome (title)	escalation (12)
unwarranted (8)	shore (12)
irrepressible (8)	kited (13)
myocardium (8)	ventricle (13)
cardiologist (10)	

My Magical Metronome

1   I woke up, late one Friday night, feeling like the Long Island Railroad thumping at top speed over a patch of bad roadbed. Doctor-fashion, I took my pulse and found it too fast to count accurately. I heaved out of bed and sat in a chair, gloomy, wondering what next. A while later the train slowed down, nearly stopped, and my pulse rate had suddenly dropped to 35. I decided to do some telephoning.

2   Next thing I knew, I was abed in the intensive care unit of the hospital down the street, intravenous tubes in place, wires leading from several places on my chest and from electrodes on my arms and legs, lights flashing from the monitor behind my bed. If I turned my head sharply I could see the bouncing lines of my electrocardiogram, a totally incomprehensible graffito, dropped beats, long stretches of nothing followed by what looked like exclamation points. The handwriting on the wall, I thought. And illiterate at that.

3   Now it was Sunday, late afternoon, the monitor still jumpy, alarm lights still signaling trouble, all the usual drugs for restoring cardiac rhythm having been tried, and handwriting still a scrawl. The cardiovascular surgeon at the foot of my bed was explaining that it would have to be a pacemaker, immediately, Sunday late afternoon. What did I think?

4   What I thought, and then said, was that this was one of the things about which a man is not entitled to his own opinion. Over to you, I said.

5   About an hour later I was back from the operating theater. Theater is right; the masked surgeon center stage, wonderfully lit, several colleagues as appreciative audience, me as the main prop. The denouement was that famous *deus ex machina* being inserted into the prop's chest wall, my gadget now, my metronome. Best of all, my heart rate an absolutely regular, dependable, reliable 70, capable of speeding up on demand but inflexibly tuned to keep it from dropping below 70. The battery guaranteed to last seven years or thereabouts before needing changing. Plenty of time to worry about that, later on.

6   Home in a couple of days, up and around doing whatever I felt like, up and down stairs, even pushing furniture from one place to another, then back to work.

7   Afterthought:

8   A new, unwarranted but irrepressible kind of vanity. I had come into the presence of a technological marvel, namely me. To be sure, the pacemaker is a wonderful miniature piece of high technology, my friend the surgeon a skilled worker in high technology, but the greatest of wonders is my own pump, my myocardium, capable of accepting electronic instructions from that small black box and doing exactly what it is told. I am exceedingly pleased with my machine-tooled, obedient, responsive self. I would never have thought I had it in me, but now that I have it in me, ticking along soundlessly, flawlessly, I am subject to waves of pure vanity.

[9] Another surprise:

[10] I do not want to know very much about my new technology. I do not even want to have the reasons for needing it fully explained to me. As long as it works, and it does indeed, I prefer to be as mystified by it as I can. This is a surprise. I would have thought that as a reasonably intelligent doctor-patient I would be filled with intelligent, penetrating questions, insisting on comprehending each step in the procedure, making my own decisions, even calling the shots. Not a bit of it. I turn out to be the kind of patient who doesn't want to have things explained, only to have things looked after by the real professionals. Just before I left the hospital, the cardiologist brought me a manila envelope filled with reprints, brochures, the pacemaker manufacturer's instructions for physicians listing all the indications, warnings, the things that might go wrong. I have the envelope somewhere, on a closet shelf I think, unexamined. I haven't, to be honest, the faintest idea how a pacemaker works, and I have even less curiosity.

[11] This goes against the wisdom of the times, I know. These days one reads everywhere, especially in the popular magazines, that a patient should take more responsibility, be more assertive, insist on second and third opinions, and above all have everything fully explained by the doctor or, preferably, the doctors, before submitting to treatment. As a physician, I used to think this way myself, but now, as a successful patient, I feel different. Don't explain it to me, I say, go ahead and fix it.

[12] I suppose I should be feeling guilty about this. In a way I do, for I have written and lectured in the past about medicine's excessive dependence on technology in general, and the resultant escalation in the cost of health care. I have been critical of what I called "halfway technologies," designed to shore things up and keep flawed organs functioning beyond their appointed time. And here I am, enjoying precisely this sort of technology, eating my words.

[13] Pacemakers have had a bad press recently, with stories about overutilization, kited prices, kickbacks to doctors and hospitals, a scandal. Probably the stories, some of them anyway, are true. But I rise to the defense of the gadget itself, in which I now have so personal a stake. If anyone had tried to tell me, long ago when I was a medical student, that the day would come when a device the size of a cigarette lighter could be implanted permanently over the heart, with wires extending to the interior of the ventricle, dominating the heart's conduction system and regulating the rhythm with perfection, I would have laughed in his face. If then he had told me that this would happen one day to me, I would have gotten sore. But here it is, incomprehensible, and I rather like it.

Glossary

denouement (5)—the ending of a serious drama in which all the loose ends are tied up and all the problems resolved

Deus ex machina **(5)**—literally, the god of the machines in Greek drama; when the gods come down and intervene to end the play

Comprehension and Discussion

1. Thomas breaks his essay into two parts—Part 1, paragraphs 1–6; Part 2, paragraphs 7–13. What does he discuss in each part? Is this a logical and appropriate organization for his essay? Discuss his organization with your classmates.

2. What is a metronome? Why does Thomas call his pacemaker "My Magical Metronome"?

3. When the cardiologist asked Thomas what he thought about putting in a pacemaker immediately, what did Thomas reply? Why do you think he replied as he did? Do you agree with him? Write a journal entry on your response to his belief. Share your entry with your classmates.

4. How did Thomas respond to the pacemaker being placed in his chest? What were his two afterthoughts when he reflected on his experience?

5. What was Thomas's attitude toward technology in medicine before he had the pacemaker in his chest? What does he mean by the phrase "halfway technologies" (12)? How did his attitude change?

Language and Technique

1. Review Thomas's description of his heart attack (1). He follows the advice of Shirley Jackson: "Show. Don't tell." Instead of saying, "I woke up one night with my chest hurting real bad," he describes how he felt in detail so that readers can feel what he felt; in other words, he *shows* the readers what happened. With a small group of classmates, discuss how the author makes this description clear, precise, and vivid.

2. How does the author describe the electrocardiogram? Is this description another instance in which he *shows* instead of just tells?

3. Study Thomas's metaphor in which he compares the operating room to a theater (5). Discuss this metaphor with your classmates.

4. How does Thomas dramatize and make specific the surprise and incomprehensibility he feels about the pacemaker? (13)

Suggestions for Writing

1. **Sentence.** Rewrite one of the following sentences to *show*, not tell. Make the reader see what you see.

   The sunset was beautiful.

   The wreck was terrible.

   The storm was bad.

   The room was crowded.

   The clothes were horrible.

2. **Paragraph.** Using Thomas's metaphor of the theater (5) as a sample, write a paragraph on one of the following metaphors:

   The Classroom as Theater

   The Classroom as a Factory

   The Automobile as an Extension of the Owner

   Human Beings as Robots

   Life as a Stage

   The Human Face as a Mask

   The Eyes as a Window of the Soul

3. **Essay.** Write a narrative-descriptive essay in which you recount a memorable experience. *Show* your readers what happened to you so that they can share your experience. Use as many appeals to the senses—sight, sound, smell, taste, feel—as possible.

4. **Essay.** Do you think technology in medicine has gone too far? Write an argumentative essay in which you take a stand in answer to this question and try to convince your readers/classmates to agree with you. Remember that specific evidence is necessary to argue convincingly.

5. **Essay.** In paragraph 4 Thomas states that putting in the pacemaker "was one of the things about which a man is not entitled to his own opinion." Do you agree with him? What do you think about a patient's responsibility for his own health (11)? What kind of patient was Thomas? What kind of patient are you? Write an essay in which you state and develop your position on how much responsibility an individual should exercise for his or her own health.

From Forced Technology to High Tech/High Touch
John Naisbitt

JOHN NAISBITT is a social forecaster and consultant to many large corporations. He studies and writes about social, economic, political, and technological movements in the United States. In 1982 Naisbitt published *Megatrends: Ten New Directions Transforming Our Lives*, an examination of the forces changing the world and shaping the future as the society moved from the industrial era to the information era. This selection is from his discussion of the second megatrend, the movement from forced technology to a balance of high tech and high touch.

Vocabulary Study

evolution (5)	pragmatic (12)
bellwether (8)	advent (12)
phenomenon (9, 11)	ballast (13)
extrapolation (10)	proliferating (15)
dynamic (10)	compensations (17)
taboos (12)	verge (21)

From Forced Technology to High Tech/High Touch

1   High tech/high touch is a formula I use to describe the way we have responded to technology. What happens is that whenever new technology is introduced into society, there must be a counterbalancing human response—that is, *high touch*—or the technology is rejected. The more high tech, the more high touch.

2   The parallel growth of high tech/high touch took place during the last three decades, a period that appeared chaotic, but that really had its own rhythm and sense.

3   The alienation of the 1950s was a response to the most intensely industrialized period in our history. During this decade of the gray flannel suit and the organization man, fully 65 percent of our workforce were in industrial occupations, many in assembly-line regimentation. More workers, 32 percent, were unionized than would ever be again.

4   During both the 1950s and the 1960s, we mass-marketed the products of that industrial era—products whose regimented uniformities mirrored their industrial base. High tech was everywhere—in the factory, at

the office, in our communication, transportation, and health care systems and, finally, even in our homes.

5 But something else was growing alongside the technological invasion. Our response to the high tech all around us was the evolution of a highly personal value system to compensate for the impersonal nature of technology. The result was the new self-help or personal growth movement, which eventually became the human potential movement.

6 Much has been written about the human potential movement, but to my knowledge no one has connected it with technological change. In reality, each feeds the other—high tech/high touch.

7 Now, at the dawn of the twenty-first century, high tech/high touch has truly come of age. Technology and our human potential are the two great challenges and adventures facing humankind today. The great lesson we must learn from the principle of high tech/high touch is a modern version of the ancient Greek ideal—*balance.*

We must learn to balance the material wonders of technology with the spiritual demands of our human nature.

High Tech/High Touch: TV, the Pill, and Hospices

8 Perhaps the most powerful technological intrusion was television, far more vivid and more engaging than either radio or the telephone. At almost exactly the time we first introduced television, we created the group-therapy movement, which led to the personal growth movement, which in turn led to the human potential movement (est, TM, Rolfing, Yoga, Zen, and so forth—all very high touch). Television and the human potential movement developed almost in lockstep, much of both in the bellwether state of California.

9 The first television generation, the baby boomers, who started out in life with *The Howdy Doody Show* and who mellowed into *The Mickey Mouse Club* and *American Bandstand,* are without a doubt the strongest proponents of the human growth movement. The need to compensate for the years of being technologically bombarded is part of the unfolding of this high-touch phenomenon.

The gee-whiz futurists are always wrong because they believe technological innovation travels in a straight line. It doesn't. It weaves and bobs and lurches and sputters.

10 We show no signs of lessening the pace with which we introduce even more technology into our society—and into our homes. The appropriate

response to more technology is not to stop it, Luddite-like, but to accommodate it, respond to it, and shape it. In the interplay of technology and our reaction to it, technological progress does not proceed along a straight course. That is why the gee-whiz futurists who said we are all going to pilot our own helicopters, or that home hookups will replace the newspaper, were mistaken. Technological innovation rarely goes the way of straight-line extrapolation, but proceeds as part of a lurching dynamic of complicated patterns and processes.

11   Examples of the high-tech/high-touch phenomenon are all around us.

- The high technology of heart transplants and brain scanners led to a new interest in the family doctor and neighborhood clinics.
- Jet airplanes, as far as I can tell, have led only to more meetings.

12   The pill is a good example of high tech/high touch. The high technology of chemistry and pharmacology led to the development of the pill, which in turn led to a whole revolution in lifestyles. Societal taboos against premarital sex are of course partly pragmatic since becoming pregnant can lead to all kinds of complications; the advent of the pill initiated widespread experimentation and adventurism, including living together, which became very widespread. Although marriage is coming back in the 1980s, during the 1970s there were days when I was sure that the only people in this society who *really* wanted to get married were priests.

The introduction of the high technology of word processors into our offices has led to a revival of handwritten notes and letters.

13   A very poignant example of what I mean by high tech/high touch is the response to the introduction of high technology of life-sustaining equipment in hospitals. We couldn't handle the intrusion of this high technology into such a sensitive area of our lives without creating some human ballast. So we got very interested in the quality of death, which led to the hospice movement, now widespread in this country.

The more high technology we put in our hospitals, the less we are being born there, dying there—and avoiding them in between.

14   The health field offers still more examples of high tech/high touch. The high-tech side has brought heart transplants into the medical mainstream; microsurgery to reattach severed limbs, and, recently, artificial pancreata; and "walking dialysis" to replace expensive and confining

hemodialysis. At the same time there is a trend toward less surgery and less radical surgery.

15 And medical care is becoming far more high touch. Home care and home births are becoming increasingly popular, while in hospitals the staff is attempting to create a more homelike atmosphere. New low-tech birthing rooms are being added to hospitals, and freestanding birthing centers, similar to hospice centers, are proliferating. Primary nursing, for example, where a nurse is responsible for the total care of a few patients, is very high touch.

16 The immensely popular movie *Star Wars* is very high tech/high touch. It portrays a contest between characters who have used technology within human control and scale and others who have been dominated by it. The good guys are not antitechnology: When Luke Skywalker flies in on that final run, the Force with him, he turns off his computer, but not his engine.

The Computer as Liberator

17 I had thought earlier that we might rebel against the computer for dehumanizing us. But now I think we are beginning to understand just how liberating the computer is in a high-tech/high-touch sense. For example, a company with 40,000 employees has treated those employees pretty much the same for generations. It had to because that was the only way to keep track of them. With the computer to keep track, the employees can be treated differently, with a unique contract for each of the 40,000. We are all slowly moving in that direction. In addition, companies are now offering a "cafeteria of compensations," for example American Can. An employee can now decide to have a certain combination of salary, pension, health benefits, flexitime, job sharing, and job objectives.

The technology of the computer allows us to have a distinct and individually tailored arrangement with each of thousands of employees.

18 Even pension plans are moving in this direction: Because we have the computer to keep track of it, an individual contributor to the pension plan can decide where that contribution is going to be invested. And that is one of the key reasons that unions are out of tune with the new computer-rich information society. The basic idea of a union is to ensure that everyone is treated the same. But now we all want to be treated differently.

• • •

The Danger of the Technofix Mentality

19   "Man is a clever animal. There is no way to keep him from devising new tools. The error lies in thinking that new tools are the solution. It could be a fatal error," writes John Hess in a *GEO* magazine article entitled "Computer Madness."

20   When we fall into the trap of believing or, more accurately, hoping that technology will solve all our problems, we are actually abdicating the high touch of personal responsibility. Our technological fantasies illustrate the point. We are always awaiting the new magical pill that will enable us to eat all the fattening food we want, and not gain weight; burn all the gasoline we want, and not pollute the air; live as immoderately as we choose, and not contract either cancer or heart disease.

21   In our minds, at least, technology is always on the verge of liberating us from personal discipline and responsibility. Only it never does and it never will.

The more high technology around us, the more the need for human touch.

22   That is why the human potential movement that advocates both discipline and responsibility is such a critical part of the high-tech/high-touch equation. By discovering our potential as human beings we participate in the evolution of the human race. We develop the inner knowledge, the wisdom, perhaps, required to guide our exploration of technology.

23   With the high-touch wisdom gained studying our potential as human beings, we may learn the ways to master the greatest high-tech challenge that has ever faced mankind—the threat of total annihilation by nuclear warfare.

24   High tech/high touch. The principle symbolizes the need for balance between our physical and spiritual reality.

Glossary

Luddite-like (10)—The Luddites were a group of British workmen who between 1811 and 1815 destroyed labor-saving textile machinery in the belief that it would diminish employment. The word has come to mean anyone who opposes change.

Comprehension and Discussion

1. What does the phrase *high tech/high touch* mean? Why did it develop?
2. According to Naisbitt, how is the principle of high tech/high touch illustrated in each of the following fields: television; health and medicine;

business? Think of other examples of the principle of high tech/high touch. Some suggested areas are computers and the Internet, your job, education, sports, the kitchen, the bathroom, the office, the automobile, telephones, musical recordings. Write a journal entry on one example, and share it with your classmates. Discuss with them some areas in which we need more balance between high tech and high touch today.

3. Who are the gee-whiz futurists (10)? What do they predict? What is Naisbitt's attitude toward them? Do you agree with Naisbitt?

4. Do you think the computer is dehumanizing or liberating? Review what Naisbitt says about computers in paragraph 17, and discuss the question above with your classmates.

5. Review John Hess's comment in paragraph 19. What does Naisbitt say about this idea? Discuss this concept with your classmates.

Language and Technique

1. In paragraphs 2–7 Naisbitt traces the parallel growth of high tech and high touch through three decades. With a small group of classmates, analyze this mini-essay. What is the main idea of this section? What are the three decades that he explains and illustrates? What paragraphs are devoted to each of the three decades? What transitions indicate movement from one decade to the next?

2. Working with a small group of classmates, analyze paragraph 12 as a paragraph of cause and effect.

3. This selection from Naisbitt is a good model of an *expository* or explanatory essay with the introduction-body-conclusion structure and a series of causal chains and examples to develop the main idea. Working with a small group of classmates, identify the thesis statement for the selection and outline its structure (introduction, section I, section II, etc., and conclusion).

4. Naisbitt uses some catchy phrases in this selection, such as *high tech/high touch, gee-whiz futurists* (10), and *cafeteria of compensations* (17). What do these phrases mean? Why does he use such phrases? Can you find others in this selection? Discuss these with your classmates.

Suggestions for Writing

1. **Sentence.** Write a sentence in which you define *high tech/high touch* in your own words.

2. **Paragraph.** Write a paragraph in which you state, explain, and illustrate one example of high tech/high touch that you have observed. See paragraphs 12 and 13 for sample paragraphs of example or illustration.
3. **Essay.** Write an essay in which you explain how a specific development in technology has affected you.
4. **Essay.** Naisbitt's book *Megatrends* has influenced the thinking of many people during the 1980s, the 1990s, and still today. Write an essay about a book that has influenced your life, and explain specifically how it has changed your thinking and your actions.
5. **Essay.** Write an essay in which you identify and explain some of the major medical advances that have occurred since 1982 in terms of the phenomenon of high tech/high touch.

Mind-Expanding Machines

Bruce Bower

BRUCE BOWER is a journalist who contributes regularly to *Science News*. He writes articles that explain complicated scientific concepts to the nonscientific community. In this essay he discusses the complex, controversial concept of artificial intelligence.

Vocabulary Study

moxie (1)	incarnations (28)
cognitive, cognition (1 ff.)	ferrets (30)
prostheses (1 ff.)	virtuosos (32)
deemed (6)	virtual (35)
myriad (9)	ensuing (37)
simulate, simulations (11, 32, 35)	collaboratively, collaborate (38, 42)

Mind-Expanding Machines

1   When Kenneth M. Ford considers the future of artificial intelligence, he doesn't envision legions of cunning robots running the world. Nor does he have hopes for other much-touted AI prospects—among them, machines with the mental moxie to ponder their own existence and tiny computer-linked devices implanted in people's bodies. When Ford thinks of the future of artificial intelligence, two words come to his mind: cognitive prostheses.

2   It's not a term that trips off the tongue. However, the concept behind the words inspires the work of the more than 50 scientists affiliated with the

Institute for Human and Machine Cognition (IHMC) that Ford directs at the University of West Florida in Pensacola. In short, a cognitive prosthesis is a computational tool that amplifies or extends a person's thought and perception, much as eyeglasses are prostheses that improve vision. The difference, says Ford, is that a cognitive prosthesis magnifies strengths in human intellect rather than corrects presumed deficiencies in it. Cognitive prostheses, therefore, are more like binoculars than eyeglasses.

3   Current IHMC projects include an airplane-cockpit display that shows critical information in a visually intuitive format rather than on standard gauges; software that enables people to construct maps of what's known about various topics, for use in teaching, business, and Web site design; and a computer system that identifies people's daily behavior patterns as they go about their jobs and simulates ways to organize those practices more effectively.

4   Such efforts, part of a wider discipline called human-centered computing, attempt to mold computer systems to accommodate how humans behave rather than build computers to which people have to adapt. Human-centered projects bear little relationship to the traditional goal of artificial intelligence—to create machines that think as people do.

5   As a nontraditional AI scientist, Ford dismisses the influential Turing Test as a guiding principle for AI research. Named for mathematician Alan M. Turing, the 53-year-old test declares that—machine intelligence will be achieved only when a computer behaves or interacts so much like a person that it's impossible to tell the difference.

6   Not only does this test rely on a judge's subjective impressions of what it means to be intelligent, but it fails to account for weaker, different, or even stronger forms of intelligence than those deemed human, Ford asserts.

7   Just as it proved too difficult for early flight enthusiasts to discover the principles of aerodynamics by trying to build aircraft modeled on bird wings, Ford argues, it may be too hard to unravel the computational principles of intelligence by trying to build computers modeled on the processes of human thought.

8   That's a controversial stand in the artificial intelligence community. Although stung by criticism of their failure to create the insightful computers envisioned by the field's founders nearly 50 years ago, investigators have seen their computational advances adapted to a variety of uses. These range from Internet search engines and video games to cinematic special effects and decisionmaking systems in medicine and the military. And regardless of skeptics, such as Ford, many researchers now have their sights set on building robots that pass the Turing Test with flying colors.

9   "I'm skeptical of people who are skeptical" of AI research, says Rodney Brooks, who directs the Massachusetts Institute of Technology's artificial intelligence laboratory. He heads a "hard-core AI" venture aimed at creating intelligent, socially adept robots with emotionally expressive faces. Brooks also participates in a human-centered project focused on building voice-controlled, handheld computers connected to larger systems. The goal is for people to effectively tell the portable devices to retrieve information, set up business meetings, and conduct myriad other activities (Science News: 5/3/03, p. 279).

10   Cognitive prostheses represent a more active, mind-expanding approach to human-centered computing than Brooks' project does, Ford argues. "This line of work will help us formulate what we really want from computers and what roles we wish to retain for ourselves," he says.

Flight Vision

11   In the land of OZ, which lies entirely within a cockpit mock-up at IHMC, aircraft pilots simulate flight with unaccustomed ease because they see their surroundings in a new light.

IHMC's

12   David L. Still has directed work on the OZ cockpit-display system over the past decade. The movie-inspired name comes from early tests in which researchers stood behind a large screen to run demonstrations for visitors, much as the cinematic Wizard of Oz controlled a fearsome display from behind a curtain.

13   For its part, Still's creation taps into the wizardry of the human visual system. In a single image spread across a standard computer screen, OZ shows all the information needed to control an aircraft. An OZ display taps into both a person's central and peripheral vision. The pilot's eyes need not move from one gauge to another, says Still.

14   A former U.S. Navy optometrist who flies private planes, Still participated in research a decade ago that demonstrated people's capacity to detect far more detail in peripheral vision than had been assumed.

15   "OZ decreases the time it takes for a pilot to understand what the aircraft is doing from several seconds to a fraction of a second," Still says. That's a world of difference to pilots of combat aircraft and to any pilot dealing with a complex or emergency situation.

[16] The system computes key information about the state of the aircraft for immediate visual inspection. The data on the six or more gauges in traditional cockpits are translated by OZ software into a single image with two main elements. On a dark background, a pilot sees a "star field," lines of bright dots that by their spacing provide pitch, roll, altitude, and drift information. A schematic diagram of an airplane's wings and nose appears within the star field and conveys updates on how to handle the craft, such as providing flight path options and specifying the amount of engine power needed for each option. Other colored dots and lines deliver additional data used in controlling the aircraft.

[17] In standard training, pilots learn less-intuitive rules of thumb for estimating the proper relationship of airspeed, lift, drag, and attitude from separate gauges and dials. With the OZ system, a pilot need only keep certain lines aligned on the display to maintain the correct relationship.

[18] Because OZ spreads simple lines and shapes across the visual field, pilots could still read the display even if their vision suddenly blurred or if bright lights from, say, exploding antiaircraft flak, temporarily dulled their central vision or left blind spots.

[19] Experienced pilots quickly take a shine to OZ, Still says. In his most recent study, 27 military flight instructors who received several hours training on OZ reported that they liked the system better than standard cockpit displays and found it easier to use. In desktop flight simulations, the pilots maintained superior control over altitude, heading, and airspeed using OZ versus traditional gauges.

[20] OZ provides "a great example" of a human-centered display organized around what the user needs to know, remarks Mica Endsley, an industrial engineer and president of SA Technologies in Marietta, Ga. The company's primary services is to help clients in aviation and other industries improve how they use computer systems.

[21] If all goes well, OZ will undergo further testing with veteran pilots as well as with individuals receiving their initial flight training. The system will then be installed in an aircraft for test flights.

What a Concept

[22] In an age of information overload, it would be nice for people to have a simple, concise way to tease out the information they really want from, say, the World Wide Web. Today's search engines usually drag along a vast amount of irrelevant data, says Alberto Canas, IHMC's associate director.

23   Enter concept maps.

24   Concept-mapping software developed by Canas and his colleagues provides a way for people to portray, share, and elaborate on what they know about a particular subject. Concept maps consist of nodes—boxes or circles with verbal labels—connected by lines with brief descriptions of relationships between pairs of nodes. Clicking on icons that appear below the nodes opens related concept maps or a link to relevant Web sites.

25   For instance, scientists at NASA's Center for Mars Exploration created a Mars concept map. A red box at the top contains the words "Exploring Mars" and connects to boxes arrayed below it, with labels such as "Search for Evidence of Life" and "Human Missions." Icons positioned below the boxes link to a variety of Mars-related Web sites.

26   A concept-map maker needs to possess a thorough grasp of his or her subject, says Canas. Such a map draws connections between essential principles in a particular realm of knowledge. IHMC researcher Joseph Novak invented a paper-and-pencil version of concept maps nearly 30 years ago.

27   These tools aren't just jazzed-up outlines of topics within a story. In a concept map, nodes contain nouns and the connecting lines are associated with verbs, thus forming a web of propositions related to a central idea. In the Mars concept map, for example, the line between "Exploring Mars" and "Study of Meteorites" brackets the phrase "is presently carried out by."

28   In one of their incarnations, concept maps provide an alternative way to organize information on Web sites so that topics can be explored quickly and efficiently rather than through haphazard hunts on search engines, Canas notes.

29   With this technology, people can convey their expert knowledge and reasoning strategies to others. In one case, concept maps developed by IHMC scientists working with Navy meteorologists plumb the knowledge of experienced Gulf Coast weather forecasters and are now used to train new Navy forecasters.

30   Perhaps the greatest potential for concept maps lies in education. Elementary and high school students in a handful of countries now use a software system developed at IHMC to build their own concept maps about academic topics and then share them over the Internet with distant classes. The computer system ferrets out and displays related claims from different maps. It also poses questions to provoke further thought about the topic. Students then critique each other's maps and, if necessary, revise them.

[31] "It's hard work to learn enough to build a good concept map," Canas says, "but it leads to far more understanding about a topic than simply memorizing information, as so often happens."

Brahms at Work

[32] In the workplace, computers are virtuosos of information storage. However, a computer system known as Brahms sings a different tune. It discerns revealing patterns in people's work behaviors and simulates ways to get their jobs done more effectively.

[33] The Brahms system illuminates the informal practices and collaborations that occur during the workday, according to IHMC computer scientist William J. Clancey. "A Brahms model is a kind of theatrical play intended to provoke conversation and stimulate insights in groups seeking to analyze or redesign their work," he says.

[34] Clancey and other scientists began working on Brahms in 1993. The system builds on social science theories that regard each person's behaviors as being structured by broad pursuits, which researchers often call activities. In an office, common activities include coffee meetings with a supervisor, reading mail, taking a break, and answering phone messages. Activities provide a forum for addressing specific job tasks. A morning coffee meeting, for example, may determine who will make an important sales call later in the day.

[35] Brahms creates a computerized cartoon of how a work group's members perform their activities and tasks. The system's software is based on simulations of interactions among virtual individuals.

[36] Brahms got its first tryout with workers at a New York telecommunications firm in 1995. Since then, Clancey has imported the system to NASA, where he helps six-person crews practice for future Mars exploration missions. Brahms portrays how a crew's members go about their daily business so that mission-support planners can evaluate the procedures for critical activities, such as maintaining automated life-support systems and conducting scientific experiments.

[37] After a crew in training spent 12 days in 2002 working out of a research station in the Utah desert, Brahms translated extensive data on crew behavior into a portrayal of how each person divvied up his or her time and moved from one place to another during each day. Ensuing simulations indicated that simple scheduling changes—eating lunch and dinner at slightly

earlier times and eliminating afternoon crew meetings—would markedly boost the time available for scientific work and other critical duties.

38   Brahms remains a work in progress, Clancey notes. He wants to use the system to study how pairs of scientists on the Mars crews collaboratively adjust their plans in the fields as they make unexpected discoveries.

39   David Woods of Ohio State University in Columbus welcomes that prospect. Traditional artificial intelligence programs treat plans as rigid specifications for a series of actions, says Woods, who studies how people use computers in air-traffic control and other complex jobs. In such difficult endeavors, however, plans often get modified as circumstances change and surprises crop up.

40   "Researchers are just beginning to look at plans as ways in which people prepare themselves to be surprised," Woods says. In other words, the best-laid plans are those that are loose enough to allow for innovation.

Big Systems

41   The sprawling IHMC facility in downtown Pensacola has witnessed its own surprising transformation. Before Ford and his computer-savvy colleagues arrived in 1990, the building housed the local sheriff's department and a jail.

42   IHMC now represents freedom, at least of the academic sort. People trained in computer science, the social sciences, philosophy, engineering, and medicine mingle and collaborate. The only requirement: Treat computers not as isolated systems of chips and codes, but as parts of larger systems also characterized by how individuals think, the type of organizations in which they work, and the settings in which labor occurs.

43   It's this big-system perspective that informs OZ, concept maps, and Brahms. "Building cognitive prostheses keeps human thought at the center of our science," Ford says.

Comprehension and Discussion

1. What is a cognitive prosthesis? How does it differ from eyeglasses as prostheses? What are some examples of cognitive prostheses?
2. What is the goal of human-centered computing? What is the goal of artificial intelligence? How do the two differ? What are some of the achievements of human-centered computing? Of AI? How does each work, and what does it contribute to humankind?

3. What are concept maps? Have any of your teachers introduced you to concept mapping? If so, discuss this activity with your classmates. How might it be helpful in a composition class?
4. What is OZ? What does it do? How has it been accepted by pilots?
5. What is intelligence? How is it measured? Are there various types of intelligence? Participate in a class discussion of human intelligence.

Language and Technique

1. Why was flight vision software named OZ?
2. Look up the phrase "information overload" (22). What does it mean? How does it affect individuals in the Information Age?
3. Identify all the experts that Bower refers to in the essay. What would the essay lack if the comments of these experts were not included?
4. Is this an *expository* essay in which Bower explains mind-expanding machines, or is it an *argumentative* essay in which the author tries to convince readers that cognitive prostheses are better than artificial intelligence? Discuss Bower's purpose with your classmates.

Suggestions for Writing

1. **Sentence.** Write a sentence in which you state Bower's main idea in your own words.
2. **Paragraph.** How do you view and treat a computer? When something goes wrong with the computer you are working on, do you blame the computer and talk to it, or do you get angry at yourself? Write a paragraph on your relationship with your computer or another technological item, such as a cell phone, DVD, TV remote, microwave, electric can opener, or others.
3. **Essay.** Do you think artificial intelligence research will ever develop a machine that duplicates the processes of human thought and decision making? Why or why not? Write an essay in which you take a stance on this question and provide evidence to support your position.
4. **Essay.** One of the ways in which our language has changed in the last generation is in the increased use of initials or abbreviations. Bower uses several in his essay—*IHMC, AI, SN, US, NASA*. One specific form of shortened forms is the *acronym*, a word that is formed from the initial letters of a group, such as *WAC* for Women's Army Corp, or by combining initial letters or parts of a series of words, such as *radar* for *radio*

*d*etecting and *r*anging. Why are shortened forms used so frequently now? Do they enhance or complicate communication? Write an essay in which you discuss some common initials or acronyms, and explain whether their use simplifies or confuses communication, especially to people outside the specific field.

5. **Essay.** Choose a scientific or technical term from one of your courses, and write an essay in which you define and explain it to someone who is not familiar with the term or with the field of science in which it is used. In your essay of definition, you may use some of the techniques that Bower uses: formal definition, negation, comparison and contrast, cause and effect, analysis and classification, examples and illustrations.

Techno-Thriller

Ian Frazier

IAN FRAZIER is a writer who regularly contributes articles, often humorous, to serious magazines such as the *New Yorker* and *Harper's*. After his family moved from Manhattan to Montana, he wrote two books about the life and culture of the American Indian, the most recent of which is *On the Rez*, published in 2000. This selection, published in *The Atlantic* magazine in 2001, is a *parody* (or takeoff) on a screenplay.

Techno-Thriller
NOW SHOWING CONTINUOUSLY AT A THEATER NEAR YOU

Opening shot of the Mall in Washington, D.C., seen from above through an office window. Then the focus becomes blurry.

Sound of clicking keys on a computer keyboard.

KEYS: *Click-click-click-click-click. Click-click-click. Click-click-click-click-click-click-click-click-click-click-click.*

(Pause.)

KEYS: *Click-click-click-click. Click. Click.*

The shot moves from the blurry window across a desk to show fingers poised above the computer keyboard. Just the ends of the fingers, not the whole hand. The fingers hover, slightly trembling, indecisive.

Close-up of an almost full cup of coffee next to the computer.

KEYS: *Click-click-click. Click . . . click . . .*

Shot of the fingers moving over the keyboard. Extreme close-up of right index finger moving slowly, slowly, to the Enter key. It pauses above the Enter key for several seconds. Then it hits the key.

Burst of loud, suspenseful music. Sudden close-up shot of computer screen. Flashing, in greenish computer type on the screen, the words ILLEGAL OPERATION ILLEGAL OPERATION ILLEGAL OPERATION

An alarm sounds:*Wee-ooo wee-ooo wee-ooo wee-ooo . . .*

Close-up of holes in the computer speaker the alarm is coming out of. Shot of fingers moving quickly on keyboard.

KEYS: *Click-click! Click-click-click! Click-click-click-click!*

Alarm stops.

Scene 2

Close-up of a satellite in outer space with Earth in the background. The satellite has radio dishes sticking out on both sides, antennae, robotic arms, etc.

Close-up of satellite's control panel. A red light on it is blinking. The red light stops blinking. After a few seconds a green light goes on.

Scene 3

Shot of same computer as before. Close-up of coffee cup. Now it is about half full.

KEYS: *Click-click-click-click-click-click-click-click.*

Close-up of computer screen. It is blank. Then moving geometric patterns appear on it, get smaller, and disappear. Again the screen is blank.

KEYS (confidently): *Click-click-click-click-click-click.*

More geometric patterns, but different ones this times. They move faster and vibrate excitedly and disappear. Then, with a tinkling three-note bell of welcome, the words ACCESSING DEFCON CODE FILES pop onto the screen. Close-up on these words until they're huge.

WHISPERED VOICE: *Bingo!*

Scene 4

Shot of microchip magnified 10,000 times. Sudden close-up of its circuitry. Burst of scary *whang-ang-ang-ang-ang* sound.

Scene 7

Shot of space station. It goes by the satellite of Scene 2. Close-up of satellite. Now many lights are flashing strangely on its control panel. One of its robotic arms begins to move.

Scene 12

Shot from an office window showing minarets, onion domes, and other foreign-looking tops of buildings.

Sound of clicking keys. These keys sound different—sharper, more sinister.

KEYS: *Cleck-cleck-cleck-cleck-cleck-cleck-cleck-cleck.*

Shot of keyboard, with fingers moving on it. They are long and slender, with manicured red fingernails.

Close-up of computer screen. Jingling tambourine-rattle of welcome as the words file access defcon coding appear. Close-up on these words until they're huge.

WHISPERED VOICE: *Bh'hatvan!*

Scene 19

Shot of big room full of computers with nobody at them. Subtitle says THE PENTAGON. Shot goes unhurriedly along row after row of computer screens, all dark. After many rows it passes a screen on which the words UNAUTHORIZED ENTRY are blinking over and over. It goes back for a close-up on that screen. Somewhere, softly and forebodingly, a military band begins to play.

Shot continues down rest of rows of blank computer screens.

Scene 26

Split-screen shot of keyboards. On left, keyboard from opening scene; on right, keyboard from Scene 12. Ordinary fingers and red-fingernail fingers typing.

KEYS (on left): *Click-click-click-click-click!*

KEYS (on right): *Cleck-cleck-cleck-cleck-cleck!*

Typing goes on getting faster, accompanied by tense music. Scene lasts about half an hour.

Scenes 30–45

Additional plot: shots of computer screens, fingers typing, frantic mouse-clicks, tidal wave, explosions, ringing phones, papers pouring from fax machine, beepers going off, etc.

Scene 51

Sudden terrifying shot of computer screen seen from below as if about to fall on you. Symbols flash rapidly across it as sound of typing and mouse-clicks becomes deafeningly loud. Nervous music rising.

Jarring full-screen shot of digital clock with glowing red numbers complete to the thousandth of a second. The numbers are moving, going backward to zero. The clock has about fifty-eight seconds on it.

Shot of fingers typing really fast.

KEYS: *Click 'ick 'ick 'ick 'ick 'ick 'ick 'ick 'ick 'ick 'ick 'ick!*

Alternating shots of clock running down and fingers typing. Music reaches crescendo.

Suddenly clock stops. There are eleven thousandths of a second left.

Scene 55

Shot of Harrison Ford and Julia Roberts embracing.

Scene 58

Shot of satellite. All its robotic arms are retracted. It is orbiting peacefully and looks fine.

Scene 60

Shot of fingers turning off computer. This takes several minutes because of the steps involved. Finally screen goes blank.

Extreme close-up of right index finger moving to turn off little yellow-green light in right-hand corner below computer screen. Tired but relieved, the finger pushes the button. Gradually, the light dims.

Triumphant music as the credits roll.

Comprehension and Discussion

1. What is this selection about? What is the subject? What happens? In your journal, write a *synopsis* (summary of the plot or events) of this play, and share it with your classmates.
2. What is the meaning of the title? What are the *connotations* of this title?
3. Working with a small group of classmates, trace each of the following throughout the play: visual scenes or shots; sounds; music. How do these elements work together and reinforce one another?
4. Why do only two people appear in the play? Why are only two words spoken by a human being? What is the significance of the ordinary fingers and the red-fingernail fingers typing? How are emotions conveyed with fingers, computer screens, and sounds? How do emotions change? What tone or mood is conveyed in the screenplay? How does that mood shift at the end?
5. What does Frazier *satirize* in this screenplay?

Language and Technique

1. What is the effect of the repetition of *click-click*?
2. How does this screenplay differ from a traditional screenplay or drama?
3. Why does the script writer omit some scenes? What effect does this have on the reader?
4. Most plays and screen scripts are written to be acted, seen, and heard. Do you think this script was written to be staged? Filmed? Why?

Suggestions for Writing

1. **Sentence.** Write a sentence in which you convey a common sound in your classroom or somewhere else on campus.
2. **Paragraph.** Write a paragraph in which you express your reaction to and opinion of this screenplay, and share it with your classmates.
3. **Essay.** Try your hand at writing a *parody* in which you mimic and hold up to ridicule the characteristic style of a specific type of writing or of a specific writer whom you know well. Some possible topics for your parody are an obituary, a computer program, rap lyrics, hard-rock lyrics, an MTV video, a real-TV program, or the acceptance speech of an award winner (such as Miss America or an Oscar winner or the owner of the Super Bowl winning team).

4. **Essay.** Write a *review* of a techno-thriller (such as a *Matrix* film) or science fiction movie (such as *Star Wars*). Include a synopsis of the plot, an analysis of the characters, and your evaluation of the movie.
5. **Essay.** Write an essay in which you describe a computer lab or an office full of computers and convey how this room makes you feel.

What Happened to ATVs?

Michael Caple

MICHAEL CAPLE was a college composition student when he wrote this essay. The assignment was to write an argumentative essay using cause and effect and examples as evidence to support the stance. He collected some of the information in his essay from various Internet sites and documented them within the text. Included here are his formal outline and the documented essay.

What Happened to ATVs?

Thesis: The banning of 3wheelers (ATV: All Terrain Vehicle) was a hasty decision.

I. ATVs have been banned.
   A. ATVs were banned because they are dangerous.
      1. Lack of proper ATV/riding training is a serious problem.
      2. Lack of proper experienced parental supervision is an issue.
      3. Lack of proper safety equipment being worn is a problem.
      4. Adults are at risk also, because they can make the same mistakes as children, if not more.
   B. ATVS were banned because manufacturers and dealers caused a lot of problems.
      1. Manufacturers have caused problems.
      2. Dealers have caused problems.
   C. ATVs were banned because of costly lawsuits.
      1. Lawsuits cause corporations to lose money.
      2. Lawsuits cause prices to increase to compensate for corporate losses.
      3. Families and friends have to re-live the fateful day of injury.
II. The banning of ATVs could have been avoided if proper safety precautions had been taken.
   A. Riders should wear proper safety gear.
      1. Helmets and goggles should be worn at all times.

    2. When riding in the woods, long pants and long sleeve shirts should be worn.

  B. Proper safety course should be taken to improve riding ability.

    1. Dealers give rider safety courses.

    2. Dealers also provide home videos for study.

  C. Riders should always ride within the limits of their abilities.

    1. Young inexperienced riders are not high-wire stunt actors.

    2. No riders should duplicate what they see on TV.

What Happened to ATVs?

By introducing something new to a culture, we can learn a lot, but mainly how to be a better person. When the first three-wheelers were introduced in 1970, the world had to learn something new. As time passed the ATVs got larger and faster, just as cars did when they were first introduced. Technological improvements also yielded better safety gear and safer riding equipment, but all these things still didn't make up for the rider. Even though the equipment changed drastically, the riders changed very little in the aspect of responsibility and experience. Many deaths and injuries occurred throughout the 1980's to present because of rider error and misjudgments of his/her abilities. In late 1987 three-wheeler manufacturers and the CPSC (Consumer Product Safety Commission) reached an agreement that three wheelers will no longer be manufactured and sold in the United States. This agreement was based on a very extensive research effort by the CPSC that determined the three-wheelers were at a serious level of dangerousness. Various law firms also contributed to the CPSC case, by supplying important information from the injury/death cases from ATV accidents. *(www.cpsc.org)*

    Three-wheelers were considered dangerous for various reasons. These facts were based on the injuries/deaths inflicted on inexperienced riders under the age of 16. One of the facts found by the review board was lack of proper ATV rider training, which taught the rider/operator how to properly operate an ATV under many adverse riding conditions. Something else found was the lack of experienced parental supervision to assist the children in how to ride and where to go to ride their ATV. Many parents would just cut their child loose in the local field or leave their son/daughter with friends unattended. No supervisor was present to tell the child to slow down or not to ride so close to the trees. The riders weren't wearing a lot of their safety equipment either. Helmets and goggles were standard items to be worn while riding; warning decals were even installed by the factory to remind riders to wear helmets and not to ride double. Riding double caused many injuries because it put all the weight on the rear axle, which caused the ATV to flip over. Many of the adults were at risk as well, because they can make the same mistakes as children if not more. Adults tend to be cockier in their attempts to do tricks and special stunts, setting a poor example for children who in turn try to do the same tricks with even less riding experience.

However, all of this isn't the rider's fault. The manufacturers failed to directly interfere with what their dealers were doing. The dealers were selling ATVs that were rated for adults to parents who were buying the ATVs for children under the age of 16. Children under the age of 16 were rated to ride 185cc and smaller ATVs that were limited to 30–35mph and intended for riding on the beach or in the woods. The "popular cool" ATVs were intended for wide-open racing and speed. These ATVs came with massive 250+cc engines that could easily exceed 70mph with little to no modifications. These Racing ATVs were the dealer's bread and butter and he wanted to sell them at every chance. One instance was reported by *www.naturaltrails.org*:

> A November 8, 2002, Good Morning America report about ATV safety included a hidden camera investigation designed to determine whether or not ATV dealers abide by this "golden rule." Good Morning America staff visited or telephoned ten randomly selected dealers nationwide and asked salespeople to recommend an ATV for a 14-year-old child. Nine of the ten recommended an adult-size ATV with the full knowledge that it was being purchased for a child younger than 16. Most dealers made this recommendation without any caveats, while one explained the age restrictions, and then proceeded to tell the producer how to evade them.

With instances like these, injuries are bound to occur, and sometimes, even fatalities. Many things play into lawsuits like the type of injury, the results on the injury, and how many were hurt. These lawsuits cost on the average of $300,000 (*http://www.bennettlawfirm.com/atv4.htm/*) just to start the investigation. If there is long-term injury and extended health care is required, an extra $5 million is an estimate for head injuries and back injuries. Robert Bennett of Bennett Law Firm (*http://www.bennettlawfirm.com/*) reported one such representation on an injury case:

> On May 19, 1994 Travis Hagy was operating a 1985 Honda 250 ES on his farm when his foot became entangled in the wheel

pulling him off the machine and throwing him to the ground. His head and body hit the ground with such a force that he suffered severe physical and neurological injuries and damage. The permanent brain damage resulting from the incident left Mr. Hagy unable to care for himself or his family.

This case resulted in a $30 million settlement from Honda Inc. Whenever a lawsuit is lost by the manufacturer, the industry takes a serious hit. Prices are raised to compensate for monetary losses and then sales drop because of these higher costs. These increases can cause a decrease in jobs to small towns reliant on these factories for jobs. Many times these accidents could've been prevented, but not all of them.

The banning of ATVs could've been prevented if the riders would've taken the responsibility to ride like they should have. *The Bennett Law Firm .com* reported another such case that represents such responsibilities:

> Jeffrey Black suffered catastrophic head injuries while operating a 1984 KLT 160. Traveling along a dirt road Jeffrey steered toward the side of the road to avoid two girls approaching on horseback. As he made the turn the three-wheeler flipped, rolling over on Jeffrey resulting in a depressed skull fracture and brain hematoma. He was not wearing a helmet at the time of his accident. Attorneys for the Plaintiffs claimed that the 3-wheel Kawasaki was defectively designed and unreasonably dangerous.

Helmets mean a lot in any circumstance, regardless if the person is riding a motorcycle or a bicycle. Helmets were in many cases included in the deal with the ATV that were purchased. If the helmet wasn't included, the dealer offered a special promotional price. The dealer and many local ATV clubs also offered videos and riding classes. These services provided by the dealer and riding clubs were intended to help all levels of riders understand how to ride, whether it was for beginner/novice 13 year old on a small three-wheeler or an experienced 30 year old learning how to attack a racecourse.

> All of the ATVs really are unstable and not particularly safe, and where they are widely used for recreation you get youngsters on them—and the average teenager hasn't got a whole lot of sense about things like this, so you put them on something that is

unstable and it's very easy to lose control. (*www.naturaltrails.com/ rueterhealthmagazine*)

These courses and videos were intended to eliminate these negative articles and dangerous accidents, but in most cases they were overlooked or avoided because of hasty people who wanted to ride too fast, too far with not enough experience.

In conclusion, people will point fingers and blame others to make them look good and make money. If buyers and dealers took responsibility for their actions, they would still be able to enjoy a lot of the things they no longer have. Too many times money and greed take control of our motives and intentions.

Checklist for Revising and Editing

Following is a list of questions to guide you in the process of revising and editing your essays. Use the following questions to respond to the essay and to check for any point of needed revision. You may also use it to respond to and evaluate essays by other writers, whether students or professional writers.

1. **Sources:** What sources of information does the author draw upon—experience and memory, observation, reading and research, conversation and interview?

2. **Purpose:** What is the author's purpose in this essay—to narrate, to develop, to explain, to argue or convince, or a combination of these? Does the author accomplish the purpose?

3. **Thesis:** What is the thesis sentence or main point? Does the author state the thesis or imply it? Does the author make the thesis clear?

4. **Unity:** Does the author stick to the thesis? Is every statement in the essay directly relate to the main idea?

5. **Structure and Organization:**

   A. **Introduction**
      1) Does the introduction make clear the subject of the essay?
      2) Does the introduction state or imply the thesis sentence clearly?
      3) Does the introduction grab your attention and interest, and make you want to read the essay?

B. **Body**

   1) What are the major points for development in the essay?

   2) How does the author organize the points of development of the essay? Is the order of points clear? Why does the author put the points in this order?

   3) Is this order appropriate for the ideas of the essay?

   4) Are there any other points or information that the author should have included? Why?

C. **Conclusion**

   1) Does the conclusion relate directly to the introduction and to the thesis, as well as to the points in the body of the essay?

   2) Does the conclusion provide a sense of finality or ending to the essay?

   3) Is the conclusion effective?

6. **Development**

   A. What kinds of development does the author use to expand, support, and clarify the general assertions—narration, description, example, process, cause and effect, classification, example, comparison and contrast, definition, negation, statistics, expert opinion?

   B. Does the author provide sufficient evidence to make the subpoints clear and persuasive?

7. **Coherence**

   A. Does the essay flow smoothly from idea to idea? From sentence to sentence? From paragraph to paragraph?

   B. How does the author connect the ideas throughout the essay? What Bridges and signposts does the author use to help the reader navigate through the essay?

      1) What key ideas, words, and phrases does the author repeat?

      2) What pronouns does the author use?

      3) What transitional words and phrases does the author use to connect paragraphs? To connect sentences within paragraphs?

8. **Rhetorical Patterns:** What rhetorical patterns does the author use—narration, description, exposition, argument, example or illustration, enumeration, cause, effect, comparison, contrast, analysis, classification, process, definition, problems to solution?

9. **Language Skills and Proofreading**

   A. Has the author proofread and edited the essay carefully for correctness, appropriateness, and effectiveness of language skills?
      * Spelling
      * Capitalization
      * Punctuation
      * Grammar
      * Sentence structure
      * Word choice

   B. What, if anything, should be changed? Why?

10. **Response and Evaluation**

   A. Does the author effectively fulfill the purpose and/or assignment in the essay?

   B. What is the strongest aspect of the essay? What do you like best? Why?

   C. What could be changed to improve the essay? Why?

Literary Acknowledgments

Literary Acknowledgments

Allen, Frederick Lewis: Excerpt from *The Big Change: America Transforms Itself 1900–1950* by Frederick Lewis Allen. Copyright © 1952 by Frederick Lewis Allen. Reprinted by permission of HarperCollins Publishers, Inc.

Alvarez, Julia: "I want to be Miss América," by Judy Alvarez. ©1998 by Julia Alvarez. First published in *Allure*, March 1995 under the title "Translating A Look," Reprinted in *Something to Declare* by Algonquin Books, Chapel Hill, 1998. Reprinted by permission of Susan Bergholz Literary Services, New York.

Angelou, Maya: "On Aging," copyright ©1978 by Maya Angelou, from *And Still I Rise* by Maya Angelou. Used by permission of Random House, Inc.

Berne, Eric: Paragraph from *The Structure of Organizations and Groups* by Eric Berne. © J.B. Lippincott Company. Reprinted by permission of Harper & Row Publishers, Inc.

Berry, Bertice: "Changing the Tapes" Reprinted with the permission of Scribner, an imprint of Simon & Schuster Adult Publishing Group, from *Bertice: The World According to Me* by Bertice Berry. Copyright ©1996 by Bertice Berry Productions, Inc.

Bly, Robert: "Watching Television" from *The Light Around the Body* by Robert Bly. Copyright ©1967 by Robert Bly. Copyright © renewed 1995 by Robert Bly. Reprinted by permission of HarperCollins Publishers, Inc.

Bottel, Helen: From PARENTS SURVIVAL KIT by Helen Bottel, copyright ©1979 by Helen Bottel. Used by permission of Doubleday, a division of Random House, Inc.

Bower, Bruce: "Mind-Expanding Machines," by Bruce Bower. From *Science News*, Vol.164, No .9, August 30, 2003, pp.136–138. ©Science News. Reproduced with permission from Science News in the format textbook via Copyright Clearance Center, Inc.

Buscaglia, Leo: "Love As a Learned Phenomenon," by Leo Buscaglia. Chapter 1 in *Love: A Warm and Wonderful Book About the Largest Experience in Life*, pp. 53–71. © 1972 by Charles B. Slack, Inc. A Fawcett Crest Book. Published by Ballantine Books, a division of Random House, Inc. Permission of Charles B. Slack, Inc.

Capel, Michael: "What Happened to ATVs?" by Michael Capel. 2003. Student at Hillsborough Community College, Brandon Campus.

Crary, David: "Some Want Curbs on Military Moms," by David Carey, AOL News, 2003. Permission from American Online Corporate Communications, Vienna, VA.

Cleland, Lindy: "Until Death Do Us Part or Until Our Feelings Change," by Lindy Cleland. 2002. Student at Hillsborough Community College, Brandon and Dale Mabry Campuses.

Collier, John: "The Chaser," by John Collier ©1940, renewed 1968 by John Collier. Reprinted by permission of Harold Matson Co., Inc.

Derek, Matthew: "My Worst Job Ever," by Matthew Derek. 2003. Student at Hillsborough Community College, Brandon Campus.

Dickey, Bronwen: "He Caught the Dream," by Bronwen Dickey, *Newsweek*, March 24, 1997 (Vol. 129, Issue 12), p. 19. "My Turn" Section. All Rights Reserved. Reprinted by permission.

Divakaruni, Chitra Banerjee: From LEAVING YUBA CITY by Chitra Banerjee Divakaruni, copyright ©1997 by Chita Banerjee Divakaruni. Used by permission of Doubleday, a division of Random House, Inc.

Dorris, Michael: "Crazy Horse Malt Liquor" from *Paper Trail* by Michael Dorris. Copyright ©1994 by Michael Dorris. Reprinted by permission of HarperCollins Publishers, Inc.

Dunbar, Paul Laurence: "We Wear the Mask," from *The Complete Poems of Paul Laurence Dunbar*. Paul Laurence Dunbar. New York. Dodd, Mead and Co. 1913.

Florand, Nathan: "Death by Video Game: Fact or Fiction?" by Nathan Florand. Student at Hillsborough Community College, Brandon Campus.

Frazier, Ian: "Techno Thriller," ©Ian Frazier; as first appeared in *The Atlantic Monthly*.

Frost, Robert: "The Road Not Taken," by Robert Frost. From *The Poetry of Robert Frost*, edited by Edward Connery Lathem. Copyright ©1969 by Henry Holt and Company, Inc. Reprinted by permission of Henry Holt & Company, LLC.

Geil, Joseph: "The Loss of Dreams," by Joseph Geil. 2003. Student at Hillsborough Community College, Brandon Campus.

Goodman, Ellen: "The Do-It-Yourself Economy," from *The Boston Globe*, February 5, 2004. ©2004 Globe Newspaper Company. Reproduced with permission from The Boston Globe in the format textbook via Copyright Clearance Center, Inc.

Greenfield, Susan: "Flexible Futures," Originally published in *People Management*, October 23, 2003, Vol. 9, No. 21, pp. 52–53 and reproduced with permission from the Author and Penguin Books, Ltd.

Hardy, Thomas: "Neutral Tones," by Thomas Hardy. From *Collected Poems of Thomas Hardy*. Permission of the Estate of Thomas Hardy.

Hemingway, Ernest: "A Clean, Well-Lighted Place." Reprinted with the permission of Scribner, a Division of Simon & Schuster Adult Publishing Group, from *The Short Stories of Ernest Hemingway by Ernest Hemingway*. Copyright ©1933 by Charles Scribner's Sons. Copyright © renewed 1961 by Mary Hemingway. All rights reserved.

Hogan, Linda: "Heritage" by Linda Hogan. Copyright ©1979 by Linda Hogan. Reprinted with permission from the author.

Horn, Gabriel: "The Door," by Gabriel Horn, White Deer of Autumn. Chapter 1, "The Door," pp. 1–5, in *Native Heart: An American Indian Odyssey*. Reprinted by Paraview Special Editions, New York, NY. Reprinted by permission from the Author.

Hughes, Langston: "Theme for English B," by Langston Hughes. From *Collected Poems of Langston Hughes*. Copyright © 1994 by the Estate of Langston Hughes. Used by permission of Alfred A. Knopf, a division of Random House, Inc.

Jackson, Shirley: "Charles" from *THE LOTTERY* by Shirley Jackson. Copyright ©1948, 1949 by Shirley Jackson. Copyright renewed 1976, 1977 by Laurence Hyman, Barry Hyman, Mrs. Sarah Webster and Mrs. Joanne Schunurer. Reprinted by permission of Farrar, Strauss and Giroux, LLC.

Keillor, Garrison: "My Family," by Garrison Keillor. From "Introduction," pp. xxiii–xxvi, *Leaving Home: A Collection of Lake Wobegon Stories*. ©1987, 1989 Garrison Keillor. First published in USA by Viking Penguin Inc., 1987. Reprinted with permission.

King, Stephen: "Why We Crave Horror Stories." Reprinted with permission. ©Stephen King. All rights reserved. Originally appeared in *Playboy* (1982).

Koch, Kenneth: "Permanently," by Kenneth Koch. From *Thank You and Other Poems*. ©1962 by Kenneth Koch. Reprinted by permission of Grove Press, Inc and the estate of Kenneth Koch.

Lalli, Frank: "Guts, Grace, and Glory," by Frank Lalli. *Reader's Digest*, July 2002, pp. 96–105. Reprinted with permission from the July 2002 Reader's Digest Assn., Inc.

Lee, Li-Young: "The Gift," by Li-Young Lee. From *Rose*. ©1986 by Li-Young Lee. Reprinted by permission of BOA Editions, Ltd. www.BOAeditions.org

Lightman, Alan P.: "In Computers," by Alan P. Lightman. Copyright ©1982 Alan P. Lightman. Reprinted by permission of the Author.

Lipscomb, David W.: "I Wish I'd Been There," by David W. Lipscomb. 2003. Student at Hillsborough Community College, Brandon Campus.

Males, Mike: "Teenagers Are Not Becoming More Violent," by Mike Males. From "Why Demonize A Healthy Teen Culture?," *Los Angeles Times*, May 9, 1999. Reprinted with permission from the Author.

Marcus, Jaime: "Sports Hero: Muhammed Ali" by Jaime Marcus from The My Hero Project. Reprinted with permission from The My Hero Project. www.myhero.com

McGovern, George: "A Painful Bashfulness," from *Grassroots*, copyright ©1977 by George McGovern. Used by permission of Random House, Inc.

Momady N. Scott: "To the Singing, To the Drums," first printed in *Natural History* (February 1975).

Naisbitt, John: "From Forced Technology to High Tech/High Touch," by John Naisbitt. From Chapter 2, *Megatrends: Ten New Directions Transforming Our Lives.* ©John Naisbitt 1982. Published by Warner Books.

Newman, Katherine S.: "No Shame in My Game," by Katherine S. Newman. Excerpt from No Shame in My Game: The Working Poor in the Inner City. Copyright ©1999 by Russell Sage Foundation. Permission of Alfred A. Knopf, a division of Random House, Inc.

Oliver, Kitty: "The Anxiety Button," from *Mama Says.* Copyright ©2001 Kitty Oliver. Reprinted by permission of the University Press of Kentucky.

Page, Clarence: "To Educate One's Children in the Rules of Race," pp.8–11 from *Showing My Color* by Clarence Page. Copyright ©1996 by Clarence Page. Reprinted by permission of HarperCollins Publishers, Inc.

P'ang, Layman: "When the Mind Is at Peace," by Layman P'ang translated by Stephan Mitchell, from *The Enlightened Heart: An Anthropology of Sacred Poetry*, ed. Stephen Mitchell. Copyright © 1989 by Stephen Mitchell. Reprinted by permission of HarperCollins Publishers, Inc.

Piercy, Marge: "To Be of Use" from Circles on the Water by Marge Piercy. Copyright ©1982 by Marge Piercy. Used by permission of Alfred A. Knopf, a division of Random House, Inc.

Rubino, Emily: "Advice to a High School Sophomore," by Emily Rubino. 2003. Student at Hillsborough Community College, Branden Campus.

Santiago, Chiori: "Families Should Attempt to Live Without Television," by Chiori Santiago. Published in the "Family Matters" column of *Diablo*,

INSTRUCTOR'S MANUAL

TABLE OF CONTENTS

INTRODUCTION

This instructional manual provides suggestions on how the information in this textbook can be used effectively in beginning composition classes. More instructional material to accompany *Bridges: A Reader for Writers* can be found at www.prenhall.com. (Contact your local Prentice Hall representative for access.)

Both writing and learning are active, not passive. Thus, *students learn to write by writing.* Reading about rhetorical patterns and grammatical conventions and analyzing sample essays help students develop a foundation for their own writing. Participating in discussions about writing as well as drill and practice of grammatical and syntactical structures helps students to begin to internalize patterns and conventions. Beginning students need guidance *during the process* of writing: they need to be *shown*, not just told what to do; they need to know *how*, not just what. With practice and feedback they gradually become familiar with the processes and procedures of composing and develop sufficient competence and confidence to write effectively on their own.

Today many entering college students have writing deficiencies combined with writing anxiety. They lack the background information and processes for thinking and writing as well as the academic requirements and behaviors for success in college writing. For effective instruction, teachers must consider both the affective and the cognitive domains. To improve writing, students need to develop both competence and confidence. This textbook provides samples and suggestions for instructors and students to work toward strengthening the students' writing competence (cognitive domain) and confidence (affective domain).

In the last 40 years empirical research has provided us information on how people—both professionals and students—write and on how we as teachers can help students improve their writing. One research study by Andrea Lunsford in which she sampled five hundred entrance exams suggests that beginning writers focus on personal experience, using it as conclusive evidence or evaluating abstract questions solely in terms of personal effects; rely on clichéd maxims in place of generalizations; see themselves as passive victims of authority; and use stylistic features (such as personal pronouns) that reflect these content characteristics. All of this suggests that basic writers are arrested in what Piaget and Vygotsky call the "egocentric stage" of cognitive development. A similar study by Susan Miller suggests that they are also stuck in what Kohlberg calls the "conventional" stage of moral development. Basic writers might be helped, therefore, by a curriculum that asks them to solve increasingly abstract cognitive problems.

This textbook is designed to address both the affective and the cognitive domains—to help students strengthen their competence and confidence in writing, and it is arranged from simple to complex, from familiar to unfamiliar, from inner world to outer world. The selections and the study aids serve three purposes: 1) they provide practice in reading comprehension; 2) they stimulate students to think, talk, remember, and thus develop confidence and discover ideas for their own writings; 3) they provide examples and models of strategies and patterns for writing and techniques for effective language use. The study aids for each selection are ordered to help students comprehend and analyze what they read before they evaluate it, and then to use what they have read and their thoughts and responses to it as a springboard and as evidence and enrichment for their own writing.

One of the best ways to help students gain confidence in their writing ability is to provide various opportunities for discussion in an atmosphere of trust and mutual respect. First, discussion will stimulate students to think about a topic, to think about it more deeply than they may have in the past, and perhaps to consider it from a stance or point of view that they may not have considered. Second, it will help them discover that they actually do know something about a subject and that they actually have something to say that is worthwhile and of interest to others. Third, it will help them remember events, ideas, and details that they have forgotten. Fourth, it will encourage them to articulate insights, to defend their opinions, and to find specific evidence to support what they say. Thus, discussion is excellent preparation for writing.

The reading passages in this reader demonstrate various writing strategies and language techniques. The Language and Technique questions lead students to become aware of and to analyze the strategies, and the Suggestions for Writing encourage students to emulate and adapt the techniques for their use. Sentences and paragraphs are considered as parts of longer discourse pieces, and students will study individual sentences and paragraphs not in isolation but in the context of the selections. Following each selection are several suggestions for writing to provide both the instructor and the students a variety from which to choose.

Suggestions for Instructional Methods

Because learning to write is active, the most effective instructional methods involve students actively, either working with their own papers or analyzing and responding to others' writings, both students and professionals.

Self Analysis and Response: Cognitive research indicates that analysis of one's own writing can lead to deeper understanding of writing in general and to improved composition in particular. To guide the students in analyzing and responding to their own writing, you may ask them to use the Checklist for Response and Revision (which is introduced in Chapter 3 and also follows each student essay in this textbook) or to use the shortened version below.

1) What is my intended <u>thesis</u>? Is it stated or implied? Why did I decide to state/imply it? If stated, where did I state it? Why did I place it here?
2) Does my <u>introduction</u> grab my readers' attention? If I read it, would I then want to read my essay?
3) Does my <u>introduction</u> indicate my subject and slant or point of view?
4) Is my <u>conclusion</u> directly related to my introduction and to my thesis? Does it provide a sense of finality to my essay?
5) How is my essay <u>organized</u>? Why did I choose this order for my essay?
6) Do I have clear signposts to guide the reader through my essay? Do I include a clear <u>transition</u> at the beginning of each paragraph?
7) Does each <u>paragraph</u> begin with a topic sentence and end with a clincher sentence?
8) Do I include sufficient <u>details</u> to make my essay clear and convincing?
9) Did I <u>proofread, edit, and revise</u> my essay well?
10) Did I budget my <u>time</u> wisely for this assignment? Should I have spent more time on it?
11) What was the <u>easiest</u> part of this assignment for me?
12) What was the <u>most difficult</u> part of this assignment for me?
13) What would I do <u>differently</u> if I could start this assignment over?

Collaborative Learning: One of the most effective methods for beginning students is collaborative learning: students at any level—with guidance from the instructor—*can* learn from each other. Some collaborative methods that work well with beginning college composition students are discussed next.

Put students in groups of three or four, and ask them to analyze an essay and report to the class. Ask one of the group to act as recorder for the group, and another student to be the reporter for presenting the conclusions of the group to the class. A brief guide follows.

1) What is the meaning of the <u>title</u>? Is the title effective?
2) What is the <u>thesis</u> sentence or main idea sentence of the essay? Is it stated or implied? If it is stated, where is it stated?

3) Is the <u>introduction</u> effective? Does it grab the reader's attention and indicate what the essay is about?
4) How is the essay <u>organized</u>?
5) What <u>method(s) of development</u> are used?
6) Does the writer provide <u>sufficient details</u> to make the essay clear?
7) What <u>devices for coherence</u> are used?
8) Is the essay <u>easy to follow</u>? Why, or why not?
9) Is the <u>conclusion</u> effective? Why?
10) What is the <u>best</u> part or aspect of the essay to you? Why?
11) What is the <u>weakest</u> part or aspect of the essay to you? Why?
12) Overall, is the essay <u>effective</u>? Why?

Peer Response: I prefer to call this activity *peer response* instead of *peer editing* because to beginning students, especially those with high levels of anxiety, the notion that they are required to edit and evaluate someone else's writing when they lack knowledge, experience, and confidence in their own writing can be quite daunting. Also, the more competent students in a class often resent being evaluated by those with evident deficiencies. However, all students can respond as readers. When students are asked to *respond* to a classmate's paper, they do so with much more ease than if they are given what they consider the instructor's job of editing and evaluating.

When you make a writing assignment, announce to the students that they are each other's audience or readers and that they will read each other's papers. On the day that the writing assignment is due, devote at least 50 minutes to allowing students to read and respond to their classmates' writings. Ask each student to staple two blank sheets of paper to the back of his or her essay. Then have the students pass the papers around, reading as many as they can, without making any comments about the papers they read. After the students have read four or five different essays, ask each student to hold on to the one he or she is now reading. Next, ask each student reader to respond to the essay on the first blank sheet at the end of the student essay. A Checklist for Response and Revision follows each of the student essays in this textbook, and it will work well for this activity. It is advisable to have students use this checklist singly and in groups for two or more professional or student essays as practice before you ask them to use it to respond to papers their classmates write. After the student has answered all the questions, if there is time, ask another student to respond to the same essay. Then as the students complete their responses, collect the papers and return them to the writers. On the second blank sheet following the paper, ask the student writer to respond to his or her own paper.

Combination of Self Response and Peer Response: It is effective to combine the two activities of self response and peer response to student writing, using the procedures and the checklists above. If you choose to do so, you may have the students evaluate their own writing before the peer response, and then respond to the following questions following the peer response.

1) Did my classmate respondent understand my thesis without difficulty?
2) Do I agree with my classmate's comments?
3) Considering my self analysis and the peer response, what could I do to improve my essay?

Writing Anxiety

Researchers have identified some common characteristics of writer's apprehensions: 1) they are frightened by a demand for writing competency; 2) they fear evaluation of their writing because they think they will be rated negatively; 3) they avoid writing whenever possible; 4) when they are forced to write, they behave destructively (such as procrastinating or not fulfilling the assignment); 5) they do not like to and do not write well about personal topics (such as personal experience narratives or personal opinion papers); instead, they prefer to respond to what other people have written, prefer to write about the outer world instead of the inner world, and prefer to write research papers. No matter how skilled or capable individuals are in writing, if they believe they will do poorly or if they do not want to take courses that stress writing, then their skills or capabilities matter little. With all this indisputable empirical evidence about writing anxiety and its impact upon writing, instructors should help students learn to cope with and control writing anxiety in order to allow them to strengthen their writing competence and confidence.

An effective beginning instructional device is to assess each student's level of writing apprehension. Several tests to measure writing anxiety are available. (One of the most reliable and most used is the Daly-Miller Scale, developed by John Daly and Michael Miller in 1975 and adapted by Michael W. Smith in 1984.)

Useful Resources for Teaching College Composition

Author: You and your students may contact the editor of this textbook Sylvia A. Holladay at <u>wordsandmore@aol.com</u>. She will be happy to answer any of your questions about writing and teaching writing and to engage in discussion of these matters with you and your students. Also you may send her any comments, questions, and suggestions you have for this textbook.

Precise Definitions: In addition to a recent college-level desk dictionary, a valuable resource for denotation and connotation of words is *Merriam-Webster's Dictionary of Synonyms: A Thesaurus Companion* (Springfield, MA: Merriam-Webster, Incorporated, 1984). It includes not only a list of synonyms for each word entry, but also a definition and example of usage of each synonym.

Literary and Rhetorical Terminology: Two excellent resources which contain an alphabetical listing of brief essays on the chief terms used in discussing literature and rhetoric, literary history, and literary criticism are:

Harmon, William, and C. Hugh Holman. *A Handbook to Literature*, 9th ed. New York: Macmillan, 2002. (Based on original by William F. Thrall and Addison Hibbard, 1951.)

Abrams, M. H. *Glossary of Literary Terms*. 7th ed. New York: Harcourt, 1998. (Based on the original first published in 1957 by Abrams.)

Suggested Syllabi

The sections in this textbook—both the order of the chapters and the order within the chapters—are arranged from simple and familiar to complex and unfamiliar, from the personal and inner world to the impersonal and outer world, from narration and description to exposition and argument. This overall easy-to-difficult order is significant in setting up the work for a college course.

This textbook integrates the information on reading and writing from these selections with the study of language skills and composition skills in the Study Aids following each selection. However, this textbook is not a complete course in composition in itself; it is designed to be used with a handbook and/or rhetoric for intense study of the conventions of language usage and of suggestions on how to write. These areas of study are not included in the sample syllabi.

The sample syllabi in this manual are set up according to a 15-week/45-hour session, but can easily be adapted to other types of academic sessions.

Various writing assignments are suggested in the Study Aids following each selection.

Syllabus #1:

This sample syllabus is a deductive syllabus: a linear, sequential, step-by-step order of instruction; moving from the general to the specific, from explanations and instructions, to examples, samples, and practice.

Week 12	Chapter 9, Popular Culture
	Writing Assignment
Week 13	Chapter 10, The World of Work
	Writing Assignment
Week 14	Chapter 11, Science and Technology
	Writing Assignment
Week 15	Review
	Final Exams

Syllabus #2:

This sample syllabus is an inductive order of instruction, moving from specific to general, from examples to explanations and instructions to writing assignment. In this syllabus, the instructor can integrate sections from Chapter 2, Responding to What You Hear and Read and Chapter 3, Writing in College into the reading selections and study aids.

Week 1	Introduction and Orientation to Course
	Chapter 1, Introduction to Students
	Diagnostic Writing
Week 2 & 3	Chapter 4, Home and Family
	Introduce Journals, Emphasizing Reader Response Entries
	Practice
	Assignment of Journal for Course
	Writing Assignment
Week 4 & 5	Chapter 5, Youth and Age
	Introduce Summarizing and Writing a Synopsis
	Practice
	Writing Assignment
Week 6 & 7	Chapter 6, Education
	Introduce Outlining of What You Read
	Practice
	Writing Assignment
Week 8 & 9	Chapter 7, Gender Roles and Relationships
	Introduce Annotating What You Read
	Practice
	Writing Assignment
Week 10 & 11	Chapter 8, Dreams, Goals, Decisions
	Work through Writing the Academic Essay
	in Chapter 3

Writing Assignment: Have students write an academic essay, and check each step in the process:

    Choosing and Restricting a Topic
    Prewriting—Title, Thesis, Plan/Outline
    Writing—Rough Draft
    Rewriting—Proofreading, Editing, and Revising for the
    Final Essay

Week 12   Chapter 9, Popular Culture
    Writing Assignment
Week 13   Chapter 10, The World of Work
    Writing Assignment
Week 14   Chapter 11, Science and Technology
    Writing Assignment
Week 15   Review
    Final Exams

Syllabus #3: Rhetorical Patterns

This sample syllabus is arranged according to rhetorical patterns for organization and development. For the list of selections according to rhetorical patterns, see the Alternate Table of Contents: Rhetorical Patterns (pp. xvii–xx). The syllabus is arranged with the simpler patterns first and the more complex patterns last. The authors of some selections use a combination of patterns, so some selections are listed in more than one category.

Week 1   Introduction and Orientation to Course
    Diagnostic Testing
    Chapter 1, Introduction to Students
Week 2 & 3   Chapter 3, Writing in College
    Narration and Description
    Assignment of Journal for Course
    Writing Assignment
Week 4   Process
    Writing Assignment with Thesis and Informal Plan Listing
    the Steps in the Process Topic
Week 5   Example and Enumeration
    Writing Assignment with Thesis and Informal Plan or
    Tree/Circle Outline Listing the Examples

Week 6	Analysis and Classification
	Writing Assignment with Thesis and Informal Plan or Tree/Circle Outline Listing the Types or Classes
Week 7 & 8	Comparison and Contrast
	Writing Assignment with Outline
Week 9	Definition
	Writing Assignment Using a Combination of the Methods Above Including Thesis and Plan
Week 10 & 11	Cause and Effect
	Writing Assignment with Thesis and Formal Outline
Week 12	Problem to Solution
	Writing Assignment with Thesis and Formal Outline
Week 13 & 14	Argumentation
	Writing Assignment with Thesis and Formal Outline
Week 15	Review
	Final Exams

Syllabus #4: Sources of Ideas for Writing

This syllabus focuses on sources of ideas for invention in writing. For a list of the selections according to sources, see the Alternate Table of Contents: Sources of Ideas for Writing (pp. xxi–xxii).

Week 1	Introduction and Orientation to Course
	Diagnostic Testing
	Chapter 1, Introduction to Students: You Are A Writer
Week 2, 3, 4	Experience and Memory
	Chapter 2, Responding to What You Read and Hear
	Chapter 3, Writing in College
	Assignment of Journal for Course
	Free Writing
	Writing Assignment with Thesis and Informal Plan
Week 5, 6, 7	Observation
	Notes on a Person, Place, or Event
	Writing Assignment with Thesis and Informal Plan
Week 8, 9, 10	Conversation and Interview
	Questions to Prepare for an Interview
	Notes from Interview

	Writing Assignment Based on Interview, with Thesis and Outline
Week 11, 12, 13, 14	Reading and Research
	Brainstorming and Free Writing to Find a Topic
	Notes from Reading
	Writing Assignment with Thesis and Formal Outline
Week 15	Review
	Final Exams

SUGGESTIONS FOR INSTRUCTION
OF SELECTIONS IN READER

CHAPTER 4 Home and Family

THE GIFT, BY LI-YOUNG LEE (PP. 53–55)

Receiving a gift is always a special occasion, and most people think of a gift as a tangible object. However, the poet Lee helps us to think about intangible, emotional, spiritual gifts, ones that we often are not aware of when we first receive them. Lee also presents an ambivalent relationship between father and son. This poem will stimulate students to think about unusual gifts and relationships between child and mentor, whether family members or not.

HERITAGE, BY LINDA HOGAN (PP. 55–59)

Prepare the students to read and discuss this poem by discussing their heritage with them. This poet discusses intangible gifts she has received from various members of her family, gifts which have become part of her heritage. This poem helps students to recall specific events and details from their childhood, specifics they can use to enrich their writing.

WHAT IS A FAMILY? BY HELEN BOTTEL (PP. 59–62)

Most students are familiar with Schulz's definition of love as a warm puppy in the comic strip "Peanuts." In this essay Bottell uses a similar technique to define a family by narrating specific events. The essay is a good model for students to define their families or other groups to which they belong as well other abstract concepts. One suggestion is to have students work in small groups of three to four to use this technique to define education before they try it alone; the practice will help them to understand how to define an abstraction and will also allay writing anxiety.

READABILITY LEVEL: 7

HE CAUGHT THE DREAM, BY BRONWEN DICKEY (PP. 62–68)

Most students have experienced the death or serious illness of a loved one, and many have felt the fear, shock, anger, lack of understanding, and loneliness that Bronwen Dickey expresses so tersely and effectively in this personal essay. This essay should help students recall and examine the significance to them of similar experiences. However, some students, especially those with high levels of writing apprehension, may be hesitant to discuss such deep, raw emotions with strangers in a classroom, and some will not choose to write about such sad experiences. The ones who do write about strong emotions will need help first to distance themselves a bit from their feelings and then to focus and carefully select the details from the total experience to support a main idea.

READABILITY LEVEL: 8

SOME WANT CURBS ON MILITARY MOMS BY DAVID CRARY (PP. 68–73)

This selection is an interesting piece that presents both sides of an argument but draws no conclusion; the author does not take a side or stance. Instead, in typical journalistic style, in an attempt to be objective, he presents quotes of spokespeople for each side. Students will be interested in this argument because of the American military troops—both male and female—now stationed around the world. And Crary's not taking a stance provides students an opportunity to draw their own conclusion for their writing.

READABILITY LEVEL: 11

BLUE WINDS DANCING, BY THOMAS ST. GERMAIN WHITECLOUD (PP. 73–82)

In this short story Whitecloud expresses very effectively how a college student feels when she or he returns home after being in the unfamiliar environment of college. This feeling of not belonging is intensified for Native Americans and other minorities. This essay is a good one for teaching narration and description as well as comparison-contrast and definition.

READABILITY LEVEL: 7

I WISH I'D BEEN THERE BY DAVID W. LIPSCOMB (PP. 82–88)

This expository narration was written by a mature student, and his maturity is evident both in his perception into the events he narrates as well as in his mature style of writing. Like Whitecloud, he deals with generational relationships and responsibilities. Like Dickey, he narrates the illness and death of a loved one. From this essay, beginning writers can learn how to select details from a broad span of years to support a thesis.

READABILITY LEVEL: 10

This student essay as well as the other student essays in the textbook is followed by a **Checklist for Response and Revision**, the same as the one in Chapter 3. Students can learn from analyzing the sample essay, written by someone similar to them in a course similar to the one they are taking at this time. The analysis and discussion will prepare the students to use this checklist for revising their own essays.

Lipscomb's essay is a good example of a reflective personal essay of expository narration. He narrates what happened over a period of years and then reflects on the meaning of these events to him. Beginning college writers can usually write a narration based on personal experience, but they often fail to reflect on the meaning and thus have little coherence in reporting the events. Analyzing Lipscomb's essay will help them understand how they can write a similar essay with a thesis idea controlling their choice of details.

CHAPTER 5 Youth and Age

THE FURY OF OVERSHOES BY ANNE SEXTON (PP. 90–93)

Through the child speaker in this poem, Sexton recalls how it feels to be a small child in a world that seems so big and frightening. After discussing the ideas and feelings expressed in this poem, students will enjoy writing about their own childhood reminiscences.

ON AGING BY MAYA ANGELOU (PP. 93–95)

The ideas expressed by the elderly speaker in this poem may seem strange to some young students. Some will be surprised that older people want to be independent, don't want sympathy, and feel like the same persons they were when they were young. This lack of understanding was brought home to me recently when as I was walking out of my office with a student, my husband called my cell phone, and the student overheard my comments to him.

Her response was, "Wow. That's neat. You talk to him just like I talk to my boyfriend." Somehow some young people don't think of older people—much less older teachers or grandparents—as having the same feelings they have. Discussion of this poem by Angelou can help students to understand and empathize with older people. It also offers an opportunity to discuss the difference between *sympathy* and *empathy*.

READABILITY LEVEL:

THE DOOR BY GABRIEL HORN, WHITE DEER OF AUTUMN (PP. 95–102)

I'll admit Horn is one of my favorite writers, and this chapter from his autobiography illustrates why. He is a master wordsmith of description, and his love and concern for Mother Earth are evident in all that he writes. You may use this essay with the one by Whitecloud (pp. 73–82) and the poem by Hogan (pp. 55–59), and ask students to compare and contrast the ideas each Native American writer sets forth.

READABILITY LEVEL: 7

THE ANXIETY BUTTON BY KITTY OLIVER (PP. 102–109)

In this excerpt from Oliver's autobiography, she illustrates through a series of anecdotes what it was like to be brought up by a loving single parent, a situation with which many students today are familiar. This childhood reminiscence works well with Horn's essay (pp. 95–102) and Sexton's poem (pp. 90–93). David Lipscomb's technique (pp. 82–88) is similar to Oliver's, selecting specific details from a span of time to support a main idea.

READABILITY LEVEL: 9

TEENAGERS ARE NOT BECOMING MORE VIOLENT BY MIKE MALES (PP. 109–114)

In this argumentative essay, Males defends teenagers and attempts to refute the widespread belief that teenagers today are more violent than those of previous generations. He contrasts the violence of teens to the violence of adults to support his argument, a rather unique stance.

READABILITY LEVEL: COLLEGE

A CLEAN, WELL-LIGHTED PLACE BY ERNEST HEMINGWAY (PP. 114–120)

This short story by Hemingway, the well-known Modernist, contrasts three generations. It illustrates several of the author's favorite techniques: 1) setting in Spain; 2) third-person objective point of view, until the end when he lets the reader into the mind of the older waiter; 3) terse, lean style, with much dialogue; 4) the Lost Generation's attitude toward life. Students may contrast the up-beat attitude of the speaker in Angelou's poem (pp. 93–95) with the attitude of the older waiter.

READABILITY LEVEL: 7

IT'S NOT JUST A PHASE BY KATHERINE E. ZONDLO (PP. 120–125)

This essay is another example of expository narration, based on Zondlo's memory. First published in the "My Turn" page in *Newsweek* magazine, the author tries to persuade adults to try to understand and respect young people better. Discuss with students the readers for *Newsweek* (primarily mature, educated, business and professional people) and whether Zondlo's essay would be successful for such an audience. The students might enjoy some role-playing in the discussion of this essay.

READABILITY LEVEL: 10

CHAPTER 6 Education

THEME FOR ENGLISH B BY LANGSTON HUGHES (PP. 127–130)

This poem is a narrative poem in which the poet uses a composition class assignment as a springboard for reflections on his search for identity and his place in the world. Students will enjoy discussing unusual school assignments or assignments that made them think deeply. Help them to realize that topics for writing are all around them, especially using what they read and what they hear as springboards for thinking and writing.

To Yrik: Of Popcorn And Unicorns by Sylvia Hicks (pp. 130–133)

This poem is about a relationship between a college professor and a student. The relationship is one in which the student came to the teacher searching for information, knowledge, and understanding, and the teacher was willing to spend time with the student to try to help him find some answers and some direction for his life. In the process of their discussions, she discovered new priorities and affirmation of the direction of her own life.

A Painful Bashfulness by George McGovern (pp. 133–136)

This autobiographical essay is one that students can use as a model for writing from experience. It is constructed of a series of narrative examples, carefully chosen and focused to the thesis. It also exemplifies how to find significance or meaning in everyday occurrences.

Readability Level: 10

Relationships 101 from Time Magazine (pp. 137–141)

This essay is a good example of an informal argument, combining information from personal experience and observation with research statistics and expert opinions. It illustrates how to incorporate statistics and quotations into the text and to cite the sources of the information right in the text. It will also help students learn how to select information that will support an argumentative stance.

Readability Level: 11

To Educate One's Children in the Rules of Race by Clarence Page (pp. 141–146)

This essay is another example of the use of personal experience as a springboard and as support for an argumentative stance. It will hit home with students from diverse backgrounds, not only African Americans, because it deals with how to assimilate into the culture without losing one's heritage and ethnic identity. On another level, it will reach many students who have been in situations in which they felt left out.

Readability Level: 8

CHARLES BY SHIRLEY JACKSON (PP. 146–152)

On the narrative level, this short story is humorous, yet it has levels of deeper universal meanings. Jackson keeps the reader in suspense and then uses her classic surprise ending. Students will probably enjoy this story, but you should steer the discussion to the deeper issues, such as going to school for the first time, the feelings, the resulting actions, and the motivations; the motivations for misbehaving and lying; whether lying is ever justified; parents not understanding their children; how going to school affects children and how they change; etc.

The readability of this story is deceptive; the reading level is determined largely by the length of sentences and paragraphs, most of which in this story are brief. Readability scales do not take into account the connotations, ambiguity, or levels of meaning—all essential of fiction.

You might discuss with students why—other than the fact that it is about a kindergarten child—this story is included in the section on "Education." Who is educated in this story? What do they learn?

READABILITY LEVEL: 6

ADVICE TO A HIGH SCHOOL SOPHOMORE BY EMILY RUBINO (PP. 152–154)

Emily Rubino was a college freshman when she wrote this essay. The in-class writing assignment was to choose a topic and write an essay drawing from her own experience. At the end of her first semester, she reflected on her experiences in college and high school and decided that what she had learned might be helpful to other students.

READABILITY LEVEL: 12

CHAPTER 7 Gender Roles and Relationships

PERMANENTLY BY KENNETH KOCH (PP. 158–160)

This is a whimsical poem which will give students a different perspective on grammar and sentence structure.

Neutral Tones by Thomas Hardy (pp. 160–162)

This poem is based on an experience that many students have experienced—the break-up of a romance or the loss of a love. However, Hardy expresses his emotions in an abstract manner that is difficult for some students to grasp. Reading the descriptive sections closely with the students and discussing the denotative and connotative meanings of the words and images will help the students understand the poem. You might discuss the difference in mood between Koch's poem "Permanently" which precedes this poem and Hardy's poem. Koch's poem which is about undying, eternal love is light and whimsical, but Hardy's poem about the end or death of love is quite serious and somber.

Friends, Good Friends—and Such Good Friends by Judith Viorst (pp. 162–169)

This essay is a good example of classification based on personal experience and developed with narrative examples. It can serve as a model for students' essays of classification.

Readability Level: 8

Will You Go Out With Me? by Laura Ullman (pp. 169–173)

This selection is a problem to a solution essay based on personal experience. The author also uses cause and effect. First, Ullman states her problem—which is not an earth-shaking one of global significance, but one that is important to her. This topic for writing illustrates that students should write about what they know and that they should not attempt to solve worldwide problems. Then she reflects on the social and personal implications of her situation—the causes and the effects. This essay is one to which students can relate their own experiences, and it will stimulate discussion on the changing roles of males and females and the social and personal results.

Readability Level: 12

LOVE AS A LEARNED PHENOMENON BY LEO BUSCAGLIA
(PP. 173–186)

In this selection Buscaglia refutes the common belief that love is innate and instinctual and asserts the position that love is learned. He carefully traces the process of learning to love and fully supports his stance with experience, observation, research, expert opinion, and examples. Although this selection is longer than most in this textbook, it is not difficult to comprehend, it is on a topic of interest to students, and student readers can identify with many of the examples. You might want to break the essay into sections for reading and discussion. One suggestion is to assign small groups of students to summarize, explain, and discuss one section with the rest of the class.

Paragraph 1–7—Introduction, with Thesis: Just as man learns to be a human being, so he learns to feel as a human being, to love as a human being.

Paragraph 8–12—Family contributions to learning to love
Paragraph 13–21—Cultural contributions to learning to love
Paragraph 22–25—Relationship of language to learning to love
Paragraph 26–29—The influence of school on learning to love
Paragraph 30–34—Mass media influences on mistaken ideas of love
Paragraph 35–38—Conclusion: It is never too late to learn to love.

READABILITY LEVEL: 10

THE CHASER BY JOHN COLLIER
(PP. 186–191)

"The Chaser" is a short, satirical story about young love, always of interest to students, and it is a good story to help students understand irony. Although the story is on the low reading level of 6 (based on the readability scales measuring primarily familiarity of words and length of words, sentences, and paragraphs), the concept load is high. Most beginning college students will need help understanding the theme that attentive love can become jealous, smothering love.

READABILITY LEVEL: 6

"UNTIL DEATH DO US PART," OR "UNTIL OUR FEELINGS CHANGE" BY LINDY CLELAND (PP. 191–196)

Lindy Cleland was a student in a college composition course when she wrote this essay. The assignment was to write an essay of cause and effect. She chose the general topic of divorce and restricted it to the major causes of divorce.

READABILITY LEVEL: 11

CHAPTER 8   Dreams, Goals, Decisions

THE ROAD NOT TAKEN BY ROBERT FROST (PP. 198–201)

This well-known poem by Frost will be familiar to most students, but it is a very teachable selection for college students. It is not a difficult poem for them to understand, they will enjoy thinking about and discussing it, and most will be able to write well in response to it. Many students have reached forks in the road of their lives so will identify with the meaning of the poem—that decisions change our lives and we cannot go back. However, students often miss the key idea in the last two lines: "I took the one less traveled by,/And that has made all the difference." They want to talk and write merely about major decisions in their lives, not taking the road "less traveled by."

DEAD MY OLD FINE HOPES, ANONYMOUS HAIKU (PP. 201–202)

Haiku is an ancient form of Japanese poetry which compresses words and ideas into a very brief package. It is a brief unrhymed poem that traditionally presents a visual image of some aspect of nature plus a reflection or comment on the image. Sam Hamill says, "A great haiku presents—through imagery drawn from intensely careful observation—a web of associated ideas requiring an active mind on the part of the listener (or reader)." In its strictest form, the haiku consists of seventeen syllables, either in four lines of 5-5-2-5, or in three lines, usually 5-7-5. However, modern poets do not follow this rigid form. This ancient poem is an example of the 5-5-2-5 form of haiku.

I WANT TO BE MISS AMERICA BY JULIA ALVAREZ (PP. 203–210)

This personal essay is a good example of childhood reminiscence. It explains how Alvarez and her sisters felt after emigrating to the United States as they tried to adapt to a new culture. The author uses narration as well as cause and effect. Because we live in a mobile society, most students have experienced situations in which they have felt like outsiders and have done unusual things to be accepted. Discuss the irony of what happened in the late 60s when the author was in college: "They wanted to look exotic—they wanted to look like us" (20), and ask the students to identify the ironies in some of their attempts to conform to a new culture or group.

READABILITY LEVEL: 8

CHANGING THE TAPES BY BERTICE BERRY (PP. 210–215)

Unlike Alvarez's autobiographical essay which is expository narration organized chronologically, this autobiographical selection by Berry is exposition with narrative anecdotes to illustrate the ideas. It is organized logically, with an introduction, body, and conclusion. Alvarez implies her thesis in the last paragraph of the essay, but Berry states her thesis in the middle of the essay (P8, S1). This essay will stimulate students to think about what the author says and to write in response to her ideas.

READABILITY LEVEL: 6

GUTS, GRACE, AND GLORY: FACE TO FACE WITH RUDY GIULIANI BY FRANK LALLI (PP. 215–225)

This long interview will hold students' attention and interest because of the subject matter—the terrorist attacks on New York on 9/11/2001, because of the interview form, and because of its readability.

READABILITY LEVEL: 6

My Family by Garrison Keillor (pp. 225–229)

Keillor's narrative poem is a short story in rhymed verse with a surprise ending. It deals with dreams and with the effects of lost dreams. Students will enjoy discussing why Keillor chose to tell this part of his family history in poetry rather than in prose, as he did the other events in his life and the lives of his family members included in his autobiographical book *Leaving Home*.

The Loss of Dreams by Joseph Geil (pp. 230–233)

This student essay of literary interpretation, written in class, compares and contrasts Willy Loman in "Death of a Salesman" to Walter Younger in "A Raisin in the Sun." It follows the academic structure of introduction with thesis, body of three points, and conclusion reaffirming the thesis. It is a good example of using evidence from literary works to support an idea.

Readability Level: 7

CHAPTER 9 Popular Culture

Indian Movie, New Jersey by Chitra Banerjee Divakaruni (pp. 235–238)

This poem focuses on the universal promise of movies—that our dreams can come true, but it has a twist in that the speaker is an emigrant from India. In the movie theater, the speaker finds escape from unpleasant realities as so many people do throughout the world. Students will be able to identify with escape and dreaming of a better world through watching movies. Discuss with them other ways of escape—soap operas, television sitcoms, video games, computer games.

Watching Television by Robert Bly (pp. 238–241)

Bly presents quite a different view of mass media than does Divakaruni in the previous poem. Whereas to Divakaruni, movies are comforting and relaxing, to Bly television is so unpleasant and violent that it causes anxiety in the human spirit. Discuss the two views with students, and ask them which they agree with.

SPORTS HERO: MUHAMMED ALI BY JAIME MARCUS (PP. 241–244)

Muhammed Ali has been a controversial cultural figure since the 1960s, and in this essay Marcus makes a strong case for Ali's being the greatest boxing champion of all time. Boxing fans will enjoy this essay, but it will also stimulate all students to think of their heroes. You might have students write essays on their heroes and submit them to The Hero Project at www.myhero.com.

READABILITY LEVEL: 12

CRAZY HORSE MALT LIQUOR BY MICHAEL DORRIS (PP. 245–249)

This essay is excellent for helping students understand tone. Dorris is angry and pessimistic over the way the image of American Indians is misused. Throughout he builds irony until the last bitterly ironic paragraph. Have students compare and contrast Dorris's tone and ideas about Native Americans with the tone and ideas of Whitecloud in "Blue Winds Dancing" (pp. 73–82) and Horn in "The Door" (pp. 95–102). This essay also illustrates the use of multiple brief examples and one extended example as evidence for arguing a position.

READABILITY LEVEL: COLLEGE

FAMILIES SHOULD ATTEMPT TO LIVE WITHOUT TELEVISION BY CHIORI SANTIAGO (PP. 249–255)

Chiori Santiago contributes regularly to the "Family Matters" column of *Diablo*, a monthly magazine that covers the East Bay area of San Francisco, California. In this column she responds to the annual National TV-Turn-Off-Week, sponsored by a Washington, D.C. based organization named TV-Free America.

READABILITY LEVEL: 10

MEDIA LITERACY EDUCATION CAN ADDRESS THE PROBLEM OF MEDIA VIOLENCE, BY ELIZABETH THOMAN (PP. 255–262)

Elizabeth Thoman is founder and director of the Center for Media Literacy, a California-based nonprofit organization that produces teacher training and community education materials designed to promote media literacy. This argument is from her testimony before the US Senate Committee on Commerce, Science, and Transportation, July 12, 1995.

READABILITY LEVEL: COLLEGE

THE PORTABLE PHONOGRAPH BY WALTER VAN TILBURG CLARK (PP. 262–270)

The reading level of this short story is deceptive, as is the level of most fiction and poetry, because the readability scales do not take connotations and levels of meaning into account. Also, some of the vocabulary is British and thus unfamiliar to American students. However, students can understand the narrative and literal level of the story, an understanding that will provide the foundation for discussion and understanding of the deeper psychological and universal levels of meaning. Clark wrote this story in 1942 during World War II, before the Atomic Age, before the Cold War, and before the conflicts in the Middle East.

READABILITY LEVEL: 7

DEATH BY VIDEO GAME: FACT OR FICTION BY NATHAN FLORAND (PP. 270–274)

Florand's defense of video games will appeal to techies and gamers alike. It will also be of interest to others who have been following the varied stories of teen violence in the media. Students may compare this essay to Males, "Teenagers Are Not Becoming More Violent" (pp. 109–114) and to Zondlo, "It's Not Just A Phase" (pp. 120–125).

READABILITY LEVEL: 12

CHAPTER 10 The World of Work

To be of use by Marge Piercy (pp. 277–279)

This poem offers the opportunity to talk about work and the American or Puritan work ethic. It will also stimulate discussion of different attitudes toward work, especially among generations. And you may bring in different ethnic attitudes toward work. Because so many college students today have already had or now have part-time or full-time jobs, most will already have developed some concepts and attitudes toward work, so their ideas will enrich the discussion.

When the Mind Is At Peace by Layman P'ang (pp. 279–281)

Layman P'ang (P'ang Yun) was a Chinese Buddhist Zen Master in the 8th century. This poem reflects the Zen attitude toward the physical world and toward work. You might ask the students to contrast P'ang's attitude toward work with that of Marge Piercy in the preceding poem, with the prevailing attitudes toward work today, and with their own attitudes toward work. Ask them to discuss what kinds of work bring them the peace of mind that P'ang discusses.

No Shame in My Game by Katherine S. Newman (pp. 281–289)

This essay is a high reading level because of the high level of vocabulary, the high concept level, the unfamiliar ideas, and the structure of sentences and paragraphs. A discussion of cognition and cognitive skills before students' reading the essay would be helpful to them. Nevertheless, many students will identify with this essay because they have had part-time jobs, maybe in fast-food restaurants, and may have had friends or relatives who looked down on such jobs as demeaning to the employees. All will be stimulated by Newman's different approach the intellectual skills that these jobs require. Newman agrees with Greenfield in the previous essay that learning-by-doing or on-the-job training are valuable, widely practiced methods of teaching and learning.

READABILITY LEVEL: COLLEGE

FLEXIBLE FUTURES BY SUSAN GREENFIELD
(PP. 289–293)

Students will probably need assistance comprehending this essay because of the unfamiliar words and concepts. However, once they grasp Greenfield's idea that people will be more in control of their own careers in the future and that this is the world in which they will work, they will enjoy discussing the potential of this notion as well as its advantages and disadvantages. Through a series of causes and effects, the author explains and argues her position.

THE DO-IT-YOURSELF ECONOMY BY ELLEN GOODMAN
(PP. 293–297)

This column is an interesting op-ed piece in which Goodman ironically takes off on both the creation of new jobs and the outsourcing of jobs to other countries, both controversial economic issues. She presents her evaluation of the situation with gentle, tongue-in-cheek humor and plenty of examples. Ask students to think of other ways that jobs have been out-sourced to us.

READABILITY LEVEL: 10

A & P BY JOHN UPDIKE
(PP. 297–305)

This short story by Updike demonstrates the effects of generational conflict in the work place, the conflict between Sammy, the narrator, and Lengel, his boss.

READABILITY LEVEL: 7

My Worst Job Ever by Matthew Derek (pp. 305–309)

This essay about Derek's job as a cook at MacDonald's works well with Newman's essay, "No Shame in My Game" (pp. 281–289). He is one of the fast-food workers that she as an anthropologist writes about. He provides the worker's point of view to this job. Also, the essay is a good example of cause-and-effect. Derek begins with the statement that this job was the worst he has ever had and then goes back to trace three causes of his opinion. Next he builds a causal chain of the results of his working at this job and the negative effects it had.

READABILITY LEVEL: 6

CHAPTER 11 Science and Technology

In Computers by Alan P. Lightman (pp. 311–312)

Today many people consider computers to be the solution of our problems, but Lightman presents a different view of computers, pointing out the shortcomings of these machines. Compare and contrast Lightman's views with those of Clark in the short story "The Portable Phonograph" (pp. 262–270).

READABILITY LEVEL:

The Leading Edge by Sylvia Hicks (pp. 312–315)

This poem is the reflection of someone steeped in the humanities on the new technologies in our society. The poet has said that she was surprised to find that the scientists, technicians, and engineers at Vancouver conference were actually more concerned about mistakes that could be made (such as someone accidentally pushing the wrong button) than she and others in the humanities and academics because the scientists were more well informed on the possibilities of what could go wrong and what might happen.